Manifest Manhood and the Antebellum American Empire

The U.S.-Mexico War (1846–8) brought two centuries of dramatic territorial expansionism to a close, seemingly fulfilling America's Manifest Destiny. Or did it? As politicians schemed to annex new lands in Latin America and the Pacific, some Americans took expansionism into their own hands. Between 1848 and 1860, there was an epidemic of unsanctioned attacks by private American mercenaries (known as filibusters) throughout the Western Hemisphere. This book documents the potency of Manifest Destiny in the antebellum era and situates imperial lust in the context of social and economic transformations that were changing the meaning of manhood and womanhood in the United States. Easy victory over Mexico in 1848 led many American men to embrace both an aggressive vision of expansionism and an equally martial vision of manhood. Debates about the propriety of aggression abroad polarized the public at home, shaping antebellum presidential elections, foreign policies, gender relations, and, ultimately, the failure of sectional compromise before the Civil War.

Amy S. Greenberg is Associate Professor of History and Women's Studies at the Pennsylvania State University. She is also the author of *Cause for Alarm: The Volunteer Fire Department in the Nineteenth-Century City* (1998).

Manifest Manhood and the Antebellum American Empire

AMY S. GREENBERG

The Pennsylvania State University

CAMBRIDGE UNIVERSITY PRESS
Cambridge, New York, Melbourne, Madrid, Cape Town, Singapore, São Paulo

Cambridge University Press
40 West 20th Street, New York, NY 10011-4211, USA

www.cambridge.org
Information on this title: www.cambridge.org/9780521840965

First published 2005

Printed in the United States of America

A catalog record for this publication is available from the British Library.

Library of Congress Cataloging in Publication data

Greenberg, Amy S., 1968–
Manifest manhood and the antebellum American empire / Amy S. Greenberg.
    p. cm.
Includes bibliographical references.
ISBN 0-521-84096-1 (hardback) – ISBN 0-521-60080-4 (pbk.)
    1. United States – Territorial expansion.   2. Filibusters.   3. United States – History –
1849–1877.   4. Men – United States – History – 19th century.   5. Masculinity – United
States – History – 19th century.   I. Title.
E179.5.G79   2005
973.6–dc22   2004020453

ISBN-13   978-0-521-84096-5 hardback
ISBN-10   0-521-84096-1 hardback

ISBN-13   978-0-521-60080-4 paperback
ISBN-10   0-521-60080-4 paperback

For Rich and Jackson

The reputations of the nineteenth century will one day be quoted, to prove its barbarism.

         – Ralph Waldo Emerson, 1850

Time will decide whether they were pirates and cutthroats, or heroes and patriots.

         – Cora Montgomery, 1851

Contents

Illustrations

Acknowledgments

Without the support of some very generous institutions and individuals, this project would never have gotten off the ground. At the Pennsylvania State University, the Department of History, the Institute for Arts and Humanities, and the Office for Research and Graduate Studies provided release time and research funds over the many years of this book's gestation. At a critical moment, the Richards Civil War Era Center at Penn State kindly bankrolled the services of a competent research assistant, Leah Vincent. The Huntington Library has been an enthusiastic supporter of my work, providing me with both Mellon and W. M. Keck fellowships. Thanks also to the Beinecke Rare Book and Manuscript Library at Yale for an Archibald Hanna, Jr., Fellowship. Librarians at the Huntington and Beinecke libraries, the Bancroft Library at the University of California at Berkeley, the Howard Tilton Memorial Library at Tulane University, the Hawaii State Archives Historical Records Branch, and the Library of Congress also deserve thanks for accommodating my ongoing and sometimes vague research demands. Eric Novotny at Penn State gets special acknowledgment for his library expertise and assistance over the course of many years.

A number of scholars have engaged with this project, and in the process have broadened my intellectual horizons, encouraged my ambition, and corrected a truly embarrassing number of factual and conceptual errors. Tyler Anbinder, Thomas Augst, Gail Bederman, Iver Bernstein, Patricia Cline Cohen, Bruce Dorsey, Richard Doyle, Alice Fahs, Gary Gallagher, the late William Gienapp, Paul Gilje, David Henkin, Nancy Isenberg, Philip Jenkins, Richard John, Patrick Kelly, Stephanie McCurry, Mark Neely, Jr., Adam Rome, Mary Ryan, Gregory Smits, and Amy Gilman Srebnick each read part or all of this manuscript and provided valuable feedback. Robert Lockhart was an enthusiastic booster of this project from an early date who helped convince me of the project's importance. Two generous colleagues who also are experts in fields closely related to this study, Anne C. Rose and Mrinilini Sinha, provided detailed comments on an early draft and went to great lengths to save me from myself. I feel remarkably fortunate for their assistance.

To review a manuscript well takes a good deal of work, and to convince a stubborn writer to change her ways takes an equally notable degree of diplomacy. Three scholars in particular deserve special credit for their achievements in these areas. Alexis McCrossen encouraged this project from its earliest stages, read the entire first draft of this manuscript within two weeks of its completion, and provided a generous and smart critique of each and every aspect of the argument. Through her daily emails she has continued to shape this project in a profound manner. Without her encouragement, suggestions for improvement, and unflagging optimism this book might never have been written. Kristin Hoganson also put a great amount of time and energy into making this book stonger. She provided me with the kind of reader's report that every writer dreams of – engaged, generous, insightful, and tough where it needed to be. She not only noted flaws in the manuscript but suggested ways I might fix problems about which I hadn't even been aware. She has continued to provide answers to my many questions with an unbeatable combination of enthusiasm and expertise in the intersection of gender and foreign relations. Robert E. May gets a special note of thanks. Bob, the dean of filibustering studies, has aided and assisted this project for about six years. He has proofread lengthy sections, pointed out countless errors of fact and interpretation, and put up with my no doubt infuriatingly scatterbrained approach to research and writing with a warmth and generosity that I certainly haven't deserved. I also have been blessed by a conscientious group of anonymous readers. Each of them carefully evaluated the strengths and weaknesses of this project, and all have strengthened this book through their suggestions and criticism. Any remaining errors of fact or interpretation are, of course, my own.

Portions of this project have been presented as papers and talks at Penn State, the University of California at Irvine, the University of California at Santa Barbara, and the University of Texas at San Antonio, as well as at meetings of the American Studies Association, the Organization of American Historians, the Social Science History Association, the Society for Historians of the Early American Republic, and the Southern Historical Association. I thank audience members and fellow panelists for their challenging questions and helpful suggestions. I also must acknowledge the great Lew Bateman and the remarkably professional staff at Cambridge University Press.

My cheerful and engaged colleagues at Penn State have provided intellectual stimulation and a nurturing work environment. Special thanks to William Blair, Karen Ebeling, Lori Ginzberg, Deryck Holdsworth, Joan Landes, Sally McMurry, Mark Neely, Jr., William Pencak, Robert Proctor, A. Gregg Roeber, Guido Ruggiero, Londa Schiebinger, Susan Squier, and Nan Woodruff for their good humor and ongoing encouragement. Thanks also to the *Journal of the Early Republic* for allowing me to reprint portions of my previously published article, "A Gray-eyed Man: Character, Appearance, and Filibustering" (vol. 20, winter 2000).

Family members know how much I rely on them. Jane Lee Greenberg and Kenneth S. Greenberg have provided me with an intellectual upbringing, encouragement for my work, and, most recently, a fine collection of rare nineteenth-century expansionist travelogues. My wonderful siblings, Mike and Ken Greenberg, Barbara Walker, and Suzann and Lowell Ball, can always be counted on to help me put my work into perspective. Alexis McCrossen, Kathy Newman, and Claudia Swan are closer to family members than to colleagues. I here gratefully acknowledge their hospitality and emotional support.

My greatest thanks, finally, goes to my partner in crime, Richard Doyle, without whom I would be far less imaginative in my scholarship and joyous in my life. Rich's work ethic is a constant inspiration. As a model for the necessity of passion in both the public and private sphere, he is without parallel. This book is dedicated to him, and to our lovely son Jackson, whose curiosity and engagement with the world bring me pleasure every day.

Abbreviations Used in the Notes

AH	Hawaii State Archives
AHR	*American Historical Review*
BL	Bancroft Library, University of California at Berkeley, Berkeley, CA
DBR	*De Bow's Review*
HL	Manuscripts Collection, Huntington Library, San Marino, CA
IINMM	*Harper's New Monthly Magazine*
JAH	*Journal of American History*
LOC	Library of Congress, Washington, DC
NEYR	*New Englander and Yale Review*
NYH	New York *Herald*
NYT	New York *Tribune*
PMM	*Putnam's Monthly Magazine*
SLM	*Southern Literary Messenger*
SQR	*Southern Quarterly Review*
USDR	*United States Magazine and Democratic Review*
WWP	Callender I. Fayssoux Collection of William Walker Papers, Latin American Collection, Howard Tilton Memorial Library, Tulane University, New Orleans, LA

Manifest Manhood and the Antebellum American Empire

Introduction

John Gast's 1872 *American Progress* is perhaps the best-known image of the nineteenth-century American concept of *Manifest Destiny*.[1] Painted twenty-four years after the United States literally "won the west," taking half of Mexico's territory as spoils of war, and eighteen years before the U.S. Census Bureau proclaimed that there was no longer an identifiable American frontier, Gast's vision of Manifest Destiny is both self-confident and self-congratulatory. American territorial expansion literally brings light to darkness in this painting. An allegorical female representation of "American Progress" (with the "star of empire" on her forehead) leads the pioneers westward, schoolbook in hand, along with the great technological advances of the era, the telegraph and railroad. Wild animals flee as she nears, and bare-breasted Native-American women make way for a white family in a covered wagon. *American Progress* was widely circulated in print form, and it quickly became one of the preeminent artistic visions of westward expansion (Figure 0.1).[2]

The first thing that strikes the viewer, of course, is the scantily clad and well-formed flying woman who dominates the painting. So focused is Gast's allegorical figure on her civilizing project that she fails to note that her translucent gown is in imminent danger of sliding off. Why did Gast represent "American Progress" as a woman, when so many of the iconic nineteenth-century images of western settlement were male? The gold-rush

[1] I will capitalize Manifest Destiny throughout this study to signify its significance. As Bruce Harvey has noted, "Manifest Destiny is one of the few ideologies, in the history of nations, that in its own time became so reified as to garner initial capitals in its name." Bruce Albert Harvey, *American Geographics: U.S. National Narratives and the Representation of the Non-European World, 1830–1865* (Stanford, 2001), 6.

[2] George Crofutt's print of *American Progress* was featured in his magazine, *Crofutt's Western World*. Crofutt was fond enough of the image to use it as the frontispiece in his guide for western travelers, in which he praised the image in great detail. George A. Crofutt, *Crofutt's New Overland Tourist and Pacific Coast Guide* (Chicago, 1878), 1, 300.

FIGURE 0.1. *American Progress* (George A. Crofutt chromolithograph, 1873, after an 1872 painting of the same title by John Gast). Library of Congress, Prints and Photographs Division [LC-USZ62-737].

migrant, the U.S.-Mexico War solider, the fur trapper, and the frontiersman were all exemplars of masculinity in the middle decades of the century. Yet it is difficult to envision "American Progress" in any of these forms, indeed in any male form at all. It is the benign domestic influence of our allegorical figure, and of the white women in that covered wagon, Gast seems to indicate, that is responsible for the smooth and uplifting transformation of wilderness into civilization. The benevolent domestic presence obscures the violent process through which the United States gained control of the region.[3]

Was Manifest Destiny gendered?[4] It is the argument of both this image and this book that it was. Gender concerns shaped both the popular

[3] R. W. Connell, *Masculinities* (Berkeley, 1995), 194; Henry Nash Smith, *Virgin Land: the American West as Symbol and Myth* (Cambridge, MA, 1950), 81–111; Richard Slotkin, *Regeneration Through Violence: The Mythology of the American Frontiér, 1600–1860.* (Middletown, CT, 1973).

[4] In using the term *gender* I mean the "ongoing construction that shapes identities and the social practices of women and men over time." Katherine G. Morrissey, "Engendering the West," in *Under an Open Sky: Rethinking America's Western Past*, William Cronon, George Miles, and Jay Gitlin, eds. (New York, 1992), ftnt. 4, 308. Joan Scott's observation that "gender is a constitutive element of social relationships based on perceived differences between the sexes, and gender is a primary way of signifying relationships of power" has shaped the approach

understanding of the meaning of Manifest Destiny and the experiences of men and women abroad in the antebellum period. Expansionism in this painting is justified largely because it is domesticated. This illustration resonated with U.S. residents in the post–Civil War era in part because the vision of expansionism as "progress," and progress defined as the introduction of domesticity to the wilderness, fit with the hegemonic gender norms of the era. After the upheaval and staggering violence of four years of Civil War, survivors turned away from heroic individualism and looked toward work and home for meaning. The growth of the country, "from sea to sea," in the decades before the war was idealized as an essentially peaceful process, a period when harmony reigned and Americans were unified in pursuit of their destiny. *American Progress* is a vision of expansionism, both domesticated and restrained.[5]

As this study will explore, expansionism didn't always look this way. In the antebellum era, many Americans justified territorial expansionism precisely because it was *not* domesticated.[6] Potential new American territories were embraced by some American men because they offered opportunities for individual heroic initiative and for success in love and war, which seemed to be fading at home. They might not wish to gaze upon an antebellum version of "American Progress," featuring a bloody soldier floating over the "new frontiers" of Central America, the Caribbean, and Hawaii, but the violent implications of such a scene would not be incompatible with their vision of America's territorial future.

While domesticated expansionism, as pictured by Gast, had its antebellum proponents, many others embraced a more aggressive expansionism, in which Manifest Destiny would be achieved through the direct and rightful force of arms. Consider the gendered resonances of an 1849 poem written

---

of this study. Joan Scott, "Gender: A Useful Category for Historical Analysis," *AHR* 91 (December 1986): 1067.

[5] Gerald Linderman, *Embattled Courage: The Experience of Combat in the American Civil War* (New York, 1987); George Fredrickson, *The Inner Civil War: Northern Intellectuals and the Crisis of the Union* (New York, 1965).

[6] Following nineteenth-century usage, this study will use the term *American* to refer to a resident of the United States, as opposed to a resident of Central America, Mexico, Canada, or South America, and *America* as a synonym for the United States. As Frederick B. Pike and Lester Langley have pointed out, while residents of other states in the Americas have just as much right to call themselves Americans as do residents of the United States, they "invariably refer to themselves by the name of their native countries." Quote in Frederick B. Pike, *The United States and Latin America: Myths and Stereotypes of Civilization and Nature* (Austin, 1992), xvi; Lester D. Langley, *America and the Americas: The United States in the Western Hemisphere* (Athens, GA, 1989), xvi–xvii. Residents of the United States, on the other hand, have historically embraced the title wholeheartedly. As the *SQR* explained in 1850, "The United States are called par eminence, America, and their citizens Americans." "The Battles of the Rio Grande," *SQR* 2 (November 1850): 429.

by Francis Lieber, a professor of history at the University of South Carolina and respected intellectual.

> Long indeed they have been wooing,
>   The Pacific and his bride;
> Now 'tis time for holy wedding –
>   Join them by the tide.
>   . . . .
> When the mighty God of nature
>   Made his favored continent,
> He allowed it yet unsevered,
>   That a race be sent,
> Able, mindful of his purpose,
>   Prone to people, to subdue,
> And to bind the lands with iron,
>   Or to force them through.

Lieber's verse in honor of a newly contracted canal project in Nicaragua initially renders the relationship between the oceans in a romantic fashion; they are a couple to be joined in holy matrimony after a lengthy courtship. But the tone of "The Ship Canal" soon shifts. Rather than peacefully supervise the ceremony, the vigorous American race subdues not only nameless people but the entire continent as well. God may have created the Western Hemisphere, Lieber suggests, but he left it to the American man to remake through force. It is the American who binds the lands with iron before forcing the oceans through them, with the inter-oceanic wedding reception effectively co-opted in a narrative of indomitable American will.[7]

Lieber suggests here that this Central American canal was a part of America's Manifest Destiny, the next stop, after victory against Mexico, in the unfolding process of American domination of the continent and hemisphere. In retrospect, of course, he would be proved wrong. By the time Gast painted *American Progress*, Americans realized that antebellum territorial expansionism ended at the Pacific Ocean and the Rio Grande. But it was not at all obvious in 1848 that the "continental frontier" marked a natural limit to the growth of the republic.

Manifest Destiny was alive and well after the U.S.-Mexico War, and the majority of Americans continued to hold expansive plans for the United States. Many Americans became commercial expansionists, and they

---

[7] Francis Lieber, "The Ship Canal," *SLM* 15 (May 1849): 266. Cornelius Vanderbilt's American Atlantic and Pacific Ship Canal Company contracted with Nicaragua to build a canal through the country at the height of the gold rush. The canal was never built, but it established America's interests there. David I. Folkman, Jr., *The Nicaragua Route* (Salt Lake City, 1972), 23–106. The idea that a romantic engagement could lead to a marriage defined by patriarchal authority and force would have fit well with nineteenth-century marriage conventions. Norma Basch, *In the Eyes of the Law: Women, Marriage, and Property in Nineteenth-Century New York* (Ithaca, 1982); Amy Dru Stanley, *From Bondage to Contract: Wage Labor, Marriage, and the Market in the Age of Slave Emancipation* (New York, 1998), 175–217.

envisioned American domination of the hemisphere or world emerging through the growth of a commercial empire. Others, who this study will term *aggressive expansionists*, advocated using force of arms to obtain new territories in Latin America and the Pacific. Aggressive expansionists were especially influential in their support for the controversial but widespread practice of filibustering. In the nineteenth century, a filibuster was not a long-winded speech in the Senate. *Filibustering* referred to private armies invading other countries without official sanction of the U.S. government. Filibusters were men who on their own initiative went to war against foreign nations, often in the face of open hostility from their own governments. The term also was used for the invasions themselves. Although the actions of these mercenaries were clearly illegal, they received the praise and even adulation of aggressive expansionists. Given that the United States has just won an enormous territorial concession from Mexico, the enthusiasm of Americans for aggressive expansionism seems, upon first examination, perplexing. It is only upon placing Manifest Destiny in its social and cultural context that enthusiasm for continued territorial annexation begins to make sense.[8]

This study investigates the meaning of Manifest Destiny for American men and women in the years between the U.S.-Mexico and Civil wars, based on written accounts from letters and journals to political cartoons and newspapers.[9] Travelers to the California gold rush left a large body of documents in which they expressed their often candid views of the lands and peoples they encountered on their voyages. Although these travelers were far more likely male than female, and were likely also to be more adventurous sorts than the neighbors they left behind, the men who crossed the isthmus on their way to California were otherwise a heterogeneous group in terms of occupation, age, and ethnicity.[10] Travel narratives and travel fiction, published

---

[8] Charles H. Brown, *Agents of Manifest Destiny: The Lives and Times of the Filibusters* (Chapel Hill, 1980), 3; Robert E. May, *Manifest Destiny's Underworld: Filibustering in Antebellum America* (Chapel Hill, 2002), xi.

[9] Antebellum newspapers provide an excellent vantage point from which to judge public opinion of expansionism, since, as Michael Warner has written, "by the Revolution ... the business of governing relocated itself from the context of town meetings and market-street conversations to the realm of a public constituted in writing and print." Michael Warner, "Franklin and the Letters of the Republic," *Representations* 16 (Fall 1986): 111. Tocqueville also noted the significance of newspapers in the construction of what scholars would later call the public sphere. "If there were no newspapers there would be no common activity. ... A newspaper then takes up the notion or the feeling that had occurred simultaneously, but singly, to each of them. All are then immediately guided towards this beacon; and these wandering minds, which had long sought each other in darkness, at length meet and unite. The newspaper brought them together, and the newspaper is still necessary to keep them united." Alexis de Tocqueville, *Democracy in America*. 1840 (New York, 1981), 409–10.

[10] Letters and diaries, like any other genres, are bound by their own representational demands and are shaped by both visible and invisible constraints. But, by and large, I would argue, they provide a less-mediated lens on the views of their writers than do other genres, like the published travelogue. On the heterogeneity of gold-rush travelers see Malcolm Rohrbough, *Days of Gold: The California Gold Rush and the American Nation* (Berkeley, 1997).

in book form and in popular periodicals, proliferated during the antebellum period and were devoured by readers. At the same time, letters from foreign correspondents became a staple of the penny press, and travelogues became a staple of magazines like the *North American Review* and *Harper's New Monthly Magazine*.[11] During the decade or so before the Civil War, politicians actively debated whether further territorial expansion was desirable, and many political tracts were published either supporting or opposing expansionism.[12]

This study argues that the American encounter with potential new territories in the antebellum period was shaped by concerns at home, especially evolving gendered ideals and practices. Dramatic changes in American society, economy, and culture reconfigured the meanings of both manhood and womanhood in the 1830s and 1840s. Antebellum Americans lived through an astonishing array of changes, including mass immigration from Europe; the emergence of evangelical Christianity in the Second Great Awakening; the end of bound labor in the North; the beginnings of a "market revolution," including specialization in agriculture and dependency on wider markets in even rural areas; changes in print technology; the decline of the artisan workshop; increasing class stratification; and universal white manhood suffrage. All of these transformations shaped the ideology and practices of womanhood and manhood, and the meaning of Manifest Destiny, as well.[13]

---

[11] Between fifteen and nineteen percent of all books charged from the New York Society Library in the 1840s were travel narratives. Ronald J. Zboray, *A Fictive People: Antebellum Economic Development and the American Reading Public.* (New York, 1993), 176–9; Mary Suzanne Schriber, *Writing Home: American Women Abroad, 1830–1920* (Charlottesville, 1997), 47–8, 57. An excellent bibliography of published American travelogues is Harold F. Smith, *American Travelers Abroad: A Bibliography of Accounts Published before 1900* (Carbondale, 1969).

[12] Thomas Hietala has suggested that "the American people as a whole may have shared their leaders' ideas, but the question of whether or not they did is less crucial to a comprehension of American expansion than identifying and examining the convictions of the public figures who attained the continental empire." Thomas Hietala, *Manifest Design: Anxious Aggrandizement in Late Jacksonian America* (Ithaca, 1985), 2–3. This study suggests that personal letters and journals provide a window on "popular opinion," while texts in popular periodicals provides a means to deduce the opinion of an "informed public," or "knowledgeable public." Several scholars have posited that the "informed public" had a significant (and at times measurable) impact on foreign policy. See Gabriel Almond, *The American People and Foreign Policy* 1950. (New York, 1960); Ernest R. May, *American Imperialism: A Speculative Essay* (New York, 1968), ch. 2; James Rosenau, *The Attentive Public and Foreign Policy: A Theory of Growth and Some New Evidence* (Princeton, 1968).

[13] It is impossible to do justice to the vast literature on these multiple subjects in a footnote. Key works that have influenced this study include Paul Boyer, *Urban Masses and Moral Order in America, 1820–1920* (Cambridge, MA, 1978); Paul E. Johnson, *A Shopkeeper's Millennium: Society and Revivals in Rochester, New York, 1815–1837* (New York, 1978); Joanne Pope Melish, *Disowning Slavery: Gradual Emancipation and "Race" in New England, 1780–1860* (Ithaca, 1998); James Oliver Horton and Lois E. Horton, *In Hope of Liberty: Culture, Community, and Protest among Northern Free Blacks, 1700–1860* (New York, 1997);

The reigning view of American womanhood in the early years of the republic, that of "republican motherhood," had, by the 1830s, been overshadowed by a new and contested ideology of domesticity. Republican motherhood posited that maternal influence would emanate outside the family home to the frontier, uplifting the values of new Americans and supporting male-initiated attempts to expand westward.[14] Domesticity idealized women as virtuous domestic beings who could change society for the better through their positive moral influence on their husbands and children, while it simultaneously demonized women who worked outside the home. By conceptualizing women as essentially domestic beings, the reigning ideology of the "woman's sphere" could isolate the wife and mother within her home, in a form of "imperial isolation."[15]

At the same time, however, women successfully used their elevated status within the home to effect change outside it. Women played key roles in many of the most significant moral and social reform movements of the antebellum era, including evangelical and anti-slavery reform, and, most notably, the Woman's Rights movement. Although by the 1850s, voting rights for white adult males had become nearly universal, women could not vote, and their legal rights in marriage were extremely limited, since it was understood that a woman transferred her civic identity to her husband in marriage. In 1848 200 women, and 40 men, gathered at a convention in Seneca Falls, New York, and adopted a statement based on the Declaration of Independence that called for expanded rights for women, especially in the areas of marital and property law. Feminists continued holding conventions on a regular basis afterwards.[16]

Charles Sellers, *The Market Revolution: Jacksonian America, 1815–1846* (New York, 1991); David Henkin, *City Reading: Written Words and Public Spaces in Antebellum New York* (New York, 1998); Stuart M. Blumin, *The Emergence of the Middle Class: Social Experience in the American City, 1760–1900* (Cambridge, UK, 1989); Sean Wilentz, *Chants Democratic: New York City and the Rise of the American Working Class, 1788–1850* (New York, 1984). One important study to place Manifest Destiny in the context of these changes is Hietala, *Manifest Design*.

[14] On republican motherhood see Linda Kerber, *Women of the Republic: Intellect and Ideology in Revolutionary America* (Chapel Hill, 1980). On domesticity see Kathryn Kish Sklar, *Catharine Beecher: A Study in American Domesticity* (New Haven, 1973); Mary Ryan, *Cradle of the Middle Class: The Family in Oneida County, New York, 1790–1865* (Cambridge, UK, 1981); Nancy F. Cott, *Bonds of Womanhood: "Woman's Sphere" in New England, 1780–1835.* Second edition. (New Haven, 1997).

[15] On imperial isolation see Mary Ryan, *The Empire of the Mother: American Writings about Domesticity, 1830–1860* (New York, 1982); Scott, "Gender: A Useful Category of Analysis," 1068. Domesticity was hegemonic if unachievable for most women. Ann D. Gordon and Mari Jo Buhle, "Sex and Class in Colonial and Nineteenth-Century America," in *Liberating Women's History: Theoretical and Critical Essays*, Berenice A. Carroll, ed. (Urbana, 1976), 284.

[16] Elizabeth Varon, *We Mean to be Counted: White Women and Politics in Antebellum Virginia* (Chapel Hill, 1998), 101; Norma Basch, *In the Eyes of the Law: Women, Marriage and*

Although delegates at Seneca Falls were split on the issue of women's suffrage, domesticity provided alternative means for women to influence the political process. The Second Party System accepted female partisanship, and the Whig Party, which blended evangelical religion with politics, was especially welcoming to women, including women as part of their vision of politics as "secular revivalism." Although Democrats initially critiqued Whig women's involvement in campaigns, slurring the party as effeminate, William Henry Harrison's victory in 1840 taught them the error of their ways. As Elizabeth Varon has shown, both parties in the 1840s and into the 1850s courted women's approval and used women in their campaigns.[17]

The economic and social upheavals that transformed the practice of womanhood had an equally profound effect on the practice of manhood, as did, of course, the new challenges to the gender order posed by female activism and the elevation of women through domesticity in the 1840s and 1850s. Competition and economic transformations eroded traditional routes of occupational advancement and made the process of both choosing a calling, and succeeding at it, more contentious and demanding for men of all walks of life.[18] A split emerged in patriarchal masculinity in the nineteenth century, as "practice organized around dominance was increasingly incompatible with practice organized around expertise or technical knowledge." For men the experience of work and home life, of social interactions, even of citizenship, was dramatically transformed from the 1830s to 1850s.[19]

Historians of gender have generally posited the crucial shift in male gender ideology in the late nineteenth century, when a "crisis of manhood" led men to reconceptualize proper male behavior.[20] In the early years of the

Property in Nineteenth-Century New York (Ithaca, 1982). On the empowering aspects of domesticity see Nancy A. Hewitt, *Women's Activism and Social Change: Rochester, New York, 1822–1872* (Ithaca, 1984); Lori D. Ginzberg, *Women and the Work of Benevolence: Morality, Politics, and Class in the Nineteenth-Century United States* (New Haven, 1990); Anne Firor Scott, *Natural Allies: Women's Associations in American History* (Urbana, 1991); Sklar, *Catharine Beecher*; Christine Stansell, *City of Women: Sex and Class in New York, 1789–1860* (Urbana, IL, 1987).

[17] Varon, *We Mean to be Counted*, 82; Ronald Formisano, *The Transformation of Political Culture: Massachusetts Parties, 1790s–1840s* (New York, 1983), 262–7; Ronald and Mary Saracino Zboray, "Gender Slurs in Boston's Partisan Press during the 1840s," *Journal of American Studies* 34 (2000): 413–46.

[18] For one moving example of the perils of the marketplace, see Paul Johnson and Sean Wilentz, *The Kingdom of Matthias: A Story of Sex and Salvation in 19th-Century America* (New York, 1994).

[19] Connell, *Masculinities*, 193.

[20] On the "crisis of manhood" see Joe Dubbert, "Progressivism and the Masculinity Crisis," in *The American Man*, Elizabeth Pleck and Joseph Pleck, eds. (Englewood Cliffs, NJ, 1980), 307; Susan Lee Johnson, "'A Memory Sweet to Soldiers': The Significance of Gender," in *A New Significance: Re-envisioning the History of the American West*, Clyde A. Milner II, ed. (New York, 1996), 257; Michael S. Kimmel, "The Contemporary 'Crisis' of Masculinity in Historical Perspective," in *The Making of Masculinities: the New Men's Studies*, Harry

republic, men had grounded their own sense of manliness in virtue, honor, and public service. By the late nineteenth century, these ideas were being supplanted by a new vision of "primitive masculinity," grounded in a selective reading of Charles Darwin's 1859 theory of evolution. Whereas an early nineteenth-century ideal of manly behavior resided largely in the life of the mind, by the end of the century, historians argue, the preeminent masculine ideal had gained important physical criteria. Middle-class men were encouraged to embrace their animal nature, to improve their physical strength, and to develop their martial virtues so that they could successfully compete with men of less-refined classes and races. Late nineteenth-century nostalgia for the sacrifices of the Civil War generation also supported the contention that middle-class men were growing soft and needed to reanimate their essential masculine virtues.[21]

In the middle decades of the century, however, there was not yet a hegemonic "primitive" masculinity. In a period before America's distinctive three-class structure had fully formed, when a middle class was only beginning to coalesce out of the transformations of work practices under industrialization, both class norms and gender norms were in flux.[22] During the period

---

Brod, ed. (Boston, 1987). For a critique of the "crisis" interpretation see Clyde Griffen, "Reconstructing Masculinity from the Evangelical Revival to the Waning of Progressivism: A Speculative Synthesis," in *Meanings for Manhood: Constructions of Masculinity in Victorian America*, Mark C. Carnes and Clyde Griffen, eds. (Chicago, 1990), 183-4.

[21] Darwin never claimed that "survival of the fittest" applied to races or to nations, (indeed the phrase was coined by Herbert Spencer) but this so-called social Darwinism justified both personal aggression and imperial domination by the late nineteenth century. Gail Bederman, *Manliness and Civilization: A Cultural History of Gender and Race in the United States, 1880–1917* (Chicago, 1995); Elliott J. Gorn, *The Manly Art: Bare Knuckle Prize Fighting in America* (Ithaca, 1986); E. Anthony Rotundo, *American Manhood: Transformations in Masculinity from the Revolution to the Modern Era* (New York, 1993); John Tosh, "What Should Historians do with Masculinity? Reflections on Nineteenth-century Britain," *History Workshop Journal* 38 (Autumn 1994): 182. On Darwin and social Darwinism see Joseph M. Henning, *Outposts of Civilization: Race Religion, and the Formative Years of American-Japanese Relations* (New York, 2000): 14–16.

[22] As Stuart Blumin, among others, has documented, "a middle class was *not* fully formed before the [Civil] war." Blumin, *The Emergence of the Middle Class*, 13. The overwhelming historical bias in favor of sources drawn from literate men of high white-collar occupations has skewed our understanding of American manhood by ignoring the practices of the vast majority of American men, or by simply equating class identity with gender identity. The experience of highly educated, upper middle-class men was not typical, yet it has too often stood in as representative of all men. Anthony Rotundo's study *American Manhood*, for instance (described as the "first comprehensive history of American manhood), relies entirely on sources drawn from the middle or upper-middle classes because "[m]iddle-class values have been the dominant values in the United States for two centuries.... If, as social critics have often written, the United States is a bourgeois society, one good way to open up a new topic like the history of manhood is to study the bourgeoisie." Rotundo, *American Manhood*, 296; see also the essays in *Manliness and Morality: Middle Class Masculinity in Britain and America, 1800–1940*, J. A. Mangan and James Walvin eds., (Manchester, UK,

covered by this study, as Clyde Griffin has written, "markedly divergent conceptions and styles of masculinity co-existed, not only between social classes but within them."[23] In the 1850s, there was no single ideal of masculinity, like the "primitive manhood" of the 1890s or the "gentry masculinity" that historians have described in the eighteenth century, that dominated expectations for American men's behavior. On the contrary, a whole range of practices of manhood competed for men's allegiances.[24]

White American men of diverse occupations could and did embrace a wide range of masculine practices in the middle decades of the century. Laborers could locate their manhood in bare-knuckle boxing, in the sentimental ideals of melodrama, or in the very different theatrical genre of minstrelsy. Some urban workers, influenced by the spread of evangelical Christianity, internalized self-restraint and moral self-discipline, while others reveled in pre-industrial work habits and physical, often bloody cultural expressions drawn from Europe. Merchants could self-identify as militia members or could join socially exclusive men's clubs. Southern gentlemen upheld dueling as a key expression of their own culture of honor. Abolitionists embraced one another as well as the language of Christian fraternal love, while some professional men embraced competitiveness and political realism. Temperance cut across the economic spectrum, as did other reform movements of the period. The preeminent social organization of the antebellum city, the urban volunteer fire company, was explicitly heterogeneous in its membership, and it unified American men, from merchant to manual laborer, Irish immigrant to native born, in a celebration of strength, camaraderie, and social service in the interest of their city. An urban sporting culture brought together young men of different occupations in the shared enjoyment of urban entertainments, including prostitution. America's mass political culture of parades, marching, elaborate ritual, and alcohol consumption likewise

1987). For a critique of the tendency of historians of masculinity to equate class and gender see Tosh, "What Should Historians do with Masculinity?" 179–202.

[23] Griffen, "Reconstructing Masculinity," in *Meanings for Manhood*, Carnes and Griffen, eds. 185. This study is one of several in recent years to emphasize the importance of the fact that there co-existed multiple practices of manhood at mid-century, none of which was hegemonic. See for example, Bruce Dorsey, *Reforming Men and Women: Gender in the Antebellum City* (Ithaca, 2002); Amy S. Greenberg, *Cause for Alarm: The Volunteer Fire Department in the Nineteenth-Century City* (Princeton, 1998); Brian Roberts, *American Alchemy: The California Gold Rush and Middle-Class Culture* (Chapel Hill, 2000); Susan Lee Johnson, *Roaring Camp: The Social World of the California Gold Rush* (New York, 2000). Several other notable studies have emerged out of a literary context. See especially Shelly Streeby, *American Sensations: Class, Empire, and the Production of Popular Culture* (Berkeley, 2002); Dana D. Nelson, *National Manhood: Capitalist Citizenship and the Imagined Fraternity of White Men* (Durham, 1998); Michael Paul Rogin, *Fathers and Children: Andrew Jackson and the Subjugation of the American Indian* (New York, 1975).

[24] Connell, *Masculinities*, 191.

unified men across occupation and ethnicity. Free black men in the North also drew on different gendered practices.[25]

This study focuses on what by 1848 had become two preeminent and dueling mid-century masculinities: *restrained manhood* and *martial manhood*. Restrained manhood was practiced by men in the North and South who grounded their identities in their families, in the evangelical practice of their Protestant faith, and in success in the business world. Their masculine practices valued expertise. Restrained men were strong proponents of domesticity or "true womanhood." They believed that the domestic household was the moral center of the world, and the wife and mother its moral compass.[26] Restrained men worked hard to follow the example of Jesus Christ and to avoid sin. They were generally repulsed by the violent blood sports that captivated many urban working men. They did not drink to excess, and were likely, after the passage of the 1851 Maine temperance law, to support legislation to prohibit the sale of alcohol in other states.

[25] Griffen, "Reconstructing Masculinity," 183–91; Mark C. Carnes, "Middle-Class Men and the Solace of Fraternal Ritual," 37–52; Donald Yacovone, "Abolitionists and the 'Language of Fraternal Love,'" 85–95; Michael Grossberg, "Institutionalizing Masculinity: The Law as a Masculine Profession," 133–51, all in *Meanings for Manhood*, Carnes and Griffen, eds. 183–91. On urban workers see Gorn, *The Manly Art*; Wilentz, *Chants Democratic*. On melodrama see David Reynolds, *Beneath the American Renaissance: The Subversive Imagination in the Age of Emerson and Melville* (New York, 1988), ch. 6. On blackface minstrelsy see Eric Lott, *Love and Theft: Blackface Minstrelsy and the American Working Class* (New York, 1993). On men's clubs see Mark C. Carnes, *Secret Ritual and Manhood in Victorian America* (New Haven, 1989); Mary Ann Clawson, *Constructing Brotherhood: Class, Gender and Fraternalism* (Princeton, 1989). On Southerners see Elliott Gorn, "'Gouge and Bite, Pull Hair and Scratch': The Social Significance of Fighting in the Southern Backcountry," *AHR* 90 (February 1985): 18–43; Kenneth S. Greenberg, *Honor and Slavery: Lies, Duels, Noses, Masks, Dressing as a Woman, Gifts, Strangers, Humanitarianism, Death, Slave Rebellions, the Proslavery Argument, Baseball, Hunting and Gambling in the Old South* (Princeton 1996); Bertram Wyatt-Brown, *Honor and Violence in the Old South* (New York, 1986). On temperance see Johnson, *A Shopkeeper's Millennium*; Dorsey, *Reforming Men and Women*, 90–135. On firefighting see Greenberg, *Cause for Alarm*. On urban sporting culture see Patricia Cline Cohen, *The Murder of Helen Jewett: The Life and Death of a Prostitute in Nineteenth-Century New York* (New York, 1998). On politics see Paula Baker, "Domestication of Politics: Women and American Political Society, 1780–1920," *AHR* 89 (June 1984): 620–47; William E. Gienapp, "'Politics Seem to Enter into Everything': Political Culture in the North, 1840–1860," in *Essays on American Antebellum Politics, 1840–1860*, Stephen E. Maizlish and John J. Kushma, eds. (College Station, 1982), 15–69. On free African-Americans in the North see James Oliver Horton, "Freedom's Yoke: Gender Conventions among Antebellum Free Blacks," *Feminist Studies* 12 (Spring 1986): 51–76; Dorsey, *Reforming Men and Women*, 136–94.

[26] Although this outlook has been represented as primarily northern in origin, Jan Lewis has documented similar sentiment in Virginia in the early republic, long before industrialization hit the region, in response to the "growth and spread . . . of commerce and the complexities of interdependent economies." Virginians found that "as the world became louder and more problematic, the home profited from the comparison." Jan Lewis, *The Pursuit of Happiness: Family and Values in Jeffersonian Virginia* (New York, 1983), 222.

By calling these men restrained, I do not mean to infer that they were weak, afraid of conflict, or feminized, although exponents of martial manhood might say all those things about them. Restrained men were often successful in business (where they might employ aggressive tactics) and in other areas of life as well. They could be found in all political parties, but the reform aspects of the Whig, Know-Nothing, and Republican parties held a special appeal. Whig men were more likely than Democrats to support the Woman's Rights movement, and they openly encouraged female participation in their campaigns. Restrained men were manly, in the nineteenth-century sense of the term. Their manhood derived from being morally upright, reliable, and brave.[27]

Martial manhood was something else entirely. Martial men rejected the moral standards that guided restrained men; they often drank to excess with pride, and they reveled in their physical strength and ability to dominate both men and women. In a period when economic transformations placed increasing value on expertise, their masculine practices still revolved around dominance. They were not, in general, supporters of the moral superiority of women and the values of domesticity. Martial men believed that the masculine qualities of strength, aggression, and even violence, better defined a true man than did the firm and upright manliness of restrained men. At times they embraced the "chivalry" of knighthood or other masculine ideals from the past.[28] Martial men could be found in all parties, but the aggressively expansionist discourse of the Democratic Party held a special appeal to these men. Martial men were not necessarily ruffians, although restrained men might say they were. Both martial manhood, and the primitive manhood that emerged in the late-nineteenth century, celebrated martial virtues, strength,

[27] I do not think it is correct to identify restrained manhood entirely with what other historians have labeled "evangelical manhood," although evangelical Christianity obviously had a strong effect on restrained men's morality. As Anne C. Rose has noted, Victorian American culture was partially defined in opposition to the religious conviction of the earlier generation of Second Great Awakening converts. The generation born between 1815 and 1837 "set out to recover in secular pursuits the gratifications once provided by religion." Anne C. Rose, *Victorian America and the Civil War* (New York, 1992), 4; Griffen, "Reconstructing Masculinity," 187–8; Johnson, *A Shopkeeper's Millennium*; Ann Douglas, *The Feminization of American Culture* (New York, 1977), ch. 7. On the appeal of different parties to men of different "character" see Lawrence Frederick Kohl, *The Politics of Individualism: Parties and the American Character in the Jacksonian Era* (New York, 1989). On the Whigs and gender see Varon, *We Mean to Be Counted*; Ronald and Mary Zboray, "Gender Slurs."

[28] Stephanie McCurry has described a "martial manhood…grounded in the household and in the prerogatives of masters," that was mobilized by South Carolina planters in order to convince yeomen farmers of the necessity of nullification in the 1830s and in 1860. A national martial manhood served a similar purpose, eliding class in the interests of a territorial expansionism grounded in masculine privilege. Stephanie McCurry, *Masters of Small Worlds: Yeoman Households, Gender Relations, and the Political Culture of the Antebellum South Carolina Low Country* (New York, 1995), 261. On "chivalry" see Isenberg, *Sex and Citizenship*, 141–7.

bravery, and idealized the adventurous outsider. But in a pre-Darwinian era, American men neither self-identified with primitive peoples nor identified themselves as having a bestial nature, as they would later in the century.[29]

While it might seem tempting to see these two expressions of manhood as essentially classed, restrained manhood was not middle-class manhood, and martial manhood was not working-class manhood. Although economic and social transformations shaped these two masculinities, they did not determine them. Some working men opposed territorial expansionism, embraced the ideal of domesticity even if it was an elusive goal, and otherwise personified restrained manhood. The often martial stance of periodicals directed to a refined reading audience, like *Harper's Monthly Magazine*, argues against generalizing about the appeal of aggressive expansionism as well. In an era when college attendance was limited to the elite, collegiate debating societies in Rhode Island, North Carolina, and Ohio addressed questions of the virtue of filibustering and whether the actions of individual filibusters were justified. College students not only advocated filibustering in debates but joined the wide array of men – from working men, to firefighters, to U.S.-Mexico War veterans – who made up filibustering armies.[30]

None the less, martial manhood held special appeal to working men by promising a reward commensurate with their martial virtues, regardless of their financial success at home. The frontier, whether in the western United States or in Latin America, appealed to martial men more than to restrained men because, as R. M. Connell has written, as the practice of manhood in cities "became more subject to rationalization, violence and license, were, symbolically and to some extent actually, pushed out" to the frontier. The economic circumstances of working men were clearly in decline in the first half of the nineteenth century. Mechanics and artisans lost much of their financial independence when the growth of factory production forced the closure of artisanal workshops. Both the pay and the respectability of skilled labor declined as a result. The appeal of the frontier, where strength, will, and bravery counted for more than a good appearance, was understandably great among those who found fewer and fewer public acknowledgements of their masculine prowess in the industrializing United States.[31]

---

[29] On primitive manhood vs. martial manhood see Rotundo, *American Manhood*, 227–31. On a fascination with adventuresome outsiders see Carroll Smith-Rosenberg, *Disorderly Conduct: Visions of Gender in Victorian America* (New York, 1985), 92–108.

[30] May, *Manifest Destiny's Underworld*, 76–77. While it is easy to correlate martial manhood with the "working-class manhood" described by Elliott Gorn and Sean Wilentz (among others), it is important to emphasize that men of different occupations and ethnic groups embraced the aggressive expansionism described in this study. Martial manhood was not defined by class. See Gorn, *Manly Art*; Wilentz, *Chants Democratic*.

[31] Connell, *Masculinities*, 194. This study will use the term *Latin America* when the territory in question extends beyond national borders, and beyond the generally accepted borders of Central America.

By singling out and labeling these two masculinities as martial and restrained, I do not wish to imply that every man, or even most men, fell
clearly into one of these two camps in the mid-nineteenth century. These
two identities easily overlapped with many others mentioned earlier. A fire-
man, merchant, politician, or even militia member could embrace martial
or restrained masculine practices. Irish laborers and southern lawyers could
find common ground with either position, although the former were far
more likely to identify with the aggressive spirit of martial manhood than
restrained manhood. There was a wide variety of gendered practices available to both men and women then, as now. But then, as now, some visions of
manhood were more dominant than others. In the mid-nineteenth century,
these two masculinities were actively embraced by large numbers of men,
and they competed for hegemony. Territorial expansionism provided one
important stage on which this battle was waged.

This book contends that aggressive expansionism, defined here as support
for the use of war to gain new American territory, between the U.S.-Mexico
War, through the filibustering of the 1850s, and up through the Civil War,
was supported by martial men, and that debates over Manifest Destiny also
were debates over the meaning of American manhood and womanhood.
Men filibustered, supported filibustering, or understood Latin America as
rightfully America's in part because of their gender practices. As one letter
writer seeking enlistment in a filibustering scheme in Cuba suggested, joining
was an excellent way for men to "show their manhood." The restrained men
who opposed aggressive expansionism also believed that America's Manifest
Destiny was yet to be fulfilled, but they envisioned it unfolding not by force
of arms but through trade and the spread of American social and religious
institutions. Manifest Destiny forced the question of what both manhood
and womanhood should look like, at home, and abroad. And if it is true,
as historians have suggested, that "Americans clearly formulated the idea
of themselves as an Anglo-Saxon race" through their confrontations with
Mexicans in the mid-1830s to 1840s, those confrontations had an equally
potent and related impact on gender ideals. Antebellum confrontations with
the new filibustering frontier enabled some Americans to equate the proper
practice of American manhood with martial virtues, during a time when
other men insisted manhood was best proven at home.[32]

This study contributes to the growing body of literature that inte-
grates America's political and cultural history in an attempt to document
America's changing relationship to the larger world.[33] It is written with the

---

[32] May, *Manifest Destiny's Underworld*, 104; Reginald Horsman, *Race and Manifest Destiny:
the Origins of American Racial Anglo-Saxonism* (Cambridge, MA, 1981), 208.

[33] The turn of the century, not surprisingly, has proven the richest field for studies of American foreign policy that mesh cultural and political history. Several of the best works,
including Kristin Hoganson, *Fighting for American Manhood: How Gender Politics Provoked the Spanish-American and Philippine-American Wars* (New Haven, 1998) and Gail
Bederman, *Manliness and Civilization*, have specifically considered the role that American

understanding that foreign policy has an important cultural component and that texts can produce meaning, not simply reflect it.[34] The consolidation of national identity and the internal American categories of race, class, and gender occurred in a framework of expansionism and imperial domination. In a period of dramatic economic, social, and cultural change, gender influenced foreign relations, and American foreign relations also had a profound impact on what it meant to be an American.[35] This study does not, for the most part, engage the reactions of the people Americans encountered in Latin American, in Hawaii, or in Japan, to aggressive expansionism, nor

manhood played in the construction of American foreign policy, and the role foreign policy played in reinforcing manhood at home. See also Amy Kaplan, "Black and Blue on San Juan Hill" in *Cultures of United States Imperialism*, Amy Kaplan and Donald E. Pease, eds. (Durham, 1993), 219–36. Eileen J. Findlay brings gender to her study of Puerto Rico in the same period. "Love in the Tropics: Marriage, Divorce, and the Construction of Benevolent Colonialism in Puerto Rico, 1898–1910" in *Close Encounters of Empire: Writing the Cultural History of U.S. Latin American Relations*, Gilbert M. Joseph, Catherine C. LeGrand, Ricardo D. Salvatore, eds. (Durham, 1998), 139–72.

There has been far less attention paid to the antebellum era. The two most significant culturally oriented studies of America's encounter with the outside world in the antebellum period, Streeby, *American Sensations*, and Harvey, *American Geographics*, have both emerged out of a literary context and place key texts at the centers of their investigations. The emphasis on the twentieth century has been particularly pronounced in the cultural study of the interrelationship between the United States and Latin America. For instance, Frederick B. Pike's superb *The United States and Latin America: Myths and Stereotypes of Civilization and Nature*, which spans from the colonial to post–Civil War periods devotes only one of ten chapters to "Early American Views of Latin Americans." John J. Johnson's *Latin America in Caricature* (Austin, 1980) includes only cartoons published after 1880. *Close Encounters of Empire* includes nothing on U.S.-Latin American relations before 1858. See also Mark T. Berger, *Under Northern Eyes: Latin American Studies and U.S. Hegemony in the Americas, 1898–1990* (Bloomington, 1995); James William Park, *Latin American Underdevelopment: A History of Perspectives in the United States, 1870–1965* (Baton Rouge, 1995); Florencia E. Mallon, "The Promise and Dilemma of Subaltern Studies: Perspectives from Latin American History," *AHR* 99 (December 1994): 1491–1515.

[34] For a explication of this position see Melani McAlister, *Epic Encounters: Culture, Media, and U.S. Interests in the Middle East, 1945–2000* (Berkeley, 2001), 5–8.

[35] An entire school of historians, literary scholars, and anthropologists have focused on the imperial encounter over the last few decades, exploring the manner in which imperialism shaped not only the foreign colony and its residents but also the imperialist power at home. Key examples of this approach are Edward Said, *Culture and Imperialism* (New York, 1993); Homi K. Bhabha, *The Location of Culture* (London, 1994); Mrinalini Sinha, *Colonial Masculinity: The "Manly Englishman" and the "Effeminate Bengali" in the Late Nineteenth Century* (Manchester, UK, 1995); Frederick Cooper and Ann Laura Stoler, eds., *Tensions of Empire: Colonial Cultures in a Bourgeois World* (Berkeley, 1997); Ann L. Stoler, "Making Empire Respectable: The Politics of Sexual Morality in Twentieth-Century Colonial Cultures," *American Ethnologist* 16 (November 1989): 634–60. Some key examples of this approach with regards to the United States include Priscilla Wald, "Terms of Assimilation: Legislating Subjectivity in the Emerging Nation," and Richard Slotkin, "Buffalo Bill's 'Wild West' and the Mythologization of the American Empire," both in *Cultures of United States Imperialism*, Amy Kaplan and Donald E. Pease, eds. (Durham, 1993), 59–84, 164–81.

does it attempt to evaluate the legitimacy of American impressions of foreign peoples or foreign territories. While these questions are obviously important, perhaps more important in some ways than those engaged here, they are unfortunately beyond the scope of this study.[36]

I make several arguments here. Manifest Destiny continued to be a vital force in American foreign relations and an object of faith among antebellum Americans after 1848, despite the fact that that war marked the end of substantial new territorial acquisitions of the period.[37] White American men from both sides of the Mason-Dixon Line internalized the ideology of Manifest Destiny and believed that destiny was yet unfulfilled in the decade or so before the Civil War. Their understanding in the 1850s of the Caribbean, the Pacific, and Central America as the "new frontier" undermines the distinction that Americanists have traditionally drawn between continental expansion, which supposedly guided nineteenth-century territorial growth, and the overseas imperialism that emerged in the turn of the century. This study supports Nina Baym's assertion that it was "the expansionist ideology of American Manifest Destiny" that "transformed republicanism into imperialism." Antebellum American culture after 1848 was clearly shaped by and grounded in what Richard Van Alstyne has called "an *imperium* – a dominion, state or sovereignty that would expand in population and territory, and increase in strength and power." The United States may not have achieved a proper empire in the antebellum era, but it was not for lack of trying.[38]

---

[36] On the need for American Studies scholars to adopt a more inclusive view of "America" and actually engage the very questions that this study does not do justice to see Annette Kolodny, "Letting Go Our Grand Obsessions: Notes Toward a New Literary History of the American Frontiers," *American Literature* 64 (March 1992): 1–18. For two different approaches to some of the same material discussed in this book see Doris L. Meyer, "Early Mexican-American Responses to Negative Stereotyping," *New Mexico Historical Review*, 53 (1978): 75–91, and Johnson, *Roaring Camp*. For a good overview of Mexican-American relations from a joint perspective see the essays in *Myths, Misdeeds, and Misunderstandings: The Roots of Conflict in U.S.-Mexican Relations*, Jaime E. Rodríguez O. and Kathryn Vincent, eds. (Wilmington, DE, 1997).

[37] The Gadsden Purchase of 1853 brought almost 30,000 more square miles of Mexico's territory into the American Southwest.

[38] Nina Baym, *American Women Writers and the Work of History, 1790–1860* (New Brunswick, 1995), 64; Richard W. Van Alstyne, *The Rising American Empire* (New York, 1974), 1. Paul Foos has similarly argued that the U.S-Mexico War was "a historic moment in the creation for an American empire rather than nation, encompassing proliferating hierarchies of race and social class, establishing the basis for oligarchic rule based partly on landed wealth." Foos, *A Short, Offhand, Killing Affair: Soldiers and Social Conflict during the Mexican-American War* (Chapel Hill, 2002), 175; see also Walter LaFeber, *The New Empire: An Interpretation of American Expansion, 1860–1898* (Ithaca, 1963). Two scholars who have utilized the idea of empire productively in studies of mid-nineteenth century America are Streeby, *American Sensations*, and Amy Kaplan, *The Anarchy of Empire in the Making of U.S. Culture* (Cambridge, MA, 2002).

But Manifest Destiny did not mean the same thing to all Americans. Some Americans, who supported a martial vision of masculinity, advocated an aggressive expansionism that supported territorial acquisition through force of arms, and particularly though filibustering. Other Americans, advocates of a more restrained vision of manhood, rejected the aggressive expansionism of filibustering and war in favor of American religious and commercial expansionism. These people believed America's Manifest Destiny would best be accomplished through the proliferation of her superior political and religious forms, without the actual annexation of new territories. In other words, competing gender ideals at home shaped very different visions of American expansionism.

Gendered visions of women and men abroad, from Latin America to the islands of the Pacific, justified and reinforced particular practices of manhood and womanhood in the United States. Martial men hoped that they could reify their masculine virtues through aggressive expansionism. In one sense they failed. Filibustering successes were short lived and few in number, and they tended to inhibit rather than further territorial expansionism. But in the 1850s the discourse of aggressive expansionism dominated the discussion of America's proper role in the world, and in doing so, it led to an unintended victory for martial manhood. It ended up exacerbating the growing sectional conflict by promoting violence as a solution to discord. Restrained men promoted their own practices of masculinity through expansionism of trade and religion, and although neither economics, religion, nor compromise was able to prevent the Civil War, the war itself led to a near total acceptance of restrained masculine practices in the post-bellum era. The victory of restrained manhood would not be long lived, however, as both aggressive expansionism and martial manhood had a rebirth at the end of the nineteenth century. Hegemonic American masculinity, this study will attempt to show, was actually made manifest through the process of antebellum territorial expansionism.

The "New Frontier" as Safety Valve

The Political and Social Context of Manifest Destiny, 1800–1860

We want almost unlimited power of expansion. That is our safety valve.

— Lewis Cass, 1847

Americans have been slow to recognize that their republic is in fact an empire, and that its imperial history stretches back almost to the American Revolution.[1] Traditionally, historians distinguished between the continental growth of the United States in the antebellum period and the imperialism that marked American foreign relations starting in the 1890s in order to prove America's exceptionalism from patterns of imperialism set by European nations. In the United States, empire was a "twentieth century aberration rather than . . . part of an expansionist continuum."[2] As proof, scholars pointed to evidence that antebellum exponents of Manifest Destiny promoted the "absorption" of foreign populations into the United States along with full citizenship rights for adult males, a concept alien to

---

[1] A summer of 2004 issue of the *New York Times Book Review* featured an interview with two leading scholars of international history that posed the question, "Does the United States have an empire?" The same issue offered a review of a book that takes as part of its thesis that "the United States is an empire, however much Americans might deny that fact." "Kill the Empire! (Or Not)," *New York Times Book Review* (July 25, 2004), 23; John Lewis Gaddis, "Colossus: The Price of America's Empire," ibid., 11. Michael Doyle provides a working definition of empire as "a system of interaction between two political entities, one of which, the dominant metropole, exerts political control over the internal and external policy – the effective sovereignty – of the other, the subordinate periphery." Imperialism is the process by which an empire is established and maintained. Michael W. Doyle, *Empires* (Ithaca, 1986), 10.

[2] Amy Kaplan, "'Left Alone with America': The Absence of Empire in the Study of American Culture," in *Cultures of United States Imperialism*, Amy Kaplan and Donald E. Pease, eds. (Durham, 1993), 17. Robert Gregg argues persuasively that "exceptionalism is, in many respects, an imperial formulation." *Inside Out, Outside In: Essays in Comparative History* (New York, 2000), 25.

reigning ideas of colonization practiced by European imperial powers at the time.[3]

That the United States was *not* imperialistic in the nineteenth century became a point of pride and honor among policy makers during the very same years in which America embraced colonialism. It was used to buttress the conviction that the United States was an exceptional liberty-loving nation that used its power, not to oppress the free, like certain European nations, but rather to free the oppressed. In the decades after World War II, the transformation of empire and conquest into pious rhetoric reached its apogee, as policy makers and pundits sought to distinguish the United States from the Soviet Union, also known as the "Evil Empire." But the differences between Britain's empire and the immediate prospects for an American empire were far less distinct during the 1850s than was later asserted.[4]

Most aggressive expansionists during the 1850s rejected European-style colonization as incompatible with American liberty, but they dreamed of an America as big or as powerful as the British Empire and actively pursued new territorial acquisitions as far away as Hawaii, Central America, and Japan. The distinctions they drew between their own "empire of Liberty" and contemporary European empires weren't always concrete. Drawing on their experiences of western settlement in the early decades of the century, they often asserted that the peoples in these new territories would "fade away" in the face of American immigration. At other times, as this study will explore, they envisioned annexation facilitated by racial mixing, the "personal annexation," as one aggressive expansionist put it, of Latin American women and U.S. men.

The ability of scholars to disavow empire and of nineteenth-century expansionists to simultaneously critique England's empire while working toward the annexation of Central America was due in large part to the remarkably malleable nature of Manifest Destiny, the guiding ideology behind

---

[3] Because it has not been automatically apparent that the British colonial experience was relevant to the United States in the nineteenth century, many historians have questioned whether imperialism is a useful conceptual frame through which to understand American foreign relations. See, for example, Edward Crapol, "Coming to Terms with Empire: The Historiography of Late-Nineteenth-Century American Foreign Relations," *Diplomatic History* 16 (Fall 1992): 573–97; and a special issue of the *Radical History Review* 57 (Fall 1993): 4–84. A few historians have made strong arguments for the existence of an American "empire" in the antebellum period. See, for example, Thomas Hietala, *Manifest Design: Anxious Aggrandizement in Late Jacksonian America* (Ithaca, 1985), 173–214; Shelly Streeby, *American Sensations: Class, Empire, and the Production of Popular Culture* (Berkeley, 2002).

[4] Charles Vevier, "American Continentalism: An Idea of Expansion, 1845–1910," *AHR* 65 (April 1960): 323; Albert Weinberg, *Manifest Destiny: A Study of Nationalist Expansionism in American History* 1935, reprint edition (Chicago, 1963), 198; William Appleman Williams, *Empire as a Way of Life* (New York, 1980), ix. One excellent recent study of antebellum American expansionism that explores the distinction between American imperialism and colonialism in depth is Streeby, *American Sensations*.

American expansionism. The term *Manifest Destiny* first appeared in print in 1839, in the politically affiliated journal, the *United States Magazine and Democratic Review*. Although the term was attributed to editor John L. O'Sullivan, it was actually one of his writers, Jane McManus Storm, also known as Cora Montgomery or simply Montgomery, who coined the term. In the famous 1845 essay "Annexation" she wrote that it was "the fulfillment of our Manifest Destiny to overspread the continent allotted by Providence for the free development of our yearly multiplying millions."[5] Never a strategic doctrine, Manifest Destiny nonetheless became an institutionally imbedded force with "determinate effects." As Anders Stephanson has written, it was "of signal importance in the way the United States came to understand itself in the world.... Not a mere rationalization, it appeared in the guise of common sense."[6]

Although the phrase came into use in the nineteenth century, the roots of the concept emerged from the Puritan vision that the American settlement would be a "city upon a hill" and beacon of light for less blessed people elsewhere. The triumph of the American Revolution (a war against British imperialism that did not reject imperialism in principle) was seen as providential by the American people, and republican ideology provided secular support to the sacred notion that Americans were a people apart. Even in the early years of the republic, many Americans accepted continental expansion as both natural and inevitable. As Jedediah Morse proclaimed in his 1789 children's geography textbook, "we cannot but anticipate the period, as not far distant, when the American Empire will comprehend millions of souls, west of the Mississippi."[7] Thomas Jefferson envisioned his "empire of liberty" in continental terms, and as a result he was revered by Gilded Age expansionists as "the first imperialist of the Republic." The Monroe Doctrine of 1823 warned European powers against interfering in the affairs of the

---

[5] "Annexation," *USDR* 16 (July–August, 1845): 5–10; With the use of a grammar-check program, Linda S. Hudson has convincingly argued that Montgomery was the author of many crucial expansionist texts previously attributed to O'Sullivan and other authors, including the essay in which the phrase was first used, "The Great Nation of Futurity," *USDR* 6 (November 1839): 426–30. Linda S. Hudson, *Mistress of Manifest Destiny: A Biography of Jane McManus Storm Cazneau, 1807–1878* (Austin, 2001), 46–8, 205–10.

[6] Anders Stephanson, *Manifest Destiny: American Expansion and the Empire of the Right* (New York, 1995), xiv.

[7] Carroll Smith-Rosenberg, "Dis-Covering the Subject of the 'Great Constitutional Discussion,' 1786–1789," *JAH* 79 (December 1992): 848; Jedediah Morse, *The American Geography*. 1789. Reprint edition (New York, 1970), 469. On Jedediah Morse and the manner in which "geographer-pedagogues deeply influenced how antebellum citizens, or citizens to be, thought of themselves and the world beyond...." see Bruce Albert Harvey, *American Geographics: U.S. National Narratives and the Representation of the Non-European World, 1830–1865* (Stanford, 2001), 26–36; David Livingstone, *The Geographical Tradition: Episodes in the History of a Contested Enterprise* (Oxford, 1992), 146.

Americas, without disavowing colonization in principle. In later decades the Doctrine would be used by expansionists to justify hemispheric domination in the name of national security. By the 1830s, a rising American Romanticism encouraged the idea that America's growth could be boundless, while evangelical religion, combined with immigration, exacerbated the tendency of Protestant Americans to view the Catholic states to the south and west of their country as a distinct challenge to their "religion, security, commercial activity and culture."[8]

Through the early decades of the nineteenth century, most Americans believed that expansionism would spread progress and enlightenment to all of mankind and that through the power of influence and persuasion America's Manifest Destiny would be revealed. Americans also believed, well into the nineteenth century, that America's territorial destiny would unfold in a peaceful and natural process, expressed through a feminized metaphor of fertility. In the expansionist vision of the 1830s, new territories would come to America, like "fruit dropping from a tree."[9] By the 1840s, however, Manifest Destiny's discourse had become largely martial in tone, nurtured by scientific race theory and a growing acceptance that the imaginary race of American "Anglo-Saxons" was destined to dominate lesser races. It was by force of arms that territorial conquest was both envisioned and undertaken. Although the German immigrant Francis Lieber grew increasingly repulsed by the bellicose expressions of America's racial mission after the U.S.-Mexico War, his "Ship Canal" poem highlights the essential aggressivity at the heart of the American project in Central America. Although a ship canal is a business venture and not a military encounter, in Lieber's vision the two meld together. Even a moderate like Lieber believed in and celebrated the martial nature of the American race as providentially selected to subdue the whole favored continent.[10]

---

[8] Mary Ann Heiss, "The Evolution of the Imperial Idea and U.S. National Identity," *Diplomatic History* 26 (Fall 2002): 516–19, Gilded Age expansionist Albert Beverage quote page 517; Peter S. Onuf, *Jefferson's Empire: The Language of American Nationhood* (Charlottesville, VA, 2000); Reginald Horsman, *Race and Manifest Destiny: The Origins of American Racial Anglo-Saxonism* (Cambridge, MA, 1981), 82–6; Weinberg, *Manifest Destiny*, 63, 388; Stephanson, *Manifest Destiny: American Expansion*, 3–27; Robert W. Johannsen, "The Meaning of Manifest Destiny," in *Manifest Destiny and Empire: American Antebellum Expansionism*, Sam W. Haynes and Christopher Morris, eds. (College Station, TX, 1997), 7–20; Thomas Schoonover, *Uncle Sam's War of 1898 and the Origins of Globalization* (Lexington, KY, 2003), 2.

[9] On land-as-woman in American writing see Annette Kolodny, *The Lay of the Land: Metaphor as Experience and History in American Life and Letters* (Chapel Hill, 1975).

[10] Key works on Manifest Destiny include Hietala, *Manifest Design*; Horsman, *Race and Manifest Destiny*; Frederick Merk, *Manifest Destiny and Mission in American History: A Reinterpretation* (New York, 1963); Weinberg, *Manifest Destiny*; Robert F. Berkhofer, Jr., *The White Man's Indian: Images of the American Indian from Columbus to the Present* (New York,

To argue as this study does, that Manifest Destiny was gendered, is on one level to state the obvious, yet as an explanatory factor it has been largely overlooked by historians.[11] During the earliest years of the republic, as Americans worked to simultaneously distinguish themselves from Europeans and dehumanize Native Americans in order to justify their displacement, editors and journalists wrote "endless articles" celebrating America's military heroes in order to confirm the masculinity of "the American republican, the Son of Liberty, the frontiersman, the empire builder." By feminizing Native Americans, white Americans could prove themselves to be the legitimate possessors of American land. This gender dynamic would help propel American expansion westward.[12]

Faith in the racial superiority of the Anglo-Saxon and in the inferiority of the "mixed race" peoples of Latin America easily translated into a gendered vision of the dominant American when expansionists turned to the south. As Frederick Pike has explored, in the view of nineteenth-century Americans, "Latin Americans, regardless of gender, were stereotyped as feminine and destined by nature to satisfy Yankee lust." The New York *Herald* concisely expressed this view, along with the widespread equation of Latin American nations with women, when it supported annexing all of Mexico late in the U.S.-Mexico war in 1847. "Like the Sabine virgins, she [Mexico] will soon learn to love her ravisher." The ubiquity of metaphors of penetration in the literature of Manifest Destiny also is striking. In one typical formulation, *De Bow's Review* celebrated America's westward settlement in 1849. "The American people ... have, while yet scarce 'hardened into manhood,' swept across the 'impassable' mountains, overspread the great valleys, and penetrated in immense numbers through the wildernesses of the Oregon, the Sacramento, and the Gila, to the very shores of the Pacific Ocean."[13]

1978), 154; Robert Johannsen, "The Meaning of Manifest Destiny," in *Manifest Destiny and Empire: American Antebellum Expansionism*, Sam W. Haynes and Christopher Morris, eds. (College Station, TX, 1997); 7–20. On Lieber, see Philip S. Paludan, *A Covenant with Death: The Constitution, Law, and Equality in the Civil War Era* (Urbana, 1975), 61–108; Horsman, *Race and Manifest Destiny*, 171–3.

[11] The gendered nature of antebellum Manifest Destiny is readily apparent but, strangely enough, has been ignored by scholars. Reginald Horsman has explored how support for Manifest Destiny became increasingly bellicose in the 1840s, attributing it to the growth of "romantic racial nationalism." But neither he nor other scholars have addressed the gendered implications of what was first and foremost a vision of American manhood. Frederick Merk compiled a long list of factors that contributed to Manifest Destiny, not including gender. Merk, *Manifest Destiny and Mission*, viii–ix. Recent accounts also fail to take gender into account. Stephanson, in *Manifest Destiny: American Expansion*, fails to mention gender. Nor do any of the authors in *Manifest Destiny and Empire*, Haynes and Morris, editors. One recent study that does consider gender is Streeby, *American Sensations*.

[12] Smith-Rosenberg, "Dis-Covering the Subject," 869; See also Richard Drinnon, *Facing West: The Metaphysics of Indian Hating and Empire Building* (New York, 1990).

[13] Frederick B. Pike, *The United States and Latin America: Myths and Stereotypes of Civilization and Nature* (Austin, 1992), 13; *NYH*, October 8, 1847; "Communication between the

Gendered rhetoric proliferated during the U.S.-Mexico conflict. Up until 1844, Whigs and Democrats alike refused to annex the Republic of Texas, which declared independence from Mexico in 1836. Mexico never recognized Texas sovereignty, and a dispute over the southern boundary of the Republic virtually guaranteed that American annexation would result in war. During the presidential campaign of 1844, Democratic supporters of annexation pictured Texas as a vulnerable European maiden, and they cast their Whig opponents as unmanly moralizers unwilling to help a damsel in distress. In other words, Democrats cloaked their aggressivity in the language of chivalry (see Figure 1.1).

Gendered rhetoric was not wholly responsible for the U.S.-Mexico War, but the chivalrous Democratic victor in that election, James K. Polk, provoked war with Mexico less than two years later. Images of attractive Mexican women and effeminate Mexican men in the popular literature of the war helped to justify aggression against Mexico. As the *Southern Quarterly Review* stated in 1847, Mexican women "are always agreeable" and "win foreigners irresistibly," but "the mass of the male sex is selfish, false, reckless and idle."[14] The poem "They Wait for Us," published in Boston in 1846 nicely summarized these stereotypes.

> The Spanish maid, with eye of fire,
> At balmy evening turns her lyre
> And, looking to the Eastern sky,
> Awaits our Yankee chivalry.
> Whose purer blood and valiant arms,
> Are fit to clasp her budding charms.
> The *man*, her mate, is sunk in sloth –
> To love, his senseless heart is loth;
> The pipe and glass and tinkling lute,
> A sofa and a dish of fruit;
> A nap, some dozen times a day;
> Sombre and sad, and never gay.[15]

Opponents of the U.S.-Mexico War also employed gendered imagery to frame their critique. Massachusetts abolitionist James Russell Lowell

Atlantic and Pacific Oceans," *DBR* 7 (July 1849): 1. On representations of Latin American nations as feminine see Michael Hunt, *Ideology and U.S. Foreign Policy* (New Haven, 1987), 59–61. On colonies as feminine see Ann Stoler, *Race and the Education of Desire: Foucault's History of Sexuality and the Colonial Order of Things* (Durham, 1995), 174.

[14] "Mexico, Her People and Revolutions," *SQR* 12 (October 1847): 371; On images of Mexican women see Robert Johannsen, *To the Halls of the Montezumas: The Mexican War in the American Imagination* (New York, 1985), 169–70, 189–91; Streeby, *American Sensations*; Eric J. Sundquist, "The Literature of Expansion and Race," in *The Cambridge History of American Literature*, Sacvan Bercovitch, ed. (New York, 1995), vol. 2: 162.

[15] Quoted in Horsman, *Race and Manifest Destiny*, 233.

FIGURE I.I. "Virtuous Harry, or Set a Thief to Catch a Thief!" (New York, J. Baillie, 1844). This gendered critique of the Whig Party's anti-Texas-annexation platform in 1844 contrasts the manliness of James K. Polk, the Democrat, with that of Whig Henry Clay, and it equates territorial annexation with the "personal annexation" of a beautiful woman. "Harry" Clay, an illustrious gambler, hypocritically spurns the young, white, female figure of Texas, saying "Stand back, Madam Texas! for we are more holy than thou! Do you think we will have anything to do with gamblers, horse-racers, and licentious profligates?" suggesting that anti-annexationists were moralists. A Quaker taps Clay on the shoulder and reminds him, "Softly, Softly, friend Harry. Thou hast mentioned the very reason that we cannot Vote for thee!" Polk and his vice-presidential candidate George Dallas, in contrast, are presented as the chivalrous protectors of womanhood, embracing Texas not out of a desire to extend slavery (as critics claimed), but because Texas is a young maiden in distress. Polk takes her hand saying, "Welcome, sister, Your Valor has won you liberty and independence, and you have fairly won the right to be identified with 'the land of the brave, and the home of the free.'" Dallas adds, "Slandered as she is, let him that is without sin, cast the first stone at her!" The demure Texas appeals to the viewer of the cartoon directly: "Shall the slanders that have been urged against your sister, sever those whose blood flows from the same fountain?" Since it was widely understood that annexing Texas would lead to war with Mexico, the reduction of the Democratic platform to chivalry, and the Whig platform to moralizing, is especially notable. Library of Congress, Prints and Photographs Division [LC-USZ62-1276].

criticized the war and the rights of Anglo-Saxon manhood in his *Biglow Papers*. In the persona of an uneducated recruit, Lowell wrote,

> It must be right, fer Caleb sez it's reg'lar Anglo-saxon
>
> . . . .
>
> Thet our nation's bigger 'n theirn an' so its
> rights air bigger,
> An' thet it's all to make 'em free that we air
> pullin' trigger,
> Thet Anglo Saxondom's idee's abreakin' 'em to
> pieces;
> An' thet idee's that every man doos just wut he
> dam pleases;[16]

The aggressive stance of a martial America was rejected during the U.S.-Mexico War by more restrained men. Might did not make right, according to Lowell, and the argument that the war was being fought to increase the liberty of the Mexican people was a transparent excuse for willful destruction. Whig congressman Alexander Stephens of Georgia, who would later become vice president of the Confederate States of America, supported Manifest Destiny through peaceful expansionism. But like many in his party he condemned the U.S.-Mexico War as the self-indulgent exercise of antiquated forms of aggression. In 1846 he declared the war to be "*downward* progress. It is a progress of party– of excitement– of lust of power– a spirit of war–aggression– violence and licentiousness. It is a progress which, if indulged in, would soon sweep over all law, all order, and the Constitution itself." More blisteringly direct was Ohio Whig senator Thomas Corwin's critique of the manhood of the proponents of war. On February 11, 1847, Corwin compared President Polk to a pirate for the "avarice which prompted us to covet and to seize by force, *that* which was not ours."[17]

Nor was the debate over the manliness of expansionists among men only. Woman's rights activists in the 1840s roundly denounced the war for upholding aggression and force as necessary characteristics of the American citizen. To those who claimed that America's national honor was at stake, journalist Jane Swisshelm compared the war to a "giant whipping a cripple." For antebellum feminists, the rise of martial manhood undermined their own claims for full citizenship.[18] The idea that aggression was an admirable quality in a man (or a nation) was rejected by opponents of the U.S.-Mexico War at the

---

[16] James Russell Lowell, *The Biglow Papers* (Cambridge, MA, 1848), 145. "Caleb" refers to Caleb Cushing, Massachusetts Democrat and brigadier general in the war. John H. Schroeder, *Mr. Polk's War: American Opposition and Dissent, 1846–1848* (Madison, 1973), 103–4, ftnt. 42.

[17] *Congressional Globe*, 29th Congress, 1st Sess., 1846, Appendix, 949–50; 29th Congress, 2nd. Sess., 1847, Appendix, 215–7.

[18] Nancy Isenberg, *Sex and Citizenship in Antebellum America* (Chapel Hill, 1998), 105, quote page 133.

same time that supporters of the war upheld aggression, and even, as this study will explore, the "virtues" of piracy.

The gendered nature of contemporary race theory had serious implications in 1848 at war's end, when some Americans demanded all of Mexico's territory as spoils of war. The all-Mexico movement never gained the support of the majority of Americans, who viewed the annexation of the densely populated southern states of Mexico in quite a different light than the annexation of the less populated north. But race theory allowed supporters of the all-Mexico movement to dismiss objections about the difficulty of assimilating this population. Thus the *Democratic Review* could openly acknowledge the concerns of anti-expansionists like the pro-slavery ideologue Senator John C. Calhoun of South Carolina that Mexicans were socially, politically, and, especially, racially inferior to Americans, but it could express utter confidence that in the end, the characteristics of the superior race would win out. As the journal wrote in February of 1847, "the Mexican race now see, in the fate of the aborigines of the north, their own inevitable destiny. They must amalgamate and be lost, in the superior vigor of the Anglo-Saxon race, or they must utterly perish" (See Figure 1.2).[19] Supporters of the all-Mexico movement argued that through the sexual union of "vigorous" American men with Mexican women, eight million Mexicans could somehow be absorbed into the "Anglo-Saxon" race.[20]

That war rewards martial excess is not surprising; nor is it surprising that gendered language would be used in wartime. The connection between masculinity and national strength is an ancient one, and well before the period under consideration in this study people at war have critiqued their opponents in gendered terms. Witnesses to any war will note that the heroic, brave, and strong seem to be limited to, or at least overrepresented, on the home team. Americans embraced war as a means to strengthen manhood at home long before war with Mexico. Jeffersonian Republicans, for instance, looked to a second war against Great Britain in 1812 as a way to reinforce martial virtue in a post-Revolutionary generation.[21] What is notable about

---

[19] "The War," *USDR* 20 (February 1847): 99–102.

[20] Historians of the all-Mexico movement have generally noted that support for the movement was predicated on the belief that Mexicans would become Americanized, but they have largely failed to consider the importance of the fact that it was through the sexual union of American men and Mexican women that this amalgamation would occur. See, for instance, Horsman, *Race and Manifest Destiny*, 165–6, 233, 246; Albert Weinberg discussed the concept of "regeneration" in some detail in the 1930s, but he did not closely examine how that regeneration was envisioned as happening. Weinberg, *Manifest Destiny*, 160–89.

[21] Joan Scott, *Gender and the Politics of History* (New York, 1988), 48; Hannah Arendt, "Imperialism, Nationalism, Chauvinism," *Review of Politics* 7 (October 1945): 441–63; Nancy C. M. Hartsock, "Masculinity, Heroism, and the Making of War," in *Rocking the Ship of State*, Adrienne Harris and Ynestra King, eds. (Boulder, 1989), 133–52; Steven Watts, *The Republic Reborn: War and the Making of Liberal America, 1790–1820* (Baltimore, 1987), 154, 168–9; Kristin Hoganson, *Fighting for American Manhood: How Gender Politics Provoked the Spanish-American and Philippine-American Wars* (New Haven, 1998), 206.

FIGURE 1.2. *Flight of the Mexican Army at the Battle of Buena Vista, Feb. 23, 1847* (New York, Nathaniel Currier, 1847). This popular lithograph of the Mexican army retreating from the battlefield after the most celebrated American victory of the U.S.-Mexico War reinforced the vision of Mexican men as cowardly and American men as heroic. Mexican troops outnumbered American troops by almost three to one at Buena Vista. The mass exodus of Mexicans from the battlefield pictured here nicely corresponds with an expansionist faith that the "inferior" peoples of Latin America "must amalgamate and be lost, in the superior vigor of the Anglo-Saxon race, or they must utterly perish." Library of Congress, Prints and Photographs Division [LC-USZ62-93028].

the period between the U.S.-Mexico War and the Civil War, and what this study seeks to document, is the extent to which gendered language and assumptions continued to frame the popular understanding of expansionism during a period when the United States was *not* at war.

Enter the Filibusters

The years between 1848 and 1860 could hardly be called a peaceful time, but at least with regards to war they were a time of peace.[22] To say that the

---

[22] The Navy did take part in several minor military encounters with China during this period, related to the Taiping Rebellion in 1854, the Arrow War in 1856, and at the Taku Bar forts in 1859, and the Army was regularly engaged with Native-American tribes within the United States.

United States was not at war between 1848 and 1860, however, is not to say that United States *citizens* were not at war, and this is precisely the distinction that makes the controversial but widespread practice of filibustering in this period so remarkable. Americans, flaunting international law, were targeting foreign countries with disturbing regularity between these two wars. Between 1848 and 1860 it was not unusual for two or more filibustering expeditions to either be in preparation or in progress in America's cities.[23]

In some sense, this seems quite strange. One might imagine that war would quench the filibustering impulse. After all, the war cost thirteen thousand American and twenty thousand Mexican lives, and it transferred 1,193,061 square miles of Mexican territory (including Texas) to the United States. Despite the claims of some historians that "many Americans saw the United States' victory [over Mexico] as fulfillment of their 'Manifest Destiny,'" there is ample evidence that many other Americans believed that northern Mexico was just the beginning of the United States' territorial expansion south.[24] For many Americans, the U.S.-Mexico War served to enflame expansionist desire, seemingly fulfilling the proclamations of the most rabid exponents of Manifest Destiny and offering a precedent for further dramatic gains. During the war, New England transcendentalist philosopher Ralph Waldo Emerson predicted that "Mexico will poison us." But even he had privately mused that "the strong British race . . . must also overrun . . . Mexico and Oregon."[25]

It was an 1844 essay of Emerson's, "The Young American," that gave name to the faction of the Democratic Party that would push hardest for territorial expansionism. "In every age of the world, there has been a leading nation," he wrote. Although Emerson conceptualized America leading the world through moral example, his essay, "The Young American," provided a justification for an aggressive approach to Manifest Destiny after the war, since where "official government" fails to act, he argued, America must rely on "the increasing disposition of private adventurers to assume its fallen

---

[23] Robert E. May, *Manifest Destiny's Underworld: Filibustering in Antebellum America* (Chapel Hill, 2002), 20.

[24] Quote in Carol and Thomas Christensen, *The U.S.-Mexican War* (San Francisco, 1998), v. Bruce A. Harvey is typical in his assertion that Central America and Polynesia "lay beyond the immediate juggernaut of Manifest Destiny." Harvey, *American Geographics*, 3. In his recent study of the U.S.-Mexico War, Paul Foos has shown that many soldiers became active in the Free-Soil movement after the war. For these men, service in the war was what limited their territorial ambitions. Paul Foos, *A Short, Offhand, Killing Affair: Soldiers and Social Conflict during the Mexican-American War* (Chapel Hill, 2002). Frederick Merk has made the most dramatic claims about the limits of expansionism, arguing that "from the outset Manifest Destiny – vast in program, in its sense of continentalism – was slight in support. It lacked national, sectional, or party following commensurate with its bigness." Merk, *Manifest Destiny and Mission*, 216. See also John Mack Faragher, "North, South, and West: Sectional Controversies and the U.S.-Mexico Boundary Survey," in *Drawing the Borderline: Artists-Explorers of the U.S.-Mexico Boundary Survey*, Dawn Hall, ed. (Albuquerque, 1996), 3.

[25] Quoted in Horsman, *Race and Manifest Destiny*, 177.

functions." Even some thoughtful opponents of war, like Emerson, held an expansive vision of America's Manifest Destiny.[26]

What other Americans may have lacked in thoughtfulness, they more than made up for in enthusiasm. The preeminent scholar of aggressive expansionism, Robert E. May, has documented that the close of the war heralded a filibustering "epidemic" in America, as recently released soldiers, urban working men, southern partisans, and ardent nationalists joined together in unsanctioned military excursions with the goal of wresting new territories out of Latin America. At the bare minimum, five thousand men participated in filibustering excursions, although many more hoped to filibuster or otherwise actively supported filibustering. Urban men from New York to San Francisco signed up to fight in Central America in the 1850s, while an army officer on the Rio Grande bemoaned the fact that some of the "best citizens" of that region "actively solicited desertions" from the Army for filibustering missions. Before the war, the expansionist *Democratic Review* regularly suggested that "the whole of this vast continent is destined one day to subscribe to the Constitution of the United States." In the early 1850s the journal pictured the southern boundary of the country "moving downward on the two sides, from California and from Texas, and in a less decided manner, extending, as it were, a penumbra over the West Indies." By the close of the 1850s, the *Democratic Review* was even more emphatic that "Mexico and Cuba . . . be numbered among the United States of America. That this is to be the certain destiny of this people, notwithstanding the delay occasioned by diplomacy, no well-informed person entertains the shadow of a doubt."[27]

Filibustering was not the invention of the interwar period. One of Tennessee's first U.S. senators, William Blount, was impeached in 1797 on charges that he was planning to invade Spanish territory. Former vice president Aaron Burr was arrested by U.S. authorities on similar charges in 1807. Spanish East Florida and Texas were popular targets of American filibusters in the eighteen-teens, and Americans were involved in many of the independence movements that reduced Spain's once mighty new-world empire to a pair of Caribbean islands by 1824. The filibustering of this period led U.S.

---

[26] Ralph Waldo Emerson, "The Young American," *Essays and Lectures* (New York, 1983), 262, 225; "Emerson, however unwittingly, did his small part in fostering the filibustering missions of the 1850s: he made available – to philosophers, poets, and freebooters alike – an elegant rhetoric and belief in the power of the American self." Brady Harrison, "The Young Americans," *American Studies* 40 (Fall 1999): 76. On the Young America movement see Edward L. Widmer, *Young America: The Flowering of Democracy in New York City* (New York, 1999); Merle E. Curti, "Young America," *AHR* 32 (October 1926): 34–55.

[27] May, *Manifest Destiny's Underworld*, 18, 91–101, 52; William Prince diary, September 22, 1851. Beinecke Rare Book and Manuscript Library; "Territorial Aggrandizement," *USDR* 17 (October 1845): 247; "The Line of Political Knowledge," *USDR* 32 (March 1853): 280; "Abrogation of the Clayton-Bulwer Treaty," *USDR* 42, (December 1858): 442. See also "The Monroe Doctrine versus the Clayton and Bulwer Treaty," *USDR* 32 (March 1853): 199.

authorities to reiterate in the clearest form U.S. support for the Law of Nations, already enshrined in the Constitution. The Neutrality Act of 1818, one of several issued during the first half of the nineteenth century, was notable because it provided for stiff fines and prison sentences for any American aiding a "military expedition...against the territory or dominions of any foreign prince or state, or of any colony, district, or people, with whom the United States are at peace."[28]

Still Americans filibustered. Canada became one of the leading targets of the 1830s, attracting attention because the border between the two countries was not clearly defined in some places and because of Canadian-led insurrectionary activities against the governments of Upper and Lower Canada. Canadian efforts at fighting ecclesiastical favoritism, high taxation rates, and the limited representation accorded them by Britain struck an understandably sympathetic cord in the United States, and those Canadian rebels who fled south found enthusiastic audiences in cities including Buffalo and Rochester. In the most famous Canadian filibustering excursion, a few hundred American "Patriots" took part in a deluded and poorly organized attempt to free Upper Canada from English "tyranny." Captured in Ontario in 1838, and convicted of "piratical invasion," almost 100 of them were shipped to a British penal colony in Australia. Canada faded as a locus of filibustering attention in the 1840s thanks to President Martin Van Buren's 1838 proclamation that the United States would enforce its neutrality acts, because the boundary between the two countries was resolved, and because the British granted Canada self government in 1842, which by 1848 had become firmly entrenched. A secret organization with the goal of driving the British out of Ireland, the Fenian Brotherhood of New York, invaded Canada in 1866 with the goal of exchanging Canadian independence for Irish independence, but in the 1840s and 1850s, filibusters looked south, and not north.[29]

Mexican Texas, occupied primarily by Americans disgruntled with Mexican law, was the other major target of aggressive expansionists in the 1830s. Robert May has called the 1835 Texas Revolution "the most successful filibuster in American History" since very few soldiers in the rebel army were permanent residents of Texas.[30] After 1848, the pace of American filibustering plots accelerated dramatically, although only a limited number of

---

[28] *Annals of Congress*, 15th Congress, 1st Sess., 2:2567–70; Congress was empowered to punish "offenses against the Law of Nations" in Article I, Section 8, of the Constitution. May, *Manifest Destiny's Underworld*, 4–7; Charles H. Brown, *Agents of Manifest Destiny: The Lives and Times of the Filibusters* (Chapel Hill, 1980), 3–13.

[29] Cassandra Pybus and Hamish Maxwell-Stewart, *American Citizens: British Slaves: Yankee Political Prisoners in an Australian Penal Colony, 1839–1850* (East Lansing, MI, 2002), quote page 44; Mark L. Harris, "The Meaning of Patriot: The Canadian Rebellion and American Republicanism, 1837–1839," *Michigan Historical Review* 23 (Spring 1997): 33–69.

[30] May, *Manifest Destiny's Underworld*, 9.

them actually made it off United States soil. Not surprisingly, Mexico remained a popular target. Texans repeatedly crossed the Rio Grande in their attempts to revolutionize neighboring Mexican states, including Tamaulipas and Coahuila. The most significant troublemaker based in Texas was the charismatic Tejano veteran of the Mexican Revolution, José María Jesús Carvajal. The light-skinned Carvajal, who spoke English fluently, had little trouble finding Anglos who were willing to follow him into Tamaulipas on three separate occasions in the early 1850s to fight for both freedom and free trade.[31]

During the same period, Californians targeted the Mexican states closest to them. Given that the vast majority of the California population had arrived as a result of the 1849 gold rush, the reported great mineral wealth of Sonora attracted a great deal of unwanted attention. California quartermaster general Joseph C. Morehead attempted to invade Sonora in 1851 but was stopped en route in Baja. The French adventurer Count Gaston de Raousset-Boulbon sent an armed expedition to Sonora from San Francisco in 1852. Newspaper editor William Walker invaded Sonora in 1853. Former California Whig state senator Henry A. Crabb became a filibuster after he failed to gain reelection to the state senate in 1854. He was executed in Sonora in 1857, along with his followers, whose bodies were left unburied in the desert. Sonoran authorities expressed their displeasure at being so often targeted by Californians by preserving Crabb's head in a jar in alcohol. Californians also took part in a multi-national filibuster against Ecuador in 1851, and they managed to convince Hawaiian authorities that they were planning attacks on the kingdom through much of the decade, despite the fact that no Hawaiian filibuster ever materialized.[32]

The strategic location, fertility, and wealth (in sugar and slaves) of Cuba made it a natural target for filibusters. Venezuelan-born Narciso López gained international attention as he repeatedly tried to liberate the island from Spain in the late 1840s and beginning of the 1850s. With the help of a wide variety of American supporters from New York to Natchez (including *Democratic Review* editor John L. O'Sullivan) and followed by an American volunteer army, López seemed unstoppable, until he and fifty-one American volunteers were captured in Cuba and put to death in the summer of 1851. This hardly dampened American ardor for the "Queen of the Antilles," and Southerners, including Mississippi governor John Quitman,

[31] Carvajal's name was also spelled Carbajal. Ernest C. Shearer, "The Carvajal Disturbances," *Southwestern Historical Quarterly* 55 (October 1951): 201–9; Brown, *Agents of Manifest Destiny*, 152–4, 156–7; May, *Manifest Destiny's Underworld*, 36–8.
[32] Joaquin Ramirez Cabañas, *Gaston de Raousset: Conquistador de Sonora* (Mexico D.F., 1941), 7–12; Brown, *Agents of Manifest Destiny*, 217; May, "Manifest Destiny's Filibusters," in *Manifest Destiny and Empire: American Antebellum Expansionism*, Sam W. Haynes and Christopher Morris, eds. (College Station, TX, 1997), 39.

and the Louisiana-based secret society, the Order of the Lone Star, continued to target the slaveholding island over the course of the decade.[33]

Although there were a greater number of attacks on Mexico and Cuba, Central America became the most famous aggressive expansionist target of the period. Only a few months after Mexico ceded control of California to the United States in the Treaty of Guadalupe Hidalgo, San Francisco newspapers began to report the discovery of gold at a nearby lumber mill. The 1849 gold rush provoked a sudden popular interest in Central America because the quickest and easiest route to the gold fields was through Panama or Nicaragua. Twenty-thousand immigrants each year traveled by sea to California, the vast majority along the Nicaragua and Panama routes. In 1855, after the Panama railway was completed at a cost of six thousand lives and $8 million, travel from New York to San Francisco could be as short as thirty days. In contrast, the Cape Horn and overland routes, both more dangerous, generally took four months. The Nicaraguan canal proposed by Cornelius Vanderbilt's American Atlantic and Pacific Ship Canal Company, (the same canal so poetically lauded by Francis Lieber) would have made the Isthmus route even shorter. The canal was never built, but it established Vanderbilt's control over transit in the country.[34]

Tennessee-born William Walker, who first rose to national attention in the fall and winter of 1853 in an aborted attempt to capture land in Sonora and Baja California, seized control of Nicaragua, which was divided by a civil war, in the fall of 1855. He became commander in chief of the republic's army, and in July of 1856 became president of the country (thereby besting Texan Henry L. Kinney, another filibuster who mounted an expedition to Nicaragua at the same time). Although Walker was originally supported by Vanderbilt, who believed the American could provide a stabilizing presence in the region, Walker undermined Vanderbilt's transit interests in Nicaragua soon after gaining control of the country. He paid a heavy price when Vanderbilt subsequently cut off all his supplies.[35] After losing a war in May of 1857 to a coalition army composed of Central Americans and the British, sponsored by Vanderbilt, Walker returned to the United States and gathered funds for another invasion of Central America in a series of speaking engagements in major cities. In November of 1857 he returned to

[33] May, *Manifest Destiny's Underworld*, 22–3, 33–5.

[34] David I. Folkman Jr., *The Nicaragua Route* (Salt Lake City, 1972), 1–11; Hudson, *Mistress of Manifest Destiny*, 139–40; Craig Dozier, *Nicaragua's Mosquito Shore: The Years of British and American Presence* (Tuscaloosa, 1985), 79, 83, 91; Earl E. Moore, "The Panama Rail Road Company," *Manuscripts* 52 (Summer 2000): 209–18; JoAnn Levy, "The Panama Trail: Short Cut to California," *Overland Journal* 10 (Fall 1992): 27; see also Ernest A. Wiltsee, *Gold Rush Steamers of the Pacific* (San Francisco, 1938). The Isthmus of Tehuantepec, in Mexico, was another site being considered for a canal or railroad, primarily because Americans held title to a million acres of land spanning the Isthmus.

[35] Folkman, *The Nicaragua Route*, 23–106; May, *Manifest Destiny's Underworld*, 174.

Nicaragua but was arrested by U.S. Commodore Hiram Paulding and was forcibly returned to the United States. On the eve of the Civil War, William Walker made one final foray to the region, meeting his death in front of a firing squad in Honduras in 1860.

Walker was president of Nicaragua for less than a year, but his was the only filibuster in the post-1848 period to achieve even limited success. Given the illegal and arguably immoral nature of aggressive expansionism, it is perhaps understandable why the failed filibustering of this period is not frequently highlighted in American history. But this short outline of some of the most significant excursions indicates that filibustering was a chronic condition in the years between the Mexican and Civil Wars. The motivations driving aggressive expansionists to target neighboring countries is a subject of this study, but it seems important to note at the outset that most post-1848 filibusters appear to have had markedly less noble motivations than those of the "Patriots" who invaded Ontario in 1838. Filibusters were usually driven by the desire to annex new territories to the United States, and they generally operated out of the conviction that American political, social, and religious forms would improve the condition of residents of new territories. The popular insurrections and revolutionary fervor of 1848 in Europe were closely followed by the American press, and they proved inspirational to many fledgling revolutionaries.

But it seems safe to say that while men who joined the post-1848 filibustering excursions to Mexico, Cuba, and Nicaragua were just as likely to speak of liberty as were the Canadian filibusters of the 1830s, they were far more likely to be motivated by concrete enticements. The United States had extensive investments in the region, beyond Vanderbilt's newly contracted canal and the proposed Panama railway. Caribbean ports were the outlets for production from the Midwest and South and were primary trading partners for the commercial centers of the Gulf coast. The control of Caribbean islands and of Latin America promised a steady source of raw materials to fuel America's industrial production and foodstuffs for its expanding urban populations. Furthermore, filibustering expedition organizers promised recruits adventure and good pay. As this study explores, the lands and peoples of Latin America and the Pacific promised other enticements as well. These "new frontiers" offered advantages in love and work the snowy north seemed less likely to provide.[36]

Political Repercussions and Responses in the Second Party System

The expansionist fervor that supported this spate of filibusters had a serious impact on U.S. foreign policy in the 1840s and 1850s. The father of the

---

[36] Pybus and Maxwell-Stewart, *American Citizens*, 1–25; May, *Manifest Destiny's Underworld*, 4–6; Schoonover, *Uncle Sam's War*, 20–2.

Democratic Party, Andrew Jackson, forced the removal of the five major Indian tribes of the Southeast – the Cherokee, Creek, Choctaw, Chickasaw, and Seminole – to west of the Mississippi along the infamous "trail of tears" in the 1830s. In doing so, he opened up extensive new lands to white settlement in the Southeast. Following in his footsteps, James K. Polk ran for president in 1844 on a ambitiously expansionist platform, including the promise that the United States would take the entire Oregon territory from the British, to "54° 40′," or he would "fight" as the slogan went (he quickly settled for half of that, angering many expansionist supporters in the North). Polk, who desired and served only one term, set a standard for the acquisition of new territories that future Democratic presidential candidates would struggle unsuccessfully to emulate. In his failed 1848 presidential bid against the Whig war hero Zachary Taylor, Michigan senator Lewis Cass did not attempt to hide his "bellicose expansionism" (see Figure 1.3). Cass stated during the war that "we want almost unlimited power of expansion. That is our safety valve." He advocated annexing the Yucatan peninsula when it declared independence from Mexico in 1847 (Mexico settled with its province before the United States could take action but not before many Americas left to help with the fighting). He was a firm and lifelong supporter of the annexation of Cuba, since, he proclaimed, the Gulf of Mexico "should be ours."[37]

Zachary Taylor, who died soon after entering office, and his vice president, Millard Fillmore, worked assiduously to stop filibustering excursions, most notably Narciso López's repeated attacks on Cuba. Fillmore originally appointed the esteemed New Hampshire orator Daniel Webster secretary of state, a post Webster had held in the early 1840s under Whig presidents William Henry Harrison and John Tyler. An opponent of the U.S.-Mexico War and aggressive expansionism generally, Webster left no question about the illegality of filibustering, and he became an object of scorn among aggressive expansionists. Massachusetts Whig Edward Everett, who succeeded to the post after Webster's death in 1852, faced fewer filibustering crises during his short tenure (López was dead by this time) and left the question of Cuba's destiny tantalizingly open. Everett asserted that the final destiny of Cuba was an American question, one which Europe had no voice in, and that the eventual annexation of the island "might be almost essential to our safety."[38]

Fillmore proved himself an avid commercial expansionist, however, by sponsoring the Matthew Perry Expedition to Japan. Perry was directed to open up commercial relations with Japan and to gain coaling bases in the

[37] Willard Carl Klunder, *Lewis Cass and the Politics of Moderation* (Kent, OH, 1996), quotes on pages 165, 173. For an excellent discussion of the role of gender in the election of 1848, see Lynnea Magnuson, "In the Service of Columbia: Gendered Politics and Manifest Destiny Expansion" (Ph.D. Diss., University of Illinois at Urbana-Champaign, 2000), 183–246.

[38] Peter H. Smith, *Talons of the Eagle: Dynamics of U.S.-Latin American Relations* (New York, 2000), 24.

FIGURE 1.3. "A War President. Progressive Democracy" (New York, Currier and Ives, 1848). This 1848 Whig critique of Democratic candidate Lewis Cass (known as "General Gas") suggests that his desire for more territory would lead the country right back into war. The machine-like Cass wields a bloody sword labeled "Manifest Destiny" while rattling off desired future territorial acquisitions, "New Mexico, California, Chihuahua, Zacatecas, MEXICO, Peru, Yucatan, Cuba." The inclusion of "Mexico" in the list (meaning Mexico City) is a reference to his support for the all-Mexico movement at the close of the U.S.-Mexico War. That Cass could be tarred the "war president" candidate in a race against an army general fresh from the field suggests how truly bellicose his positions were. Library of Congress, Prints and Photographs Division, [LC-USZ62-10789].

area to facilitate the newly growing China trade. Although Fillmore acknowledged the significance of the Hawaiian Islands to this trade, his vision of American trade did not include an American Hawaii. This put him at odds with many in the Senate, which twice unsuccessfully requested information from him on a supposed proposition by the king to transfer sovereignty of the islands to the United States. Amidst calls for the immediate annexation of the island chain in Congress, Fillmore held firm.[39]

---

[39] Sylvester Stevens, *American Expansion in Hawaii, 1842–1898*, (Harrisburg, PA, 1945), 43–5; Ralph S. Kuykendall, *The Hawaiian Kingdom 1778–1854, Foundation and Transformation* (Honolulu, 1957), 409–10; May, "Manifest Destiny's Filibusters," 146–8, 168.

New Hampshire Democrat Franklin Pierce, elected in 1852, also made territorial expansionism an explicit goal. His administration would "not be controlled by any timid forebodings of evil from expansion," he stated in his inaugural address. He directed James Gadsden to bully or bribe Mexico into selling the United States enough land for a southern route for a transcontinental railroad. The Gadsden Purchase in December of 1853 added an extra 45,535 square miles to the Southwest.⁴⁰ This brought him singular success among Democratic presidents of the era, all of whom hoped to acquire extra land from Mexico. His efforts to acquire Cuba through negotiation with Spain were seriously hampered, however, by the public leak of the Ostend Manifesto, a document drawn up by three of Pierce's European diplomats in 1854 after the minister to Spain, Pierre Soulé of Louisiana, bungled negotiations over the sale of the island. Soulé, along with the minister to Great Britain, James Buchanan, and the minister to France, John Mason, declared in the Manifesto that the United States should forcibly take Cuba if Spain refused to sell it. "We shall be justified in wresting it from Spain if we possess the power," the Manifesto stated. The outcry against a document that seemed to license outright robbery was overwhelming, and the new secretary of state, William L. Marcy of New York, was forced to repudiate it (see Figure 1.4).⁴¹

On the other hand, Pierce's decision to withhold recognition of William Walker's regime in Nicaragua cost him friends among the aggressive expansionists who had celebrated the Gadsden Purchase and Ostend Manifesto. One 1855 ditty titled "Nicaragua Ho!" bemoaned the fact that "We ain't got room enough to spread; our eagle's mighty pinions/ Are clipped and fastened to his sides by Pierce and his cuss'd minions."⁴² Pierce hesitated when faced with other opportunities as well. Special agent to the Dominican Republic, William Cazneau, pushed him to annex that nation. Commodore Matthew Perry, who successfully "opened up" Japan to American trade in 1854 with

---

⁴⁰ Weinberg, *Manifest Destiny*, 190; The Gadsden Purchase occurred after Congress rejected the efforts of Whig appointee John Russell Bartlett of Rhode Island to mark the boundary between the United States and Mexico in 1853 as too conciliatory to Mexico. Pierce appointed a "tougher" new Democratic supervisor of the project and left Bartlett's reputation in tatters. The 1850s was a disastrous decade for the Whig Party, and it was almost as bad for Whig expansionists. Key primary sources on the Boundary Commission dispute include John Russell Bartlett, *Personal Narrative of Explorations and Incidents in Texas, New Mexico, California, Sonora, and Chihuahua*, (New York, 1854); William H. Emory, *Report on the United States and Mexican Boundary Survey, made under the Direction of the Secretary of the Interior* (Washington, DC, 1857–1859), 34th Congress, 1st Sess., Ex. Doc. No. 135.

⁴¹ Smith, *Talons of the Eagle*, 24–5; Soulé's limitations as a diplomat are suggested by the fact that while in Spain he fought a duel with the French ambassador over the issue of Mrs. Soulé's "immodest" dress. Janet L. Coryell, "Duty with Delicacy: Anna Ella Carroll of Maryland," in *Women and American Foreign Policy: Lobbyists, Critics, and Insiders*, Edward P. Crapol, ed. (New York, 1987), 49.

⁴² On Pierce and Walker see the anti-Pierce (Know-Nothing Party) newspaper, *Young Sam*, which inveighed against Pierce's Walker policy (and his manliness) for months. Quote from "Nicaragua Ho!," *Young Sam* 1 (January 1856): 67.

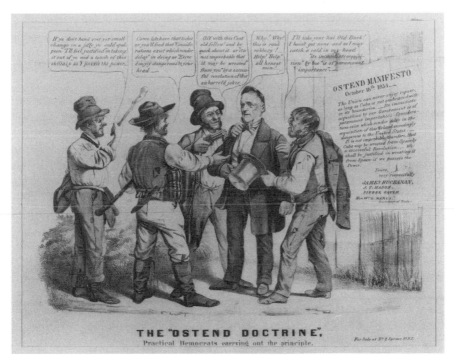

FIGURE 1.4. "'The Ostend Doctrine', Practical Democrats carrying out the principle." (New York, Currier & Ives, 1856). This critique of the Ostend Manifesto
and one of its authors, James Buchanan, equates the 1854 Manifesto's claim that
the United States "shall be justified in wresting" Cuba "from Spain if we possess
the power" with highway robbery. Four thugs threaten Buchanan while quoting his
manifesto. A ragged Irishman holding a club warns, "If ye don't hand over yer small
change in a jiffy ye ould spal-peen 'I'll feel justified' in taking it out of ye wid a
touch of this shillaly as 'I pozziz the power'" while another hoodlum flaunting a
large revolver warns "Off with this Coat old fellow! and be quick about it or 'it
is not improbable that it may be wrested' from you 'by a successful revolution' of
this six barrel'd joker." The unmanly Buchanan cries out, "Why! Why! this is rank
robbery! Help! Help! all Honest men!" This critique of martial manhood equates
filibusters with robbers, and it implies that aggressive expansionists were unmanly,
since, despite all their bluster, they were supposedly the first to cry for help when
threatened. Library of Congress, Prints and Photographs Division [LC-USZ62-9177].

the use of heavily fortified Navy vessels, encouraged Pierce to annex the
islands of Ryukyu. The president ignored both suggestions.[43] Pierce had

[43] Hudson, *Mistress of Manifest Destiny*, 152–5; *U.S. Congress. Senate. Message of the President of the United States, Transmitting a Report of the Secretary of the Navy... Relative
to the Naval Expedition to Japan* Senate Executive Document 54 Washington, DC, 1855,
108–10; Matthew Calbraith Perry, *The Japan Expedition, 1852–1854: The Personal Journal
of Commodore Matthew C. Perry*, Roger Pineau, ed. (Washington DC, 1968), 86.

hoped to annex the Kingdom of Hawaii, and his commissioner gained King Kamehameha's agreement to draft a treaty of annexation in 1854. But the movement stalled, in part because of fears of American filibustering among Hawaiian residents, and the island chain remained independent until the turn of the century.[44]

The public backlash against the Ostend Manifesto did not prevent one of its authors, Pennsylvania Democrat James Buchanan, from winning election in 1856 on an openly expansionist platform (see Figure 1.5). In a classic equation of expansion and manliness, Buchanan argued that "expansion is in the future the policy of our country, and only cowards fear and oppose it." Lewis Cass, now Buchanan's secretary of state, was even more enthusiastic, writing that the United States "requires more land, more territory upon which to settle, and just as fast as our interests and our destiny require additional territory in the North, or in the South, or on the Islands of the Ocean, I am for it." Cass authorized the American minister to Mexico to offer $15 million for lower California and parts of Sonora and Chihuahua, an offer that was repeatedly rebuffed by Mexico. The Buchanan administration also worked toward purchasing Cuba. Any hopes in that direction were thwarted, however, by the exploding sectional conflict, including violence in Kansas between Free-Soil and slaveholding settlers, the Dred Scott Decision, and the new Fugitive Slave Act, and also by a serious financial panic in 1857 that hit the manufacturing sector of the Northeast particularly hard. When the Louisiana Democrat, Senator John Slidell, introduced a bill in January of 1859 allocating $30 million toward the acquisition of Cuba, it was shot down by northern opponents who expressed horror that so much money would be devoted to the purchase of slave territory during a period of financial instability.[45]

The Anglophobic Cass loudly fought British territorial claims in Central America, particularly British efforts to maintain sovereignty over British Honduras and to act as protectorate to the Mosquito Indians in Nicaragua contrary to the 1850 Clayton-Bulwer Treaty (in which both Britain and the United States promised not to colonize Central America). Threats of war against Britain, as well as the suggestion that British actions had nullified the treaty, encouraged filibusters to the region, as did Buchanan's less than wholehearted enforcement of America's neutrality laws.[46]

---

[44] Proclamation of King Kamehameha, December 8, 1854, Official Dispatches, Hawai'i (reel 6); May, "Manifest Destiny's Filibusters," 146–8, 168.

[45] Weinberg, *Manifest Destiny*, 201; Klunder, *Lewis Cass*, 289–90, quote on page 289; Alexander DeConde, *Presidential Machismo: Executive Authority, Military Intervention, and Foreign Relations* (Boston, 2000), 95–7; Elbert B. Smith, *The Presidency of James Buchanan* (Lawrence, 1975), 78.

[46] Klunder, *Lewis Cass*, 291–3. Robert May has argued that Buchanan worked diligently to prevent filibusters, even at the expense of his support in the South. Robert E. May, "James Buchanan, the Neutrality Laws, and American Invasions of Nicaragua," in *James Buchanan and the Political Crisis of the 1850s*, Michael J. Birkner, ed. (Selinsgrove, PA, 1996): 123–45.

FIGURE 1.5. "A Serviceable Garment – or Reverie of a Bachelor" (New York, Currier & Ives, 1856). In a complex commentary on both bachelordom and the appeal of Cuban annexation in 1856, this Currier and Ives cartoon shows a poverty-stricken James Buchanan, the Democratic presidential candidate, sewing a patch that says "Cuba" on his very worn coat. Buchanan says, "My Old coat was a very fashionable Federal coat when it was new, but by patching and turning I have made it quite a Democratic Garment. That Cuba patch to be sure is rather unsightly but it suits Southern fashions at this season, and then. (If I am elected,) let me see, $25,000 pr. annum, and no rent to pay, and no Women and Babies about, I guess I can afford a new outfit." Buchanan's Ostend Manifesto of 1854, which threatened to take Cuba by force if Spain wouldn't sell it, helped endear the Pennsylvanian to southern slaveholding expansionists. The anti-slavery Nathaniel Currier here equates both bachelordom and filibustering with a lack of respectability, while simultaneously questioning Buchanan's manliness (by representing him doing a woman's work, sewing). Library of Congress, Prints and Photographs Division, [LC-USZ62-59105].

In short, while filibustering was illegal in this period, and no president openly supported filibustering, aggressive expansionists could and did take comfort from the mixed message emanating from Washington. Democratic administrations came packaged with openly expansionistic platforms, even if, as in the case of Pierce, they didn't always follow through on their implied promise to aid and abet filibusters, while even officials in Whig administrations, like Edward Everett, waffled on the question of the desirability of further territorial growth.

The possibility, then, say, that Nicaragua, Cuba, or even distant Hawaii could become a new state seemed far more likely after the dramatic (if ill-gotten) gains of the 1840s than it had before. Manifest Destiny was not in "eclipse" in the 1850s. If anything, the 1850s were, as Albert K. Weinberg has put it, "the heyday of 'spread-eagleism' when lack of luck rather than boldness limited the decade's achievements." The U.S.-Mexico War only marked an end to antebellum territorial expansion in retrospect. At the end of the 1840s it seemed rather to open the door to it.[47]

Section, Class, and Race: The Horizontal Comradeship of Manifest Destiny

Given the support of the Young America faction of the Democratic Party for territorial expansionism, it is tempting to label the Democratic Party the party of aggressive expansionism. To a certain extent, this designation holds true, although filibustering Whigs, like Henry Crabb, were not unknown. Expansionists also were careful to make their appeals non-partisan whenever possible. Other divisions between supporters and opponents of aggressive expansionism also suggest themselves. As Thomas Hietala has argued, the expansionist policies of the 1840s "developed in the shadow of the unwanted black," and debates over territorial expansionism were inseparable from the issue of slavery. Filibustering, the most dramatic expression of the culture of aggressive expansionism, found its strongest and most passionate support in the southern states, where many viewed the possibility of gaining new slave states in Central America and the Caribbean as the best means for maintaining parity in the Senate with the increasingly more populous, and more powerful, North. Southerners led the majority of filibustering expeditions, and they contributed more than their fair share of soldiers to those expeditions. Certainly most supporters of Cuban filibustering by the late 1850s were southern. It is not true, however, as some have suggested,

[47] Weinberg, *Manifest Destiny*, 190; Luis G. Zorrilla, *Historia de las relaciones entre México y los Estados Unidos de América, 1800–1958*. 1965. Second edition (Mexico, 1977), 1: 368–94; Thomas Schoonover, *Dollars over Dominion: The Triumph of Liberalism in Mexican-United States Relations, 1861–1867* (Baton Rouge, 1978), 5–6.

that the post-1848 filibustering movement was simply a desperate act of an increasingly marginalized slave power.[48]

While some filibusters, like John Quitman, were openly pro-slavery partisans who looked abroad for new opportunities for slavery and slaveholders, many of the Mexican filibusters from California had no interest in extending slavery. William Walker's stated views on slavery changed dramatically in the course of his adventures. As a newspaper editor in New Orleans and San Francisco in the early 1850s, Walker professed Free-Soil views – he endorsed the idea that newly acquired territories should be kept free from slavery. He continued to be known as a Free-Soil man after his trip to Mexico, and at the outset of his Nicaragua campaign. Once in possession of that country, however, Walker found himself a popular hero back home, but one without strong political allies in the United States. Desperate for the southern political support that he believed would lead to American recognition, in 1856 Walker reintroduced African slavery into Nicaragua, where it had long been illegal. "The slavery decree," Walker later wrote, "was calculated to bind the Southern States to Nicaragua, as if she were one of themselves."[49]

By the time he returned from Nicaragua in 1857, Walker had moved from a restrained anti-slavery position to a rabid pro-slavery one, and he was not shy about declaring his new beliefs. During a trial in New Orleans for violating neutrality laws in 1857, Walker used his new pro-slavery stance to gain his freedom. Appealing to a courtroom packed with Southerners, Walker said he doubted "that men, seeking to maintain their rights in the perpetuation for Southern institutions, of which they have been unjustly deprived by foreign and abolitionist interference, are to be restrained by a Southern jury." Not only was Walker freed, but he was reportedly "carried out of the building on the shoulders of the spectators." His 1860 narrative of his experiences in Nicaragua proudly proclaimed his belief in the "really beneficial and conservative character of negro-slavery" and the need to extend slavery throughout Latin America, and even to England, if possible. A

---

[48] Hietala, *Manifest Design*, 10. On the same point see Kaplan, *The Anarchy of Empire in the Making of U.S. Culture* (Cambridge, MA, 2002), 18. The classic statement of the view that filibustering was a southern phenomenon can be found in John Hope Franklin, *The Militant South, 1800–1861* (Cambridge, MA, 1956), 96–128.

[49] William Walker, *The War in Nicaragua* (Mobile, 1860), 266. The slavery decree did "bind the Southern States to Nicaragua." A southern steamboat guide published in 1857 declared Walker's "a cause in which the whole South is interested. . . . it is the interest of the South to sustain Walker." W. *Alvin Lloyd's Steamboat and Railroad Guide* (New Orleans, 1857), xi. And a letter to the Philadelphia *Public Ledger* in July of 1858 warned of plans for another Walker expedition and noted that "it would appear, according to Southern journals, that, in two states – Alabama and Mississippi – the filibuster spirit rages to a greater extent than ever." Letter to the "Public Ledger," from Washington DC, July 8, 1858 – undated article, Ephraim George Squier's Collection of Newspaper Clippings on Central America, 1856–1860, HL.

pro-slavery Walker was widely seen in the South as a symbol and hope for their cause, and it was in the South that "Walker was hailed as a hero and a martyr, and his bitterest enemies were silenced for the time." Even after his death in 1860, Southerners continued to embrace Walker as "the remarkable man whose life is a sacrifice to his devotion to Southern interest and Southern expansion, and who failed in his magnificent plans only because he had to contend against the two greatest powers in the world – Great Britain, and the United States of America."[50]

But Walker also was embraced in the urban North, in spite of his slavery proclamation. Some of his strongest supporters were northern urban working men, for whom a pro-slavery Walker became a "race hero."[51] The best evidence for his continuing support in the North is in the composition of his army. The register of the Army of the Republic of Nicaragua indicates that fifty-nine percent of Walker's American-born soldiers, recruited before Walker issued his slavery decree in Nicaragua, were born north of the Mason-Dixon Line. And years after Walker was firmly entrenched in the southern camp, twenty-eight percent of the men willing to "emigrate" to Central America as part of his 1860 attack on Honduras were born north of the Mason-Dixon line.[52] Walker also had better luck raising money for his forays in New York than in the South and found his greatest degree of public adulation in New York. *Harper's Monthly Magazine* reported that "beyond a very limited circle of admirers" his 1857 tour "attracted little attention," but that in New York, Walker was forced to repeatedly deliver speeches "in reply to the cheers with which he was greeted" when he appeared in the city. A later witness remembered that "Walker's reception in New York, on his return to the United States, was like that of a conqueror. . . . tens of thousands of citizens flocked to see the hero." While in power in Nicaragua, Walker was widely praised as an exponent of heroic masculinity in national journals

[50] Charles W. Doubleday, *Reminiscences of the Filibuster War in Nicaragua* (New York, 1886), 96; Walker, *War in Nicaragua*, 259. Walker also claimed in his book that he had held pro-slavery views before his Nicaragua journey but had failed to share them with anti-slavery allies like John C. Frémont, the first Republican candidate for president. Writing in the third person, Walker stated that "it was due probably, to both Colonel Frémont and Mr. Palmer, to state that they were not fully aware of all the views Walker held on the subject of slavery; nor, indeed, was it necessary at that time for those views to be expressed." Walker, *War in Nicaragua*, 29; James Jeffrey Roche, *The Story of the Filibusters* (New York, 1891), 159; pro-Walker quote, *Mobile-Register*, n.d., Folder 160, WWP.
[51] On Walker as a race hero see Richard Slotkin, *The Fatal Environment: The Myth of the Frontier in the Age of Industrialization, 1800–1860* (New York, 1985), 245–61, quotation page 252.
[52] Army of the Republic statistics tabulated by Dr. Alejandro Bolaños Geyer, Masaya, Nicaragua, 1972. From the Guide to Item 120, Register of the Army of the Republic of Nicaragua, WWP; 1860 "emigrant" statistics based on data in Folder 85: Men and Stores sent to Caribbean Sea, 1860, #1 (arrivals on 4/20, 4/23, 4/25, 5/5, 5/18, 6/2, 6/5, 6/13, 6/23, 7/5, 8/30, 9/16), Folder 85, WWP.

critical of the expansion of slavery, including *Harper's* and *Putnam's* monthly magazines.[53]

Nor was Walker the only filibuster to gain significant urban support in the North. Cuban filibuster Narciso López was lauded across urban America. Mexican filibusters Henry Crabb and Gaston de Raoussett-Boulbon were widely popular in San Francisco. Smaller California towns like Stockton had meetings of secret filibustering societies in 1850s, and even the Louisiana-based Cuban filibustering organization, the Order of the Lone Star, had a branch in New York. The anti-slavery New Haven publication the *New Englander and Yale Review* bemoaned the fact in 1859 that "it is hardly more difficult now than it was ten years ago, to enlist men in the Southern States, or in the great cities, for a foray into some country with which our own country is in friendly relations. Any captain of banditti who can succeed in effecting the temporary overthrow of an unstable government . . . becomes a 'gray-eyed man of destiny,' the hero of the hour in the popular feeling of the South, aye, and of the great masses of people in such cities as Philadelphia and New York."[54]

Clearly, filibustering exacerbated sectional tensions, but even as some aggressive expansionists looked south for new slave territories, others asserted that the pursuit of new territories could actually counter sectionalism. *De Bow's Review* editor William M. Burwell suggested in 1856 that both Northerners and Southerners could support the expansion of the South in a "south and southwest, rather than west and northwest" direction, because this would keep slaves out of northern territories. Looking even further south, naval scientist Matthew Maury of Virginia made the same claim about the unifying possibilities of territorial expansion in his 1853 book *The Amazon, and Atlantic Slopes of South America*. The discourse of expansionism, however divisive in reality, held the potential to create a fictional unified American community in a decade in which debates over the extension of slavery into new territories became a matter of national life and death.[55]

[53] Letter from Walker to Callendar Fayssoux, September 18, 1858 and emigration circular dated October 10, 1858; both in Folder 66, WWP; *HNMM* XV, (July 1857): 402; Roche, *The Story of the Filibusters*, 159.

[54] May, *Manifest Destiny's Underworld*, 33, 74–6, 249–79. May points out that support for filibustering in the North ebbed after Walker's failure in 1857, and that some filibusters, like John Quitman, never had substantial support in the North. "Slavery so tainted the image of filibustering by the late 1850s that many expansionist Northerners found the expedition less appealing and certainly less politically palatable, than they had in earlier years," 268; "The Moral of Harper's Ferry," *NEYR* 17 (November 1859): 1073.

[55] W. Burwell, Esq., "The Policy of the South – Suggestion for the Settlement of Our Sectional Differences," *DBR* 21 (November 1856): 469–90; Matthew F. Maury, *The Amazon, and Atlantic Slopes of South America* (Washington, DC, 1853); Jane McManus Storm Cazneau (Cora Montgomery) made similar arguments in the *USDR* and in *The Queen of Islands and the King of Rivers* (New York, 1850), and she also emphasized the importance of Cuban trade to all sections of the country. On the potential of expansionism south to solve sectional

Territorial expansionism provided a fictional space where men could join in a common celebration of American might and where American men, struggling through a period of economic and social transformations, could find redemption. Latin America held the potential of becoming the "new frontier," after 1848, complete with the regenerating promise of limitless space and opportunity that the western frontier held in the nineteenth-century American imagination.[56] The literature of Manifest Destiny, in the 1850s as in earlier decades, obscured the ugly side of expansionism, and especially the displacement of native peoples through violence, by focusing on the unifying aspects of the endeavor. As Benedict Anderson has explained, the ability of nationalism to turn "chance into destiny" is dependent on participants imagining a community or nation "as a deep horizontal comradeship," regardless of "actual inequality and exploitation."[57] Territorial expansionism enabled participants to imagine themselves part of the American community.

Walker's vocal support among working men suggests that, at least in northern cities, supporters and opponents of filibustering may have been divided along class lines. Working men flocked to the support of filibusters and saw in their actions a validation of the masculine qualities they held dear. But public meetings in support of filibustering were heterogeneous gatherings, and filibustering was popular in part because it held the potential to undermine emerging class divisions by unifying American men in a celebration of national destiny, by publicly acknowledging the masculinity of filibusters and other "daring men," and by providing opportunities to men whose prospects for economic advancement were deteriorating at home.

As Shelly Streeby has written, the popular literature produced during and about the U.S.-Mexico War worked to popularize "an ideology of imperial U.S. American manhood that promised to transcend internal divisions such as class and region." Representations of American expansion after the

tensions see Robert Walker, *Letter of Mr. Walker, of Mississippi, Relative to the Reannexation of Texas: in Reply to the Call of the People of Carroll County, Kentucky, to Communicate his views on that subject* (Philadelphia, 1844), 13–5; Frederick Merk, *Fruits of Propaganda in the Tyler Administration* (Cambridge, MA, 1971), 21–6; George Fredrickson, *The Black Image in the White Mind: The Debate on Afro-American Character and Destiny, 1817–1914* (New York, 1971), 140–1. See also "The Black Race in America," *SLM* 21 (November 1855): 676–81.

56 Slotkin, *The Fatal Environment*, 41–3, 161–90. Frederick Jackson Turner famously suggested in 1893 that the frontier made Americans the outgoing, energetic, and self-reliant people they liked to believe themselves to be. *Frontier and Section: Selected Essays of Frederick Jackson Turner*, Ray Allen Billington, ed. (Englewood Cliffs, NJ, 1961), 37–62; Billington, *America's Frontier Heritage* (New York, 1966), 1–22.

57 Benedict Anderson, *Imagined Communities: Reflections on the Origin and Spread of Nationalism* (London, 1991), 7. Stephen John Hartnett has explored the manner in which Robert J. Walker's writings helped create exactly this sort of fictional space supporting Manifest Destiny. *Democratic Dissent and the Cultural Fictions of Antebellum America* (Urbana, 2002), 93–131.

war served the same purpose. Antebellum booster travel narratives regularly obscured issues of class while highlighting issues of gender. In speeches at public meetings and in fiery editorials, expansionists drummed up support for their agenda among men of different occupations. Egalitarian rhetoric, once employed by artisan editors as a weapon against the oligarchy, had become by the 1840s "a means of obscuring newly developing class separations." The largely Democratic penny press of America's big cities was particularly unified in their support for territorial expansionism. By focusing on Central America, or Hawaii or Mexico, as a land where white men could thrive without excessive competition, supporters of aggressive expansionism produced a highly attractive fictional space that not only justified warfare but also might subvert emerging class, ethnic, and sectional divisions. What is particularly notable here is that the imagined white nationalist community excluded not only racial others, but, as this study will reveal, white women as well.[58]

Aggressive expansionism was shaped by what Reginald Horsman has called America's "romantic racial nationalism." It affirmed the whiteness that unified European-Americans at the expense of non-whites in the nineteenth century. Other scholars have explored the way in which Manifest Destiny and the U.S-Mexico War simultaneously racialized Latin Americans and provided opportunities for European immigrants (especially the Irish) to be absorbed into an American Anglo-Saxon racial identity.[59] The assimilation of white ethnic groups proved equally important to the development of aggressive expansionism after the war because territorial expansionism offered another opportunity for European immigrants to assert the advantages of whiteness. One of the remarkable features of the literature of expansionism, and of the letters and diaries of travelers through Latin America, is the general uniformity of opinion expressed about America's destiny and about the peoples and territories the travelers encountered, despite the ethnicity of the writers. Gender and race were mutually constitutive in the expansionist

---

[58] Streeby, *American Sensations*, 91. See also Slotkin, *The Fatal Environment*, 173–90; Mary Suzanne Schriber, *Writing Home: American Women Abroad, 1830–1920* (Charlottesville, VA, 1997), 86–7. On the relationship between class and gender in antebellum literature see David Leverenz, *Manhood and the American Renaissance* (Ithaca, 1989), 72; egalitarian rhetoric quote in Alexander Saxton, *The Rise and Fall of the White Republic: Class Politics and Mass Culture in Nineteenth-Century America* (London, 1990), 100–5; see also Ronald J. Zboray, *A Fictive People: Antebellum Economic Development and the American Reading Public* (New York, 1993), 6–16; Hartnett, *Democratic Dissent*, 144–7; Frederic Hudson, *Journalism in the United States from 1690 to 1872*, (New York, 1873), 443, 476, 480.

[59] Horsman, *Race and Manifest Destiny*, 165. On whiteness and Manifest Destiny see also David Roediger, *The Wages of Whiteness: Race and the Making of the American Working Class* (London, 1999); Neil Foley, *The White Scourge: Mexicans, Blacks, and Poor Whites in Texas Cotton Culture* (Berkeley, 1997); Noel Ignatiev, *How the Irish Became White* (New York, 1996); Eric Lott, *Love and Theft: Blackface Minstrelsy and the American Working Class* (New York, 1993), 201–7; Streeby, *American Sensations*.

encounter, highlighting the difference of the Latin American while erasing differences among American observers. Boosters claimed that territorial expansionism provided opportunities for all white men. The manhood made manifest here was a white and (for European men) inclusive Anglo-Saxon manhood, and the exponents of Manifest Destiny were, by and large, white American men.[60]

The "deep horizontal comradeship" of Manifest Destiny did not include everyone of course. Those Americans who were not part of the privileged white race were deliberately excluded. This is not to say that non-white men had no voice in territorial expansionism or that territorial expansionism did not shape the meaning of manhood and womanhood for non-white men and women. The black abolitionist Martin Delany argued forcefully in the mid-1850s that African-American manhood would be best served through emigration to a new state, possibly in Latin America or the Caribbean. In *The Condition, Elevation, Emigration, and Destiny of the Colored People of the United States* (1852), Delany offers a vision of the climate and agriculture in Central America as effusive as any found in the booster literature of the region, and he suggests that Nicaragua presents "opportunities for us to rise to the full stature of manhood.... You have all the opportunities for elevating yourselves as the highest, according to your industry and merits." Whether his readers chose Nicaragua or some other state in Central or South America, Delany made clear his view that "that country is best, in which our manhood can be best developed."[61]

Although Delany, like most African-American men, opposed Liberian colonization, the movement of freed slaves to Liberia was one of the most significant foreign encounters in the decades before the Civil War. As historians have shown, competing ideologies of masculinity shaped the way northern black men understood Liberian emigration. Some black men saw the potential for the reinvention of black manhood in Liberia. Augustus Washington, a New England artist, offered his view that Liberia was the perfect land for the "development of their manhood and intellect," while envisioning the "bosom" of Africa as a place where "all the fruits of... a tropical clime" repose "in exuberance and wild extravagance." Had Liberian colonization been more successful, the expansionist encounter in Liberia

---

[60] Shelly Streeby points out that issues of Irish ethnicity are central to the storybook literature on the war, yet they are of minor significance in the private writings, booster literature, and newspaper accounts that form the basis of this study. Streeby, *American Sensations*, 102–38.

[61] Martin Delany, *The Condition, Elevation, Emigration, and Destiny of the Colored People of the United States* (Philadelphia, 1852), 184, 189. On Delany see Harvey, *American Geographics*, 194–241; Sundquist, "The Literature of Expansion and Race," in *The Cambridge History of American Literature*, ed. Bercovitch, vol. 2: 306–7. Robert May has noted that at least two African-Americans went to Nicaragua to "seek their fortune." But given Walker's views on slavery, his appeal among African-Americans was understandably limited. May, *Manifest Destiny's Underworld*, 197.

might have played a similar role in the formation of antebellum African-American manhood as did Manifest Destiny for white American manhood. But because the colonization of Liberia was guided by the desire to remove an undesirable population from the United States rather than to incorporate new territory into the nation, Liberia never earned a place in the expansionist vision of white men, and it was seen as problematic by most black American men as well.[62]

There was another group that was excluded from the "horizontal comradeship" of aggressive expansionism, and, like African-Americans, their exclusion was not a matter of chance. In the aggressive expansionist imagination, white American women were to be left at home. Like African-American men, white American women had their own expansionist encounter in the years after the U.S.-Mexico War. But just as aggressive expansionism was explicitly raced, so too was it explicitly gendered.

Filibustering as Seduction: Two Interpretations

One way to understand the gender dynamic orienting debates over territorial expansionism is to look closely at two stories published in popular periodicals during the late 1850s. In 1857, *Littell's Living Age* reprinted "Gaston, the Little Wolf," originally published in the middle-class British publication *Household Words*. The following year, the *Southern Literary Messenger* offered readers "The Story of Blannerhassett [sic]." Each follows the tragic career of a foreigner who moves to America in search of opportunity and who becomes obsessed with plans to conquer territory outside the borders of the United States. In each story the "American" (or white) qualities of the European protagonist are emphasized. Each story also features a heroic love interest of great beauty and courage who passively suffers in the course of the tale. Each was loosely based on a true story. Finally, and most importantly, each story makes a clear argument about the effect of filibustering on manhood. Despite their similarities, these are two dramatically different stories, each of which brings a different gendered analysis to its interpretation of the dangers and possibilities of aggressive expansionism.

"Gaston, the Little Wolf" heroized a figure familiar to most Americans at the time of the story's publication. Gaston de Raoussett-Boulbon was an aristocratic Frenchman who, after squandering his inheritance and failing as a gold miner, made repeated filibustering forays into Mexico in the early 1850s from a base in San Francisco. Eventually executed in Sonora as an (obviously ineffective) example to future filibusterers, Raoussett-Boulbon gained a great

---

[62] On the role of gender in black emigrationist plans see Bruce Dorsey, *Reforming Men and Women: Gender in the Antebellum City* (Ithaca, 2002), 154–86, Washington quote, 157; see also Wilson Moses, ed., *Liberian Dreams: Back-to-Africa Narratives from the 1850s* (University Park, PA, 1998).

deal of press and sympathy from Americans, and he seriously compromised U.S.-Mexican relations at a time when the countries were attempting to amicably resolve boundary differences emerging out of the Treaty of Guadalupe Hidalgo. Raoussett-Boulbon, it can safely be said, was a man who never succeeded at anything in his life.[63]

This is not the view held by the author of "Gaston, the Little Wolf." In the author's romantic vision, Raoussett-Boulbon represented much finer ideals than his career, marked by burning ambition and disdain for international law, might suggest. "Here were grand talents, and a rich nature lost, which under more favorable circumstances might have revolutionized a hemisphere." Here also was a remarkable example of manhood, one that male readers who had themselves faced unfavorable circumstances might take pride in emulating. Raoussett-Boulbon was not American of course, but his character is marked by a very American independence, even in the nursery. Young Raoussett-Boulbon rejects the authority of household servants, his grandmother, and the Catholic church – he is expelled from school at age seventeen when he refuses to kneel before a priest. "I will only kneel before God" he tells the Jesuit, in a strangely Protestant interpretation of doctrine designed to appeal to anti-papist readers. The Little Wolf asserts his manhood by breaking with his father over the question of facial hair, or rather over the question of his father's authority over his "very fine" beard, as well as the cigar he insists on smoking. He leaves France for a life of "brilliant actions as a military volunteer" in Algeria, daring sportsmanship, and a love of liberty and republicanism that is tested, but not destroyed, by the revolutions of 1848.

His pursuit of liberty and republicanism translates, once in America, into a plan to establish a "valiant French barrier" in Sonora between the "weak" Mexicans and the Americans they hate. His career in Mexico is marked by its "vigor" and by a wholly fictional relationship with Antonia, the "tall, proud, and beautiful" daughter of "one of the principal authorities of Sonora." The young Mexican woman, "fair as a Saxon," also rejects the authority of the patriarch by declaring her allegiance to Raoussett-Boulbon in front of her father. "I do love this pirate, as you call him. Yes; I love him!" she announces. Simultaneously asserting her virtue as a lover of martial manhood and liberty while betraying her virtue as a woman, she leaves her father's house and goes to "the pirate-count's camp, and into the tent" in the "sight of six thousand people."[64]

Despite the love of a fair lady, who drops out of the story immediately after entering the pirate's tent, Raoussett-Boulbon does not succeed in his

---

[63] Joseph A. Stout Jr., *Schemers and Dreamers: Filibustering in Mexico, 1848–1921* (Fort Worth, 2002), 26–8, 30–3, 48–50; Horacio Sobarzo, *Cronica de la Aventura de Raousset-Boulbon en Sonora*, 2nd edition (Mexico D.F., 1980).

[64] "Gaston, the Little Wolf," *The Living Age* 54 (September 26, 1857): 769–824.

plan to create an independent French state in Sonora. The reader is assured, however, that the failure of his Mexican scheme is outside his control and that he always exhibits bravery and an iron will. Even his demeanor in the face of the firing squad illustrates his manliness. "He refused to allow his eyes to be bandaged, and met his death with a calm, grave courage that had something truly heroic in it." In the selective reading of the author, it is not Raoussett-Boulbon's business failure, foreignness, peripatetic career, or flouting of law that merit emphasis but his aristocratic origins, American independence from all authority, especially that of the Catholic Church, and hyper-masculine characteristics (the beard, the cigar, the public seduction).

A dramatically different moral is offered by "The Story of Blannerhassett [sic]," published by the *Southern Literary Messenger*. Harman Blennerhassett was a wealthy Irish immigrant who was implicated in Aaron Burr's 1805 conspiracy to possibly carve an empire out of Mexico or the valley of the Mississippi. Burr, descendent of leading New England Puritans who nearly beat Thomas Jefferson in the 1801 presidential election, was condemned as a libertine by his many political opponents after killing Alexander Hamilton in a duel while serving as vice president. Burr was never convicted for his filibustering, but Blennerhassett's name and fortune were destroyed by the accusations.[65]

In this retelling of the story, Blennerhassett lives an idyllic life in a bucolic "Eden" in a mansion in the western territories with two "blessed" children and a wife known not only for her "extraordinary beauty" but also for her "mental attractions ... fully commensurate with her physical charms." His days pass "in the cultivation of his literary, artistic and scientific tastes."

Once Burr arrives, all this changes. Burr resembles Raoussett-Boulbon in many ways. He is a handsome man and "very resolute – but impatient of control." He has a great power of leadership, immense ambition, and a seductive personality. While the author of "Gaston, the Little Wolf" suggests these are ideal attributes for a man, in this anti-filibustering cautionary tale

---

[65] Blennerhassett's name is misspelled throughout the "The Story of Blannerhassett," *SLM* 27 (December 1858): 457–68. The Blennerhassett story was first popularized in William Wirt's famous speech during Burr's treason trial. The 1850s saw a revival of interest in Blennerhassett with the 1850 publication of William H. Safford's *The Life of Harman Blennerhassett. Comprising an authentic narrative of the Burr expedition: and containing many additional facts not heretofore published* (Chillicothe, Ohio, 1850); and John P. Kennedy's *Memoirs of the Life of William Wirt* (Philadelphia, 1850). "The Story of Blannerhassett" was not the only fictional representation of Burr published during this period. For a far more flattering representation of Burr and martial manhood written by a southern Democrat see Jeremiah Clemens, *The Rivals: A Tale of the Times of Aaron Burr and Alexander Hamilton* (Philadelphia, 1860). On Burr as an extremely polarizing model of manhood see Nancy Isenberg's, "The 'Little Emperor': Aaron Burr, Dandyism, and the Sexual Politics of Treason," in *Beyond the Founders: New Approaches to the Political History of the Early American Republic*. Jeffrey L. Pasley, Andrew W. Robertson, and David Waldstreicher, eds. (Chapel Hill, 2004), 129–58.

they signify the exact opposite. Burr is a destroyer of happiness, a "bold bad man" for whom "female chastity and manly honour were . . . words of no import." With the highest praise, one author describes Raoussett-Boulbon as a "Cortes slain at the outset." With the strongest contempt, this author quotes Hamilton that Burr was "an embryo Caesar."[66]

Blennerhassett, seduced by Burr's schemes, "embarked all, fortune, fame, and life, and the domestic happiness, dearer to him than life, in the adventure, and wrecked them all together." Ignoring his wife in favor of the "cannon's roar," Blennerhassett brings literal destruction down upon his home. After Burr's arrest, an unruly posse of militia members descends on the Blenner-hassett home:

They wantonly mutilated and defaced rare and valuable books and paintings, shattered the broad mirrors and discharged their rifles into the ornaments of the ceiling. One brawny, whiskered fellow, of six feet high, was seen with a delicate French hat of Mrs. Blannerhassett's stuck atop his fiery poll and a richly figured shawl thrown across his broad shoulders, while a stripling of seventeen . . . was aping with drunken gravity, the gestures and protestations of an enamoured lover to the psuedo lady.

The cross-dressing rioters within the Blennerhassett home exemplify the disarray that ensues when martial manhood invades the domestic sphere. Gender is turned upside down, the cultural markers of domestic respectability are destroyed, and courtship and even womanhood itself are mocked. Only the real Mrs. Blennerhassett has the capacity to defuse the situation, and the "dignity of her bearing" shames the drunken soldiers into leaving. "They slunk back abashed and shame-faced, before the strength of her weakness, and her anxious and care-stricken beauty."[67]

While "The Story of Blannerhassett" was set in 1805, the contemporary relevance would have been obvious to antebellum readers. The author labels Burr as the "great Filibuster," father of antebellum aggressive expansionism.[68] "Filibustering was not so much in vogue then as it has gotten to be since, and met with by no means so much countenance from the public," the author explains with evident regret. The lesson to readers is clear. A man has no one to blame but himself if he allows the lure of the "cannon's roar" to upsets his domestic order. Indeed, only by guarding against men like Burr can domestic order be protected. "From the hour that dark and incomprehensible man . . . crossed the threshold, the doom of that house was written." The Blennerhassett home, destroyed by martial manhood, becomes in this analogy domesticity personified. As in "Gaston, the Little Wolf," the

[66] Henry de la Madelene, quoted in "Gaston, the Little Wolf," 824; Alexander Hamilton, quoted in "The Story of Blannerhassett," *SLM* 27 (December 1858): 462.

[67] "The Story of Blannerhassett," *SLM* 27 (December 1858): 457–68.

[68] According to Charles Brown, Burr was a "prototypical filibuster." Brown, *Agents of Manifest Destiny*, 6–13.

exertions of filibustering allow the ethnicity of the protagonist to fade into a generalized white American manhood. That Blennerhassett is Irish is of no importance in this story. What is important is that as an American man he failed to protect the sanctity of his family home.[69]

These two stories effectively frame the American debate over manhood and aggressive expansionism, since, as this study argues, when American men looked abroad they saw, first and foremost, reflections of themselves and of the men they chose to be. Aggressive expansionists believed that new territories offered an exceptional sphere for manly activity, a place where martial men could express their talents, unlike the United States where submission and conformity seemed to be increasingly rewarded. Raoussett-Boulbon is at his best in battle, and he is at his worst in the rarified atmosphere of his aristocratic French home. Restrained men, on the other hand, condemned the values of the aggressive expansionists as antiquated and retrograde.

In each story, an "innocent" is seduced by a filibusterer, and the sanctity of the family home is destroyed. In "Gaston, the Little-Wolf," the seduction proves the admirable masculinity of the filibuster. In "The Story of Blennerhassett," the seduction of the title character reveals Burr's corrupt and retrograde nature. Blennerhassett has everything necessary for his happiness on his estate but is led astray by visions of empire. This story suggests that American men had best look to the home and to the example offered by women, rather than abroad, for their salvation.

The gendered debate here was not only about manhood. Women in each of the stories play important and contrasting roles. In the aggressive expansionist position, a woman is an important indicator of a man's virility, expected to support her man while remaining otherwise passive. The ideal woman in the martial-manhood fantasy is sexually available, attractive, and supportive – and without strong moral positions. In a sense, the relationship between a martial man and his ideal woman was closer to that of the cross-dressing soldier and his seventeen-year-old suitor in "the Story of Blannerhassett" than to the domestic ideal of companionate marriage.[70]

The model woman in the anti-filibustering tale, as "The Story of Blannerhassett" makes quite clear, is the moral compass for her husband, the light of his life, the center of his home, in short, the "true woman" idealized in the ideology of domesticity. When a man strays from the example set by the domestic star of his household, be it his wife, sister, or mother, the result is chaos and disaster. It is not that women were more important to restrained men than to martial men but that different sorts of women were important to each. To a great degree, the aggressive expansionist ideal

[69] "The Story of Blannerhassett," SLM 27 (December 1858): 463.
[70] On the companionate ideal see A. James Hammerton, Cruelty and Companionship: Conflict in Nineteenth-Century Married Life (London, 1992), ch. 3–4; Rotundo, American Manhood, 163–4.

of "personal annexation," or Manifest Destiny accomplished through the union of white American man and Latin American woman, was dependent upon the rejection of the ideal of domesticity. While martial men imagined such a union promoting the uplift of the woman, or at the least a pleasing dalliance, for restrained men the embrace of a racially, religiously, or culturally "inferior" woman would necessarily lead to the moral downfall of the man. Ideals of manhood and womanhood are mutually constitutive, and even when debates over expansionism appear to have been debates between men, over manhood, transformations in the ideology and practices of womanhood were never far from the surface.[71]

One further contrast between these two stories is worth noting. Each was published in a journal with a strong regional affiliation, but the affiliations were not what one might expect. It was the *Southern Literary Messenger*, a Whig journal published in Richmond, Virginia, that printed "The Story of Blannerhassett," the anti-filibustering cautionary tale. The northern publication, *The Living Age*, was the magazine that suggested in "Gaston, the Little Wolf" that filibustering was an appropriately challenging activity for vigorous men.[72] While it is true that by the 1850s most of the strongest voices in favor of expansionism were southern and the most adamant anti-expansion voices could be found in New England, the dichotomous views of the relationship between manhood and territory offered in these stories, as well as in the following chapters of this study, reflect the diversity of views held in each section of the country up until the Civil War. Indeed, the author of "The Story of Blannerhassett," uses Burr's moral failings as a way to rail against talk of nullification in the North and the South. "How is it to-day? We daily hear the value of the Union estimated, see its laws nullified . . . and we are not horrified. Were our ancestors better men and purer patriots than we . . . ?"[73] Both martial and restrained men would answer, emphatically, that America was still producing pure patriots and that those patriots could be found among men who embraced their particular masculine practices. Restrained men grounded their patriotism in their respect for the patriarchal legal system, and they expressed their devotion to their country through

---

[71] Even when this study focuses on manhood, it does so in the understanding that a truthful history of gender needs to be, as Bruce Dorsey has put it, a "holistic history of gender." Dorsey, *Reforming Men and Women*, 4.

[72] *Littell's Living Age* was published in New York City. *Household Words*, a British "weekly miscellany of general literature," was edited by Charles Dickens for a middle-class audience. The *Southern Literary Messenger* was explicitly directed at educated southern readers. The magazine's first editor, James A. Heath, attempted to develop southern patriotism through the magazine. "[W]e who live on the sunny side of Mason and Dixon's line are not yet sufficiently inspired with a sense of importance of maintaining our just rights, or rather our proper representation in the Republic of Letters." Frank Luther Mott, *A History of American Magazines, Vol. II, 1850–1865* (Cambridge, MA, 1938), 631.

[73] "The Story of Blannerhassett," 468.

their committed attention to family and workplace. Martial men pointed to their aggressive pursuit of new territories, and to their will and strength, as evidence of their own patriotism.

Perhaps Americans were unwilling to let Manifest Destiny die after the U.S.-Mexico War because it held too much promise to too many people. It remained, in Lewis Cass's words, a "safety valve" for the wide variety of pressures facing antebellum Americans. Democrats could use it to rally support to their cause and to make their opponents appear weak and emasculated; working men and immigrants could improve their economic and social status by embracing it. It could both empower the South and possibly unify Southerners and Northerners during a period of increasing sectionalism. For martial men it offered a means to affirm masculine practices that were increasingly marginalized at home. As the following chapter will explore, Manifest Destiny was alive and well in the 1850s, evident in a booster literature designed to justify the annexation of portions of Latin America and in the writings of travelers through the region as well.

2

An American Central America

Boosters, Travelers, and the Persistence of Manifest Destiny

> Various parties in America, who agree about nothing else, unite in desiring the annexation of the Central American States.... The American government ... and office-holders who extol the Monroe Doctrine, and believe in a 'Manifest Destiny' of their own devising, naturally strive to engross the Isthmus which is about to become the highway of the world. The blustering element vociferates for war; the industrialist seeks so fair a field for migration; the owners of exhausted lands long for the rich savannahs of Costa Rica and San Salvador; and the ambitious see what may be made of so noble and diversified a territory so scantily peopled, and so degenerate in importance.
>
> – *London Daily News*, July 7, 1858

The *London Daily News*, a paper that promoted British territorial expansion in Central America, was hardly pleased by the annexationist desires of the North Americans. Expansionist James Buchanan was president, and his Anglophobic secretary of state, Lewis Cass, seemed committed to undermining British interests in Central America through the threat of arms, loudly insisting that the British withdraw their support from the Mosquito protectorate in Nicaragua. A majority of the American public seemed to support the Buchanan administration's foreign policy, and, the paper marvelled, even the illegal activities of filibuster William Walker, who maintained his Nicaraguan citizenship and threatened to reclaim power in Central America. A region once "so degenerate in importance" had captured the attention of otherwise antithetical factions in the United States, the *London Daily News* concluded:

The Slaveholders (not quite all, however) covet the extension of tropical territory at their command. A portion of the Free-soil party hope to plant down free labour on the fertile terraces of Honduras and Guatemala with their temperate climate, with the great object of establishing a barrier against the spread of slavery southwards. Adventurers are eager to seek their fortunes in a region so rich. Merchants anticipate the opening of vast new markets. Speculative capitalists look to the exploitation of silver-mines, old and new and to the profits of the transit.[1]

For a period in the 1850s, it did seem as though a fever for Central America had infected the country and that territorial expansionism in the region could bring together laborer and merchant, adventurer and farmer, slaveholders and those who desired new territory free from the taint of slavery.

In the eyes of many observers, the mania had uncomfortably familiar resonances to developments a decade or more earlier. The U.S.-Mexico War was, among other things, the culmination of a propaganda campaign by Democratic aggressive expansionists. Popular periodicals, especially those aligned with the Democratic Party, offered regular calls to war in the mid 1840s and also offered readers a portrait of northern Mexican territories that would make desirable possessions for the United States. But aggressive expansionists were not limited to the Democratic Party. When Waddy Thompson, a South Carolina Whig and former American plenipotentiary to the Republic of Mexico, published his *Recollections of Mexico* in 1846, the New York *Albion* was only one of many papers and journals to afford it a lengthy review. Thompson, the reviewer archly commented, "is remarkably proud of his own race, and religiously believes that the Anglo-Saxons are destined to conquer the whole continent with their – civilization." On the eve of the war with Mexico, Thompson promoted an activist version of Manifest Destiny that would bring that country under United States' control, even suggesting that California was worth a "'twenty years' war." His portrait of Mexico is a highly biased one, emphasizing Mexico's mineral riches and the fertility of her soil, as well as the burdensome nature of the Catholic Church. A classic booster narrative, Thompson's *Recollections* both inspired and justified aggressive expansionism in Mexico. Importantly, Thompson grounded his critique of Mexico in a gender analysis – he decried the lackadaisical attitude of Mexican men toward work and offered a highly romantic portrait of the women of the country. As later chapters will explore, these tropes provided the structure for Manifest Destiny's literature after the war as well.[2]

The Latin American booster narrative, designed to encourage American lust for the region, did not decline in popularity after war's end. On the contrary, the expansionist travel narrative flowered between 1848 and 1860,

[1] *London Daily News*, July 7, 1858. Squier Collection of Newspaper clippings on Central America, 1856–1860, HL. The 1823 Monroe Doctrine did *not* by any means advocate continental domination but was frequently cited by expansionists in the antebellum period and later as justifying incursions south in the name of national security.

[2] "Recollections of Mexico," New York *Albion*, reprinted in *The Living Age* 10 (July 11, 1846): 57–63; Waddy Thompson, *Recollections of Mexico* (New York, 1846); Eric J. Sundquist, "The Literature of Expansion and Race," in *The Cambridge History of American Literature*, Sacvan Bercovitch, ed. (New York, 1995), 2: 157–9; Reginald Horsman, *Race and Manifest Destiny: the Origins of American Racial Anglo-Saxonism* (Cambridge, MA, 1981), 212.

propelled by Central America's new geopolitical importance.[3] As gold-rush pioneers heading to California landed in Panama, Nicaragua, and Mexico, and as business and political leaders started shipping lines through the region and began constructing a railroad across Panama, Latin America, in general, and Central America, in particular, drew the attention of previously oblivious Americans, as did ongoing disputes with the British over the 1850 Clayton-Bulwer Treaty (renouncing colonization in Central America). The exploits of William Walker, and increasing traffic across the Isthmus, opened up the possibility that Nicaragua, or another portion of Central America, could become the next Texas or California in the 1850s.

A booster literature, steeped in Manifest Destiny, encouraged the fantasy of Central American annexation. In the mid to late 1850s, in fact, it would have been difficult to examine a selection of popular periodicals without finding a travelogue to the region. Book-length narratives were published throughout the decade, and they were both reviewed and serialized in popular journals.[4] Almost all of these narratives were inflected with an expansionist ethos, and they functioned to reassure readers that American activity in territories far removed from Boston, New York, and even Texas, was desirable and to suggest ways in which Nicaragua, or Panama or Honduras, could fit into the United States. The ideological bent of these writings is particularly notable when compared with those authored by non-Americans. Although Europeans, especially the British, had their own dreams of a Central American outpost, European-authored travelogues from the same period tended to be more evenhanded and less rabidly expansionistic than the American narratives.

Several of the most prolific boosters of Central American annexation had clear political or financial interests in the region. Ephraim George Squier, a respected ethnologist and fervent aggressive expansionist, was the author of ten books and fifty articles or pamphlets on Central America, and by the mid-1850s he had invested heavily in plans for an inter-oceanic railroad line across Nicaragua. Although Squier was appointed chargé d'affaires to the Central American nations by a Whig president, his views were those of the Young America movement, the faction of the Democratic Party that took its name from Emerson's essay and pushed for territorial expansionism, free trade, and support for democratic movements abroad. Squier was one of the most vocal advocates of William Walker's attempts to take over Central America.[5]

[3] Raymund A. Paredes, "The Mexican Image in American Travel Literature, 1831–1869," *New Mexico Historical Review* LII (January 1977): 5–6.

[4] David C. Miller, *Dark Eden: The Swamp in Nineteenth-Century American Culture* (New York, 1989), 118.

[5] Ephraim George Squier published voluminously on the broader Americas, as well. While his earlier archeological writing on the mounds of the Midwest was objective, his primarily "propagandistic" work on Central America was "designed principally to justify his own actions

William Vincent Wells, another important booster, traveled to Central America as an agent of the Honduras Mining and Trading Company and was appointed consul-general of Honduras. His paid employment during much of the 1850s involved him attempting to obtain grants from Central American governments for foreign capitalists, but he worked with equal fervor to sell Honduras to Americas. Author of *Explorations and Adventures in Honduras* and a number of travelogues published in *Harper's New Monthly Magazine* in the mid 1850s, Wells also penned a heroizing account of Walker's rise to power, *Walker's Expedition to Nicaragua*, in 1856. According to Wells, Honduras needed only energetic men and good equipment to produce more gold than California, and it boasted the finest resources, weather, and women in the Western Hemisphere.[6]

That these men, and others with a clear financial interest in the American annexation of Central America, would tout the virtues of potential new territories, is not surprising.[7] What is notable is the number of authors with no explicit political or economic stake in the region who suggested during this period that Latin America was an appropriate arena for American domination. Popular periodicals with no political affiliation, including *Harper's Monthly* and *Putnam's Monthly Magazine*, published rabidly expansionistic travelogues to Cuba, Mexico, and Central America with some regularity during the 1850s.

Educated readers were exposed to an expansionist vision of Latin America in a period of great popular interest in travel writing. In the late 1840s, nineteen percent of the books charged from the New York Society Library by men and fifteen percent of the books charged by women were travel narratives.[8] While it is always difficult to judge a reader's response to a text, there

as chargé d'affaires, to influence the policy of the United States and Great Britain toward Central America and toward each other, and to publicize the isthmian region to the reading public of the United States and Europe." Charles Stansifer, "The Central American Career of E. George Squier" (Ph.D. Diss., Department of History, Tulane University, 1959), 133–4, quoted in Michael D. Olien, "E. G. Squier and the Miskito: Anthropological Scholarship and Political Propaganda," *Ethnohistory* 32 (1985): 125, 115. On Squier's financial investments in the Honduras Interoceanic Railway see Squier's Honduras Interoceanic Railway manuscript collection, HL.

6 William V. Wells, *Explorations and Adventures in Honduras*, excerpted in "Adventures in the Gold Fields of Central America," *HNMM* 12 (February 1856): 315–36.

7 Jane McManus Storm Cazneau (Cora Montgomery) had financial interests in virtually every territory she touted. She invested heavily in transit routes across the Isthmus of Tehuantepec before pushing for the annexation of the Yucatan peninsula, and she held rights to a silver mine in Nicaragua under William Walker at the time she pushed for the recognition of his presidency. For Cazneau's particular vision of Manifest Destiny see Chapter 6 of Linda S. Hudson, *Mistress of Manifest Destiny: A Biography of Jane McManus Storm Cazneau, 1807–1878* (Austin, 2001), 92, 163.

8 Ronald J. Zboray, *A Fictive People: Antebellum Economic Development and the American Reading Public* (New York, 1993), 176–9; Mary Suzanne Schriber, *Writing Home: American Women Abroad, 1830–1920* (Charlottesville, VA, 1997), 47–8, 57.

is evidence that many Americans shared the expansionist sentiments of authors during this period, ranging from confidence that American enterprise could improve the country to the annexationist frenzy that motivated and supported filibustering.[9] Thousands of American men participated in filibustering expeditions to Latin America in the antebellum period, and many thousands more planned to participate. Many more encountered Latin America as tourists. Tens of thousands of California-bound men and women traveled by ship to Central America, crossed the Isthmus in Panama or Nicaragua, and then boarded another ship on the Pacific Coast to take them to San Francisco. Along the way, they often stopped in Cuba and coastal Mexico. The average if adventuresome gold-rush traveler in the late 1840s and 1850s revealed privately, in letter and journal, expansionist views about the future destiny of these lands that were often indistinguishable from the writings of annexationist boosters.[10]

This chapter will look closely at the role of Manifest Destiny in both public and private travel narratives and in other popular writings on Latin America between 1848 and 1860. It will focus in particular on discussions of the most physically distant filibustering target, Central America, in order to understand how Americans imagined that a region far from U.S. borders could be incorporated into a continental republic. Despite the claims of some historians that Manifest Destiny was on the decline after 1848 or that expansionism was "limited to specific maritime objectives" and as an ideology

---

[9] On the difficulty of judging antebellum responses to texts see Mary Kupiec Cayton, "The Making of an American Prophet: Emerson, His Audiences, and the Rise of the Culture Industry in Nineteenth-Century America," AHR 92 (June 1987): 597–620.

[10] Of course letters and diaries are not necessarily objective. Not only do individuals bring their own personal biases to travel, but the very practices of tourism may have shaped their reactions in a gendered manner. As William Stowe has written, travel provoked gendered responses from an American man, encouraging him to think of himself "as a deservedly masterful member of a deservedly dominant gender, class, and ethnic group." In particular, Brian Roberts has noted that gold-rush narratives (including many of the sources considered here), often greatly exaggerated the dangers of the journey and worked to structure the relationship between the writer (male) and reader (female). "She would have to admit that gold or no gold, proof or not, the California experience was the harshest form of reality, and that the gold seeker, in turn, was the most real of men." Ralph Waldo Emerson saw the process of reading travel narratives as reinvigorating their virility, by giving them "surcharge of arterial blood." William W. Stowe, *Going Abroad: European Travel in Nineteenth-Century American Culture* (Princeton, 1994), 47; Brian Roberts, *American Alchemy: The California Gold Rush and Middle-Class Culture* (Chapel Hill, 2000), 217; Bruce Albert Harvey, *American Geographics: U.S. National Narratives and the Representation of the Non-European World, 1830–1865* (Stanford, 2001), 10. On ethnocentricity in nineteenth-century travel writing see also John Pemble, *The Mediterranean Passion: Victorians and Edwardians in the South* (New York, 1987), 67, 142; William L. Vance, *America's Rome* (New Haven, 1989), vol. 2: 77–102, 144–60; Dean MacCannell, *The Tourist: A New Theory of the Leisure Class* (New York, 1976), 177–9; Judith Adler, "Origins of Sightseeing," *Annals of Tourism Research* 16 (1989): 7–29.

"does not bear close scrutiny," both popular travelogues and the private writings of travelers in Latin America during the 1850s suggest otherwise.[11] An examination of expansionist themes in writings on Central America during the antebellum era reveals that the ideology of Manifest Destiny was healthy and vibrant at the close of the U.S.-Mexico War. While territorial expansionism was a failed project in the 1850s, for Manifest Destiny's literature, the inter-war years were a golden age.

Natural versus National Borders: Redrawing the Map

That the United States had no imperial ambitions before the Spanish-American War has long been a truism of the U.S. position on empire, setting the United States apart from imperialist powers like Britain, France, and, especially during the Cold War, the Soviet Union. That the "benevolent assimilation" of continental expansion marked the difference between the United States and those powers that practiced overseas colonization in the nineteenth century was not simply retrospective nostalgia: critics of Britain in the antebellum period also made the point that the British were oppressors of colonized peoples, while America, born of revolution, was dedicated to liberating oppressed peoples. But the distinction between Britain and the United States posed certain difficulties for American writers who contemplated the annexation of overseas territories of their own from 1848 to 1860.[12]

Advocates of the annexation of Cuba, Mexico, and Central America attempted to justify and make legitimate the conquest of overseas lands after 1848 in a number of ways. Foremost among them was by culturally reconstructing United States boundaries to include new territories. Authors of Latin American travelogues suggested in both explicit and implicit manners that significant portions of other countries belonged not in those countries but in the United States, offering a vision of national boundaries as fluid or even inconsequential and in the process working to justify the incorporation of overseas territories into the United States.

It was not automatically apparent how any of the filibustering targets of the post-1848 period could "fit" into an American republic, or even into

---

[11] Quotes in Norman Graebner, *Empire on the Pacific: A Study in American Continental Expansion* (New York, 1955), vi, 217, 218. Michael A. Morrison's contention that "[a]lthough Manifest Destiny was not in eclipse, to a growing number of Americans in 1851 expansion no longer appeared to promote automatically the ideals of liberty and emancipation" is reasonable. But for an equally significant number of Americans, as this book will reveal, it is not true that "López was no Sam Houston. Caution and introspection began to overshadow the sense of boundlessness of the previous decade." Michael A. Morrison, *Slavery and the American West: The Eclipse of Manifest Destiny and the Coming of the Civil War* (Chapel Hill, 1997), 133.

[12] Mary Ann Heiss, "The Evolution of the Imperial Idea and U.S. National Identity," *Diplomatic History* 26 (Fall 2002): 511–40.

an American empire. As Robert W. Johannsen shows in *To the Halls of the Montezumas*, adjacent Mexico contained a landscape essentially alien to the American soldiers who traveled there during the war, a landscape that provoked fears by many Americans that Mexico's territory, and the residents of that territory, were too foreign to integrate into the United States. This fear helps to explain the failure of the movement to acquire all of Mexico after U.S. troops captured Mexico City in 1847. While it seemed only logical to some to simply take all of Mexico as booty of the war, cut Mexico up, and turn it into new territories and states, most Americans rejected this idea. They did so because central Mexico was densely populated. While contemporary science argued that an inferior Mexican "race" could be absorbed by the stronger American or Anglo-Saxon race, without harm to the Anglo-Saxon, many Americans feared the result of the integration of Mexico's people into the United States. Critics also doubted whether Americans could be happy in the alien landscape of central and southern Mexico.[13]

By the 1850s expansionists were promoting the incorporation of territory even farther away than Mexico, territory with an equally alien landscape and population. One of the most extreme cases was Central America. The importance of the Isthmus on transit routes and William Walker's exploits drove both the friends and foes of expansionism to imagine that Central America might be the next step in America's destiny. For this to happen, of course, Americans needed to be convinced that Nicaragua or some other portion of Central America could fit into the United States. To this end, authors worked hard to sell Central America to the public, to reconstruct natural boundaries so that Central America might fit within America's national boundaries, and to make American activity in the region appear natural and desirable.

A region of diverse micro-climates, extremely varied terrain, and indigenous peoples of widely varying cultures and traditions, Central America defies easy categorization, except insofar that most of it is, in many respects, quite unlike the United States. On the basic level of word choice and metaphor, expansionist travel narratives worked to tie the United States to Latin America. As Mary Louise Pratt notes in *Imperial Eyes: Travel Writing and Transculturation*, nineteenth-century European travel writers employed adjectives designed to tie the landscape of South America explicitly to the home culture of the explorers. This same use of adjectival modifiers, chosen to add material referents into the landscape, was made by American expansionists. In descriptions of the Nicaraguan landscape, for example, "plum colored" volcanoes rise "like spires" to heaven and the landscape is "rose colored." These adjectives are not chosen at random, they do actual

---

[13] Robert Johannsen, *To the Halls of the Montezumas: The Mexican War in the American Imagination* (New York, 1985), 144–74. For a different view of the failure of the all-Mexico movement see John Douglas Pitts Fuller, *The Movement for the Acquisition of All Mexico, 1846–1848* (Baltimore, 1936).

work for those who would like to claim that Nicaragua is more familiar than foreign. These terms work to relate potentially alien visions – the volcano and desert landscape – in comfortably familiar terms. Volcanoes are essentially like the spires of churches while the landscape wears the appearance of the favorite temperate-climate flower, the rose, and familiar plum. Thomas Francis Meagher, an Irish nationalist who became a firm supporter of both filibustering and an Isthmus canal after fleeing Britain for the United States in 1852, offered a typical expansionist paean to Costa Rica, "of all tropical countries . . . the best adapted for the North American and European emigrant" in 1859 to 1860 in *Harper's Monthly Magazine*. Repeatedly comparing the climate and landscape to the United States, Meagher asserted that all the familiar crops of North America – "English wheat and clover, the Irish potato, the American pumpkin, peaches, apple, plums, quinces and strawberries" – grew in Costa Rica's valleys as well as did the less familiar tropical fruits.[14]

Other images in the popular literature about Latin America seem to have been chosen for the additional associations they created in the minds of readers. For instance, those volcanoes are perpetually bathed in a "golden" light, while the mountains of Nicaragua are frequently described as "steel colored." One later author described Lake Nicaragua in a similar manner: "In the glowing light of the evening it seemed like a sea of gold, studded with emerald isles." In other words, "the landscape is represented as extremely rich in material and semantic substance" in these accounts and is, thus, theoretically at least, rendered appealing and familiar – not threatening or foreign.[15]

This vision of the metallic landscape nicely complemented one of the most seductive claims made by boosters about Central America – that it contained gold and silver mines that would eventually put California to shame. This was an attraction that proved remarkably successful in attracting filibusters to Sonora, Mexico, in the first half of the 1850s. When Walker left Sonora for Nicaragua, so to speak, he brought the claim with him. An "Officer in the service of Walker" reported that there was gold and silver in the Isthmus as did an 1860 recruiting letter for Walker's army in Honduras in the New Orleans *Delta*. Honduras, the author wrote, "is a Land of Gold! . . . The bed of nearly every river here about is enriched with this metal, and the women wash sufficient in one day to support themselves and their families for weeks." One booster noted that Nicaragua's "rivers have gold dust, her mountains the ore of gold," while the late vice counsul for Nicaragua claimed

[14] Mary Louise Pratt, *Imperial Eyes: Travel Writing and Transculturation* (New York, 1992), 204; Thomas Francis Meagher, "Holidays in Costa Rica," *HNMM* 20 (December 1859): 34.

[15] E. G. Squier, "Nicaragua: An Exploration from Ocean to Ocean," *HNMM* 11 (June 1855): 754; William E. Simmons, *Uncle Sam's New Waterway* (New York, 1899), 134; Pratt, *Imperial Eyes*, 204.

that that country's "minerals are gold, silver, copper and iron; lead nearly virginal has been found, fully ninety per cent, and the residue silver."[16]

Perhaps the most enthusiastic account of the mineral riches of Central America appeared in *Harper's Monthly* in May of 1856. The anonymous author of "A Visit to the Silver Mines of Central America," described "veins of silver" in the "centre of some of the richest gold fields of the continent," single mills that yielded five to ten thousand dollars a day, a "cool and comfortable climate," and silver mines that "never give out; they vary in width, but are indefinitely continued. Their supply is inexhaustible." Add to this a labor force of "mild, industrious, and obedient" Indians, and a local gentry that tells the author "if your countrymen, los Americanos del Norte, that great and happy people, would but come here . . . how rich and happy we should become!" and the author's claim seems well founded that with "Anglo-Saxon industry" and "prophetic intelligence" Honduras could easily dwarf California as a field for mineral wealth. Walker's supporter William Wells drew similar connections between the Honduran landscape, material riches, the familiar colors of fall, and California. He and his reader delighted in a landscape "retiring with richest verdure into the hues of autumn, brought vividly to mind the scenery of California, where the foot-hills of the Sierras decline westward as do these northward. An ocean of gold and green undulating in the perfect tints of sunset."[17]

Central America also was equated to parts of the United States through analogy and metaphor in the popular literature of expansionism. Central America was "three times and one third larger than the State of New York," in one analogy, and had a "claim to territory about as large as that of the united six states of New England" in another. Peter Stout, late vice consul of Nicaragua, described that country as "about seven times the extent of Massachusetts" with a climate that in places "resembles that of the Middle States of America."[18]

Nicaragua's fertility and bounty loomed large in the expansionist vision, a reflection of what one scholar has identified as the transformation of a nurturing feminized American landscape into wealth in the mid-nineteenth

[16] "An officer in the service of Walker," *The Destiny of Nicaragua: Central America as it was, is, and may be* (Boston, 1856), 35; "Our Special Correspondent at Truxillo, August 18, 1860," New Orleans *Delta*, September 4, 1860; W. J. A. Bradford, "Central America," *DBR* 21 (July 1856): Pg 2; Peter F. Stout, *Nicaragua: Past, Present and Future; a Description of Its Inhabitants, Customs, Mines, Minerals. Early History, Modern Fillibusterism, Proposed Inter-Oceanic Canal and Manifest Destiny* (Philadelphia, 1859), 85.

[17] "A Visit to the Silver Mines of Central America," *HNMM* 12 (May 1856): 721–33; William V. Wells, *Explorations and Adventures in Honduras, comprising sketches of travel in the gold regions of Olancho, and a review of the history and general resources of Central America. With original maps, and numerous illustrations* (New York, 1857), 267. Wells traveled in 1854.

[18] Bradford, "Central America," *DBR* 21 (July 1856): 4, 16; Stout, *Nicaragua: Past, Present and Future*, 17, 85.

century. Wrote William Frank Stewart in 1857, "Nicaragua is a magnificent spot of earth – a sort of literal 'paradise lost' whose luxuriant soil teems in prolific abundance with every variety of herb, tree and living thing which the ardor of a tropical sun can coax into existence." Nicaragua could therefore be described as not only like the United States but, in terms of its natural resources, in many ways superior. According to E. G. Squier, Honduran pine was just one of the trees of the region "generally considered, for every necessary purpose, greatly superior to what can be imported from the United States." William Wells also affirmed that the pine of the sierra in the Cordilleras of Central America has a bark and inner wood that "compared favorably with the best Northern lumber."[19]

The rivers and lakes of Central America were likewise similar to but better than U.S. counterparts. Lake Nicaragua, according to Squier, was "half the size of lake Erie" although more impressive looking, despite a mouth as swampy as "the mouth of the Mississippi." The Gulf of Fonseca was "one of the best havens on the Pacific, and is equal to the bay of San Francisco in size, position, beauty, depth and grandeur." William Wells agreed that the Bay of Fonseca was "inferior in no respect to that of San Francisco" and then placed the United States there in the reader's vision. "It would be safe to say that the whole mercantile fleet of America might ride in security together in this great southern bay... bordered by three states possessed of the greatest natural resources within the tropics, their hills stored with the richest mineral deposits in Spanish America." Expansionist descriptions of the landscape were filled with references familiar to North Americans, but they almost always made the point that the Central American versions were superior.[20]

For territorial expansionists, the Central American climate was a serious stumbling block. As travelers through Panama or Nicaragua could and did testify, the tropical lowlands were unpleasantly hot, "95 degrees Fahrenheit in the shade" as one distressed traveler put it. Much of the region also was plagued by mosquitoes. William Denniston, native of Orange County, New York, traveled through Nicaragua on his way to California in 1849. He complained in his journal about rainy nights "fighting the mosquitoes which congregated in great numbers, singing in our ears, doubtless with the intention of singing us to sleep, they misjudged the effect of their music." The

---

[19] On the feminized landscape see Annette Kolodny, *The Lay of the Land: Metaphor as Experience and History in American Life and Letters* (Chapel Hill, 1975), 134; Stewart, *Last of the Filibusters*, 61. See also "An officer in the Service of Walker," *The Destiny of Nicaragua*, iii; E. G. Squier, *Observations on the Archaeology and Ethnology of Nicaragua. 1852* (Culver City, CA, 1990), 5; E. G. Squier, *Notes on Central America: Particularly the states of Honduras and San Salvador* (New York, 1855), 181; Wells, *Explorations and Adventures in Honduras*, 176.

[20] E. G. Squier, "Art. II – Reminiscences of Central America," *DBR* 29 (July–December 1860): 422; Wells, *Explorations and Adventures in Honduras*, 118.

gold-mining guide Daniel B. Woods wrote in the early 1850s explicitly warned travelers of the mosquitoes plaguing the Central American routes. And there were other less familiar pests to worry about. William Elder described seeing passengers "devoured" by alligators in a letter to his cousin Catherine, while another traveler cursed Panama as a "God-forsaken country" full of "monkeys, baboons, and lizards, to say nothing about the poisonous reptiles."[21]

Disease was a constant worry in the tropics, especially in the port towns where travelers spent much of their time while waiting for transportation across the Isthmus and on to California. In 1855 *Putnam's Monthly Magazine* noted that "the danger of contracting fever" in Central America was "so imminent as to deter persons in any stage of health from choosing that route." Travelers learned that the Panamanian town of Chagres was "the most unhealthy port on the American continent." One traveling physician wrote that "the exhalations from its malarious atmosphere are extremely prejudicial to the health of a newcomer." Another doctor described outbreaks of elephantiasis among travelers throughout the Isthmus. Passengers universally feared yellow fever, known at the time as "Panama Fever," but were unsure how to prevent against it. According to prevailing miasmatic theories of disease, the sticky climate could itself generate disease.[22]

Addressing the issue of the unhealthiness of the region, *Gregory's Guide for California Travelers*, published in 1850, issued a blanket warning. "Persons who regard their health, will avoid exposure or hard work in the sun, during the middle of the day.... It is considered highly dangerous, and by many residents on the Isthmus as almost certain death, to drink ardent spirits after eating tropical fruit, as it produces fermentation in the bowels, which

---

[21] Diary of Alonzo Hubbard, Volume 1, March 19, 1852, HL; William Franklin Denniston, "Journal of a voyage from New York to San Francisco via Nicaragua...; mining near Mariposa, California; return via Panama. 1849–1850," April 15, 1849, HL; Daniel B. Woods, *Sixteen Months at the Gold Diggings* (New York, 1852); William Elder Correspondence, BL; Charles Ross Parke, *Dreams to Dust: A Diary of the California Gold Rush, 1849–1850*, ed. James E. Davis (Lincoln, 1989).

[22] "The Hawaiian Islands," *PMM* 5 (March 1855): 242; Society of First Steamship Pioneers, *First Steamship Pioneers* (San Francisco, CA, 1874), 70; James L. Tyson, M.D. *Diary of a Physician in California: Being the results of Actual Experiences including Notes of the Journey by Land and Water, and Observation on the Climate, Soil, Resources of the Country, etc.* 1850 (Oakland, 1955), 2; Charles Parke journal ("Journal of a trip across the plains from Illinois to California by way of Laramie and the Donner pass; mining on the Feather river; and a voyage from San Francisco to New Orleans via Nicaragua"), HL; Jane McDougal diary, 1849, in *Ho for California! Women's Overland Diaries from the Huntington Library*, Sandra L. Myers, ed. (San Marino, 1980), 1. See also Robert Tomes, *Panama in 1855: An Account of the Panama Rail-Road, of the Cities of Panama and Aspinwall, with Sketches of Life and Character on the Isthmus* (New York, 1855), 51. Panama was particularly deadly in the mid-nineteenth century. As late as the 1880s there was still a death rate around 60 per 1,000 for residents. Stephen Frenkel, "Jungle Stories: North American Representations of Tropical Panama," *The Geographical Review* 86 (July 1996): 320, 326.

seems to defy the influence of all medical skill." While traveling through Nicaragua, Illinois resident Charles Parke mused in his diary that "if civilized man ever thinks of connecting the two oceans through this river, the first thing to do would be to have the natives deaden all the trees, and vines, for $\frac{1}{4}$ of a mile back from this river on both sides and burn them. This would let in the air and sun and dry the upper soil, thus greatly improving the healthfulness of the locality."[23]

Those who hoped to see an American Central America also had to contend with a popular belief in the enervating effects of a tropical climate. The social science theory of environmental determinism, prevalent in the mid-nineteenth century, held that the tropics inhibited civilization, induced indolence, and would eventually adversely affect any settler.[24] "The climate is undoubtedly debilitating to our Northern constitutions" wrote one traveler to his wife, while Robert Tomes declared after traveling through Panama that the area was utterly unsuitable for white settlement because of the "pestilential climate, with which no race of men and no strength of constitution can contend. . . . It is fearfully probable that no race of whites can escape deterioration upon the Isthmus. The indomitable energy which braves every hardship, and overcomes every visible obstacle, yields to the fatal influence of the climate; and each generation sinks lower than the one that proceeded it." A later author agreed: "Americans permanently residing in Central America in one or two generations always come to the ways of the country. Their descendants become Central Americans. The type yields to the climate. No matter what the ancestry, the training, or the resolution, the children will be modified by the climate."[25]

Central American boosters addressed these concerns directly and with great frequency – such fears were unmerited. "Tales of its poisonous miasma; its inviting exterior, concealing savage beasts of prey and venomous reptiles; its dark jungles, the birth-place of malaria, and its luxuriant foliage, exhaling the vapors of disease and death – these have passed away as idle dreams; and no longer deter the march of the adventurer" wrote William Wells.[26]

[23] *Gregory's Guide for California Travelers; via the Isthmus of Panama* (New York, 1850), 7; Charles Parke journal, November 22, 1850, HL.

[24] For an excellent overview of the ambivalent reaction to the tropics in the nineteenth century see Miller, *Dark Eden*. On environmental determinism see J. M. Blaut, *The Colonizer's Model of the World: Geographical Diffusionism and Eurocentric History* (New York, 1993), 69; David Livingstone, "The Moral Discourse of Climate: Historical Considerations on Race, Place, and Virtue," *Journal of Historical Geography* 17 (October 1991): 413–34; Frenkel, "Jungle Stories," 325; George Fredrickson, *The Black Image in the White Mind: The Debate on Afro-American Character and Destiny, 1817–1914* (New York, 1971), 137–8, 142–3.

[25] William Elder Correspondence. Letter to his wife Sarah, June 17, 1850, Panama, BL; Robert Tomes, *Panama in 1855: An Account of the Panama Railroad* (New York, 1855), excerpted in "A Trip on the Panama Railroad," *HNMM* 11 (October 1855): 620, 621; Henry Isaac Sheldon, *Notes on the Nicaragua Canal*. 1897. (Chicago, 1902), 118.

[26] Wells, *Explorations and Adventures in Honduras*, 30.

Boosters assured readers that the climate of Central America was neither enervating nor unhealthy, but rather superior to the climate of most regions of the United States. One pro-emigration letter published in 1857 in the southern journal, *De Bow's Review*, claimed that soldiers in Nicaragua were never sick and "began to wear that rugged, bronzed look that is produced by exposure in a healthy atmosphere" as soon as they arrived. According to *De Bow's Review* publisher W. J. A. Bradford in an article on Central America in 1856, "[t]he heat is never in that raging excess which we experience in the *northern* latitudes of the United States for some days in the summer.... This highest mark is not so high as is sometimes marked in summer in New York or Boston." In case the point were lost on readers, Bradford continued his discussion of Nicaragua's temperature for two pages, at the conclusion of which he summarized: "With a range of less than forty degrees, with the extremest [*sic*] heat not above 90 degrees – the variation for the year being less than that for our summer in the northern states of the Union, and the highest point below our greatest summer heat; it must be no less salubrious than agreeable." Another account made the same point. "Nothing is more absurd, or farther from the truth, than our popular dread of these 'unknown regions under the Tropics.' The sandy horrors of Sahara, or the Colorado, are not here. Here the sun neither scorches the skin nor dries the blood; the earth is warm, but not infectious. Throughout all the new countries of our Western States, the local unhealthiness is prevalent and hard to be resisted, even by good constitutions.... fevers are slight, and not so prevalent as on the Ohio or Mississippi."[27] Nor was this misrepresentation limited to Central America. The Mexican travelogue, "A Trip from Chihuahua to the Sierra Madre," published in 1854 in *Putnam's Monthly Magazine* was equally effusive and unrealistic in its account of the climate and fertility of the Mexican countryside. Northern Mexico, in reality extremely hot and arid, is represented in this travelogue as a beautiful, healthful region where familiar fruits grow in abundance and the earth holds "immense treasures of gold and silver."[28]

Authors of expansionist travelogues never mentioned mosquitoes, unless to explicitly deny their existence. About Nicaragua, one author wrote,

---

[27] "Nicaragua," *DBR* 22 (January 1857): 107, 108; Bradford, "Central America," 1, 4–6. See also Squier, "Nicaragua: An Exploration from Ocean to Ocean," 757 and "Art. II – Reminiscences of Central America," 423; William V. Wells, *Explorations and Adventures in Honduras,* excerpted in "Adventures in the Gold Fields of Central America," *HNMM* 12 (February 1856): 330.

[28] "A Trip from Chihuahua to Sierra Madre," *PMM* 4 (October 1854): 408–21. On Mexico's "elysian" climate see also Nahum Capen, *The Republic of the United States of America: Its Duties to Itself, and Its Responsible Relations to Other Countries. Embracing also a Review of the Late War between the United States and Mexico; Its Causes and Results; and of those measures of Government which have characterized the Democracy of the Union* (New York, 1848), 160.

"scarcely any mosquitos [*sic*] are met with, and this fact runs counter to the preconceived ideas of nearly all newcomers." Alligators and snakes provide color to some narratives, but rarely present any danger to the narrator himself. After describing "an appalling list of deadly snakes, to say nothing of the tamaulipas, tarantula, scorpion, and centipede" in Honduras, William Wells offered the fairly unconvincing reassurance that "though these all exist, as in most inter tropical countries, they are not found in such numbers as to be dangerous."[29]

The contrast between these booster narratives and those written by Europeans at the same time is instructive. With a claim to Central America at least as strong as that of the United States, British expansionists made an effort to encourage British settlement in the region, especially in British Honduras. In November of 1856, for example, the *London Daily News* published a booster account of Honduras, drawn from a letter to the minister plenipotentiary of Honduras in London. "What gives most importance to the plateau of Honduras, apart from its fertility, and temperature of perpetual spring is the salubrity of its climate," according to the author. This climate "allows colonists from the northern regions to cultivate the soil, and pursue their avocations without danger to their health." Indeed, the plateau of Honduras offered the best climate for agriculture in the New World. "A delicious climate permits the emigrant to labor and follow his avocations the entire year. With less effort he obtains ten times the product which he could secure in Europe."[30]

But even openly expansionistic British writers tended to be more subdued in their claims for Central America than their American counterparts. John Baily's 1850 *Central America: Describing each of the States of Guatemala, Honduras, Salvador, Nicaragua, and Costa Rica; their Natural Features, Products, Population, and Remarkable Capacity for Colonization....* was written with the explicit goal of encouraging British settlement in Central America. He was typical in attempting to make Latin America familiar to the British. Guatamala, he wrote, offered districts "resembling the finest part of England on a magnificent scale," as well as peach trees and fields of wheat.[31]

But Baily was unwilling to countenance the stories of mineral riches that circulated among American expansionists. In Nicaragua, "there are many situations where gold is said to be found, and doubtless it is occasionally met with," he wrote cautiously. "Yet there are grounds for being sceptical

---

[29] "An officer in the service of Walker," *The Destiny of Nicaragua*, 24; Wells, *Explorations and Adventures in Honduras*, 405.

[30] *London Daily News*, November 22, 1856. From Squier's Collection of Newspaper clippings on Central America, 1856–1860, HL.

[31] John Baily, Esq., *Central America: Describing each of the States of Guatemala, Honduras, Salvador, Nicaragua, and Costa Rica* (London, 1850) quoted in *The Living Age* 27 (November 2, 1850): 198.

[*sic*] as to the abundance that common report assigns to it; for the vulgar, when they discover any glittering mineral of a yellow color, are too apt to be confident that it is the precious metal, and are not easily convinced of the contrary, even after frequent disappointments."[32]

Other British writers were lukewarm at best about Central America and the Caribbean. Writing in 1853, Edward Sullivan was "excessively disappointed in the fruits" of the Caribbean, "finding none at all equal in flavour to our British productions." Indeed, many of the most popular British travel narratives to the Caribbean and Latin America were written with the intent of critiquing slavery, and they substituted tones of outrage and disgust for the expansionist enthusiasm that marked the accounts discussed here.[33]

Other Europeans contributed to the expansionist canon of the period. The Viennese physician Carl Scherzer and his travel companion Moritz Wagner concluded after traveling through Costa Rica in 1854 that "a small band of resolute men, uniting courage with discipline, would find no difficulty in gaining and holding this entire state. . . . It is only by some thorough admixture with a more energetic northern race, that these people can be saved from utter demoralization."[34] Their Costa Rican travelogue proved popular and was reviewed in both the United States and Britain. Both British and American reviews quoted the duo extensively on the usual expansionist themes: the fine weather and healthy state of agriculture, the political calm of the country, and the "effeminate Creole people of these zones," who have no interest in commerce or enterprise. Importantly, however, British reviewers quoted the authors on the plague of mosquitoes that made sleep impossible for the German travelers. American expansionists never mentioned mosquitoes, and American reviews of Scherzer and Wagner's book also failed to mention this portion of their narrative. With a comparative lack of passion, one British review concluded, "Central America is, in all probability, destined yet to become a great nation, and it will be our own fault if we allow the Americans to derive the exclusive benefit of its rise and progress."[35]

American expansionists appear to have been both more creative and more committed than their British peers in their attempts to connect portions of Latin America to their home countries. But the fact remained that Nicaragua

[32] Baily, *Central America*, 123.

[33] Sir Edward Robert Sullivan, *Rambles and Scrambles in North and South America* (London, 1853), 241. On abolitionist travelogues see, for example, John Glanville Taylor, *The United States and Cuba: Eight Years of Change and Travel* (London, 1851).

[34] "A Central American Paradise," *Ladies' Repository* 17 (July 1857): 431.

[35] "Costa Rica," *The New Monthly Magazine*, reprinted in *The Living Age* 51 (December 27, 1857): 769–82; "A Central American Paradise," *Ladies' Repository* 17 (July 1857): 431; Moritz Wagner and Carl Scherzer, *Die Republik Costa Rica in Central America* (Leipzig, 1856). The Jamaican Mary Seacole's narrative of life in Panama also emphasised the less romantic aspects of Central America – bugs, cholera, and crocodiles, in particular. Mary Seacole, *Wonderful Adventures of Mrs. Seacole in Many Lands*. 1857 (New York, 1988).

lay a thousand miles south of New Orleans, a seeming problem for a new state in a period when the United States were *physically* united states. Given the reigning geographical determinism of the nineteenth century, when educated people believed they could determine God's intended plan from spatial configurations, the relative positions of the United States and its next states in the Caribbean or Central America was a matter of some importance. New Orleans, Florida, Texas, and, finally, the Mexican territory gained in the war had all entered the union buttressed by strong cartographic arguments as to their "natural" connection to the United States. During debates over whether to annex all of Mexico in January of 1848, New York senator Daniel S. Dickinson argued that "North America presents to the eye one great geographical system.... laws more potent than those which prescribe artificial boundaries, will ordain that it shall be united." Unfortunately for Central American boosters, and those who hoped to take Cuba as well, geographical determinism clearly suggested that American territorial expansionism be limited to adjacent mainland territory, since no natural frontier was as obvious or limiting as an ocean or sea. Thus the intentions of Providence regarding Cuba, and Central America, would seem clear. They were not destined to join the United States because they could not be naturally united.[36]

Supporters of Cuban annexation had an easier time finessing this issue than did supporters of expansionism in Central America. Journalist and proponent of the Young America movement, Cora Montgomery, elided both the fact that Cuba belonged to Spain and that it was an island when she argued in the 1850 tract *The Queen of Islands* that "no one state of the Union is so accessible to all the others as Cuba." James Buchanan and the other Democratic authors of the explosive 1854 Ostend Manifesto, which attempted to justify taking Cuba from Spain by force, stated that it "must be clear to every reflecting mind" that Cuba "belongs naturally to that great family of States of which the Union is the Providential Nursery." From the opposite end of the political spectrum, New York abolitionist and U.S. senator William H. Seward took the family metaphor a step further. Seward made the case that Cuba was actually born from the United States. "Every rock and every grain of sand in that island," he argued in 1859, "were rifted and washed out from American soil by the floods of the Mississippi, and the other estuaries of the Gulf of Mexico." One of the founders of the Republican Party, Seward opposed the Ostend Manifesto and filibustering in Cuba, but he never lost his taste for territorial expansionism. At various points in his political career he

---

[36] *Congressional Globe*, 30th Congress, 1st Sess., Appendix, 86–7 (January 12, 1848); Albert Weinberg, *Manifest Destiny: A Study of Nationalist Expansionism in American History*. 1935, reprint edition (Chicago, 1963), 33–71; Anders Stephanson, *Manifest Destiny: American Expansion and the Empire of the Right* (New York, 1995), 43–4; Livingstone, *The Geographical Tradition*, 149–55, 174–5.

pushed for the annexation of Santo Domingo and Hawaii, and the purchase of not only Cuba but also the Danish Virgin Islands and Puerto Rico. In 1867 as secretary of state under Andrew Johnson he negotiated the purchase of Alaska from Russia ("Seward's Folly").[37]

Central America presented more of a challenge, but boosters of annexation in that region rose to the occasion. The Isthmus might not be contiguous to other American territory, but it shared a natural border with the United States, none the less, via nautical trade routes. Nicaragua's potential alliance with the great ports of the United States offered expansionist authors a way to collapse the vast distance separating the two countries. Not only were the ports of Nicaragua superior to those elsewhere, or as Squier put it, "the best on the whole Pacific coast of America," but they were, expansionists argued, firmly tied or connected to the United States through use and geography. *Harper's Monthly* reported that San Juan de Nicaragua was on the "natural highway between the oceans," a quick pit stop from America's ports. Filibusters helped to create new borders, by "seeking to break down the barriers which divide [the oceans], and to mingle their as yet estranged waters." American control of Nicaragua, then, might create a new national border where a natural one had already existed. The idea that the United States already shared a natural relationship with Nicaragua was explored in another popular image employed by expansionists, the flow of Americans across the Central American peninsula. The flow of Americans through Nicaragua was represented as a natural process, a "tide of immigration" that "poured its floods . . . upon the glittering shores of California."[38]

In visions of Nicaragua's relationship to the United States the "natural" almost always trumps the national. Bradford elaborated on the collapsing barriers between the Atlantic and Pacific, and between the United States and Nicaragua, in his work. He developed an analogy that reconceptualized Central America by destabilizing the actual physical location of the Central American Isthmus:

There are two remarkable geographic characteristics in the relations of the Isthmus with the rest of the world. Separating by a narrow strip of rock, the two great oceans of the globe, it is open at contiguous points, to the commerce of both; and central as to latitude and productions to both; and connecting by a monopoly of transit in one

[37] Cora Montgomery, *The Queen of Islands and the King of Rivers* (New York, 1850), 8; "The Ostend Manifesto," Robert H. Holden and Eric Zolov, eds. *Latin America and the United States: A Documentary History* (New York, 2000), 37; *Congressional Globe*, 35th Congress, 2nd Sess., 539; Richard Drinnon, *Facing West: The Metaphysics of Indian Hating and Empire Building* (New York, 1990), 272.

[38] Squier, "Nicaragua: An Exploration from Ocean to Ocean," 762, Squier, "San Juan de Nicaragua," *HNMM* 10 (December 1854): 51, 50; Squier, *Notes on Central America*, 18. The authors of the Ostend Manifesto made a similar argument about Cuba. Holden and Zolov, *Latin America and the United States*, 37.

direction, ocean to ocean; it links by a like monopoly in another direction, the two great parts of the western hemisphere, holding in poise these to the north and south, those to the east and west.

His not very surprising conclusion: "Commercially, socially, and politically, it [Central America] invites especially the interests and sympathies of the people of the United States." John L. Richmond, undersecretary of state for the Republic of Nicaragua during Walker's reign, argued the same point in his tract, *Mexico and Central America: The Problem and its Solution*. If Americans "were looking toward Mexico and Central America, merely for the cheapest and best means of connecting the Atlantic and Mississippi Valley with the Pacific" he wrote, "we should select Nicaragua for the field of operations." In other words, the fact that this land was noncontiguous to the United States was irrelevant if it provided a better, quicker, cheaper means of transport from the East to the West Coast of the United States. Because it was quicker, it was a more natural transit route than the overland route. Of course, by claiming a "natural" connection when a national one was so clearly lacking, expansionists justified the flouting of international law in the name of a higher law, or natural destiny.[39]

The "natural" connection or affinity between the United States and Central America also was represented visually in maps of the region published during the period (see Figure 2.1). The "Map Showing the Proposed Routes of Interoceanic Communication" that appeared in Squier's 1855 *Notes on Central America* is illuminating in its framing. The Gulf coasts of Louisiana and Texas, hotbeds of filibustering activity, stand at the center of the map. Potential lines of trade are emphasized, while political divisions are barely noted. The border between the United States and Mexico, only settled a few years before, is barely perceptible. America's southern border is notably fainter than its border with Canada, which is itself fainter than the line marking the coasts and rivers of North America. Cities appear not on the basis of population but, in part, on the basis of potential and proven mercantile significance. In the place of a key, the map provides relative distances between New York and San Francisco via different Central American routes. The rhetorical functions of this map are clear; the demands of trade, and not

---

[39] Bradford, "Central America," 2; John L. Richmond, *Mexico and Central America: The Problem and its Solution* (Washington, DC, 1858), 6. Frederick Church's monumentally successful paintings of the tropics served a similar purpose, according to one scholar. They provided another way to "erase the property lines (and the title deeds) of real space" and thus offered "the visual apparatus or discipline by which such imperious claims could be not only imagined, but daily reenacted as an essential component of each person's *physical and spiritual self*." Deborah Poole, "Landscape and the Imperial Subject: U.S. Images of the Andes, 1859–1930," in *Close Encounters of Empire: Writing the Cultural History of U.S.-Latin American Relations*, Gilbert M. Joseph, Catherine C. LeGrand, and Ricardo Salvatore, eds. (Durham, 1998), 116.

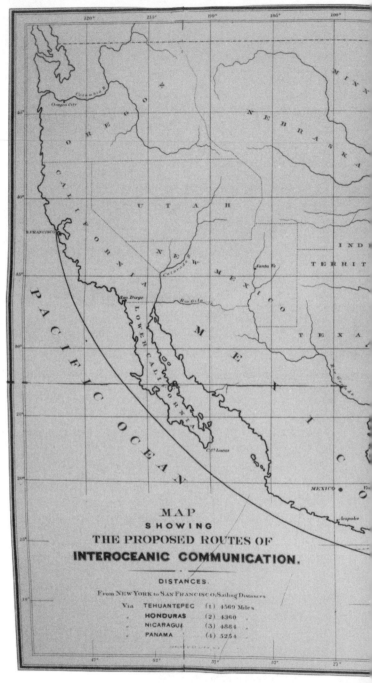

FIGURE 2.1. "Map Showing the Proposed Routes of Interoceanic Communication." The natural (trade) trumps the national (political division) in this expansionist representation of the United States and Central America. From Ephraim G. Squier, *Notes on Central America: Particularly the States of Honduras and San Salvador* (New York: 1855), 238.

political division, shall determine how the Americas are to be viewed and utilized best.[40]

Squier further destabilized existing national boundaries by revealing the manner in which the more important natural connection was already at work. Not only did Americans already flow, like a tide, through Nicaragua, but a reverse tide brought Nicaragua's vast natural resources back to the United States. In San Juan de Nicaragua, Squier wrote, "the woods and hides pass chiefly to the United States who have the greater portion of the carrying trade." Trade routes thus had already rendered national borders obsolete, connecting the two countries not just physically but culturally as well. In an article in *Harper's* in 1854, he asserted that the Americanization of Nicaragua was already under way, and he asked readers, "Is it not significant that the English language now dominates in Panama?"[41]

America was already at work in Central America, this argument claimed, and lest scrupulous Americans worry about the native inhabitants, readers were assured that the hand of America was welcome. "The Bishop of Nicaragua" was reported to have told an American visitor that "we want only an infusion of your people to make this broad land an Eden of Beauty and the garden of the world." Squier likewise emphasized the enthusiasm of Central Americans for their northern neighbors in his writing. In "Adventures and Observations in Nicaragua," in *The International Magazine of Literature, Art and Science* in 1851, Nicaraguans offer that "we trust in the Almighty, that the flag of the United States may soon become the shield of Nicaragua on land and sea." William Wells reported a similar conversation in a Honduran field where gold dust supposedly clung to the roots of corn, and

the two daughters of Maria Saenz found their famous 'windfall,' four pounds of gold in two days! 'Gold!' continued my friend, pulling nervously at the *cigarro* he held firmly in his thumb and finger, 'gold! There is as much of it here, Don Guillermo, as in California. We only need the energy to get it out – the enterprise and *work* of the great American people. The very walls of our houses are impregnated with gold!'[42]

---

[40] Squier, *Notes on Central America*, map following page 238. Cora Montgomery suggested that it was "only with the map of North America distinctly before, that the importance of Cuba, as a point of reception and distribution, can be fairly understood." Montgomery, *The Queen of Islands and the King of Rivers*, 7.

[41] Squier, "Art. II – Reminiscences of Central America," 411; Squier, "San Juan de Nicaragua," *HNMM* 10 (December 1854): 50. The argument that a natural tide of trade tied Cuba to the United States was frequently invoked by Cuban annexationists. See, for example, the Ostend Manifesto. Holden and Zolov, *Latin America and the United States*, 37; Montgomery, *The Queen of Islands and the King of Rivers*.

[42] Bradford, "Central America," 9; E. G. Squier, "Adventures and Observations in Nicaragua," *The International Magazine of Literature, Art and Science* 3 (July 1851): 438; Wells, *Explorations and Adventures in Honduras*, 304.

Boosters made similar claims about the Mexican Isthmus of Tehuantepec, an alternative route to California that expansionists worked hard to
secure during Buchanan's presidency. Assistant U.S. engineer J. J. Williams
was wildly effusive about Mexico's natural resources in *The Isthmus of
Tehuantepec: Being the results of a survey for a Rail-road to connect the
Atlantic and Pacific Oceans, made under the direction of Maj. J. G. Barnard*,
published in 1852. Arguing in favor of a railroad route through Tehuantepec,
Williams presented not only scientific data drawn from the survey but also
his observations about "one of the most delightful regions on the globe."
Tehuantepec was, according to Williams, "designed to be the great highway
of nations, it teems with the elements of wealth, and offers inducements to
emigration that it will be difficult to resist" including "truly magnificent"
forests, vines "more than a foot in diameter" full of "pure, sweet water,"
flowers everywhere, and air scented with vanilla. All of these bring charm to
a productive landscape where virtually every staple crop grows with "greatest abundance" and very little labor. In short, "[i]t is impossible to give an
adequate idea . . . of the boundless vegetable riches that nature has lavished
upon the Isthmus of Tehuantepec."[43]

When Marvin Wheat wrote *Travels on the Western Slope of the Mexican
Cordillera* in 1857 (under the pseudonymn "Cincinnatus"), he did so "not
with any overweening notions as to American Destiny, but as it appeared
to me during my sojourn, and from information obtained through official
reports and surveys." Given that the official reports he relied upon included
Williams's railroad survey, Wheat not surprisingly concluded that a railroad
route from Mazatlan to the mouth of Rio Grande was "the most practicable"
one available to those who wish to link ocean to ocean with a "*desirable* and
national iron band." Wheat relied on the image of a natural, as opposed to
national, trade route to support this assertion. A road "binding the Gulf of
Mexico and the Pacific Ocean," would function "as a natural band to anni-
hilate comparative distances," but only with American help. "This portion
of Mexico wants the people, possessing the industry, enterprise and intelligence, so commonly visible in the Republic of the United States in order to
develop those latent properties of the earth, which a Wise Providence has
laid up in store, to be measured out as great occasions and a great people,
may seem to require."[44]

---

43 John J. Williams, *The Isthmus of Tehuantepec: Being the Results of a Survey for a Rail-road
to Connect the Atlantic and Pacific Oceans Made by the Scientific Commission under the
direction of Maj. J. G. Barnard* (New York, 1852), 47; "The Isthmus of Tehuantepec," *DBR*
13 (July 1852), 52. Similar claims were made about Cuba. See Montgomery, *The Queen of
Islands and the King of Rivers*, 5–15.

44 "Cincinnatus" (Marvin Wheat), *Travels on the Western Slope of the Mexican Cordillera
in the form of Fifty-One Letters* (San Francisco, 1857), preface, 209, 43–4, 360. The gendered metaphor of the iron band was popular among expansionists, Squier also lauded a
proposed railroad through Nicaragua as evidence that only the people of the United States

Americans were welcome for a good reason, according to expansionists – it was only through their energy and labor that the countries of Central America would be "regenerated." By presenting a picture of Central American lands as underused, expansionists drew upon the Enlightenment justification of "best use" used to displace Native-American tribes from the colonial period forward. Especially important were Emmerich de Vattel's widely read arguments, cited by Jefferson and John Adams, among others, that Indian land rights could be extinguished by virtue of failing to bring arable lands into cultivation.[45]

Here the same justification served to destabilize national boundaries. Nicaragua "possesses an enormous wealth of cabinet and dye-woods, mines of precious metals, rivers of considerable extent, whose banks require only willing arms to reclaim them from entire neglect" offered one booster. Another claimed that "[n]ature has done its part; it needs but encouragement and enterprise to fulfill the most sanguine predictions." In fact, not much labor was required in the "garden spot of the world," as Joseph Stout called Nicaragua. "Why those glorious valleys and rich savannahs should not tempt the hardy and thrifty Anglo-Saxon, I cannot imagine. A living is certain, for the banana and plantain are indigenous, as also the nutritious and sweet orange. A comfortable cane hut can be soon erected, vegetation is everblooming, and the changes of temperature are neither sudden or great. A patch containing two acres, planted with plantains alone, would sustain a settler, and his labor would be rewarded in the vegetables he would easily and speedily raise." He concluded that "on a trifling annuity a foreigner could live as happily as heart need desire."[46]

Marvin Wheat, who in 1857 asserted that the "annexing [of] Lower California, Sonora, and Cinaloa," by the United States was a forthcoming event, also asserted that American intervention in Mexico was a natural process,

could "bound the Atlantic to the Pacific with an iron band" "San Juan de Nicaragua," 50. Bruce Harvey reads talk of "girding the oceans" as "National chauvinism" taking on a "psychodynamic cast; the romance of republican imperialism begins to sound, as it were, like a Freudian family romance . . . For Squier, the interoceanic canal would be the site where Northern masculinist enterprise consummated a wedding between East and West." Bruce Albert Harvey, "American Geographics: The Popular Reproduction of the Non-European World, 1830–1860," (Ph.D. Diss., Stanford University, 1991), 188.

45 On the regeneration of Central America see Richard Slotkin, *The Fatal Environment: The Myth of the Frontier in the Age of Industrialization, 1800–1860* (New York, 1985), 245–61; Emmerich de Vattel, *The Law of Nations: or Principles of the Law of Nature Applied to the Conduct and Affairs of Nations and Sovereigns* (London, perhaps 1773), 28. On "best use" see Robert F. Berkhofer Jr., *The White Man's Indian: Images of the American Indian from Columbus to the Present* (New York, 1978), 120–1, 138; Pratt, *Imperial Eyes*, 51–2; Alexander Saxton, *The Rise and Fall of the White Republic: Class Politics and Mass Culture in Nineteenth-Century America* (London, 1990), 53; Weinberg, *Manifest Destiny*, 72–99.

46 Stout, *Nicaragua: Past, Present and Future*, 85, 163, 38; Wells, *Explorations and Adventures in Honduras*, 41–2.

desired by all involved. Mexico offered easy farming and potential riches to the settler. "Few of these States there are, which would not open to an industrious, well governed, and intelligent people, a far more magnificent field to operate in, than even the great State of California, either with respect to mineral resources, or grazing and agricultural wealth, yet to be developed." But it was only the Anglo-Saxon American who could properly utilize the land. "It is now for a new race, a race possessed of iron will, to turn the fertile plains, the rich meadow lands, the forests, the mountains, the rivers and the ports, to account."[47]

But America could not simply sit back and wait for the fruit of Manifest Destiny to fall into its lap. If the Isthmus was at the axis of both the Pacific and Atlantic, and of North and South America, then it would obviously present an appealing target for expansionist efforts by countries other than the United States. Expansionists regularly exaggerated the threat posed by England to whip up Anglophobia and support their own aggressive agenda.[48] The popular weekly *Frank Leslie's Illustrated Newspaper* fumed in 1858 that it was only due to foreign interference that America had not taken "Cuba and Central America long ago."[49]

Furthermore, if the United States was willing and able to legitimate annexation based on its economic interest, then there was little stopping other nations that could profit from controlling these trade routes from doing the same. *De Bow's Review* made exactly this point in 1858 when it emphasized the necessity of quick action on this account, since "unless we can command all convenient transits across the Isthmus to California and Oregon, they will quit us, become independent, or annex themselves to the nation that does command those routes or transits." Expansionists also employed a version of the domino theory to support their agenda. Nicaragua, so distant from the United States in some ways, could prove the key to the ultimate success of America's Manifest Destiny, and expansionists like Richmond promised that "with Nicaragua Americanized, all Mexico and Central America would soon fall into the hands of our race.[50]

It is perhaps further evidence for the strength of expansionist ideology in this period that even narratives about areas beyond filibustering interest came

---

[47] Wheat, *Travels on the Western Slope*, 37, 360, 407.

[48] David M. Pletcher, *The Diplomacy of Annexation: Texas, Oregon, and the Mexican War* (Columbia, 1973); Sam W. Haynes, "Anglophobia and the Annexation of Texas: The Quest for National Security," in *Manifest Destiny and Empire: American Antebellum Expansionism*, Sam W. Haynes and Christopher Morris, eds. (College Station, TX, 1997), 115–145; Weinberg, *Manifest Destiny*, 109–13, 382–92; Paul Varg, *United States Foreign Relations, 1820–1860* (East Lansing, MI, 1979), 140.

[49] *Frank Leslie's Illustrated Newspaper*, November 6, 1858. On the threat to the United States of a British Cuba see Montgomery, *The Queen of Islands and the King of Rivers*.

[50] "Acquisition of Mexico – Filibustering," *DBR* 25 (December 1858), 616; Richmond, *Mexico and Central America*, 13.

packaged with expansionist rhetoric. In 1855 *Harper's Monthly* published an article about the Araucanians, an isolated tribe in Southern Chile, drawn from the report of a member of the U.S. Navy Astronomical Expedition to Chile. The article's editor concluded on an expansionist note: "Chili [*sic*] now begins to feel the awakening influence of the Anglo-American race. The indolence of the descendants of its Spanish conquerors must soon be replaced by the bustling energy of a more strenuous race. Will the Araucanians be able to maintain their existence in the face of these new influences? Or are they, like all the other red races of this continent, doomed to speedy extinction? A few years will bring an answer to these questions." Yet Edmund Reuel Smith's *The Araucanians*, from which the *Harper's* piece was drawn, neither posed, nor attempted to answer that question. Although Smith's Chilean travelogue was almost completely free of expansionist rhetoric, the *Harper's* editor clearly saw the larger importance of the piece in expansionist terms. Antebellum novels also could come packaged in expansionist wrappings. The preface to Joseph Warren Fabens's anti-expansionist *Story of Life on the Isthmus* (1853) proudly announced that "it was not until Anglo-Saxon enterprise strode over" the Isthmus of Darien that "the world saw upon its front the nascent lineaments of a great empire." This suggests that in the mid 1850s, the reading public was primarily interested in reading about territories open to the "bustling energy of the more strenuous race." Expansionist travelogues in the popular press thus not only shaped an expansionist ideology among readers but reflected it as well.[51]

Manifest Destiny and the Traveler's Encounter with Central America

That expansionist boosters were infused with the spirit of Manifest Destiny in the years after the U.S.-Mexico War is not surprising. By picturing Mexico, Cuba, and even distant Central America as natural extensions of the United States and by playing up the advantages of the land and climate while ignoring unpleasant realities such as mosquitoes, they crafted a vision of potential new territories that they believed would justify and promote territorial expansion to their audience.

Central America boosters like Squier and Wells hoped to influence readers into condoning expansion into the region, and perhaps even emigrating. At times they were explicit about this. Joseph Stout admitted in his Nicaragua booster account that "I cannot believe that the far-seeing, thrifty American who has partially scanned this hitherto sealed book, will not refer to some of its bright pages when he shall have returned to his home, and ere many years shall have circled, I predict that many listeners to his strange truths will

---

[51] "The Araucanians," *HNMM* 65 (October 1855), 616; Edmond Reuel Smith, *The Araucanians: or, Notes of a Tour among the Indian Tribes of Southern Chili* (New York, 1855); Joseph Warren Fabens, *A Story of Life on the Isthmus* (New York, 1853), vii.

emigrate to this rude Eden, prepared for labor."[52] The number of expansion-ist accounts that were published in this period and the wide circulation of periodicals like *Putnam's* and *Harper's* monthly magazines argue in favor of a wide diffusion of these ideas. But it is difficult to determine the efficacy of booster arguments by looking solely at the accounts themselves.

Fortunately, a large number of gold-rush travelers left correspondence and memoirs from this period, offering a means of determining the extent of Manifest Destiny's hold on average Americans, at least in regard to the fu-ture destiny of Central America. An examination of these accounts indicates that travelers were influenced by travel writing, and that many of them also envisioned Central America as potential U.S. territory. This suggests that the ideology of Manifest Destiny was much more than simple political rhetoric. Even in the 1850s it resonated as a deeply held belief among many ordinary Americans.[53]

As a later chapter will explore, a number of recruits to filibustering ex-peditions recounted that they were drawn south by the same promises of riches repeatedly made by boosters. The chorus to a song sung by Cuban filibusters put it eloquently: "O Cuba is the land for me, I'm bound to make some money there! And set the Cubans free–!" Antebellum travel writers rou-tinely invoked other travel writers in order to prove their own preparation for the journey and general intelligence. Soldiers in the U.S.-Mexico War carried copies of the best-seller *History of the Conquest of Mexico* by the esteemed Massachusetts historian William Prescott, and they experienced Mexico in part through Prescott's romantic vision of the European conquest. Prescott influenced many to view Latin America as a stage for romantic and excit-ing adventures among an effeminate and weak race. As *New York Tribune* journalist Bayard Taylor wrote from his Panama-bound steamer in 1849, "passengers clustered on the bow . . . talking of Ponce de Leon, De Soto, and the early Spanish adventurers. It was unanimously voted that the present days were as wonderful as those, and each individual emigrant entitled to equal credit for daring and enterprise."[54]

---

[52] Stout, *Nicaragua: Past, Present and Future*, 85.

[53] Graebner, *Empire on the Pacific*, vi. Notably, travelers appeared to be less enthusiastic about the future of Manifest Destiny in the Caribbean. Although R. G. S. Ten Broock, for example, was effusive about the possibilities of a Panama under the control of Americans, he expressed no such interest in Jamaica, where he stopped on the way to the Isthmus: "This is certainly a beautiful place to look upon, but the 'emancipation' has ruined it entirely and what was once a prosperous thriving city is now but a nest of irate, thieving, negroes." Journal of R. G. S. Ten Broock M.D. U.S. Army. 1854. April 12, 1854, HL.

[54] Song quoted in May, *Manifest Destiny's Underworld*, 81; David Deaderick, III, "The Expe-rience of Samuel Absalom, Filibuster," *Atlantic Monthly* IV (December 1859): 653; William H. Prescott, *History of the Conquest of Mexico* (Chicago, 1843); Bayard Taylor, *Eldorado: Adventures in the Path of Empire* 1850 (Santa Clara, CA, 2000), 3; On Prescott see Jenny Franchot, *Roads to Rome: The Antebellum Protestant Encounter with Catholicism* (Berkeley, 1994), 35–62; Schriber, *Writing Home*, 68; Sundquist, "The Literature of Expansion and

Jessie Benton Frémont, daughter of Missouri senator Thomas Hart Benton, and wife of the explorer and Bear Flag Revolt leader, John C. Frémont, made the passage in 1849 in order to join her husband in California. She also turned to Prescott in order to understand Latin America: "From a mountain top you look down into an undulating sea of magnificent unknown blooms, sending up clouds of perfume into the freshness of the morning; and thus from the last of the peaks we saw, as Balboa had seen before us, the Pacific at our feet. There I felt in connection with home, for Balboa and Pizarro meant also Prescott's history of the conquest, and family readings and discussions. . . . " [55]

John Lloyd Stephens was another popular author among travelers. Stephens published several amply illustrated volumes describing his experiences in South and Central America looking for archeological ruins after being appointed to a confidential diplomatic mission in the region by President Martin Van Buren in 1839. His work was serialized in popular magazines, and it helped create the popular image of Latin America in the 1840s. A strong exponent of America's Manifest Destiny in the region, Stephens would go on to serve as vice president of the Panama Railroad Company in 1849, helping to establish the first commercial transportation across the Isthmus. His narratives display great expectations about the future relationship between Central America and the United States. In his *Incidents of Travel in Central America, Chiapas, and Yucatan*, published in 1841, he mused over the lack of industry in Costa Rica. "In the same situation, one of our backwoodsmen, with his axe, his wife, and two pair of twins, would in a few years surround himself with all the luxuries that good land can give." At a particularly stunning Nicaraguan volcano he admitted that he "could not but reflect what a waste this was of the bounties of Providence in this favored but miserable land! At home this volcano would be a fortune; there would be a good hotel on top, with a railing round to keep children from falling in, a zigzag staircase down the sides, and a glass of iced lemonade at the bottom." Stephens also argued in favor of a Nicaraguan canal. [56]

Stephens was cited in the diaries and letters of several travelers through the region. Theodore Taylor Johnson, a miner who quoted Stephens in his diary, went on to publish his Central American travel narrative in 1851, thus further spreading Stephen's observations on the region. Other travel narratives

---

Race," vol. 2: 159–60. Prescott's writings also had a great influence on Frederick Church and his hugely popular tropical landscapes in the middle decades of the century. Poole, "Landscape and the Imperial Subject," 112–3.

[55] Jessie Benton Frémont, *A Year of American Travel: Narrative of Personal Experience*. 1878 (San Francisco, 1960), 34.

[56] Katherine Manthorne, *Tropical Renaissance: North American Artists Exploring Latin America, 1839–1879* (Washington DC, 1989), 60–1; John L. Stephens, *Incidents of Travel in Central America, Chiapas, and Yucatan*. 1841 (New Brunswick, 1949), vol. 1: 306, 237, 336–7; vol. 2: 8.

were cited by Americans passing through Central America. Bayard Taylor reported that passengers on a steamer heading to Panama discussed the western explorations of William Emory and John C. Frémont, explorations that were themselves suffused with the Manifest Destiny driving expansionism in the American Southwest and West.[57]

Perhaps the best-read account of Latin America was provided by the Boston Brahmin, Richard Henry Dana, whose narrative of life aboard a merchant ship engaged in the California trade, *Two Years Before the Mast*, was first published in 1840. Dana expressed amazement at the popularity of his own book, noting in the 1859 edition that "every American in California has read it, for when California 'broke out' as the phrase is, in 1848, and so large a portion of the Anglo-Saxon race flocked to it, there was no book upon California but mine." Although Dana did not travel through Central America, his descriptions of California, then part of Mexico, stuck to familiar booster themes. Dana raved about the climate, healthfulness, and fertility of the region, its fine forests, harbors, and rivers, and he asked readers, "[i]n the hands of an enterprising people, what a country this might be!" Nor was his enthusiasm limited to California. Dana's first Latin American stop was the island of Juan Fernandez, 300 miles off the coast of Chile. An enraptured Dana raved over the fertile, well watered, and picturesque island, which he declared "the most romantic spot on earth."[58]

The journals and letters of men traveling through Central America express a clear expansionist bent, which is somewhat surprising given the context in which they were written. Many travelers approached Central America with some trepidation, and with good reason. The Panama and Nicaraguan crossings, although potentially quicker than other routes, were hard work. Panama travelers sailed to the Atlantic port, Chagres, where they traveled by canoe and mule (later by train) across the Isthmus. Natives poled upriver in rough dugout canoes called *bungoes* at a rate of a mile an hour. After transferring to mules they underwent a harrowing trip over an ancient and unmaintained Spanish trail to Panama City, where they waited, often for weeks, for connecting transit to San Francisco.[59]

The Nicaraguan route was twice as long but less harrowing. Passengers boarded small and often dangerously overcrowded steamboats at the Atlantic port of San Juan del Norte (also called Greytown), traveled about seventy-five miles up the San Juan River, transferred to larger ships for a trip of equal length across Lake Nicaragua, and then rode mules for the final

---

57 Theodore Taylor Johnson, *Sights in the Gold Region, and Scenes by the Way* (New York, 1849), 47; Taylor, *Eldorado*, 4. See also Loyall Farragut, "Autobiography (1844–1872)" typescript, HL, 12.
58 Richard Henry Dana, *Two Years Before the Mast*. 1840. (New York, 1945), 394, 181, 48–9.
59 JoAnn Levy, "The Panama Trail: Short Cut to California," *Overland Journal* 10 (Fall 1992): 27; John H. Kemble, *The Panama Route*, 1848 to 1869 (Berkeley, 1943).

thirteen miles of the voyage. On both routes lodgings were primitive, and on the *bungoe* portion of the Panama voyage, often non-existent. Theft, price gouging, and lost luggage were regular events on both routes. Provisions were hard to come by and dear to purchase. Logistical difficulties, the great expense of travel, and long delays helped sour many Americans on a region they might appreciate under different circumstances. There was a lot for a resident of Boston, or Baltimore, not to like about Central America.[60]

None the less, many travelers agreed with boosters that Central America was lovely in a familiar way. New Yorker Peter DeWitt Jr. wrote his mother from Panama in April of 1850 that the Chagres River was the "most beautiful stream" he was ever on, with both scenery and "cool and delightful" nights "just as you could find them in Sullivan County."[61] William Elder also wrote that the Chagres River "will compare favorably with most rivers of its size" in the United States.[62]

Nor did all travelers find the climate intolerable. Orange County, New York, native, William Denniston sounded more like William V. Wells or E. G. Squier than an average forty-niner, when he wrote in his journal in April of 1849 that "the climate too is delightful and the heat not oppressive, for the trade winds sweeping across the country greatly equalize the temperature. The city is very healthy and none of our company experienced any very serious sickness while here." Army doctor Ten Broock also declared the weather in Panama in April "delightful" in his diary.[63]

Travelers who were less than enthusiastic about the weather were often amazed by the natural resources of the Isthmus. Precious metals were, not surprisingly, of interest to men heading to the gold fields. Lucian Wolcott heard that there was "[g]old, silver, and copper in this country" from an American who came out of the mountains of Nicaragua with thirty ounces of gold dust. James S. Barnes wrote from Panama to his friends in New York State in 1849 that "there has been a gold mine discovered about 25 miles from this place I have seen some of the gold dust a great many people have gone out to it."[64]

The fertility of the land was widely commented on. James Tyson found the earth so bountiful "it was a perfect fairy-land." William Elder marveled at the great stands of timber. Theodore Johnson also described the timber of the Isthmus, as well as marshes adapted to growing rice and sugar plantations

[60] Levy, *They Saw the Elephant: Women in the California Gold Rush* (Hamden, CT, 1990), 47.

[61] Typescript of letter from Peter DeWitt Jr. to his mother from Panama, April 27, 1850. DeWitt Family Papers, BL.

[62] "Letter to Cousin Catherine," William Elder Correspondence, June 10, 1850, BL.

[63] Denniston, "Journal of a voyage," April 28, 1849, HL; Journal of R. G. S. Ten Broock, 1854. April 17, 1854, HL.

[64] Lucian Wolcott "Journal," vol. 2. May 24, 1851, HL; James S. Barnes correspondence, 1849–1857, December 23, 1849, BL.

"growing in the greatest luxuriance, and without apparent cultivation." He concluded in his guide for travelers to California that "[i]n short, this is the real El Dorado, which so many of our countrymen have undertaken a voyage of 17,000 miles to behold in California."[65]

There is nothing surprising about North Americans expressing wonder at the climate and flora of the tropics, especially after leaving the Eastern seaboard in the winter months.[66] What is notable is that Americans did not simply appreciate the tropical beauty of the region as short-term travelers but seem to have imagined themselves, or other Americans, living there. Many who passed through the region agreed that the fertile lands of Central America, apparently under-exploited, called out to the North American. Rinaldo Taylor wrote his wife that in Panama, "[t]hey cultivate nothing whatever. The finest land in the world lies just as nature made it, at the very gates of Panama." Dr. William McCollum declared that "[t]he soil is teeming with the evidences of its richness – inviting the hand of man to its cultivation, by showing what it is capable of doing without it...." Lucian Wolcott wrote in his diary from Nicaragua that "I believe a young man would become a fortune by working here – buy and cultivate a few acres, raise vegetables, natives won't do it to any extent." John Udell also considered the future of Nicaragua with different residents. "Could this country be settled with civilized, industrious people, it would, I think, be one of the best farming countries in the world. It is somewhat broken, but can almost all be cultivated, and will yield nearly all the fruit of the temperate and tropical zones."[67]

John Letts, who traveled through the Isthmus twice on the way to and from California and who wrote a guide for travelers based on his experiences, was overwhelmed by the fertility of Panama's Chagres River: "One can hardly conceive of a county susceptible of a higher cultivation. They have a perpetual summer; tropical fruits grow spontaneously; they have the finest bottom lands for rice, tobacco, cotton, corn, or sugar plantations perhaps on this continent; yet, with the exception of a very little corn and sugar, nothing is cultivated. The enterprise of the States would make the country

---

[65] James L. Tyson, M.D., *Diary of a Physician in California*, 19; "Letter to Cousin Catherine," William Elder Correspondence, June 10, 1850, BL; Johnson, *Sights in the Gold Region*, 29, 80.

[66] Caribbean tourist boards still market the region as "paradise on earth." Polly Pattullo, *Last Resorts: The Cost of Tourism in the Caribbean* (London, 1996), 141–2.

[67] Rinaldo Taylor to his wife, July 8, 1849. Letters, Massachusetts Historical Society, quoted in Rohrabough, *Days of Gold*, 59; William McCollum, M.D., *California as I Saw it: Pencillings by the Way of its Gold and Gold Diggers! and Incidents of Travel by Land and Water*. Dale L. Morgan, ed. (Los Gatos, CA, 1960), 94; Lucian Wolcott "Journal," vol. 2, May 16, 1851, HL; John Udell, *Incidents of Travel to California, across the Great Plains; Together with the return trips through Central America and Jamaica; to which are added sketches of the Author's Life* (Jefferson, Ohio, 1856), September 14, 1851, 45.

a paradise." He had no problem imagining himself living there, and after camping in "one of the most delightful spots I ever saw," picked out the land "for my own use – as a rice and sugar plantation – but have not *yet* had the title examined."[68]

There was little question to the Americans traveling through the region that it was their own countrymen who could best effect change in Central America. American enterprise could "make this a choice spot on earth" South Carolinian Daniel Horn wrote from Panama. "This country in the hands of an industrious, enterprising people like the Americans would be the finest in the world," he predicted, despite the fact that "as it is now, it is about the most miserable country in this hemisphere." William McCollum viewed the movement of settlers across the Isthmus as the clear workings of Manifest Destiny, and he suggested that others felt the same way:

We sojourners upon the Isthmus of Panama, hailing from that glorious confederacy of States that had thus from a small and feeble beginning, gone on to extended empire – strengthening, laying broader and deeper the foundation as it advanced in magnitude; were walking over and straying among the ruins that marked the splendor and wide rule of a decaying monarchy of the Old World; on our way to help people – to carry our laws and institutions, to a new accession upon the shores of the Pacific! . . . We sang "Hail Columbia," and whistled "Yankee Doodle," with zest that we could hardly have enjoyed at home.[69]

Others were less subtle in their view of the relationship between North and Central America. Theodore Johnson reported that when boatmen in Panama overcharged their North American passengers in 1849, the passengers cried out for revenge and for the immediate American annexation of the region: "Whip the rascal, fire his den, burn the settlement, annex the Isthmus were heard on all sides."[70]

Echoing booster claims for the naturalness of the Americanization of the region, travelers through Central America, even in the first years of the gold rush, expressed pleasure at the American presence in the region. On a stop in Acapulco, Mexico, in June of 1851, Goldsborough Bruff noted that a lot of residents spoke English. He was told: "'Yes, Sir, every body here will soon learn that.' So I thought then a good deal of 'inevitable destiny.'" Bruff also commented that Chagres, Panama, "is almost entirely American," and noted that Americans there were flying their own flag. "The authorities of the town expressed great indignation at this innovation of the rough Yankees."

---

[68] John M. Letts, *A pictorial view of California: Including a description of the Panama and Nicaragua routes, with information and advice interesting to all, particularly those who intend to visit the gold region, by a returned Californian* (New York, 1853), 25.

[69] James P. Jones and William Warren Rogers, "Across the Isthmus in 1850: The Journey of Daniel A. Horn," *Hispanic American Historical Review* 41 (November 1961): 546–7; McCollum, *California as I Saw it*, 107.

[70] Johnson, *Sights in the Gold Region*, 14.

Other travelers proudly noted when American flags were flown. "Our patriotic countrymen . . . appropriately celebrated the birthday of Washington," Theodore Johnson wrote, by hoisting the flag in the town square in Panama. Daniel Woods relayed that the wife of the American consul in Tampico, Mexico, hoisted the flag, and "maintained it, in spite of the threats of the Mexicans."[71]

Bayard Taylor claimed that as early as 1849, the city of Panama "was already half American. The native boys whistled 'Yankee Doodle' through the streets. . . . Nearly half the faces seen were American, and the signs on shops of all kinds appeared in our language." William McCollum described Panama in 1850 as presenting "quite a business-like appearance about these days, being surrounded with Americans who make it a kind of Broadway. . . . It will soon bear marks of Yankee enterprise which will astonish the natives." Another traveler noted that in Gorgona, an "enterprising" Yankee "named John Smith, of course" ran a popular restaurant.[72]

Most travelers agreed that their countrymen had had a positive overall effect on Central America, at least as far as commerce and industry were concerned. Panama was "greatly on the decline" according to Daniel Horn, but the "tide of immigration to California" has left it in "rather more flourishing condition." Ten Broock agreed. The City of Panama, once a town of some importance, had become "the mere shadow of its former self . . . 'los yanks' however are building it up again and when the Rail Road is completed, it will once more be a place of considerable commercial importance." Peter DeWitt wrote to his mother about the improvements Americans had made to the city of Panama, describing in great detail the settlement of Cocoa Grove, a ten-minute walk from Panama, where "some gentlemen from New Jersey" were constructing a "large and handsome" hotel. John Letts expressed pleasure that a Philadelphian, ironically named "Mr. Priest," was turning a convent into a hotel in Granada, Nicaragua.[73]

Travelers also agreed with boosters that the native inhabitants of Central America seemed anxious for further Americanization. Hiram Dwight Pierce, a blacksmith from Troy, New York, was pleased to find that the Nicaraguans "are very friendly and think much of the Americans." Theodore Johnson claimed that "great is the anxiety of the people of New Granada to

---

[71] J. Goldsborough Bruff, *Gold Rush: The Journals, Drawings, and Other Papers of J. Goldsborough Bruff, April 2, 1849– July 20, 1851*, Georgia Wills Read and Ruth Gaines, eds. (New York, 1949), 498, 516; Johnson, *Sights in the Gold Region*, 30. See also Jones and Rogers. "Across the Isthmus in 1850," 551; Woods, *Sixteen Months*, 22, Letts, *A pictorial View*, 39, 146, 186.

[72] Taylor, *Eldorado*, 23; McCollum, *California as I Saw it*, 101; Johnson, *Sights in the Gold Region*, 27.

[73] Jones and Rogers, eds., "Across the Isthmus in 1850," 543; Journal of R. G. S. Ten Broock, April 17, 1854, HL; typescript of letter from Peter DeWitt Jr. to his mother from Cocoa Grove, Panama, July 28, 1851, DeWitt Family Papers, BL; Letts, *A pictorial View*, 159.

cultivate friendly relations with us, and acquire our language, that we hope an American newspaper will in due time be permanently established among them."[74]

William Denniston wrote in his journal that the Central Americans

evidently look to our government as an example which they are desirous to follow and wish to receive from it protection and support, if not to become annexed to it. For they receive Americans with open hearts and hands and greet them as brothers who they are desirous of welcoming to their country; and no other passport is necessary to ensure safety of person and a hospitable reception than to be known as a citizen of the United States.

Denniston believed this attitude was the result of Central American fear of British expansionism in the region. Striking a note that would not be out of place in *De Bow's Review*, Denniston explained that "the citizens appear to be very desirous that their country should be connected to the United States; as they are afraid of falling into the hands of the English, for whom they entertain the most bitter hatred, and their own government is too weak to afford protection to person or property."[75]

Expansionist travelogues proliferated between 1848 and 1860, shaping and reflecting expansionist ideology in the United States. However unified Americans might have appeared in their hopes for an American Nicaragua in the mid to late 1850s, the annexationist dreams of boosters like Squier and Wells evaporated in the harsh light of the growing sectional conflict. What this close exploration of the literature of Manifest Destiny reveals, however, is the strength of the ideology of Manifest Destiny after the U.S.-Mexico War. By arguing for a natural connection between Central America and the United States, one based on trade routes and the increasing presence of Americans in the Isthmus, expansionists justified the flouting of international law in the name of a higher law, or natural destiny. These boosters asserted that other territorial configurations were just as "natural" as its current continental form, and in order to undermine the claims of Latin Americans to their own lands, they drew on the same justifications that enabled Americans at home to displace and exterminate Native Americans in the name of destiny. Evidence from the letters and diaries of travelers suggests that at least some average Americans internalized these same arguments in favor of America's destiny in Mexico and Central America. Manifest Destiny was not simply a rhetorical tool of Democratic Party expansionists in the 1850s; in the years leading up to the Civil War it was also a deeply held belief among many Americans.

---

[74] Hiram Dwight Pierce, *A Forty-Niner Speaks*, Sarah Wiswall Meyer, ed. (Sacramento, 1978), 69; Johnson, *Sights in the Gold Region*, 67.

[75] Denniston, "Journal of a voyage," May 20, April 28, 1849. John Letts also ranted against Great Britain. Letts, *A pictorial View*, 164.

The claim for the primacy of natural over national borders was neither the only nor the most important claim made by aggressive expansionists in favor of absorbing new territories. It complemented a fantasy of racial and gender domination formed in the context of economic and social change at home in the United States. For many Americans, potential new territories abroad offered opportunities that seemed increasingly remote in the United States. Latin America was hardly "virgin land," even in comparison with the western United States, where the baseless cliché reigned, but boosters and travelers alike agreed that it was underused by the current "unmanly" residents.[76] Their critique of labor and manhood in Central America was hardly peripheral to the other claims for the naturalness of an American presence in the region. As the following chapter will explore, nothing was considered more natural than the ultimate triumph of white American manhood.

[76] On the significance of the concept of virgin land to western expansion see Henry Nash Smith, *Virgin Land: the American West as Symbol and Myth* (Cambridge, MA, 1950).

3

American Men Abroad

Sex and Violence in the Latin American Travelogue

> I would recommend you, if the country should be acquired, to take a trip of exploration there, and look out for the beautiful senoritas, or pretty girls, and if you should choose to annex them, no doubt the result of this annexation will be a most powerful and delightful evidence of civilization.
>
> – Sam Houston, January, 1848

During his long and eventful life, Sam Houston served as governor of two states, U.S. senator from one, and as twice-elected president of a republic. He was undoubtedly a martial man. He rebelled against the authority of his older brothers by running away from his Tennessee home as a teenager. He distinguished himself repeatedly in battles, from Horseshoe Bend in 1814, where under Andrew Jackson he helped defeat the Creek Indians, through the Battle of San Jacinto in 1836, when he led the forces that defeated General Antonio López de Santa Anna's Mexican troops in the key battle for Texas independence. He was injured repeatedly in battle, sustained a bullet wound that never healed, drank so heavily that the Osages called him "Big Drunk," and assaulted a congressional representative from Ohio in the streets of Washington with a hickory stick over a political difference. An acolyte of Jackson, his one-time commanding officer and political benefactor, Houston eventually split with the Democrats to support the Know-Nothing Party, but he remained an advocate of aggressive expansionism. In 1860, at the age of sixty-seven, he considered leading a filibuster into Mexico. He was serving as governor of Texas at the time.[1]

At an 1848 public meeting in New York City, Houston eloquently defined the relationship between sex with the "beautiful senorita" and the civilizing

---

[1] Thomas Kreneck, "Houston, Samuel" in *The Handbook of Texas Online*. Available online at: http://www.tsha.utexas.edu/handbook/online/articles/view/HH/fho73.html; Randolph B. Campbell, *Sam Houston and the American Southwest* (New York, 1993), 35; Robert E. May, *Manifest Destiny's Underworld: Filibustering in Antebellum America* (Chapel Hill, 2002), 43–4.

function of Manifest Destiny. A strong advocate of the annexation of all of Mexico as spoils of war, Houston could find no stronger appeal to the thousands of men who attended the meeting than that of Latin American womanhood, or more rightly, girlhood. In Houston's understanding, annexation was not only a national matter, it was a personal one as well. The national victory could, and would, correspond with a "delightful" personal victory for the man willing to make a trip south. In both the national and the personal case, annexation was the choice of the American alone – neither Mexico nor the Mexican woman is given a voice in the matter. Also notably absent from this equation are Mexican men. The claims of Mexican patriarchy on both the national and family level are completely discounted. In both the national and personal cases, the result of annexation would be civilization, with the personal victory emerging as the more significant, powerful, and pleasant civilizing encounter. In Houston's equation, Manifest Destiny was grounded in the womanhood of Mexico. For the individual listener, he argued, territorial expansionism meant sex and love with a desirable, available, and willing partner.[2]

Houston married a Cherokee woman, Diana Rogers Gentry, during a period of self-imposed exile with the tribe in Indian territory (now Oklahoma), in the years before he achieved his legendary status in Texas. Houston took a Cherokee wife at the same time that Andrew Jackson was working to displace the Five Civilized Tribes of the Southeast in order to effectively annex their lands. By 1848, when Houston spoke in favor of personal annexation, he had divorced Gentry and had married a white Alabama woman twenty-seven years his junior, but he spoke from personal experience when he equated sex with civilization and personal victory with national victory.[3]

Nor was Houston alone in conceptualizing aggressive expansionism in sexual terms. William Swain, editor of the Philadelphia *Public Ledger*, used the same reasoning in December of 1847 in response to those who claimed Mexicans were too foreign to annex. "Our Yankee young fellows and the pretty senoritas will do the rest of the annexation, and Mexico will soon be Anglo-Saxonized, and prepared for the confederacy." Gendered language and idealized accounts of Mexican women both supported and defined the U.S.-Mexico War in the American popular imagination. Fictional accounts of what Shelly Streeby has called the "international race romance" attempted to transform American force during the war "into Mexican 'consent' by

---

[2] "The Great War Meeting," *NYH*, January 30, 1848. According to Reginald Horsman, Houston's views of race were more informed by "romantic racial nationalism" than were those of many of his peers, who visualized the extermination of other races in the face of Anglo-Saxon dominance. Reginald Horsman, *Race and Manifest Destiny: The Origins of American Racial Anglo-Saxonism* (Cambridge, MA, 1981), 213.

[3] Kreneck, "Houston, Samuel." Although Gentry was "no more than one-quarter Indian," because her mother was Cherokee, she, too, was a full member of the matrilineal tribe. Campbell, *Sam Houston*, 33–4.

recasting violent inter-American conflicts as romantic melodramas." In one typical example of the genre, Charles Averill's *The Secret Service Ship* (1848), the white protagonist wins the hand of a Mexican beauty, figuring territorial conquest as conjugal union in much the same way as Houston had.[4]

Non-fictional travelogues published during the war frequently carried a similar message. Waddy Thompson's 1846 publication, *Recollections of Mexico*, for example, offers several anecdotes to illustrate his belief that Mexico's women are brave and virtuous, and that they would make superb wives for Americans. While they are not, in Thompson's view, the equal in appearance of the ladies in the United States, he suggests that in some ways they are the superiors of women up north. While generally poorly educated and extravagantly dressed, "in the great attributes of the heart, affection, kindness, and benevolence in all their forms. . . . in many of the qualities of the heart which make women lovely and loved, they have no superiors." Furthermore, they are sexually available to the man clever enough to gain access to them. Mexico's ladies "are brought up with an idea that the temptation of opportunity is one which is never resisted." As if that weren't enough attraction, Americans will find that while walking the streets "if you meet a woman with a fine bust, which they are very apt to have, she finds some occasion to adjust her rebozo, and throws it open for a second."[5]

The same perceptions of sex, gender, and race that shaped the view of the Mexican woman during the war continued to inform American understandings of expansionism after 1848. The preeminent metaphor of Manifest Destiny, that of fruit falling off a tree, could take on decidedly sexual overtones. The manly narrator of an 1860 *Atlantic Monthly* travel narrative marveled over the transformation of a "doe-eyed child of easy confidences into a quiet and somewhat distant girl, full in figure, with a glance which sometimes betrayed the glow of latent, but as yet unconscious passion." His analysis of the situation: "In these sunny climes the bud blossoms and the young fruit

---

[4] Philadelphia *Public Ledger*, December 11, 1847; Shelly Streeby, *American Sensations: Class, Empire, and the Production of Popular Culture* (Berkeley, 2002), 86; Charles Averill, *The Secret Service Ship; or, the Fall of the Castle San Juan d'Ulloa* (Boston, 1848). On sex and the U.S.-Mexico War see also Robert Johannsen, *To the Halls of the Montezumas: The Mexican War in the American Imagination* (New York, 1985), 169–70, 189–91; Eric J. Sundquist, "The Literature of Expansion and Race," in *The Cambridge History of American Literature*, Sacvan Bercovitch, ed. (New York, 1995), vol. 2:162; Richard Slotkin, *The Fatal Environment: The Myth of the Frontier in the Age of Industrialization, 1800–1860* (New York, 1985), 192–8.

[5] "Recollections of Mexico," New York *Albion*, reprinted in *The Living Age* 10 (July 11, 1846): 57–63; Waddy Thompson, *Recollections of Mexico* (New York, 1846); Raymund A. Paredes, "The Mexican Image in American Travel Literature, 1831–1869," *New Mexico Historical Review* (January 1977): 15. American men abroad did not "discover" (or first admire) Latin American women in the 1840s. See, for example, John M. Forbes, Chargé d'Affaires to John Quincy Adams, Secretary of State, Buenos Aires, July 10, 1822, in William R. Manning, ed., *Diplomatic Correspondence of the United States concerning the independence of the Latin American Nations*, 3 vols. (New York, 1925), vol. I:606.

ripens in a single day."[6] The fruit of Manifest Destiny was female, not only for this narrator but for American men in general.

What both Houston's analogy and the *Atlantic Monthly* image of ripe young fruit bring into relief is the essentially gendered character of aggressive expansionism. American men who were writing travelogues and visiting the region based their assumptions about the nation's future in their dismissal of Latin American manhood and envisioned Latin American womanhood in a manner that justified aggressive expansionism. Thompson's *Recollections of Mexico* fits, to a limited degree, the reigning convention of nineteenth-century travel writing, in which descriptions of foreign women are used to highlight the superiority of women back home. But Thompson's expression of national chauvinism was *not* representative of the American expansionist travelogue to Latin America. The majority of this genre, as well as many of the letters and diaries of ordinary male travelers in the region, do not acknowledge the superiority of American women but instead focus on the irresistible qualities of local women.[7] They also are unified in their assessment of the dismissible qualities of local men. This chapter will examine the views expressed by American male travelers of Latin American men and women. White male masculinity at home was constructed not only in relation to black men and white women but also to the racially mixed peoples of Latin America. The highly gendered foreign encounter of both travelers and readers of travelogues offered support to the aggressive practices of martial manhood by constructing the "new frontier" as a region where masculine practices organized around dominance were highly valued. Travel accounts also encouraged national expansionism by connecting it to the fantasy of personal annexation with Latin American women.

Race and Manifest Destiny

Reginald Horsman has convincingly argued that race was central to the understanding of America's mission to the world. "By the 1850s it was generally believed in the United States that a superior American race was destined to shape the destiny of much of the world. It was also believed that in their outward thrust Americans were encountering a variety of inferior races incapable of sharing America's republican system and doomed to permanent subordination or extinction."[8] Of course Eurocentric racism was neither an American invention nor specific to the antebellum period. Europeans arrived in America in the seventeenth century with a well-defined sense of

---

[6] "Hunting a Pass: A Sketch of Tropical Adventure," part 2. *The Atlantic Monthly* 5 (April 1860): 449.

[7] Mary Suzanne Schriber, *Writing Home: American Women Abroad, 1830–1920* (Charlottesville, 1997), 80–2.

[8] Horsman, *Race and Manifest Destiny*, 6.

racial superiority, and once here, they defined the original Native-American inhabitants they encountered as "non-persons" in order to dispossess them of their lands. As Richard Drinnon has written, racism "was in a real sense the enabling experience of the rising American empire."[9]

An examination of the popular literature of aggressive expansionism in the post–U.S.-Mexico War period and of the letters and diaries of travelers in the region suggest that the same justificatory racism shaped the Central American encounter. The idea that Latin Americans were in need of American guidance justified arguments for the uplifting nature of America's role in the region, while a sense of racial superiority (based in a fictional Anglo-Saxon unity) gave white American men confidence in their ability to dominate or even exterminate the "weaker" races – be they Native American, African-American, or Mexican. What has been largely ignored in studies of race and gender in the antebellum period is the manner in which gendered stereotypes about Latin American men justified a particular vision of manhood at home in the United States. In the same manner that "Indian hating identified the dark *others* that white settlers were not and must not under any circumstances become," the dismissal of Latin American manhood allowed American men, both abroad and at home, to celebrate their own masculine virtues. The aggressive expansionist encounter was not only supported by martial men, it in turn supported martial manhood as well.[10]

The mutually constitutive nature of aggressive expansionism and martial manhood is apparent across the spectrum of expansionist writing. Antebellum scientific efforts were openly directed to the service of Manifest Destiny. The very first lecture in 1852 of the newly formed American Geographical Society, for instance, declared that "it was both a matter of pride and commercial necessity that the U.S. should dominate the other Americas."[11] Ethnological works by Albert Gallatin, Josiah C. Nott, E. G. Squier, and others on the Americas provided grist for pseudo-scientific musing on the inevitable fate of the "lesser" races. By the middle of the 1840s, scientific theories of the natural inequality of the races were being widely disseminated in popular periodicals. Based in part on the increasing marginalization of American Indian tribes, Americans grew to accept that inferior races would simply disappear under pressure from the imagined Anglo-Saxon "race" of European-Americans. Especially provocative was Samuel George Morton's work on skulls, which meshed nicely with the newly popular "science" of phrenology to prove that "the large heads . . . have, every where, outstripped and ruled the small-headed races among men." In an 1853 review of recent

---

[9] Richard Drinnon, *Facing West: The Metaphysics of Indian Hating and Empire Building* (New York, 1990), xxvii.
[10] Ibid., xxvii–xxviii. Italics in original quotation.
[11] Quoted in Bruce Albert Harvey, "American Geographics: The Popular Reproduction of the Non-European World, 1830–1860" (Ph.D. Diss., Stanford University, 1991), 184.

ethnological publications, including Morton's, the *Southern Quarterly Review* found it worth mentioning that "an Army officer, of high standing, who accompanied our army in its march through Mexico during the late war . . . told us he could not find, in a large hat store in Tampico, a single hat which would go on his head" despite the fact that his head "is below the average size of the Anglo-Saxon race."[12]

The craniological argument was a gendered one, since those with small brains generally also lacked aggressive qualities. According to craniologist J. S. Phillips, the early indigenous peoples of Mexico, "with small brains, were evidently inferior in resolution, in attack and defense, and the more manly traits of character" to the Aztecs who defeated them. "These facts afford very instructive material for reflection," the *Southern Quarterly Review* concluded. "We here see one race, with the larger though less intellectual brains, subjugating the less warlike and half civilized race; and it seems clear that the latter were destined to be swallowed up by the former, or exterminated. Who can doubt that similar occurrences have been going on over this continent for many centuries, or even thousands of years." Following the general nineteenth-century scientific equation of "inferior" races with women, other exponents of what George Frederickson has called "romantic racialism" argued that "smaller brained" Africans were more "effeminate" and less aggressive than Caucasians. "Africa is like a gentle sister in a family of fierce brothers," New England reformer Samuel Gridley Howe wrote. The implications for American manhood were clear: While the large-headed American was destined to prevail, aggressiveness and a war-like nature also was predetermined, the result of brain size. Ultimately, ethnology claimed, a war-like nature was a positive, indeed crucial, characteristic for the race. In this manner, popular science supported a martial vision of Anglo-Saxon manhood at the expense of restrained manhood.[13]

---

[12] "Aboriginal Races of the Americas," *The Southern Quarterly Review* 8 (July 1853): 59–92; Albert Gallatin, *Notes on the Semi-Civilized Nations of Mexico, Yucatan, and Central America* (New York, 1845); Ephraim George Squier, *Ancient Monuments of the Mississippi Valley* (New York, 1848); Samuel George Morton, *Catalogue of Skulls of Man and the Inferior Animals, in the collection of Samuel George Morton* (Philadelphia, 1849); also see ibid, *Crania Americana* (Philadelphia, 1839); E. G. Squier, "American Ethnology," *The American Whig Review* 9 (April 1849): 385–99. See also William Stanton, *The Leopard's Spots: Scientific Attitudes toward Race in America, 1815–1859* (Chicago, 1960); Horsman, *Race and Manifest Destiny*, 139–57; George Fredrickson, *The Black Image in the White Mind: The Debate on Afro American Character and Destiny, 1817–1914* (New York, 1971) 71–96. Ethnology also was used to prove the indigenous origins of America's Indians, proving that America had as old a history as did Europe. Stanton, *Leopard's Spots*, 86–9.

[13] "Aboriginal Races of the Americas," *SQR* 8 (July 1853): 68–70; Howe quoted in Fredrickson, *The Black Image in the White Mind*, 163–4. Nancy Leys Stepan has shown that in the nineteenth century "gender was found to be remarkably analogous to race, such that the scientist could use racial difference to explain gender difference, and vice versa." "Race and Gender: The Role of Analogy in Science," *ISIS* 77 (June 1986): 263.

Race shaped the imperial encounter on the new frontier of Latin America, as it had on the old frontier in encounters with Native Americans. But many Americans, coming from a racially binary society, had difficulty evaluating race in Latin America. The wide range of skin tones and extent of racial mixing in the region confused American observers when they first entered the region. The popular author Francis Parkman claimed that Mexicans were "by no means" white but left unsaid that they were not obviously non-white, either. Although some Southerners, especially, found the racially mixed character of Latin Americans incompatible with the idea of citizenship, for others, the salient fact about the people of Latin America was that so many of them were clearly not black. Article VIII of the 1848 Treaty of Guadalupe Hidalgo set a legal precedent for this perspective when it conferred rights of U.S. citizenship on all Mexican men residing in the new U.S. territories, regardless of race. Since United States citizenship was reserved for white men, article VIII implied that Mexican-American men were indeed white.[14]

Travelers to Latin America revealed their own racial suppositions, informed by race relations at home, in their evaluations of Latin Americans. South Carolinian Daniel Horn constantly compared the Latin American to the African-American, sometimes to the detriment of the former. "The natives are, perhaps a majority of them, full blooded Negroes, one-third Indians, the balance mixed, with here and there a Spaniard. Their language [is] a mongrel Spanish, and their appearance not as respectable as our Negroes." Even light-skinned Creoles (residents of European descent) appeared to him sub-human. "Negroes, Indians, and Creoles, nearly or quite naked; rolling up the whites of their eyes at us, and vociferating for cargo in tones that were a caution to Ourang-outangs" he wrote to his family.[15]

---

[14] Parkman quoted in Brian Roberts, *American Alchemy: The California Gold Rush and Middle-Class Culture* (Chapel Hill, 2000), 123; Neil Foley, *The White Scourge: Mexicans, Blacks, and Poor Whites in Texas Cotton Culture* (Berkeley, 1997), 17–24, 107. On the racial stereotyping of Latin Americans see Arnoldo De León, *They Called Them Greasers: Anglo Attitudes toward Mexicans in Texas, 1821–1900* (Austin, 1983); Frederick Pike, *The United States and Latin America: Myths and Stereotypes of Civilization and Nature* (Austin, 1992); Paredes, "The Mexican Image," 5–29; David J. Weber, "'Scarce more than apes.' Historical Roots of Anglo-American Stereotypes of Mexicans in the Border Region," in *New Spain's Northern Frontier: Essays on Spain in the American West, 1540–1821*, David J. Weber, ed. (Albuquerque, 1979), 295–307; Richard Griswold del Castillo, *The Treaty of Guadalupe Hidalgo: A Legacy of Conflict* (Norman, OK, 1990).

[15] The very architecture of the Latin American town associated itself in Horn's vision with slavery. The houses of Chagres he wrote "are only hovels that, in the States, would not even do for Negro Quarters or even for a respectable cow house. The whole town does not look near so well as the quarters on a Southern plantation." James P. Jones and William Warren Rogers, "Across the Isthmus in 1850: The Journey of Daniel A. Horn," *Hispanic American Historical Review* 41 (November 1961): 534–5; Theodore Taylor Johnson, *Sights in the Gold Region, and Scenes by the Way* (New York, 1849), 9.

Most travelers recognized dark-skinned Latin Americans as racially distinct from African-Americans, however, and they decreed the Latin Americans superior. William McCollum was typical in his understanding that "the natives of this portion of New Granada, are a mixture of the Spanish, Indian, and African. They are nearly as black as African negroes, but better formed." New Yorker J. A. Clarke wrote that in Panama "I was crowded by Natives, men and women, some of whose Faces were as black as ebony, but there was nothing of that offensive odor that accompanies a Negro, thus showing a different race from the negro, although black."[16]

Nor did a recognition of racial difference translate in all cases into automatic condemnation. Travelers were obviously impressed by the appearance of Latin American women, and the appearance of Latin American men impressed some visitors as well. Michigan native Milo Goss wrote home that "[t]his country is romantic and beautiful – the natives are much better in all respects than I expected to find them, very neat in their persons, countenances expressive and intelligent, their features small and well formed, their complexions of a dark copper colour." J. Goldsborough Bruff described his admiration for a "well-formed" man of "olive complexion" on his return from the gold fields.[17]

American men expressed interest in the "well formed" bodies they encountered, and not only the female ones. Journalist Bayard Taylor noted about his nude boatmen that "the clothing of our men was likewise waterproof, but without seam or fold. It gave no hindrance to the free play of their muscles, as they deftly and rapidly plied the broad paddles." He clearly admired those muscles, commenting at another point that "their naked, sinewy forms, bathed in sweat, shone like polished bronze." One early California pioneer recalled his Panamanian boatmen being "stalwart men of mixed Spanish and Indian blood – muscular, strong, and well skilled in the use of the pole, but they would not wear a particle of clothing."[18]

While American men sometimes admired the appearance of Latin American men, it was far rarer for them to admit them as equals in ambition, strength, or character. Interactions with Native-American tribes on the western frontier suggested to white Americans that a highly muscled body could be as incompatible with republican virtue as effeminacy. As one traveler put

[16] William McCollum, M.D., *California as I Saw it: Pencillings by the Way of its Gold and Gold Diggers! and Incidents of Travel by Land and Water* Dale L. Morgan, ed. (Los Gatos, CA, 1960), 88; Journal of J. A. Clarke, April 5, 1852, HL.

[17] Milo Goss Letter to Catherine Goss, Galgona, New Granada, May 19, 1850. Goss Family Letter Collection, 1849–1853, BL; J. Goldsborough Bruff, *Gold Rush: The Journals, Drawings, and Other Papers of J. Goldsborough Bruff, April 2, 1849–July 20, 1851*, Georgia Wills Read and Ruth Gaines, eds. (New York, 1949), 498.

[18] Bayard Taylor, *Eldorado: Adventures in the Path of Empire*. 1850 (Santa Clara, CA, 2000), 15, 18; Society of First Steamship Pioneers, *First Steamship Pioneers* (San Francisco, CA, 1874), 77.

it, the natives were certainly strong, "but very little above the brutes."[19] A critique of Latin American manhood is one of the most outstanding characteristics of travelogues of the region and of the private writings of travelers. In his evaluation of the Latin American man, the white male traveler not only expressed his racial superiority, but also revealed his concerns about manhood at home.

Looking at the Latin American Man

Recent studies of American filibustering have noted that Americans who opposed illegal expeditions often held Latin American men in such low esteem that they hoped the filibusters might succeed. Even officials whose job it was to enforce neutrality laws more often than not felt sympathy for the expansionist goals of the filibusters. Commodore Hiram Paulding became one of the most high-profile filibustering opponents in America when he arrested William Walker during his second invasion of Nicaragua in 1857. He declared himself "no filibuster," yet he also hoped that America's "enterprising race" would use their "stouter hearts and stronger hands" to redeem Nicaragua. Naval Commander Charles H. Davis believed that Central American troops had no chance against Walker because they were unmanly. In a letter to his superior office he noted the "strong contrast between the serious count[en]ances, and the personal proportions of the men of Northern origin" and the "mild unthoughtful faces (with large womanly eyes) and the full round forms" of the Central Americans.[20]

American travelers expressed similar opinions. Ordinary travelers, boosters, and filibusters alike condemned the Latin American man for what they saw as his "supine sloth."[21] Richard Henry Dana set the standard for representations of lazy Latin American men in his best-selling 1840 travel narrative, *Two Years Before the Mast*. From the first Latin American men he encountered off the coast of Chile, whom he described as "the laziest of mortals," to the "idle, thriftless people" of California, Dana's portrait of Latin American manhood was unvaried. Another popular nineteenth-century

---

[19] Mary Jane Megquier, *Apron Full of Gold: The Letters of Mary Jane Megquier from San Francisco, 1849–1856*, 2nd ed., Polly Welts Kaufman, ed. (Albuquerque, 1994), 18. In her study of representations of Native Americans in the United States in the nineteenth century, Susan Scheckel has argued that accounts of Indian effeminacy fit into an antebellum context whereby manliness and republican virtue were believed to be expressed physically. Neither the well-muscled Indians represented in sculptures from the period nor effeminate Indians passed the test of republican virtue. *The Insistence of the Indian: Race and Nationalism in Nineteenth-Century American Culture* (Princeton, 1998), 138.

[20] Quoted in May, *Manifest Destiny's Underworld*, 128–9.

[21] On the convention of "othering" indigenous males in nineteenth-century travel writing see Schriber, *Writing Home*, 78–81.

travel writer described Latin Americans as "beggars on golden stools," incapable of exerting enough energy to support themselves despite the remarkable resources at hand. A Honduran travelogue published in *Harper's* in 1856 noted that "the inhabitants of Omoá, like those of most of the tropical towns, are rather indolent, their principle business of the day being the *siesta*." Guidebook author Theodore Johnson prepared readers for what they would find upon landing in Chagres: "Laziness and listlessness seemed to prevail among all. Every house has the everlasting hammock, in which they sleep at night and lounge all day.... A flock of buzzards would present a favorable comparison."[22]

Gold-rush travelers agreed. Wisconsin native Joseph Warren Wood was typical in his diary notation that the "natives appear like a lazy set." New Englander Henry Peters discounted Panamanians as "a miserable, degraded race with no trade, ambition or anything else desirable." Another remarked that in Panama "the people [are] indolent, sloven [*sic*]; nothing showing prosperity or comfort...." Although Lucian Wolcott found the Nicaraguans "hospitable" and "kind," he also complained that "the people are very indolent, can't do much work." James Tyson imagined that "slothful, and adverse to exertion, they see nature with a prodigal hand scattering around her rich and precious fruits, which they are content to pluck and eat."[23]

Travelers condemned the Central American man for his laziness, and expressed surprise at his lack of "education" as well. John Udell noted upon landing in Nicaragua in 1851, "The inhabitants here are almost savage in their manners, and know but little of the arts and sciences." Milo Goss reported to family at home that while many he had met were "in their manners polite and civil," overall "They are uneducated and consequently know nothing of the benefits of a higher state of civilization." What little education they had sometimes seemed not for good, concluded those who condemned the Latin American man for his untrustworthiness. Theodore DeWitt wrote to his mother from Panama in September of 1850 that "the inhabitants appear to have learned but one thing and that is to lie and cheat, which they

[22] Richard Henry Dana, *Two Years Before the Mast*, 1840. (New York, 1945), 48–9, 79; Baron Alexander von Humboldt, quoted in Pike, *The United States and Latin America*, 70; "Scraps from an Artist's Notebook," HNMM 14 (December 1856): 23; Johnson, *Sights in the Gold Region*, 13. See also Nahum Capen, *The Republic of the United States of America: Its Duties to Itself, and Its Responsible Relations to Other Countries. Embracing also a Review of the Late War between the United States and Mexico; Its Causes and Results; and of those measure of Government which have characterized the Democracy of the Union* (New York, 1848), 101. On laziness on the western frontier see Ray Allen Billington, *The Far Western Frontier, 1830–1860* (New York, 1956), 40.

[23] Joseph Warren Wood diary (in 6 volumes). 1849–1852. October 20, 1852, HL; Henry Hunter Peters diary (transcript), March 5, 1850, Box 1, Folder 9, Peters Collection, New York Public Library; Jones and Rogers, "Across the Isthmus in 1850," 547; Lucian Wolcott "Journal," 2 vols. May 10, 1851, HL; Tyson, *Diary of a Physician in California*, 30.

do to perfection and in other respects resemble a Hog who has received a poor education."[24]

Many Americans blamed the laziness and ignorance they perceived in the region on the Catholic Church. A critique of Roman Catholicism was a common feature of travelogues and other accounts of the period. America was a virulently Protestant nation, and by the 1830s, anti-Catholicism had become a vigorous movement in the United States in the face of increasing Catholic immigration from Germany and, especially, from Ireland. By 1860, the Catholic Church had 3.1 million American adherents, and it had become the single largest religious body in United States. As Jenny Franchot has shown, the Catholic Church was pictured by Protestants as the feminine "other" in the antebellum era, suggesting that Catholic Latin American men were feminized in the eyes of American Protestants by virtue of their religion. Prominent authors like the inventor of the electric telegraph, Samuel Morse, published scurrilous attacks on Catholics and on the Catholic Church. Anti-Catholic violence, from harassment at the voting booth to full-scale riots against Catholic institutions like monasteries and schools, became an uncomfortably common feature of urban life from Baltimore to Boston. By the 1840s, nativists capitalized on anti-Catholic hysteria to become a significant political force in opposition to immigration and in favor of limiting the rights of immigrants once arrived. At the time of the U.S.-Mexico War, there were six members of the nativist American Party serving in the Twenty-Ninth Congress from Pennsylvania and New York alone.[25]

Nativists were divided on the question of territorial expansionism. Given the nativist desire to limit Irish Catholic immigration in the 1840s and 1850s, it is hardly surprising that many opposed expansionism because Mexicans, Central Americans, and Cubans also were Catholic. As the nativist

---

[24] John Udell, *Incidents of Travel to California, across the Great Plains; Together with the return trips through Central America and Jamaica; to which are added sketches of the Author's Life.* (Jefferson, OH, 1856), 45; Milo Goss Letter to Catherine Goss, Galgona, New Granada, May 19, 1850. Goss Family Letter Collection, 1849–1853, BL; typescript of letter from Theodore DeWitt to his mother from Panama, September 29, 1850. DeWitt Family Papers, BL.

[25] Paredes, "The Mexican Image," 8. See, for example, Capen, *The Republic of the United States of America,* 161. On the nativist movement in the United States see Tyler Anbinder, *Nativism and Slavery: The Northern Know-Nothings and the Politics of the 1850s* (New York, 1992); Ray Allen Billington, *The Protestant Crusade, 1800–1860: A Study of the Origins of American Nativism.* 1938 (Chicago, 1964); Jenny Franchot, *Roads to Rome: The Antebellum Protestant Encounter with Catholicism* (Berkeley, 1994), xx. On nativist rioting see Paul Gilje, *Rioting in America* (Bloomington, 1996), 64–9; Michael Feldberg, *The Turbulent Era: Riot and Disorder in Jacksonian America* (New York, 1980), 19–20. Some key anti-Catholic tracts from the period include Lyman Beecher, *A Plea for the West.* 1835 (New York, 1977); Samuel F. B. Morse, *Foreign Conspiracy against the Liberties of the United States: the numbers of Brutus* (New York, 1835); ibid., *Imminent Dangers to the Free Institutions of the United States through Foreign Immigration, and the Present State of the Naturalization Laws.* 1835 (New York, 1969), 8–28.

Philadelphia *Daily Sun* put it in 1846, "if we look towards Mexico, we are menaced by the accession of *eight millions of foreigners*, not only entirely ignorant of our institutions, but ignorant of everything, uncultivated in mind, brutal in manners, steeped in the worst of all superstitions, and slaves to the tyranny of monks...."[26] During the U.S.-Mexico War, nativists criticized Polk and the Democratic Party for appointing Catholic priests to serve with the Army, and suggested that the Democrats supported efforts to create a vast Catholic state in the western regions of North America.[27]

But the same scientific logic that supported territorial expansion in the belief that inferior races would either die out or be "regenerated" by the Anglo-Saxon race drove many nativists to embrace expansionism as a means of undermining the power of the Catholic Church in the Western Hemisphere. Most nativists believed their own Protestant faith to be so much more compelling than Catholicism that simple exposure to the creed within America's enlightened political structure would be sufficient to cause mass conversion away from the "Romish enemy." The Philadelphia *Daily Sun*, for instance, was a supporter of the movement to annex all of Mexico as spoils of war. "On general principles, Americans are bound to the diffusion of our own system of government over every enslaved people," the journal wrote. "In poor, degraded Mexico, even the first elements of civilization are wanting – and these are, respect for property, and the right to worship God according to their own conscience. To extend our free system into such a country would be the brightest stretch of mercy."[28] The supposed "degradation" of Catholics was therefore informed by ideas of both gender and race.

While many travelers held Catholicism accountable for the dearth of ambition they perceived in Latin America, others suggested that there might be a method to the Latin American man's lack of energy. It was one traveler's conclusion that "[t]he people certainly are blessed. Providence or nature provides for all their wants. Pigs, chickens, plantains, oranges ... grow all around them without the aid of labor ... nothing to do but enjoy themselves, and they do it." Another asked, "Why should they exert themselves, when nature has so abundantly supplied their wants?" These relativists were in the minority, however. Most travelers criticized Latin American "sloth" wherever they found it. Drawing on the vision of "best use" that supported colonization of the New World, as well as the removal of Native Americans from east of the Mississippi, prominent nineteenth-century expansionists claimed that

[26] Philadelphia *Daily Sun*, July 18, September 16, 1846, quoted in John C. Pinheiro, "'On Their Knees to Jesuits': Nativist Conspiracy Theories and the War with Mexico, 1846–1848." Unpublished paper presented at the annual meeting of the Organization of American Historians, 2003, 17.

[27] Pinheiro, "'On Their Knees to Jesuits'"; Richard Hofstadter, *The Paranoid Style in American Politics and Other Essays* (New York, 1965), 21; William D. Hogan, *High and Low Mass in the Roman Catholic Church; with Comments* (Nashua, NH, 1846).

[28] Philadelphia *Daily Sun*, July 4, 1846, quoted in Pinheiro, "'On Their Knees to Jesuits,'" 18.

the lazy character of the Latin American man justified U.S. annexation of the region.[29]

Ordinary travelers held the same opinion. James Tyson wondered at the fact that "the strange and worthless set of beings living here in thatched huts, should neglect the culture of such prolific soil, and appear so apathetic in regard to the magnificent prospects presented on every hand." But he also believed that while the native residents of Panama passed their time in "drowsy languor and supine sloth . . . the influence of men from rougher climes and bleaker regions will probably exercise a salutary influence, by showing them the advantages of industry and patient toil." The early gold-rush pioneer Edward Dunbar imagined that "[t]he dusky natives with their squalid children, their dogs and pigs, the monkeys, alligators, snakes, and all created things of the aligerous [sic] order, were roused from their dreamy lethargy by this sudden irruption of the Northern white race. The hubbub was terrific."[30]

William Denniston suggested that it was not innate laziness that prevented Central America's men from applying themselves but the political instability of the region: "Such is the insecurity of life and property under its present political institutions that few seem desirous of accumulating property, but only seek to supply the immediate wants of nature." Of course the annexation of the region to the United States would provide a solution to this problem, as well.[31]

Americans understood their relationship with Latin America in gendered terms. The United States was the dominant power because it was vigorous, and the states of Latin America should be submissive because they were not. The pro-slavery ideologue George Fitzhugh, writing in *De Bow's Review*, declared that Mexico should be filibustered because it was, in essence, effeminate. "Her mixed population has all the vices of civilization, with none of its virtues; all the ignorance of barbarism, with none of its hardihood, enterprise, and self-reliance. It is enervate, effeminate, treacherous, false, and fickle." The *Democratic Review* made a similar argument in favor of aggressive expansionism in 1857: "We entertain a settled conviction that at

---

[29] Lucian Wolcott "Journal," vol. 2, May 13, 1851; Mrs. D. B. Bates, *Incidents on Land and Water, or Four Years on the Pacific Coast* (New York, 1858), 308. On the extinction of Indian land rights by virtue of failing to bring arable lands into cultivation see Emmerich de Vattel, *The Law of Nations: or Principles of the Law of Nature Applied to the Conduct and Affairs of Nations and Sovereigns* (London, perhaps 1773), 28: Capen, *The Republic of the United States of America*, 161–5; Alexander Saxton, *The Rise and Fall of the White Republic: Class Politics and Mass Culture in Nineteenth-Century America* (London, 1990), 53; Albert Weinberg, *Manifest Destiny: A Study of Nationalist Expansionism in American History*. 1935, reprint edition (Chicago, 1963), 72–99.

[30] James L. Tyson, M.D., *Diary of a Physician in California*. 1850 (Oakland, 1955), 22, 18; Edward E. Dunbar, *The Romance of the Age; or, the Discovery of Gold in California* (New York, 1867), 57.

[31] Denniston, "Journal of a voyage," May 20, 1849.

no distant period Central America will become a part either of the territory of the United States, or of a second system of American republics.... The present inhabitants of these regions are a short lived and constitutionally feeble race."³²

Travelers regularly described the men they encountered in Latin America as effeminate as well. Theodore Johnson believed that Mexicans "appear effeminate in their fancy *serapes*," while William McCollum imagined himself "in the midst of an inferior race of men, enervated by the climate...." Richard Henry Dana saw the essential effeminacy of the Latin American in the behavior of Cuban boys. "In their recreations they were more like girls, and liked to sit a good deal, playing or working with their hands.... The son of an American mother ... had more pluck than any boy in the school." Dana also contrasted the "timorous, sallow, slender, small-voiced" Cuban boy with "boys from the Northern States ... with fair skins and light hair, strong, loud-voiced, plainly dressed, in stout shoes, honest and awkward." Dana's view of the weakened nature of Latin American manhood extended to other species. Even the horses at a bullfight were "such feeble animals that, with all the flourish of music and the whipping of drivers, they are barely able to tug the bull."³³

Those travelers who expressed respect for Latin American culture generally tended to patronize the men of the region. Bayard Taylor strongly condemned the bad behavior of Americans on the Isthmus. "It is no bravery to put a revolver to the head of an unarmed and ignorant native," he wrote, and the "faithful, hard-working, and grateful boatmen have sense enough to be no longer terrified of it." Even a considerate observer like Taylor regularly enfantilized the Latin American man, as when he described a male salesman as having a "childish head."³⁴

It was a standard assertion of the Latin American travelogue that the Latin American man was a coward and a thief. This stereotype was supported by what many travelers believed to be excessive charges for the transportation, housing, and food provided them, and by the efforts Latin Americans made to avoid the wrath of the violent "overcharged" Americans. Peter DeWitt wrote his mother from his Panama crossing in April of 1850 that "the natives are great thieves although a cowardly set."³⁵

³² George Fitzhugh, "Acquisition of Mexico – Filibustering," *DRB* 25 (December 1858): 613; "Central America – The Late War in Nicaragua," *USDR* 40 (July 1857): 20–1; May, *Manifest Destiny's Underworld*, 111.

³³ Johnson, *Sights In the Gold Region*, 190; William McCollum, M.D., *California as I Saw it: Pencillings by the Way of its Gold and Gold Diggers! and Incidents of Travel by Land and Water*. Dale L. Morgan, ed. (Los Gatos, CA, 1960), 88; Richard Henry Dana, *To Cuba and Back: A Vacation Voyage* (Boston, 1859), 87, 24, 200–1.

³⁴ Taylor, *Eldorado*, 16, 12.

³⁵ Paredes, "The Mexican Image," 6; typescript of letter from Peter DeWitt Jr. to his mother from Panama, April 27, 1850, DeWitt Family Papers, BL. William McCollum put his own

Latin American men had good reason to fear American travelers. John Letts suggested to readers of his guide to California travel that "it is well understood that no one started for California without being thoroughly fortified." On his trip through the Isthmus, passengers proved that their weaponry was not just for show.

As we had arrived at a place (the mouth of the Chagres river) where, we thought, there must be, at least, *some* fighting to do, our first attention was to our *armor*. The revolvers, each man having at least two, were first overhauled, and the six barrels charged. These were put in our belt, which also contained a bowie knife. A brace of similar pistols are snugly pocketed inside our vest; our rifles are liberally charged; and with a cane in hand (which of course contains a dirk), and a *slung shot* in our pockets, we step off and look around for the enemy.[36]

Theodore Johnson, for whom the racial difference of the Panamanian and his inherent cowardice were linked, believed that what he saw as price gouging was best addressed with violence. On one occasion, when passengers threatened their boatmen, Johnson smugly remarked that "the dirty brown of their complexion speedily changed to a livid white, and they came down in their villainous demands." In a separate interaction between white passengers and native boatmen, "the one who had been in close proximity to the pistol, however, was transmuted by his fright from a dark darkey into a milky Creole." In these accounts violence was justified by a white supremacist view that racial inferiors will only listen to force, and that cowardice will prevent any reciprocal violence by the boatmen. Violence against racial inferiors, like other race reversals, worked to distance "perversity from whiteness," thus ensuring the continued superiority of the white American traveler.[37]

Not surprisingly, travelers had nothing good to say about Latin American soldiers, the group that should have most impressed proponents of martial manhood. After watching Mexican soldiers drill in 1835 in California, Richard Henry Dana expressed his conviction that "a dozen of Yankees and Englishmen, were a match for a whole regiment of hungry, drawling, lazy half-breeds." Representations like these led Americans to believe that they would encounter little resistance in Mexico in 1846. Despite facing fiercely

perspective on the price-gouging of the natives. "I should like to see...a community of genuine Yankees enjoy the monopoly of a few canoes, to transport a crowd of eager adventurers, willing to pay almost any price to get ahead; I opine, there would be such fleecing and extortion as the Isthmus has not yet witnessed." McCollum, *California as I Saw it*, 89.

[36] John M. Letts, *A pictorial View of California, including a description of the Panama and Nicaragua routes, with information and advice interesting to all, particularly those who intend to visit the golden region* (New York, 1853), 13–14.

[37] Johnson, *Sights in the Gold Region*, 14, 38. On social reversals strengthening proper standards of behavior see Roberts, *American Alchemy*, 122. See also David Goodman, *Gold Seeking: Victoria and California in the 1850s* (Stanford, 1994); Marianna Torgovnick, *Gone Primitive: Savage Intellects, Modern Lives* (Chicago, 1990); Edward Said, *Culture and Imperialism* (New York, 1993).

determined troops during the U.S.-Mexico War, relatively easy victory in that war served to reinforce these beliefs. Not surprisingly, many Americans carried these same assumptions about Latin American effeminacy as they traveled during the following decade. Daniel Horn took the soldiers he saw, "all Indians & Negroes . . . to be a worthless, inefficient set," while Theodore Johnson commented that they "forcibly remind[ed] one of Jack Falstaff and his buckram warriors." John Letts suggested that it would be a simple matter to take over Acapulco, Mexico, because the castle was "garrisoned by only a few barefooted soldiers," and included an image of a single lame soldier in his drawing of the Acapulco marketplace (Figure 3.1).[38]

Latin American men were stereotyped as cowardly but also, at times, as overly brutal. The image of the barbaric Latin American was rooted in a Protestant perception of the depravity of the Spanish who colonized the region, as well as the Indian cultures they subdued.[39] In the description of one traveler, Central Americans were "ignorant and superstitious . . . cowardly bandits." Americans explained this seeming contradiction by noting the underhanded techniques or treachery employed by the violent Latin American. While Theodore Johnson reported with zeal instances of Americans threatening or attacking unarmed Panamanian guides and boatmen, he had a less charitable opinion of the same behavior by Latin Americans. Johnson described the "gleaming, treacherous eyes" of the "lower class of Mexican" who "invariably conceal the ready and cowardly knife."[40]

Travelers claimed that the sadistic character of the Latin American was also revealed in his love of cockfighting and bullfighting. John Stephens, who seemed generally horrified by Latin American male culture, included a description of a cockfight in his *Incidents of Travel in Central America*. "The eagerness and vehemence, noise and uproar, wrangling, betting, swearing, and scuffling of the crowd, exhibited a dark picture of human nature and a sanguinary people." Others viewed these blood sports as evidence of the Latin American's essential immaturity. Theodore Johnson spoke for his traveling companions when he claimed that cockfighting "appeared to us

[38] Dana, *Two Years Before the Mast*, 179; Jones and Rogers, "Across the Isthmus in 1850," 544; Johnson, *Sights in the Gold Region*, 51; John M. Letts, *A pictorial View of California*, 143. Of course this view was not limited to American men. Mary Seacole of Jamaica agreed that the soldiers "were a dirty, cowardly, indolent set." *Wonderful Adventures of Mrs. Seacole in Many Lands*. 1857 (New York, 1988), 43. On gendered representations of Mexican soldiers, see Streeby, *American Sensations*, 102–38; Slotkin, *The Fatal Environment*, 185.

[39] De Léon, *They Called Them Greasers*, 63–74. See also Philip Wayne Powell, *Tree of Hate: Propaganda and Prejudices Affecting United States Relations with the Hispanic World* (New York, 1971), 118; Cecil Robinson, *With the Ears of Strangers: The Mexican in American Literature* (Tucson, 1963), 190. Popular representations of Mexicans were full of these images. See, for example, "Colonel Yanez: A Mexican Story of the Present Day," *The Living Age* 4 (February 8, 1845): 376–8; *Frank Leslie's Illustrated Newspaper*, July 2, 1859.

[40] Woods, *Sixteen Months*, 31; Johnson, *Sights in the Gold Region*, 290. See also Dana, *Two Years Before the Mast*, 84.

FIGURE 3.1. "Market Place, Acapulco." Many travelers were charmed by Acapulco, a regular stop on sea routes to California, and not only because the women of the city were "celebrated for their beauty, finely developed forms, and graceful bearing, as well as for their vivacity and winning pathos in conversation." The increasing Americanization of Acapulco also was lauded by visitors from the United States. But the behavior of these travelers did not endear them to Mexican residents. John Letts's illustration of the marketplace in Acapulco captured some of the attractions and tensions of a public space that desirable Mexican women largely controlled. "The stands are mostly attended by females. The first salutation upon entering the market-place is from the little girls, who hail you with 'Say, Americano! Lemonade, picayune?' holding up to you a plate containing a glass of lemonade, as will be seen by the accompanying plate." The scene includes not only a "demure" saleswoman, with a basket of shells on her head, but examples of the kind of relationships that might flourish in such a setting. "At the left, in the foreground, is seen a Señora making love to an *hombre* who looks from underneath his huge *sombrero*, and seems to hold the tighter, his lemon basket and jug." But in the middle-ground right a less pleasant interaction is occurring. "The man is a Californian; he was brought ashore by the boy, but does not seem anxious to pay his fare. The boy has his hand full of stones, by which he designs to convince the man that he had better pay. During the parlay, a female runs out recognizing the man as having got his dinner of her without paying for it, she says, 'Ah! You thought I wouldn't know you, but I do know you.' This was coming too thick for the man, and giving a kind of 'b'hoy' bend of the knee, he runs both hands into his pockets, with a 'well, I guess if I owe you anything, I can p-a-y.'" The marketplace could be a site of both sexual adventure and mortification for American men. Will further Americanization resolve these tensions? While Letts does not openly encourage the filibustering of Acapulco, he does note that it would be easy to invade since the castle is "garrisoned by only a few barefooted soldiers." Note the soldier in the right-hand middle-ground, whom Letts describes as appearing "lame in one foot." John M. Letts, *A pictorial View of California* (New York, 1853), 145.

cruel, disgusting, and puerile, but is, nevertheless, the grand entertainment among these people." Richard Henry Dana noted "the meanness, and cruelty, and impotency" of the audience at a bullfight who reminded him of "children at a play."[41]

Given the low opinion in which American travelers held Central American men, the frequency of violent encounters between the two groups is not surprising. There were two major riots in Panama between American travelers and locals. The first, in Panama City in 1850, resulted in at least four deaths. The second, in October of 1851, left twelve Americans dead. Even avid expansionists like Daniel Horn were forced to conclude that "the Americans were wholly to blame" in these cases. "The riot was brought on by their own high-handed measures, contrary to law, in a way that could not be submitted to in any civilized country" he reported about one such encounter, although he added that "the Americans did not use their usual bravery or more damage would have been done."[42]

More common than rioting was a low-level violence and intimidation that reflected the white supremacist view that the domination of inferior races was no crime.[43] The Jamaican hotel keeper Mary Seacole pitied the boatmen and muleteers of Panama who were "terribly bullied by the Americans." Seacole connected their treatment directly to the slave system in the United States and to aggressive expansionism abroad. The Panamanians were "reviled, shot, and stabbed by those free and independent filibusters, who would feign whop all creation abroad as they do their slaves at home." Examples of Americans mistreating Central American men, with no remorse, fill the accounts of travelers through the region. Usually travelers excused their behavior by pointing to some perceived slight, such as price gouging, that provoked the response. In some cases, the perceived slight was much less obvious. One "little Creole" who was "dancing with his might and main," made the mistake of "danc[ing] close to us, with a sort of challenging, swaggering air," Theodore Johnson reported. His punishment was swift. "Watching him a moment, and seeing that he was half intoxicated, and would soon give out if put to the test, one of our party commenced a regular hoe-down, knocking his shins with heavy boots when opportunity offered, by way of *tattoo*, thus provoking him and keeping him to his own game, till, at last, he became quite

[41] John L. Stephens, *Incidents of Travel in Central America, Chiapas, and Yucatan.* 1841 (New Brunswick, 1949), vol. 1:209; Johnson, *Sights in the Gold Region*, 64; Dana, *To Cuba and Back*, 203–4.

[42] Jones and Rogers, "Across the Isthmus in 1850," 542. On riots see *NYH*, June 6, 1850; Roberts, *American Alchemy*, 140–1.

[43] As Arnoldo De León has written about relations between Mexicans and whites in Texas, "the image whites held of Mexicans as depraved and brutal folk determined the careless regard Anglos held for them as human beings. Whites seldom manifested guilt or restraint in committing acts for the preservation of white supremacy." De León, *They Called Them Greasers*, 74.

exhausted, and fairly broke down." Johnson justified his behavior not only because the man dared swagger in his presence but also based on his presupposition about Central American cruelty and depravity. "He was evidently a bully among the men, and cock of the walk" according to Johnson.[44]

By feminizing Latin American men and Latin American nations, Americans justified their aggression against both individuals, as in the case of Theodore Johnson and the swaggering dancer, and also against entire countries. As Sam Houston put it at the all-Mexico rally, "your ancestors, when they landed at Plymouth.... from the first moment ... went on trading with the Indians, and cheating them out of their land. Now the Mexicans are no better than Indians, and I see no reason why we should not go on in the same course now, and take their land."[45]

The vision of the cowardly Mexican contributed to the inflated expectations Americans had about an easy victory in the U.S.-Mexico War, and to the chances badly prepared filibusters might have in Mexico, Cuba, or Central America. But the vision of the effeminate Latin American man also was employed by restrained opponents of aggressive expansionism. The *American Whig Review*, a strong opponent of the U.S.-Mexico War, quoted one typical account of Mexican soldiers in a contemporary travelogue: "Discipline they have none. Courage a Mexican does not possess." And it raised the question of why Americans had fought them in the first place. The war was wrong, in the anti-war position, in part because the two sides were so badly matched. This view, diametrically opposed to that of aggressive expansionists, reflected a concern with fairness shared by proponents of restrained manhood. "It would be better if, while we admit the strength of our nation's right hand, we could defer awhile rejoicing over the blows it has struck in an unjust contest," concluded the journal.[46] The critique of Latin American manhood need not necessarily lead to cries for annexation, but the restrained opinion of the *American Whig Review* was a minority view in Central American matters between 1848 and 1860.

The Manly American

In his study of the gold rush and middle-class culture, Brian Roberts has argued that many of the characteristics ascribed by forty-niners to Latin Americans – their economic irresponsibility, laziness, sexuality, and overuse of tobacco, alcohol, and chocolate – were exactly those qualities that attracted Americans to the region. "Obviously, many would find ways to

---

[44] Seacole, *Wonderful Adventures*, 41; Johnson, *Sights in the Gold Region*, 32.

[45] "The Great War Meeting," *NYH*, January 30, 1848.

[46] G. W. Peck, "Adventures in Mexico," *American Whig Review* 7 (March 1848): 307, 308, 314; see also George F. Ruxton, *Adventures in Mexico and the Rocky Mountains* (New York, 1848).

embrace these apparently quintessential Latin American expressions and behaviors" he writes. Some men clearly reveled in the difference of Latin America and embraced it wholeheartedly. Milo Jasper Goss went so far as to write to his wife from Panama: "You would hardly know me, were you to see me now; I am quite fleshy and as black as an Indian and health excellent."[47]

Generally, however, the embrace of the other was not self-conscious. According to travelers, many American men behaved as badly as the Latin Americans they critiqued. The gold rush attracted a heterogeneous body of travelers, including many rowdy workingmen who felt no hesitation about expressing their aggressive masculine culture. T. Robinson Warren claimed that Chagres was full of "the very lowest and vilest wretches from the purlieus of New York and New Orleans." Mary Seacole agreed. "The crowds to California were of the lowest sorts," she wrote. While dismissive of Central American men in general, Daniel Horn admitted that Americans in Panama "are far more dishonest than the natives." Edward Dunbar was shocked at the cowardice of fellow travelers who deserted a colleague suffering from cholera. Francis Edward Prevaux reported to his parents in Massachusetts that "were I in want of men to engage in the most daring, hazardous and bloody undertaking possible, I would seek for them and find them here.... the greatest cutthroats in the world are found on the Isthmus."[48] The image of the disorderly forty-niner was mocked in Nathaniel Currier's 1849 lithograph, "The Way They Wait for 'The Steamer' at Panama." Drunken Americans fight one another and hold an "indignation meeting" in which they threaten to declare "war" on all foreign countries (see Figure 3.2).

Others travelers seemed to lose their moral compass once they arrived. Mary Jane Megquier, who made three trips across the Isthmus in the late 1840s and early 1850s, claimed that the bearded Americans in Panama looked "less like civilization than the natives." Milo Goss suggested that Americans engaged in behavior in Central America they would never have participated in at home. "Rioting, debauchery in all its different forms, prevails here, in all its deformity. The Sabbath day is a day of revelry among the Spanish and of drinking and gambling with the Am[erican]s, and all kinds of sin is committed with more boldness than one performs a good act...."[49]

---

[47] Roberts, *American Alchemy*, 128; Milo Goss Letter to Catherine Goss, New Granada, Panama, May 22, 1850. Goss Family Letter Collection, 1849–1853, BL.

[48] T. Robinson Warren, *Dust and Foam; or, Three Oceans and Two Continents* (New York, 1859), 156; Seacole, *Wonderful Adventures*, 51–2; Jones and Rogers, "Across the Isthmus in 1850," 535; Dunbar, *The Romance of the Age*, 58–60; Francis Edward Prevaux, "Letters to his Family in Massachusetts," 1846–1859, undated letter from Prevaux to his parents, 1, BL.

[49] Extract from the Norway (ME) *Advertiser*, Friday, June 1, 1849 in Megquier, *Apron Full of Gold*, 21; Letter from Milo to Catherine Goss, Panama, June 18, 1850. Goss Family Letter Collection, 1849–1853, BL.

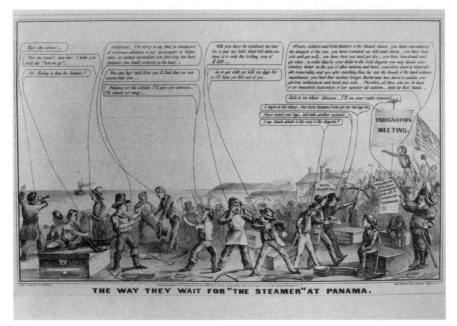

FIGURE 3.2. "The Way They Wait for 'The Steamer' at Panama." (New York, Nathaniel Currier, 1849.) Nathaniel Currier mocked the drunken, rowdy behavior of Americans in Panama in this popular print representing the difficulties of the Isthmus passage. Although several of the pugilistic forty-niners sport caricatured Irish features, the orator at the "indignation meeting" suggests to his enthusiastic crowd that they immediately "declare war against all nations" in order to prevent "insolent foreign Barbarians" from mining gold in California. There are no recognizably Panamanian characters in this print, and no women. Library of Congress, Prints and Photographs Division [LC-USZ62-26406].

While some men may have embraced "quintessential Latin American expressions and behaviors," many more defined their own masculine virtues in contrast to the Latin American. Indeed, one of the most outstanding aspects of the Central American encounter for men was the opportunity it provided to assert one's own masculinity. Every quality that the American man found lacking in the Latin American man – bravery, hard work, intelligence, and strength – reflected a quality that he claimed for himself, and one that was becoming increasingly difficult to prove at home. By projecting onto Latin American men "all that they feared or disliked in themselves," American travelers reassured themselves about their own masculine virtues. Indeed, martial men traveling through Latin America constructed their own martial masculinity in relation to the men they encountered, dominated, and abused.[50]

[50] Quote in Pike, *The United States and Latin America*, 30; R. M. Connell, *Masculinities*, 75.

By picturing the Central American as lazy, travelers highlighted the success a non-lazy man was certain to find. Richard Henry Dana made the projection of undesirable American qualities onto the Latin American man explicit when he offered his observation that "there are no people to whom the newly invented Yankee word of 'loafer' is more applicable than to the Spanish Americans." Central America, with its fertile land, mineral riches, and gentle climate, offered unequalled opportunities for hard working Americans, boosters argued. "Little can be expected from those who have been reared from infancy to consider labor as degrading; but he who will settle in Nicaragua, willing 'to take the chances,' may rest assured he holds trumps in the plow, the hoe, and a civil tongue" wrote one booster account.[51] While laborers in the United States faced falling wages due to industrialization and immigration, laborers in Central America, boosters and travelers agreed, could count on their work ethic to bring them success.

By envisioning the Central American as cowardly, American men asserted their own bravery. This dynamic is apparent in travelers' descriptions of violent interactions on the Isthmus. Theodore Johnson reported that when faced with price gouging, "Our Yankee friend...deliberately knocked our belligerent *hombre* down, adding his rapid rise by a kick. This *argumentum ad hominem* he perfectly understood, and nimbly picking up the game, trotted off in the required direction."[52] Images of brave Americans dominating cowardly Latinos also fill fictional accounts of the Latin American encounter, from the sensational accounts of the U.S.-Mexico War to travel fiction like Ephraim George Squier's anonymously authored Central American adventure story, *Waikna: Adventures on the Mosquito Shore* (see Figure 3.3). The demonstration of physical prowess and bravery was central to the practice of martial manhood.[53]

By focusing on the ignorance of the Central American, the American man's enlightenment could shine brightly. Even men who would never brag about a fistfight felt confident about their physical abilities in Central America and could exercise that confidence in defense of American values, including,

[51] Dana, *Two Years Before the Mast*, 48. At other points, Dana makes it clear that it is only the men who are lazy. On Juan Fernandez, for example, "the men appeared to be the laziest of mortals," and habitually occupied in "doing nothing," 48–9; Peter F. Stout, *Nicaragua: Past, Present and Future; a Description of Its Inhabitants, Customs, Mines, Minerals. Early History, Modern Fillibusterism, Proposed Inter-Oceanic Canal and Manifest Destiny* (Philadelphia, 1859), 165.

[52] Johnson, *Sights in the Gold Region*, 72.

[53] E. George Squier (as "Samuel A. Bard"), *Waikna: Adventures on the Mosquito Shore*. 1855 reprint (Gainesville, FL, 1965); Waikna was re-released in the 1890s under Squier's name as *Adventures on the Mosquito Shore* (New York, 1891). On *Waikna* see Bruce Harvey, *American Geographics*, 180–90. On sensational literature in the U.S.-Mexico War see Streeby, *American Sensations*; Slotkin, *The Fatal Environment*, 192–8.

AND I TOOK DELIBERATE AIM AT HIS BREAST, AT A DISTANCE OF LESS THAN
FIVE YARDS. "MOTHER OF MERCY!" HE EXCLAIMED——

p. 50.

FIGURE 3.3. "And I took deliberate aim at his breast...." Aggressive expansionist Ephraim George Squier promoted the annexation of Nicaragua in his 1855 novel, *Waikna: Adventures on the Mosquito Shore*, by highlighting the attractions of Central America to martial men, including the ability to dominate the cowardly (or simply unarmed). Fictional representations of the Latin American encounter from this period often highlighted the martial manhood of the Anglo-Saxon protagonists in scenes of domination of Latin American men. E. George Squier, *Adventures on the Mosquito Shore* (New York, 1891 edition), 50.

significantly, American Protestantism.[54] The strongly anti-papist William Elder revealed both his biases and his confidence in American pugilism in a tale he related to family back home. "Yesterday," he wrote from Panama City,

[t]hey carried the host through the streets in a very pompous manner.... I noticed one honest looking man who kept his hat on. One of the officials being within reach politely knocked it off him. The man seemed at a loss to know whether to get angry or not, but picking it up he put it on again. The same man knocked it off a second time. The man a second time picked it up and put it on as if nothing had happened. It was well for the priest that the man was so forebearing. There are not a great many of the Americans would have submitted to the insult so tamely.[55]

In Elder's understanding, the refusal to remove one's hat in the face of an il-legitimate religion is "honest," and the "forebearing" American an anomaly. Interestingly, Elder seems unimpressed by the valor of the priest who defends his religion in the face of insult, and he is so confident in American man-hood that he witnesses this interaction without questioning his presupposi-tions about either the courage of American men or the cowardice of Latin American men. Elder's response to the pompous priest helps to explain why Americans who were terrified of the increasing power of Catholics at home nonetheless might support expansionism into Latin America; expansionism offered an opportunity to impress the superiority of Protestant manhood on Catholic men.

Finally, by asserting that the Central American was effeminate, the Amer-ican male could reinforce his own masculinity. This logic took into account the individual effeminacy of the Latin American man, as well as of the whole region. Latin America offered men countless opportunities to prove them-selves sexually, but only because Americans imagined themselves so much more appealing than Latin American men. A Honduran priest reportedly expressed his fears to booster William Vincent Wells that if Americans were to arrive in the region in large numbers, they "will quarrel with our young men.... And then you have another fault, worse than that – you deceive our women, young man." Another expansionist argued that the effeminacy of the whole Spanish "race" would rebound to the benefit of the American. "I have often heard it remarked that one's stock is running out from want of changing of the bread; perhaps this might not be inapplicable to the Spanish race in Mexico. A young Mexican ... suggested this view of his country's fair

---

54 Theodore DeWitt, for example, wrote to his mother from Panama, "a more miserable set of hipocrites [*sic*] than their priests are you would have some difficulty in finding." Letter from Theodore DeWitt to his mother from Panama, September 29, 1850, DeWitt Family Papers, BL.

55 Letter to "Cousin Catherine," from Panama, June 10, 1850, William Elder Corresponde-nce, BL.

sex to my consideration, and cited the United States with their millions of emigrants from different nations, in proof of this remark or suggestion."[56]

The dialectic between the effeminacy of the Latin American man and the masculinity of the American also is a key theme in the travel narratives of Central America, Mexico, and Cuba that ran in national magazines and newspapers in this period. In one 1854 Nicaraguan travel narrative that ran in *Harper's*, a German-American settler named Hipp "made extensive clearings on both banks of the river" and had "started a flourishing plantation." As an unmarried man, Hipp is at first forced "to do his own cooking," and as an American abroad he is also unsure about the ability of Nicaragua's government to uphold his land claims. Both of these dilemmas are easily resolved in the course of the tale. Hipp protects his property rights by pummeling some trespassers, and proudly raising an American flag. Soon after, he slips a letter into the narrator's hand, to be delivered to a "dark-eyed damsel in Granada."[57]

As the story of Hipp indicates, there was no better land than Central America for the martial white man. For recent immigrants to the United States, be they from Ireland or Germany, Central America offered a means of Americanization, where the "changing of the bread" could be accomplished by beating Latin American men and seducing women. Given the opportunities to prove oneself in Central America, it is no wonder that proponents of martial manhood clung to the idea of the Americanization of the region. As the chances for success in increasingly competitive America shrank, Central America offered a world of possibility.

Looking at Latin American Women

To one outside observer, Americans in Panama were "hot-brained armed men" who "loitered on the verandah, smoking, and looking at the native women." No figure looms larger in the Latin American travelogues that were published in the United States in the late 1840s and 1850s than the lovely Latina, illuminating the fact that the intended audience of these pieces was male. Not only do booster narratives tout the opportunities for labor and business in the region, they generally also include ample discussion of the greatest of all natural resources – the beautiful and available women of the region.[58]

56 William V. Wells, *Explorations and Adventures in Honduras*, excerpted in "Adventures in the Gold Fields of Central America," *HNMM* 12 (February 1856): 331; "Cincinnatus" (Marvin Wheat), *Travels on the Western Slope of the Mexican Cordillera in the form of Fifty-One Letters* (San Francisco, 1857), 50.

57 E. G. Squier (as anon.), "San Juan," *HNMM* X (December 1854): 59, 60; see also Dana, *Two Years Before the Mast*, 393.

58 Seacole, *Wonderful Adventures*, 22. For gendered reports of Nicaragua, see, for example, "Three Weeks in Nicaragua," *San Francisco Herald*, January 14, 1856; unsigned letter from

While it would be wrong to say that success in love had become as difficult to achieve in the United States by the late 1840s as success in work, young unmarried men in America's cities faced dismal marriage prospects. Unmarried men outnumbered unmarried women by a substantial margin in most cities in the 1850s. In St. Louis, for example, there were three adult men to every two adult women, and less than twenty-five percent of unskilled workers and nineteen percent of clerks had wives. San Francisco's sex ration was far worse. The gold rush attracted an almost exclusively male population, and in 1860, there were still two men for every woman. The censuses of 1850 and 1860 noted a fall in the incidence of marriage in America and a rise in the age of marriage for both men and women. A growing urban sex trade and a proliferation of brothels in America's cities serviced this bachelor population, while a growing hysteria over the "epidemic" of masturbation pointed to social concerns about the problematic sexuality of the period. The unskilled worker or clerk, living in a boarding house with other unmarried men, would have a difficult time finding a wife in urban America. If he chose to follow his luck to California, he could expect his marriage prospects to decline further. It is hardly surprising that American travelers would look fondly on Latin American women under these circumstances.[59]

American travel narratives were far more enthusiastic about the women of Latin America than were European travel narratives to the region published at the same time. The foreign narratives tended to present mixed assessments of the women of Latin America. The Viennese physician Carl Scherzer complemented the "extraordinarily beautiful" hair and "very transparent" chemises of Costa Rican women, but he also claimed that their "broad" noses ruined the effect. A British traveler to Cuba suggested that he would have been attracted to the beautiful women of the country had they not been such sloppy dressers.[60]

American travelers were less ambivalent. As one traveler wrote about Mexico's women, "I could almost say that to see her is to love her." Nor was the attraction merely skin deep. T. Robinson Warren claimed that their "inexhaustible spirits, their quick perception of the ridiculous, their love

Granada to the editor of the *San Francisco Herald*, dated February 19, 1856, in the Wheeler Collection, LOC, series I, vol. 12: 96.

59 Amy S. Greenberg, *Cause for Alarm: The Volunteer Fire Department in the Nineteenth-Century City* (Princeton, 1998), 43; G. J. Barker-Benfield, *The Horrors of the Half-Known Life: Male Attitudes Toward Women and Sexuality in Nineteenth-Century America*, 2nd ed. (New York, 2000), 14 15; Patricia Cline Cohen, *The Murder of Helen Jewett: The Life and Death of a Prostitute in Nineteenth-Century New York* (New York, 1998), 69–86; Timothy Gilfoyle, *City of Eros: New York City, Prostitution, and the Commercialization of Sex, 1790– 1920* (New York, 1992).

60 "Costa Rica," *The New Monthly Magazine*, reprinted in *The Living Age* 51 (December 27, 1857): 769–82; Moritz Wagner and Carl Scherzer, *Die Republik Costa Rica in Central America* (Leipzig, 1856); Sir Edward Robert Sullivan, *Rambles and Scrambles in North and South America* (London, 1853).

of quizzing, and their gentle affectionate manner," made Mexican women "agreeable companions for anyone." Perhaps the most effusive booster of the women of Latin America was also one of the most prolific authors on the region, E. G. Squier. As the *London Literary Gazette* commented, "Our American envoy's appreciation of female charms is so intense, that he cannot pass a pretty woman without inscribing a memorandum respecting her in his note-book, afterwards to be printed more at length with additional expressions of admiration."[61] Squier penned two typically effusive travelogues (one anonymously) in *Harper's Monthly Magazine* in December 1854 and October 1855. Squier's narratives are representative of the Latin American travelogue genre in the degree to which ideas of gender and sex shaped the vision of these territories. As Squier makes clear, Nicaragua is a perfect place for men to succeed in both work and love.

The women in Squier's narratives, like those in other published travelogues, are beautiful, friendly, and scantily clad. In one port, the Nicaraguan women wear shirts which "left exposed a strip of skin at the waist, which the wanton wind often made much wider. They all had their hair braided in two long locks, which hung down behind, and gave them a school-girly appearance – quite out of keeping with the cool, deliberate manner in which they smoked their cigars." At Lake Masaya, women bathe nude, while in the next village "Indian women, naked to the waist, sat beneath the trees spinning snow-white cotton." On the way to Leon, the American visitors encounter washer women, who "when occupied with their work" wear less of a costume "even than that of the Georgia Major, which was catalogued as a shirt-collar and a pair of spurs." Squier waxes poetic about virtually every woman he sees in Nicaragua, whether naked or clothed. One "dark-colored Ceres, her hair stuck full of flowers, displays a dozen baskets heaped up with ripe and luscious fruits, and chants, with a musical voice,

> 'tengo narangas, papayas, jocotes,
> Melones de agua, de oro, zapotes!
> Quieren á comprar?'"

Like the ripe fruit of Manifest Destiny, and like Nicaragua itself, these women are lovely, fertile, and ready to be bought.[62]

[61] Albert M. Gilliam, *Travels over the Table Lands and Cordilleras of Mexico* (Philadelphia, 1846), 134; Warren, *Dust and Foam*, 199; "Mr. Squier on Nicaragua," *London Literary Gazette*, quoted in *The International Magazine of Literature, Art and Science* 5 (April 1852): 474–6; E. G. Squier, "Adventures and Observations in Nicaragua," *The International Magazine of Literature, Art and Science* 3 (July 1851): 438. The *London Literary Gazette* believed that Squier's "affection for the ladies is only equaled by his dislike of the 'Britishers.' The handsomest girl and the ugliest idol could scarcely distract his thought from the vices and crimes of England and the English," 474.

[62] Translation: "I have oranges, papayas, jocotes, watermelons, musk melons, and zapotes. Would you buy some?" E. G. Squier (as anon.), "San Juan," *HNMM* X (December 1854):

Thomas Francis Meagher's *Harper's* Costa Rica travelogue also focused on the appeal of the country's women. "The *mestizas* – the women of the country – in very loose low-necked dresses of white or colored calico, with bare arms and feet, sit behind their *serones* of fruit and vegetables... and with accents as liquid and refreshing as the *guarapo*, and with a shy gracefulness if the passer-by happens to be a stranger, expatiate upon the merits of their merchandise." Meagher, like Squier, intimated that the Latina had more to sell than produce. "Besides their very loose and low-necked dresses of white or colored calico," he continued, "these winsome merchants sport the prettiest pert little hats.... They are perfect heartbreakers – those pert little hats! – and to settle the business, the young women of Costa Rica are decidedly handsome. Their figures are full and round, their features regularly cut, their eyebrows richly penciled."[63]

The author of a Honduran travelogue was equally smitten by that country's women, noting in particular the "loose and flowing" costume that leaves the "neck and arms exposed." He was most impressed by one woman, of "mixed blood, but figure of faultless beauty" including a "bust surpassing that of the Venus de Medici in 'its audacious press of full-breathed beauty.'" This author chose to sketch this beauty as "Liberty," suggesting the possibilities for the incorporation of "mixed-blood" Central American women, into the symbolic heart of the North American family.[64]

Ordinary men travelling through the region on the way to California were almost as smitten as the boosters. In part, the sensual nature of the environment was to blame. According to Bayard Taylor, Panama appeared to be a place where "plantains take root in the banks, hiding the soil with their leaves, shaken and split into immense plumes by the wind and rain." Given the luxuriance of the tropics and the fact that, in America, the metaphor of land-as-woman was embraced as literal truth, it isn't surprising that some travelers got carried away. Edward Dunbar marveled at the "lovely Indian maidens, who dreamed away life in a voluptuous atmosphere" in Panama. They invited the traveler to "blissful relaxation and repose, bathed in rockbound pools of cool, crystal waters, found in picturesque recesses hidden by

---

52; E. G. Squier, "Nicaragua: an Exploration From Ocean to Ocean," *HNMM* XI (October 1855): 755. On Squier see Albert Z. Carr, *The World and William Walker* (New York, 1963), 112. The anonymous author of "A Ranger's Life in Nicaragua" also, incongruously, remarked on the beauty of the scantily clad Nicaraguan women in the middle of his critique of the Nicaraguan war. "A Ranger's Life in Nicaragua," *Harper's Weekly*, vol. 1 (April 18, 1857), 249. On the representation of Mexican women as ripe fruit in the twentieth century see María del Carmen Suescun Pozas, "From Reading to Seeing: Doing and Undoing Imperialism in the Visual Arts," in Gilbert M. Joseph, Catherine C. LeGrand, Ricardo D. Salvatore, eds., *Close Encounters of Empire: Writing the Cultural History of U.S. Latin American Relations* (Durham, 1998), 534–5.

[63] Thomas Francis Meagher, "Holidays in Costa Rica," *HNMM* 20 (February 1860): 310.

[64] "Visit to the Guajiquero Indians," *HNMM* 19 (October 1859): 609–10.

a network of foliage and flowers." Other travelers were less florid but no less impressed. Lucian Wolcott, traveling through Nicaragua in 1851, repeatedly noted the "beautiful" women of the country, including "[a] beautiful young senorita standing in the door of a thatched bamboo or cane house" who "beckoned me with a banana...." John Letts waxed rapturously about virtually every woman he encountered. "Never did I look upon such specimens of feminine grace and loveliness. Their eyes were dark and lustrous, and their countenances, like their native clime, always beaming with sunshine."[65]

The "busts" of Latin American women were not the only features to attract attention. The dark eyes of many Latinas were considered especially evocative. Goldsborough Bruff described one "dark female" he met in Acapulco in 1851, "with the usual large lustrous black eyes, of the clime and the people." James Tyson also noted the "rather pretty faces and particularly fine eyes" of the women he met in Panama. Theodore Johnson visited a nunnery with some friends, and remarked that "seeing only the flash of their brilliant black eyes through a knot hole in the wheel, we imagined ourselves transferred to the famed Alhambra."[66]

Female nudity was a favored topic in the diaries and letters of male travelers through Central America. William Denniston repeatedly noted running across attractive women bathing themselves, once in a fruit-laden orchard no less. Other male travelers actively searched out nude women at the public baths of Panama. "We cast frequent glances through the bamboo sides of our modest retreat, fearing some young Señorita might linger in the grove to lave in turn her own fair form, or rather twilight skin. But in this, alas! We were not so fortunate...."[67]

Even clothed women appeared virtually nude to travelers used to different standards of propriety. As Brian Roberts has written, "the forty-niner vision seemed capable of passing right through loose clothing to focus on heaving breasts." Theodore Johnson spoke for many American men when he noted that "the costume of the women of Panama especially attracted our attention. Although appropriate enough to the climate, it was rather different from our

---

[65] Taylor, *Eldorado*, 13; Dunbar, *The Romance of the Age*, 70; Lucian Wolcott "Journal," 2 vols., HL; Letts, *A pictorial View of California*, 148. According to Annette Kolodny, the mid-nineteenth century saw a conversion of "the pastoral possibility into the exclusive prerogative of the single male figure, living out a highly eroticized and intimate relationship with a landscape at once suggestively sexual, but overwhelmingly maternal." *The Lay of the Land: Metaphor as Experience and History in American Life and Letters* (Chapel Hill, 1975), 134, 6. On the "porno-tropics" in European thought see Anne McClintock, *Imperial Leather: Race, Gender, and Sexuality in the Colonial Context* (New York, 1995), 21–4. For an analysis of forty-niner racial and gender attitudes in California see Susan Lee Johnson, *Roaring Camp: The Social World of the California Gold Rush* (New York, 2000), 157–68.

[66] Bruff, *Gold Rush*, 498; Tyson, *Diary of a Physician in California*, 17; Johnson, *Sights in the Gold Region*, 61.

[67] Denniston, "Journal of a voyage," HL; Johnson, *Sights in the Gold Region*, 64; see also, Letts, *A pictorial View of California*, 14, 25.

preconceived ideas of modesty and propriety." James Tyson thrilled to getting coffee "handed by a damsel nearly *nude*," and also admired "younger" females "entirely *model artiste* at least as far as clothing was concerned." But the "shock" of abbreviated clothing wore off quickly. Peter DeWitt wrote to his mother that "the climate requires but little clothing, and it might give somewhat of a shock to your sense of propriety at first on account of their manner of dressing, but you soon get used to it...."[68]

The American sense of propriety was not only shaken by the apparel of the Latina but also by behavior that suggested lax morality. Milo Goss wrote to his cousin Catherine back in Michigan that "the ladies all smoke, which looks odd enough." Daniel Horn wrote his family that "all smoke segars [*sic*], men, women, children." Published narratives were more direct in their assertion that sometimes a cigar wasn't just a cigar. "School-girly" looking women smoke cigars in a "cool, deliberate manner" in Squier's narratives. The cigar becomes yet more erotic in one of Stephen's travelogues. "I had been dozing, when I opened my eyes and saw a girl about seventeen sitting sideways upon it, [his hammock] smoking a cigar. She had a piece of striped cotton cloth tied around her waist and falling below her knees. The rest of her dress was that which Nature bestows alike upon the belle of fashionable life and the poorest girl.... At first I thought it was something I had conjured up in a dream."[69]

Not even smoking, however, attracted as much comment as the "lewd" and "barbaric" fandango, which travelers both condemned and searched out. Bayard Taylor expressed his ambivalence about these "half-barbaric orgies" that could be best seen "in the pure and splendid light poured upon the landscape from a vertical moon." Theodore Johnson also noted that the motions in the fandango are "often indecent and disgusting" but none the less described the dance for the benefit of readers. Other travelers were less judgmental. Daniel Horn regretted that he missed a fandango in Cruces, while for the Troy blacksmith Hiram Pierce, the fandango was an opportunity to admire the feet of the female dancers. The "females have a singular way of wearing their shoes" he wrote. "They appear just large enough for them to slip the forepart of the foot into, leaving the back part out, and shuffle along with a wagging slipshod shuffling gate." Given the attractiveness of the Latina, and the sexual nature of the dance, it was perhaps not surprising that, as Charles Ross Parke wrote in his diary, some men attended the fandango every night: "Our American boys, especially Boston and

[68] Roberts, *American Alchemy*, 135; see also Pike, *The United States and Latin America*, 10–13; Johnson, *Sights in the Gold Region*, 68; Tyson, *Diary of a Physician in California*, 24, 17; typescript of letter from Peter DeWitt Jr. to his mother from San Francisco, May 27, 1850, DeWitt Family Papers, BL.

[69] Milo Goss Letter to Cousin Catherine, June 18, 1850, Goss Family Letters, BL; Jones and Rogers, "Across the Isthmus in 1850," 538–9; E. G. Squier (as anon.), "San Juan," *HNMM* X (December 1854): 52; Stephens, *Incidents of Travel*, vol. 1:41.

N. York boys, can easily be persuaded to take a drink with the dusky señoritas when away from home. In fact, would be too polite to refuse her."[70]

Charles Parke's image of the American "boy," or young urban man, purchasing drinks for the "dusky" skinned Latina when away from home, conforms to a popular image – that American men were only interested in Latin American women when the sex-ratio was skewed and lighter-skinned women were unavailable. A corollary holds that white American men searched out the lightest skinned women available, and that the only acceptable marriage partners were the "European" looking women of the region. As John Stephens put it, although he admired women of all colors, "I have seen enough of fancy colors in women to remove some prejudices, but I retain an old-fashioned predilection for white faces."[71]

Certainly some American travelers carried their racial prejudices to Latin America. William Wells was "disappointed" that the "habit of intermarrying practiced by whites, Indians, mestizos, and even negroes, has done much to deteriorate female beauty in Central America." W. H. Hecox wrote home from Panama that "the Senoritas are not fascinating, because they are not pretty.... I must confess I prefer something lighter – and less greasy." Other travelers emphasized that the women they were attracted to were of European rather than Indian extraction. Thomas Francis Meagher makes it clear in his booster narrative that there are many European women in Costa Rica, whose "complexion, generally speaking, suggests a *conserve* of cream and roses." Charles Parke expressed his approval of a Baltimorean who became infatuated with the eighteen-year-old daughter of a "pure Castillian, no mixed blood" family that flew the "Stars and Stripes" over their house, and who chose to remain with her rather than continue across the Isthmus. Henry Peters expressed regret that "lovely specimens of Spanish beauty" and "pure Castillian blood" were so rare in Panama.[72]

What is equally notable is the number of travelers who either failed to note the complexion of the women they admired or ignored the supposed racial heirarchy of attractiveness. It seems unlikely that Charles Parke would

---

[70] Taylor, *Eldorado*, 19; Johnson, *Sights in the Gold Region*, 32; Jones and Rogers, "Across the Isthmus in 1850," 538–9; Hiram Dwight Pierce, *A Forty-Niner Speaks*, Sarah Wiswall Meyer, ed. (Sacramento, 1978), 19; Parke, *Dreams to Dust*, 133.

[71] Stephens, *Incidents of Travel in Central America*, vol. 1:139; De León, *They Called Them Greasers*, 41. Other popular accounts clearly distinguished the "unusually beautiful" women of European extraction from the "degraded and miserable" mixed-race women. See for example, "Sketches of Lally's Campaign in Mexico," *USDR* 27 (November 1850): 419.

[72] William V. Wells, *Explorations and Adventures in Honduras, comprising sketches of travel in the gold regions of Olancho, and a review of the history and general resources of Central America. With original maps, and numerous illustrations* (New York, 1857), 74; Letter from W. H. Hecox, Panama, February 28, 1849, in McCollum, *California as I Saw it*, 185; Meagher, "Holidays in Costa Rica," *HNMM* 20 (February 1860): 310; Charles Parke journal, November 13, 1850, HL; Henry Hunter Peters diary (transcript), March 5, 1850, Box 1, Folder 9, Peters Collection, New York Public Library.

be as approving of the Baltimorean had he affiliated himself with a "mixed blood" woman, but William Denniston had no qualms with such a match. "In this village N. Bowers fell in love with a pretty Indian girl," he wrote. "if the present symptoms does not speedily abate, I think if he does not conclude to remain here he will return as soon as he has filled his coffers with the yellow dust of California." William McCollum expressed no prejudice when he noted that "[t]he natives of this portion of New Granada are.... nearly as black as African negroes, but better formed; the females especially, have good forms, and many of them have good expressions of countenance. The women are slightly, but neatly dressed." In the view of Peter Stout, race was relatively unimportant in Nicaragua: "The dark-eyed daughters of Seville, and the nut-brown lasses of Nicaragua, have the same origin; their language, mayhap, is partially changed, yet their spirits, their souls, are identical."[73]

Squier rarely let an opportunity slip by to complement the busts, coloring, feet, ankles, eyes, or hair of almost any woman he encountered in Latin America, regardless of race. In Subtiaba, Nicaragua, he noted that the indigenous women, whether shirtless or in holiday finery, entwined flowers in the "luxuriant locks of their long black hair" (see Figure 3.4).[74] Indeed, he suggests, it was exactly the racial diversity of Latinas that rendered a visit or stay in the region so enchanting.

As tastes differ, so may opinions as to whether the tinge of brown, through which the blood glows with a peach-like bloom, in the complexion of a girl who may trace her lineage to the Caziques upon one side, and the haughty grandees of Andalusia and Seville on the other, superadded, as it usually is, to a greater lightness of figure and animation of face, – whether this is not a more real beauty than that of the fair and more languid Senora, whose white and almost transparent skin bespeaks a purer ancestry. Nor is the Indian girl, with her full, lithe figure, long, glossy hair, quick and mischievous eyes, who walks erect as a grenadier beneath her heavy water-jar, and salutes you in a musical, impudent voice, as you pass – nor is the Indian girl to be overlooked in the novel contrasts that the "bello sexo" affords in this glorious land of the sun.

Squier's vision of Central America as home to a rainbow of lovely women was regularly cited in reviews of his work and was plagiarized in later work on the region.[75]

---

[73] Denniston, "Journal of a voyage," May 17, 1849, HL; McCollum, *California as I Saw it*, 88; Stout, *Nicaragua; Past, Present and Future*, 34.

[74] Ephraim G. Squier, *Nicaragua: Its People, Scenery, Monuments, Resources, Condition and Proposed Canal* (New York, 1860), 273–4.

[75] "Mr. Squier on Nicaragua," *London Literary Gazette*, quoted in *The International Magazine of Literature, Art and Science* 5 (April 1852): 474–6: E. G. Squier, "Adventures and Observations in Nicaragua," *The International Magazine of Literature, Art and Science* 3 (July 1851): 438. For an example of the plagiarism of Squier see "Visit to the Guajiquero Indians," *HNMM* 19 (October 1859): 609–10.

AN INDIAN GIRL OF SUBTIABA IN HOLIDAY COSTUME.

FIGURE 3.4. "An Indian Girl of Subtiaba in Holiday Costume." Ephraim G. Squier, *Nicaragua: Its People, Scenery, Monuments, Resources, Condition and Proposed Canal* (New York, 1860), 274.

Yet however heterogeneous his taste in women might appear to be, even Squier occasionally exhibited anxiety about both racial purity and female sexuality in Latin America. In his novel *Waikna*, he presents a version of the fandango in which the participants "gave themselves up to the grossest and most shameless debauchery" and contrasts a powerful mixed-blood Mosquito Indian matriarch, described as "a hideous old woman," with a "perfectly formed" young pure-blood Indian, "The Mother of the Tigers"

"THE MOTHER OF THE TIGERS."

FIGURE 3.5. "The Mother of the Tigers." A model of feminine beauty and decorum, the author described the pure-blooded "Mother of the Tigers" as "certainly not over twenty, tall, and perfectly formed.... after all only a shy and timid Indian girl." Ephraim G. Squire (as "Samuel A. Bard"). *Waikna: Adventures on the Mosquito Shore* (New York, 1855), 256.

(see Figure 3.5). The Afro-Amerindian Mosquito population of Honduras and Nicaragua claimed British protection, and they were thus the key to British claims to the region in the 1850s. Squier worked tirelessly to undermine the claims of both the Mosquito and the British in Central America.

Given his political stance, what is perhaps most notable about *Waikna* is not the degradation of the Mosquito matriarch but the perfection of the young Indian girl.[76]

While explicit statements in support of the advantages of racial mixing are rare in Latin American travelogues, an underlying tolerance for or appreciation of beauty not strictly European in origin is absolutely central to the encounter between American man and Central American woman. The most radical writers on the racial dominance of the Anglo-Saxon in the antebellum era argued that the white race would never "deteriorate" in the face of unions between white men and women of any other race, since through such unions "the ovum is improved."[77]

Many Americans, however, viewed the racial inferiority of Latin Americans as a major impediment against the absorption of territories to the south. Latin Americans, by virtue of their mixed ancestry and Christianity, were never fully affected by nineteenth-century taboos against interracial sex as they existed in the United States. There were no laws against marriage between Mexicans and Americans, as there were against marriage between black and white Americans, and although Anglos in Texas and California rarely included men of Mexican descent in their descriptions of whiteness, there was a long precedent in both places for Mexican women becoming "Spanish" and thus white, once they married Anglo men. Even a South Carolinian like Daniel Horn, who repeatedly equated Latin Americans with slaves in his descriptions of Central America, reported favorably on the appearance of Latin American women. "Some of the females are quite good looking and fond of dress; frill as much showy lace as they can about the neck and arms," he wrote. He also added, however, that they "have a very tawdry appearance" and "show that they are but little better than savages, so far as civilization is concerned."[78]

Clearly sex and race existed uneasily in Horn's mind, and his ambivalence about the "quite good looking" but racially suspect women he encounters

---

[76] Squier, *Waikna*, 223–3, 255–7. On Squier and his writings see Harvey, "American Geographics," 195–6. Harvey reads this work as evidence of Squier's obsession with racial purity, but as the Mosquito were the special objects of Squier's expansionist disdain, his critique of them might not be generalizable to other women, or men, in Central America. On Squier's lack of objectivity regarding the Mosquito see Michael D. Olien, "E. G. Squier and the Miskito: Anthropological Scholarship and Political Propaganda," *Ethnohistory* 32 (1985): 111–33.

[77] Theodore Poesche and Charles Goepp, *The New Rome; or, The United States and the World* (New York, 1853), 55–7; Horsman, *Race and Manifest Destiny*, 294–6. Horsman points out that Poesche and Goepp were "justly obscure," 296.

[78] Jones and Rogers, "Across the Isthmus in 1850," 535; De León, *They Called Them Greasers*, 48; Martha Hodes, *White Women: Black Men: Illicit Sex in the Nineteenth-Century South* (New Haven, 1997); Foley, *The White Scourge*, 24; Antonia I. Castañeda, "The Political Economy of Nineteenth-Century Stereotypes of Californianas," in *Between Borders: Essays on Mexicana/Chicana History*, Adelaida R. Del Castillo, ed. (Encino, CA, 1990), 223–4.

reveals that the appeal of personal "annexation" in Latin America was not universal. Of course, many virulent expansionists would find the prospect of romance with a Latina inconceivable for racial, religious, or cultural reasons. Likewise, many men who opposed aggressive expansionism found Latin American women appealing. The appeal of personal annexation was not universal, nor was it a necessary correlative to the support of national annexation. The prevalence of the beautiful and willing Latina in the discourse of aggressive expansionism, however, reveals the degree to which fantasies of male success abroad, and anxiety about that success at home, underlay expansionist desire.

The Irresistible American

While American travelers disagreed on the relationship between skin tone and beauty, they agreed that Latin American women of all shades found white American men irresistible. Given prevailing scientific views of the inevitable disappearance of inferior races in the face of Anglo-Saxon dominance, the vision of the irresistible American man was perhaps predetermined. In an 1849 review essay of California travel narratives, the *Southern Quarterly Review* explained that "the señoritas of California, as of all other countries, preferring brave men, did not permit a moment's rivalry between the races. The Anglo-Saxon, or Norman races were invariably preferred."[79] The image of the sexually available Latina was a major component of the booster narrative about Central America. Men were told that whatever luck or lack of luck they might have with women at home, in Central America they would be embraced with open arms.

Frederick Pike has argued that the image of the willing Latina was part of a larger conceptualization in which Americans linked the Latina with "wanton sexuality." She was a source of "available sex proffered by inferior creatures who ostensibly welcome seduction and subjugation." The image of the sexually wanton African-American woman legitimated the sexual exploitation of slave women in the United States and shaped the response of many Americans to the differently raced women they met while traveling. Arnoldo De León has pointed out that in nineteenth-century Texas, white men were only able to overcome their inhibitions about interracial sex by casting Mexican women as the aggressors. To a certain degree, both of these observations hold for the encounter between American men and Latinas in Central America and Mexico. In descriptions of the fandango, especially, the vision of prostitution was very thinly veiled. W. H. Hecox was just one traveler who found the women of Panama "very willing to be gazed at," although he expressed distaste at their appearance. Other travelers reported

---

[79] "The Conquest of California, and the Case of Lieutenant Col. Fremont," *SQR* 15 (July 1849), 420.

that the scantily clad local women "seemed transported with the novelty and excitement" when American men appeared.[80]

Popular representations of the region in periodicals also made use of this image. An 1849 article in *The Knickerbocker* reminded readers that while visitors might "indulge in...[a] thousand delights" in the tropics, virtue was primarily limited to white women. "Truth, goodness, and virtue flourish in far greater beauty" at home "than the wild flowers of the tropics" the piece concluded. *Harper's Monthly Magazine* reinforced the vision of the wanton, easily dominated Latina in an 1858 account of seventeenth-century piracy, "An Old Filibuster." The title character, while French, is also a superbly martial man who becomes a pirate at an early age and ends up in what will become Nicaragua. In Central America he and his men enjoy the "freebooter's paradise" in a town "distinguished for its beautiful women" (wearing only "a native cloth from the waist downward") and for its "loose morals" as well. The local men are no competition for the handsome and active newcomers. "Laden with spoils, with an abundance to eat and drink, nothing to do, and crowds of beautiful women to minister to their pleasures, they passed the time in a round of gayety and dissipation." The women of the town "soon found many of the handsome, well-formed pirates far preferable to the fat monks of Queaquilla, and passionate and romantic like their race, became enamored of their captors and the wild life they led." The protagonist breaks the heart of a beautiful Spanish widow "in the most approved French style," and although the freebooters eventually set their female prisoners "at liberty" some did not want to leave. "Some of these beautiful women had become so attached to their captors that they wept bitterly at parting."[81]

The idea of the promiscuous Latina could be based in assumptions about race and sexuality, yet the image was not limited to women of mixed-race descent. One traveler reported flirting with "Spanish women, all vivacious, and rather pleasing in their manners." Bayard Taylor claimed that in the city of Panama, "senoritas of the pure Castilian blood sang the Ethiopian melodies of Virginia." Thomas Francis Meagher also claimed that the fair-skinned women of Costa Rica were great flirts. In short, the conception of

---

[80] Pike, *The United States and Latin America*, 10–13; De Léon, *They Called Them Greasers*, 42–4; Deborah Gray White, *Ar'n't I a Woman? Female Slaves in the Plantation South* (New York, 1985), 29–31; Letter from W. H. Hecox, Panama, February 28, 1849, published in McCollum, *California as I Saw it*, 185; Johnson, *Sights in the Gold Region*, 12. See also Letts, *A pictorial View of California*, 143. Frederick B. Pike points out that a lack of sexual restraint and monogamy were both key elements in the stereotyping of Latin Americans. Pike, *The United States and Latin America*, 53–6.

[81] John Esaias Warren, "The Romance of the Tropics," *The Knickerbocker* 33 (June 1849): 504, quoted in Bruce Albert Harvey, "American Geographics," 165–6; "An Old Filibuster," *HNMM* XVIII (December 1858): 20–6.

the Latina as "primitive sensualist" was not necessarily a result of her racial makeup.[82]

The vision of the Latina as naturally wanton was clearly an element of the American expansionist encounter. But to reduce the encounter to this alone is to miss an equally important dynamic. As Sam Houston's 1848 statement about civilization and the *señorita* suggested, the Latin American woman was above all, a worthy partner. For many American men, the vision of the willing Latina was less about subjugation than success. American men could attract Latina women, not necessarily because the women were wanton but because "annexation" was natural and ordained by God himself.

American men were irresistible, and their victory, like that of the United States itself, was seen to be a victory for civilization. The encounter legitimated short-term dalliances but could also support long-term relationships. Since marriage was understood as a relationship between a dominant man and subservient woman, marriage between a white American man and Latina did not upset the American concepts of racial hierarchy that held all Latin Americans as naturally inferior. Nor were religious differences between Catholic women and Protestant men insurmountable in the mid-nineteenth century. As Jenny Franchot has written, "the romance of the [Catholic] Church was inextricably bound into the Protestant imagination." As antebellum natiyist exposés, and Theodore Johnson's comment about seeing "flashing eyes" at a convent suggested, Catholic religious institutions held an erotic appeal grounded in an "anticlerical eroticism" and were buttressed by what Protestants considered "eroticized architecture" (see Figure 3.6).[83]

As a Nicaraguan official supposedly told an officer in Walker's army, "we must have the sexes equalized, and when we have conquered a peace, immigrants will come. They will marry our forlorn girls, they will infuse a new sprit into the country, become a component part of the population, and in this way we look to the regeneration of Central America." Given the implications of contemporary racial theory, family formation between American men and Latinas would assist in the rightful domination of the

---

[82] McCollum, *California as I Saw it*, 103; Taylor, *Eldorado*, 23; Thomas Francis Meagher, "Holidays in Costa Rica," *HNMM* 20 (February 1860): 310; Pike, *The United States and Latin America*, 8. Americans used the term "Spanish" to designate Latinos of supposedly pure-European heritage.

[83] Pike, *The United States and Latin America*, 9. On marriage contracts in the mid-nineteenth century see Norma Basch, *In the Eyes of the Law: Women, Marriage, and Property in Nineteenth-Century New York* (Ithaca, 1982); Amy Dru Stanley, *From Bondage to Contract: Wage Labor, Marriage, and the Market in the Age of Slave Emancipation* (New York, 1998), 175–217. On the tolerance for mixed-faith marriages in nineteenth-century America see Anne C. Rose, *Beloved Strangers: Interfaith Families in Nineteenth-Century America* (Cambridge, MA, 2001); Maria Monk's expose of sexual misconduct, *Awful Disclosures of the Hotel Dieu Nunnery* (New York, 1836) sold three hundred thousand copies before the Civil War; Franchot, *Roads to Rome*, 126, 154–61, quotes on pages 203, 121.

FIGURE 3.6. Nicaraguan Convent. Although antebellum Protestants were generally repulsed by Catholicism, the Catholic Church held a romance in the Protestant imagination that lent itself easily to visions of "personal annexation" in Latin America. *Harper's Weekly* 1 (May 16, 1857): 312.

Anglo-Saxon race. "It seems . . . to be in the order of Providence, that these women, so justly to be admired, are to become wives and mothers of a better race," one correspondent wrote approvingly about the marriages that took place between American soldiers and Mexican women during the war.[84] Of course the equation between beautiful *señorita* and Latin American republic only functions if the woman is herself worthy of annexation.

The vision of the available Latin American women, as it circulated in travel narratives, was based in the idea that she was available to the manly men of America in particular because Latin American men were unmanly. Marvin Wheat claimed that the women of Mexico were "kinder to strangers than the gentlemen usually are" because "many have married foreigners, who are found to be more attentive to their wants, and better providers than the Mexican gentlemen themselves." In his account of filibustering with William Walker, James Carson Jameson made the same claim about Nicaragua. In that country the "charm and beauty" of the women softened "the hearts of even warlike 'filibusteros'" and the "dark-eyed beauties" could not resist "supplicants to their love" made by the manly Americans. Nor were these supplications for short-term romance only. "A number of the Americans married estimable Nicaraguan women, and became citizens of that country – like the Lotus-Eaters, they never returned to their native land."[85]

Central American travelogues asserted that regardless of their wealth or appearance, men could succeed in these fertile new territories not only in business but with women as well.[86] As E. G. Squier's *Harper's Monthly Magazine* travelogues make clear, conquest of the Latin American woman stood for American success on both the individual and national levels. Squier pictures Nicaragua as a perfect place for manhood to be regenerated, a land where beautiful women wear little clothing and are readily available to American men. In one story, a talented guitar player, "might have won unbounded popularity among the dark-skinned beauties of Nagorote had he remained there." But the interest of the lovely women of Nicaragua is not drawn solely to the musically inclined. In comparison with local men, who recline on hammocks "in attitudes suggestive of intense laziness," any American looks good. Even a Nicaraguan guide faints repeatedly and has to quit when escorting Americans on a climb up a volcano. After their successful assent and descent, the American men "passed the evening in recounting

[84] Bell, "Confessions of a Filibuster," *Golden Era*, July 23, 1876; Johannsen, *To the Halls of the Montezumas*, 170.

[85] Wheat, *Travels on the Western Slope*, 75–6; James Carson Jamison, *With Walker in Nicaragua or Reminiscences of an Officer in the American Phalanx* (Columbia, MO, 1909), 115–6; see also Letts, *A pictorial View of California*, 143.

[86] For gendered reports of Nicaragua see, for example, "Three Weeks in Nicaragua," *San Francisco Herald*, January 14, 1856; unsigned letter from Granada to the editor of the *San Francisco Herald*, dated February 19, 1856, in the Wheeler Collection, LOC, series I, vol. 12: 96.

the wonders of the mountain to a bevy of attentive Señoritas, who opened wide their big lustrous eyes, and ejaculated *mira!* at every pause in the narrative." According to Squier's narratives, Nicaragua, and its women, were ripe for adventurous men.[87]

American men reinforced the idea that they were irresistible to Central American women by repeating stories of part-American children doted on by their Latina mothers. Hiram Dwight Pierce wrote home from Panama that "many of the women showed us their white picanininies, and said, Americano. They feel very proud of them." An *Atlantic Monthly* travelogue to Honduras featured a "yellow dame" who proudly shows off her "blue-eyed, flaxen-haired child" to his "countrymen." The bemused narrator reports that the mother "gloried" in her "*escapade*" with the child's American father.[88] These stories encouraged the idea that whatever the appearance of the mother, the offspring of the union would appear, and in fact be, white. The triumph of American Manifest Destiny is represented here as a triumph of both American manhood and of the Anglo-Saxon race over the "inferior" races of Latin America.

This is not to say that the relationship envisioned in travel writing between a white American man and a Latina was to be a relationship between equals, or even as equal as a patriarchal relationship between a man and his wife in the United States would be at the time.[89] The emphasis on youth and girlishness in accounts of attractive Latinas reinforces the presupposition of superiority that underlay both visions of "annexation" – the personal and national ones. America (and the American man) would bring civilization to the inferior Latin American country (or woman). The infantilizing of both the Latina and her country is revealed in descriptions (or the lack thereof) of older women in Latin American travel narratives. The beauty of the young

---

[87] E. G. Squier (as anon.), "San Juan," 52; Squier, "Nicaragua: an Exploration From Ocean to Ocean," 754, 759. Squier faced his own crisis of manhood when researching *Nicaragua: Its People, Scenery, Monuments, and the Proposed Interoceanic Canal*. According to Bruce Harvey, Squier was under such extreme pressure to make some major archeological discoveries that when he failed to uncover anything of significance he was forced to emphasize "the masculine labor required to bring the monuments to light. Typically, he and his crew of diggers uncover the idols with 'every muscle swell[ing]' or, he muses 'with the complacency of a father contemplating his children' upon his 'singular discoveries.'" His focus on phallic looking idols bears note as well. The "prostrate figure . . . represented a human male figure, of massive proportions." Quoted in Harvey, "American Geographics," 190.

[88] Pierce, *A Forty-Niner Speaks*, 70; "Hunting a Pass: A Sketch of Tropical Adventure," part 3, *The Atlantic Monthly* 6 (July 1860): 57.

[89] While some Americans embraced the companionate ideal of marriage during this period, given the inferior legal and social status of American women not even these marriages could be accurately described as relationships between equals. On the companionate ideal see James A. Hammerton, *Cruelty and Companionship: Conflict in Nineteenth-Century Married Life* (London, 1992), ch. 3–4; E. Anthony Rotundo, *American Manhood: Transformations in Masculinity from the Revolution to the Modern Era* (New York, 1993), 163–4.

Latina, like that of flowers, or fruit for that matter, was fleeting. Travelers like J. Goldsborough Bruff noted seeing "[a] great many aged females" during their passage through the Isthmus. William Walker's supporter William Wells admitted about Honduras that "[i]n no country that I have visited does age follow so closely upon womanhood, nor in any do the charms of youth more quickly fade." In his booster narrative, Thomas Francis Meagher offered that Costa Rican women over the age of forty (and thus beyond reproductive age) lost all charms.[90] Once a Latin American girl became a woman, many Americans asserted that she was no longer desirable.

Although the physical attractions of the Latin American girl might fade with age, one aspect of Latin American womanhood, much commented on by American men, did not decline over time. Latin American women were not only attractive because of their physical appearance, their sexuality, and the promise of success they offered the irresistible American man. Their work ethic also inspired comment among travelers, offering a vision of womanhood that was highly appealing to some men. The public labor of the Latin American woman stood in stark contrast to her lazy male counterparts. Given that antebellum Americans believed that releasing their own wives from labor outside the home was a positive good (while ignoring women's work within the home), it is hardly surprising that they would comment on the different relationship between gender and work in Latin America.[91]

Travelers frequently remarked on women's labor. It was almost a cliché of the travelogue that, as Daniel Woods put it in his guide for gold miners, the women of Latin America were "far superior to the men in industry and intelligence." Because of the strong rights of inheritance and property ownership held by women under Mexican law, Mexicanas maintained their economic power when the economic status of women north of the border was becoming increasingly tenuous. In the antebellum United States, industrialization resulted in the movement of production outside the home, while the ideology of domesticity redefined women as consumers and devalued women's labor as "housework." Antonia Castañeda has suggested that it was potential economic worth that in 1840s California transformed a Mexicana into a "Spanish Lady" or Californiana in the vision of Anglo male travelers and settlers and rendered her fit to marry. Economic worth trumped race in California.[92]

[90] Bruff, *Gold Rush*, 503; Wells, *Explorations and Adventures in Honduras*, 74; Meagher, "Holidays in Costa Rica," *HNMM* 20 (February 1860): 310.

[91] Jeanne Boydston, *Home & Work: Housework, Wages, and the Ideology of Labor in the Early Republic* (New York, 1990); Daniel T. Rodgers, *The Work Ethic in Industrial America, 1850–1920* (Chicago, 1974), 182–209.

[92] Woods, *Sixteen Months at the Gold Diggings*, 24; Castañeda, "The Political Economy of Nineteenth-Century Stereotypes of Californianas," 223–4; Ann D. Gordon and Mari Jo Buhle, "Sex and Class in Colonial and Nineteenth-Century America," in *Liberating Women's History: Theoretical and Critical Essays*, Berenice A. Carroll, ed. (Urbana, 1976), 278–300; Boydston, *Home & Work*.

C. V. COOPER DEL.

ON STONE BY J. CAMERON

BATHEING AND WASHING CORN.
AT CHINANDAGA.

Some men found women's work erotic, as in Squier's description of the "school-girly" fruit merchants. For Theodore Johnson, tortilla making provided an opportunity to admire his favorite part of the female anatomy. "Two young girls were busily engaged in pounding it between large, smooth stones. One of these *señoritas* was quite pretty, and as she gracefully bent forward in her useful employment, displayed a bust which Saratoga might envy...." Charles Ross Parke was most impressed by the labor of "two of the olive colored ladies washing corn" and then stamping on the corn with their bare feet. "Corn cake made from this meal is sweeter than ours.... I saw the feet when they came out, and I know they were *clean*. Every time after when I ate a tortilla, I imagined I could see those beautiful clean feet."[93] John M. Letts celebrated naked woman and tortilla preparation in one remarkable illustration in his guide for travelers to California (see Figure 3.7).[94]

That Latin American women worked hard was generally viewed as attractive by male observers, in part, perhaps, because "annexation" with such a woman could release a man from some of his responsibilities as breadwinner. John Stephens, who liked to remark upon entering a town that "as usual, while the don was lolling in his hammock, the women were at work," also commented admiringly on the business skills of Costa Rica's women. "All the ladies were what might be called good businessmen – they kept stores, bought and sold goods, looked out for bargains, and were particularly

[93] Johnson, *Sights in the Gold Region*, 193; Parke, *Dreams to Dust*, 128. Other observers found female labor less than arousing. George Schenck wrote that in Gatun he saw "one of the natives, a girl of about sixteen or seventeen years... go out and get a piece of sugar-cane, and commence chewing it, and occasionally she would eject the juice from her mouth into the coffee while it was being prepared outside the hut. Swain asked me if I was going to have some more coffee. I declined...." Oscar Lewis, *Sea Routes to the Gold Fields: The Migration by Water to California in 1849–1852* (New York, 1949), 178.

[94] Although Letts's illustrations were of questionable quality, and seem, in most cases, to represent "typical" experiences rather than actual events, he was adamant in the introduction to his gold-rush travel guide that "[t]he illustrations are truthful and can be relied upon as faithfully portraying the scenes they are designed to represent." They "were drawn on the spot and in order to preserve characteristics, even the attitudes represented are truthfully given." Letts, *A pictorial View of California*, p. iii.

FIGURE 3.7. "Batheing [sic] and Washing Corn at Chinandaga." Scantily clad Latin American women attracted a great deal of attention in male-authored travel narratives. Letts's guide for travelers to California provided an illustration of the "beautiful" women of Chinandaga, Nicaragua, at work and play. As women shift from bathing to working, tortilla making becomes sexualized. "In the pool are seen both sexes, the Señoritas displaying their graceful forms, without the least reserve or sense of impropriety... here is seen a party of females preparing corn for 'tortillos'; they boil it in water into which is thrown a handful of ashes; it is then put into a basket and the hull removed, by getting in with their feet; it is then washed, dried, and parched...." John M. Letts, *A pictorial View of California* (New York, 1853), 151.

NICARAGUA MEAT MARKET.

FIGURE 3.8. "Nicaraguan Meat Market." Exactly what was for sale in representations of Latin American saleswomen? Ephraim G. Squier, *Nicaragua: Its People, Scenery, Monuments, Resources, Condition and Proposed Canal* (New York, 1860), 120.

knowing in the article of coffee." The business acumen of businesswomen earned the respect of many observers, including John M. Letts, who pictured a woman shaming one deadbeat American into paying her in his illustration of the marketplace at Acapulco (see Figure 3.1). Of course it was only the unattached Americans who need fear the wrath of a Latin American businesswoman, since an "annexed" woman was happy to do his bidding. A recruiting letter from C.A., the "Special correspondent in Truxillo" to the New Orleans *Delta*, in 1860, combined a claim that Honduras was "a Land of Gold!" with the promise that a well-connected man needed to do nothing to reap the reward. "The women wash sufficient in one day to support themselves and their families for weeks" the author claimed.[95]

Some sources went so far as to suggest that American women could learn something from the laboring practices of the Latina. Visitors often remarked on the "erect and stately carriages" of some Latin American women,

[95] Stephens, *Incidents of Travel*, 1:42, 301; "Our Special Correspondent at Truxillo, August 18, 1860," New Orleans *Delta*, September 4, 1860.

especially Indian women, which was always attributed to carrying "great loads" on their heads. "The fact is suggestive" one travelogue concluded, "for, if the girls of more favored homes" in the United States "were habituated to a daily exercise in this sort of *head-work*, there would perhaps be fewer of the high shoulders, crooked backs, and puny lungs so frequently met with in these degenerate days"[96] (see Figure 3.8).

The conquest of an attractive Latina, then, could be a simple sexual escapade, but in the expansionist vision it could be much more. The discourse of the beautiful, available, and hard-working Latina complemented that of the natural resources and business opportunities of the country. For the individual American man, sex and love, and the opportunity to assert his virility presented yet another arena in which success in Latin America could come more easily than in the United States. This vision also complemented the understanding of Latin American manhood as inferior to American manhood. That the conquest of the Latin American woman could also further America's Manifest Destiny, and that individual annexation could stand for national annexation, was an added advantage.

Latin American travelogues proliferated in the 1840s and 1850s, equipped with a fairly uniform set of gendered stereotypes that promoted American expansionism in the region. Foremost among these were the assertions that Latin American men were lazy and effeminate and that Latin American women were both captivating and easily captivated by American men. Ordinary male travelers in Central America seem to have concurred with these assessments. For many of them, the experience of Latin American travel was marked by the opportunity to embrace martial practices they might have disavowed at home. Americans in Central America drank, seduced, and fought, and they brought these experiences with them when they arrived in California or back in the eastern United States, disseminating and promoting martial manhood.

Gendered expectations about the proper behavior of both men and women were central to both the constitution of martial manhood on the new Latin American frontier and the popular representation of the region as within the scope of America's Manifest Destiny between 1848 and 1860. The small skull of the Latin American man, ethnologists argued, proved that he was destined to fall to the larger-skulled American. He was, in short, a perfect foil for the American man, who was bound to appear manly, brave, and virile in comparison.

The Latin American woman, by contrast, was strong where the Latin American man was weak, brave where he was cowardly, and both beautiful and hard working. In her own way, she was also a foil for the American

[96] Oran, "Tropical Journeyings," *HNMM* 16 (March 1858): 470–1. There were very few American authorities recommending strenuous exercise for middle-class women in the antebellum era. One of the few was Catharine Beecher. See, for example, Catharine Beecher and Harriet Beecher Stowe, *The American Woman's Home* (New York, 1869).

man, whom she found irresistible. In his domination over both men and women in Latin America, the American man, even one who had limited success in the United States, could prove that he was successful and manly. The conquest of the Latin American woman offered tangible evidence of the success of aggressive American manhood, and the success of Manifest Destiny as well. At the same time that the Latin American woman offered the greatest possible evidence that annexation was a civilizing force, the effeminacy of the Latin American man assured martial men that victory in the region would come easily. It should come as little surprise that some Americans were willing to follow the implications of the Latin American encounter to its logical conclusions, and, like Sam Houston, plan or join a filibuster.

4

William Walker and the Regeneration
of Martial Manhood

> Character is what involuntarily commands respect.... what makes itself felt, whether its owner be clothed in rags, or in purple and fine linen.... The man who has character must be independent, fearless, and discriminating in his judgment. He is not influenced by the position a man holds, or the clothes he wears, in forming the estimate of him.
>
> – *Putnam's Monthly Magazine*, 1854

William Walker, or the "gray-eyed man of destiny" as he was commonly known, rose to fame in 1855 on the basis of a remarkable accomplishment. With a band of fifty-eight recruits from San Francisco, he was able to seize control of the government of Nicaragua, becoming commander in chief and later president of the country. Alone among filibusters in a decade that saw repeated attempts to capture new territory in the Western Hemisphere, Walker could claim success, if only for a limited period. In May of 1857 Walker surrendered to the commander of the United States Navy after falling to the combined pressure of a Central American army, Great Britain, and thwarted American shipping interests. One of the preeminent models of martial manhood, Walker was fearless in the face of battle, independent of both family and law, and supremely self-confident. He returned to the region for two more failed filibustering forays before meeting his death, at age thirty-six, in front of a Honduran firing line in 1860.[1]

William Walker became one of the key cultural icons of the 1850s as a result of these exploits. His whereabouts in Nicaragua and in the United States were closely watched and reported in newspapers across the country. He was especially popular among working men in the South and in cities from San Francisco to New York.[2] At one of the many public meetings held

---

[1] The best book-length biography of Walker is Albert Z. Carr, *The World and William Walker* (New York, 1963).

[2] Walker had little problem recruiting men in any of these places in the late 1850s. In April of 1859 Walker was still a commanding figure in San Francisco, although one observer doubted

for Walker in New York City in 1856, Roberdeau Wheat, an experienced filibuster and southern gentleman who fought in the U.S.-Mexico War, with López in Cuba, as well as with Walker, addressed his requests to "the poor, the noble, it is to them that I would appeal – to the poor men, the laboring men of the city." Wheat's request resulted in $1,300 in support of Walker.[3] According to *Harper's New Monthly Magazine*, Walker was encouraged to speak "in reply to the cheers with which he was greeted" whenever he appeared in public in New York City, while one witness remembered that "Walker's reception in New York, on his return to the United States, was like that of a conqueror. . . . tens of thousands of citizens flocked to see the hero." Visitors to New York City in 1856 might not get to meet Walker himself, but they could attend a three-act musical set in Nicaragua, featuring "General Walker, the Hope of Freedom." Theaters in San Francisco and Sacramento also presented Walker dramas that year, starring an actor who had actually been to Nicaragua during Walker's presidency.[4]

In late 1859, as Walker toured the country raising money for what would be his final invasion of Central America, *The Atlantic Monthly* featured "The Experience of Samuel Absalom, Filibuster," a two-part memoir anonymously penned by David Deaderick, a young veteran of Walker's first Nicaraguan campaign.[5] Like many of Walker's recruits, Deaderick's alter ego, "known

that he wanted to return to Nicaragua. "Walker is . . . endeavoring to raise a party to invade Sonora and avenge the murder of Henry A. Crabb and his party. There is but little doubt of his ability to get a thousand men to go with him to Sonora but it is thought that he will never again attempt to invade Nicaragua so long as the English and French are on the alert for him." Billington Crum Whiting letter to Susan Helen (Coligrove) Whiting, April 3, 1859, HL.

[3] "Aid for Walker and the Filibusters, Great Sympathetic Meeting in the Tabernacle," *NYH*, December 21, 1856; see also "The Great Walker Meeting in the Park at New York," *New York Evening Mirror*, May 24, 1856; "Nicaragua at Tammany Hall," and "Walker Visits Wallack's Theater," unidentified clippings, John Hill Wheeler Manuscript Collection, Series 1, #11: 202, LOC; also "City News: Sympathy for Nicaragua," Wheeler Collection, Series 1, #12: 97; Charles Dufour, *Gentle Tiger: The Gallant Life of Roberdeau Wheat* (Baton Rouge, 1957), 77–99.

[4] *HNMM* XV (July 1857), 402; James Jeffrey Roche, *The Story of the Filibusters* (New York, 1891), 159; Robert E. May, *The Southern Dream of a Caribbean Empire, 1854–1861* (Baton Rouge, 1973), 77; Robert E. May, *Manifest Destiny's Underworld: Filibustering in Antebellum America* (Chapel Hill, 2002), 71. The Know-Nothing journal *Young Sam* parodied the popularity of filibustering theater and Secretary of State William Marcy's inability to deal with the Nicaragua situation in "The Central America in Broadway." Dialogue includes Marcy desperately pleading for help when he sees a filibuster, who, on closer examination, turns out to be a pig. *Young Sam* 1 (January 26, 1856): 84.

[5] "The Experience of Samuel Absalom, Filibuster." *Atlantic Monthly* IV (December 1859): 653–66, V (January 1860): 38–60. That Deaderick based "The Experience of Samuel Absalom, Filibuster" on his own experience is supported by manuscript materials in the LOC. See the typescript, "The Stirring Adventures of a Lad from Knoxville, Tennessee, David Deaderick III, Who fought with Filibuster William Walker in Nicaragua. (With partial list of companions).

somewhere as Samuel Absalom," decides to join Walker on his journey to Nicaragua after bad fortune in the gold mines.[6] Reduced in California to donning flour sacks for clothing, he is embarrassed by his appearance and depressed by his failure. Deaderick makes clear at the outset that the increasing class stratification in California has rendered his own situation untenable. "Once, no man knew but this battered hat I sit under might partially cover the head of a nobleman or a man of honor; but men begin to show their quality by the outside, as they do elsewhere in the world, and are judged and spoken to accordingly."

With Walker's promise of 250 acres of land in Nicaragua, and $25 a month soldier's wages, Deaderick takes off to an unknown land to risk his life for the glory of the soldier's uniform. He hopes to improve his appearance and to prove himself a man of character among the sort of "Men of Character" described in *Putnam's Monthly Magazine* in 1854, independent, fearless men who are not "influenced by the position a man holds, or the clothes he wears."[7] Deaderick flees to Nicaragua in order to change his luck and find a place where the martial virtues count more than the appearance of financial prosperity in determining a man's fate. Unfortunately Deaderick finds manly character in Nicaragua as difficult a thing to judge, and to reveal, as it was in San Francisco. By the close of the narrative, Deaderick has lost his illusions about Nicaragua and the opportunity for proving his manhood on the filibustering battlefield. The author's message is clear: Walker's behavior has made a mockery of his idealistic pronouncements in both 1856 Nicaragua and 1859 America. Martial manhood will not be vindicated through filibustering.[8]

Typewritten Notes presented to the LOC by George Magruder Battey III, Washington D.C. January 23, 1940." See also "The Diary or Register of David Anderson Deaderick, esq. Of Knoxville, Tennessee, born 1797, died 1873. Intimate Family glimpses, natural phenomena, scourge of the civil war, customs of the times, 1824–July, 1872," 19, LOC Manuscript Division; Charles H. Brown, *Agents of Manifest Destiny: The Lives and Times of the Filibusters* (Chapel Hill, 1980), 159.

[6] In 1855 James Carson Jamison was a young Missourian mining gold in Northern California when he "heard of Walker's battles in Nicaragua" and joined the filibuster. "My blood grew hot at the thought of the stirring adventures that awaited me if I could attach myself to Walker's army." James Carson Jamison, *With Walker in Nicaragua or Reminiscences of an Officer in the American Phalanx* (Columbia, MO, 1909), 60. Another filibuster remembered in February 1857 that recruits from gold country were being courted. "Placerville, Coloma, and other mountain towns, were literally illuminated with flaming posters, bearing, in mammoth type, the eye-catching motto, 'Ho, for the sunny south!'" William Frank Stewart, *Last of the Fillibusters* (Sacramento, 1857), 7. On gold miners as recruits see also Carr, *The World and William Walker*, 116.

[7] "Men of Character," *PMM* III (March 1854): 267–9.

[8] "The Experience of Samuel Absalom, Filibuster." *Atlantic Monthly* IV (December 1859): 653; "Men of Character," 267–9.

"The Experience of Samuel Absalom, Filibuster" is a remarkable narrative. Not only does it provide a lens on the world of filibustering in its account of the motivation of the leadership and troops in Nicaragua and the relationship between the American troops and the Nicaraguan people, it also proves revealing of American culture back home. Specifically, Deaderick's narrative illuminates the tensions in antebellum America over economic success, over the relationship between a man and his occupation, and over the increasing importance of appearance in the public evaluation of character. Deaderick is drawn to Nicaragua, he tells us, because he, like other American men, perceives that the growing importance of the appearance of prosperity, in contrast to his manly virtues, has limited his opportunities in America. He believes that "once, no man knew" or could judge for certain, just who was a "nobleman or a man of honor" based on the clothing that a man wore. But by the 1850s, Deaderick claims, "men begin to show their quality by the outside" and appearance, particularly the appearance of propriety, had become the measure of character. Deaderick's story is as much a tale of the difficulties that martial men faced proving their manly character in the changing social and economic conditions of antebellum America as it is a critique of William Walker's Nicaraguan project.

Deaderick's crisis would have resonated with many readers – he was not alone in struggling to reconcile with the increasing demand that a man of quality also be a man of good appearance. Americans were divided over the propriety of aggressive expansionism, and especially Walker's ventures in Central America, for a host of reasons. Not only was filibustering illegal, but it was critiqued by some Northerners as an immoral technique on the part of a southern "slave power" to create new slave states out of "redeemed" territory. But as the national debate over filibustering reveals, supporters and opponents were often divided as well over Walker as a model of manly action. This chapter will explore how the American reception of William Walker's Nicaraguan adventures was shaped by the contested nature of class and manhood in 1850s America and by the perception that the appearance of financial success had replaced "traditional" martial virtues as the measure of a man. Debates over Walker recorded in the press of the time and memoirs and contemporary fiction about Nicaragua reveal that the parameters of appropriate and inappropriate masculine practices were being actively contested by antebellum Americans who projected their own anxieties about a changing American society onto Walker and his project in Central America. This chapter will argue that the reception of foreign relations in the 1850s was influenced by cultural considerations, and by a desire among some struggling white American men to make a hero of William Walker, the man who promised, but finally could not deliver, martial manhood triumphant over money, appearance, and racial inferiors.

Substance versus Trappings in the Construction of Manly Character

The phrase *manly character* is somewhat redundant, since character, as understood by antebellum Americans, was attributed almost exclusively to white men. Character was an internal state that theoretically was not signified by dress or appearance but which should "make itself felt," as *Putnam's* put it, none the less. But it is significant to note that when antebellum Americans talked about character among men, they also were talking about masculinity, about the practices that "embodied the currently accepted answer to the problem of the legitimacy of patriarchy, which guarantees (or is taken to guarantee) the dominant position of men and subordination of women."[9]

The economic and social transformation of the antebellum period posed new challenges to older models of patriarchy. "More and more rapid industrialization and urbanization, the flood tide of immigration, the possibility of women's rights – all were felt to contribute to the further erosion of male identity." In the face of these threats, martial and restrained men divided over their definitions of character and the proper means of displaying their masculinity. Historians have explored the role that the protection of honor played in the antebellum South in promoting male violence. Honor shaped the day-to-day oppression of African-Americans in slavery, it provided support for dueling in the South, long after it died out in the North, and it helped exacerbate the sectional conflict by turning political differences into injuries that demanded personal responses. Because southern men talked about their honor so much, and because southern men sometimes responded to insults in a radically different manner than northern men, it is tempting to see honor as a sectional phenomenon.[10]

The southern honor code was not that different, however, from codes of behavior that guided many northern men. While it is true that southern white men of radically different economic statuses proved ready to uphold any perceived threat to their honor through violence, as Eliott Gorn has shown in his study of bare-knuckle boxing, many urban working men and recently arrived immigrants in the North shared the understanding that violence was an appropriate means for proving their manhood. Nor were supporters of the physical display of manhood limited to a particular ethnicity or class. Men of radically different occupations could and did display their strength,

---

[9] R. W. Connell, *Masculinities* (Berkeley, 1995), 77. On the gendered nature of character see Mary Ryan, *Women in Public: Between Banners and Ballots, 1825–1880* (Baltimore, 1990).

[10] G. J. Barker-Benfield, *The Horrors of the Half-Known Life: Male Attitudes Toward Women and Sexuality in Nineteenth-Century America*, 2nd ed. (New York, 2000), 189. On southern honor see Kenneth S. Greenberg, *Honor and Slavery: Lies, Duels, Noses, Masks, Dressing as a Woman, Gifts, Strangers, Humanitarianism, Death, Slave Rebellions, the Proslavery Argument, Baseball, Hunting and Gambling in the Old South* (Princeton 1996); Edward L. Ayers, *Vengeance and Justice: Crime and Punishment in the Nineteenth Century American South* (New York, 1984); Bertram Wyatt-Brown, *Southern Honor: Ethics and Behavior in the Old South* (New York, 1982).

concentration, and will in public, by participating in athletics, by fighting fires as part of economically heterogeneous volunteer fire companies, or by going to war. Whether northern or southern, Irish or native-born, merchant or mechanic, these martial men believed that their power as men lay in their ability to publicly display masculine attributes like physical strength and bravery.[11]

Restrained men agreed with martial men that it was of great importance to uphold and display their manhood. But because the meanings of manhood for restrained men were so different from those of martial men, they naturally displayed their manliness through different actions. Restrained men demonstrated their manliness through their religious faith, their domestic virtue and treatment of family members, their ability to abstain from drinking alcoholic beverages, and their success as breadwinners. Since many of the accomplishments that restrained men valued were domestic, most of their displays of their own manly character occurred in the home, or in semi-private settings like the office, church, or temperance meeting. Martial men, by contrast, placed their character on display in highly public arenas like the street or pub. As a result of this imbalance between the largely private nature of restrained manhood and the public nature of martial manhood, martial men depended on the public display and acknowledgement of their masculinity to a far greater degree than did restrained men.

As Deaderick makes clear, it was not manly activity but the appearance of prosperity and "quality" that was too often taken as the measure of character in antebellum America. As an advertisement for a San Francisco clothier asked in 1856, "Who is there that does not feel averse to stand and talk with a man in a mean garb?"[12] High rates of geographic mobility were a fact of life in antebellum America, and not only in the overnight gold-rush metropolis of San Francisco. Less than twenty-two percent of residents of Cincinnati in 1840, for example, still resided in that city in 1861.[13] Among the transient antebellum population it was hardly possible

---

[11] Elliott J. Gorn, *The Manly Art: Bare Knuckle Prize Fighting in America* (Ithaca, 1986). Urban volunteer firefighters were active supporters of filibusterers. New Orleans firemen fought and died under Narciso López in Cuba, and San Francisco firemen fought and died under William Walker in Nicaragua. *Daily Alta California*, January 5, 1856; May, *Manifest Destiny's Underworld*, 102. One San Francisco fire company in 1856 sent its stock of muskets to Nicaragua to aid Walker. As the San Francisco *Herald* reported, "Just previous to the sailing of the steamer it was ascertained that a number of percussion lock muskets, belonging to the Manhattan Fire Company of this city, were taken from the engine-house during the night." "The Departure of the Walker Reinforcements from San Francisco," San Francisco *Herald*, October 6, 1856, quoted in "Nicaragua and the Filibusters," *The Living Age* 49 (April 19, 1856): 139. On volunteer firefighting as a display of manliness see Amy S. Greenberg, *Cause for Alarm: The Volunteer Fire Department in the Nineteenth-Century City* (Princeton, 1998).

[12] "A good dress is the best mark of gentility," *San Francisco Morning Globe*, July 12, 1856.

[13] Steven J. Ross, *Workers on the Edge: Work, Leisure, and Politics in Industrializing Cincinnati, 1788–1890* (New York, 1985), 162.

that a man could be universally known, and judged, on the basis of his character.

In the absence of real knowledge of a person, strangers turned to the outer man for confirmation of character. In this way, character was rendered transparent – revealed through appearance. It is for this reason, as Karen Halttunen has documented, that hundreds of etiquette manuals and advice guides were directed toward improving that first impression. "The art of engineering all outward expressions of the self in order to impress others had become a central concern" in the antebellum period. John Kasson has posited a similar explanation for the increasing emphasis placed on rituals of polite behavior among the emerging middle-class. Both martial and restrained men agreed with *Putnam's Magazine* that a true man of character could, in theory, be dressed in rags. But because martial men depended on the public display of their masculinity to a much greater degree than did restrained men, the increasing focus on appearance as the sole marker of character in public proved far more devastating to the martial man, whatever his financial status, than it did to the restrained man. Given that restrained men, basing their identity in their success as breadwinners, were more likely to have achieved financial success than martial men, they also were more likely to appear well in the first place.[14]

The meaning and display of character was thus contested territory in the 1850s. American men were divided over what manly character was and how manly men should act. A man of character might be "clothed in rags" like the hypothetical man of character described in *Putnam's Magazine*. But as Deaderick's experience in San Francisco makes clear, a good character, and martial virtues, were of little use to a financial failure if others believed they could judge him on the basis of appearance. Although *Putnam's* might caution readers that a man of character is "not influenced by the position a man holds, or the clothes he wears," it was clear to the reader of advice guides, to a stranger walking down the street, and to David Deaderick, that the man of character also should be a man of good appearance. After all, even *Putnam's* agreed that "character.... makes itself felt." The dismay

[14] Karen Halttunen, *Confidence Men and Painted Women: A Study of Middle-Class Culture in America, 1830–1870* (New Haven, 1982), 40; John Kasson, *Rudeness and Civility: Manners in Nineteenth-Century Urban America* (New York, 1990). On character in general, and the relationship between the inner and outer man, see Thomas Augst, *The Clerk's Tale: Young Men and Moral Life in Nineteenth-Century America* (Chicago, 2003); Tamara Plakins Thornton, *Handwriting in America: A Cultural History* (New Haven, 1996), 42–107; Warren I. Susman, "'Personality' and the making of Twentieth-Century Culture," in *New Directions in American Intellectual History*, John Higham and Paul Conklin, eds. (Baltimore, 1979), 212–26; E. Anthony Rotundo, *American Manhood: Transformations in Masculinity from the Revolution to the Modern Era* (New York, 1993), 222–7; Roberta J. Park, "Biological Thought, Athletics, and the Formation of the 'Man of Character': 1830–1900," in *Manliness and Morality: Middle Class Masculinity in Britain and America, 1800–1940*, J. A. Mangan and James Walvin, eds. (Manchester, UK, 1987), 7–33.

that Deaderick expresses about men displaying their "quality" externally is the fear that character had in fact become transparent – readily visible to all. Deaderick becomes a filibuster in order to escape from the increasing antebellum focus on appearance. In Nicaragua, he believes, he will be able to prove his manly character through martial acts and find an arena where the outward man, or appearance, is not a transparent indicator of the inward man, or character. In Nicaragua, Deaderick believes, his martial manhood will finally become manifest.

It quickly becomes clear to Deaderick that appearance and character are no more easily resolved in Nicaragua than in San Francisco, in part because no one in Nicaragua appears well. Walker's "yellow-faced, ragged, and dirty" cavalry is mounted "on horses or mules of every color, shape, and size." Only their "deadly garniture, rifles, revolvers, and bowie-knives, and their fierce and shaggy looks," keep the new recruits from bursting into laughter when they appear in port. Soon Deaderick looks no better. Food, clothing, and supplies are strictly rationed by Walker's bankrupt army. A general lack of morale takes external expression in the troops. "There was a morbid, yellowish glaze, almost universal, on their faces, and an unnatural listlessness and utter lack of animation in all their movements and conversation, which contrasted painfully with the boisterous hilarity and rugged healthiness of our late Californian fellow-travelers."

Deaderick's hopes for an improved wardrobe also are dashed. He enviously recounts the uniform of the "soldierlike and respectable" foot soldier, "black felt hats, blue cotton trousers, brogans, and blue flannel shirts, with the letter of their company and the number of the regiment sewed upon the breast in characters of white cloth." Yet even though their uniforms had "become somewhat greasy and louse-seamed" by the time he arrived in Nicaragua, Deaderick finds it difficult to obtain any sort of uniform or exterior marker of his new status as a man of character. Most troops have no "soldier's uniform ... only the poor man's uniform of rags and dirt, and the spirit of careless, disease-worn, doomed men." He is dismayed that even in Nicaragua he is forced to remain "poor" in appearance. Respectability, in the form of a proper uniform, is beyond his grasp.[15]

---

[15] "The Experience of Samuel Absalom, Filibuster," *Atlantic Monthly* IV, 654, 656–7, 665. The poor appearance of Walker's troops was regularly commented on both by his own soldiers and by outside observers. James Carson Jamison remembered that "[t]he Americans were uniformed in motley fashion. There was no regulation army uniform, and even if there had been the government was without funds for its maintenance. Most of the officers wore the uniform of their rank in the United States army, many bringing their uniforms with them to Nicaragua." William Frank Stewart claimed that the filibusters were so poorly clothed that as they fled Nicaragua for the US on the frigate *Roanoke*, the first lieutenant ordered them "to throw into the sea every article of clothing which we possessed" because they were "literally swarming with vermin." Jamison, *With Walker in Nicaragua*, 119; Stewart, *Last of the Fillibusters*, 56, see also 46.

With his appearance in crisis, his behavior quickly degenerates. Like other soldiers, Deaderick is forced to steal to survive. First he takes only food, later he takes a mule from a priest. Deaderick addresses the reader directly on this issue: "Let no one reflect upon the writer" he states. "For him there was no choice; and if he is chargeable with moral depravity, it must be elsewhere, – forsooth, in joining with one who made war unprovided with a military chest sufficient to cover expenses. However this is no matter, one way or the other. The private character of the relater, Samuel Absalom, is not before the reader; nor is it expected that he will care to turn his eye upon it for a moment."

Of course, it is exactly the private character of the man that is of importance here. The public man has already been found wanting in appearance in San Francisco, and now in Nicaragua he is riding a stolen mule without a proper uniform for a cause that Deaderick refers to as "the squalid game." But what Deaderick recognizes in his statement is the difficulty of representing character, and revealing it. He reminds the reader that character is not evident from appearance, even the appearance of moral depravity presented by his theft. Character is not transparent, a thing that can be discerned with a momentary turn of an eye. Deaderick clings to the belief that his character will reveal itself through martial acts, even if unmanly acts do not besmirch it. But the fact that he places blame on Walker's lack of money, rather than the manner or cause of the war in Nicaragua, indicates how difficult it is for even as thoughtful a man as Deaderick to separate the question of character from appearance, or from that key to a good appearance, money.[16]

Deaderick's fictional alter ego and the non-fictional Walker shared difficulties in displaying their manly character through their appearance. Few military leaders have been less physically impressive looking than the "gray-eyed man of destiny."[17] The adoring and verbose poet Joaquin Miller said simply that "Walker was not of imposing presence." *Blackwell's Magazine* informed its British readers that "[i]n personal appearance he is not at all what one would suppose such a daring and successful filibuster to be" with features, another source commented, "of no particular significance." *Harper's Weekly* called him "effeminate in appearance" (see Figure 4.1).[18]

---

[16] "The Experience of Samuel Absalom, Filibuster," *Atlantic Monthly* IV, 654–8.

[17] At the time of his initial victories, there was some difference of opinion about his actual appearance. One minister reported to have gathered from others that "in personal appearance, Walker was tall and handsome, with a muscular though slender frame and a commanding figure. His forehead was prominent, his lips firm, his big grey [sic] eyes keen and penetrating, and his well-set jaws indicated decision of character." Daniel B. Lucas, *Nicaragua: War of the Filibusters* (Richmond, 1896), 18.

[18] Joaquin Miller, "With Walker in Nicaragua" (1871), in *The Complete Poetical Works of Joaquin Miller* (New York, 1972), 18; "Nicaragua and the Filibusters," *Blackwell's Magazine*, quoted in *The Living Age* 49 (April 19, 1856): 138; Lucas, *Nicaragua: War of the Filibusters*, 116; *Harper's Weekly* 1 (March 7, 1857): 151.

GEN. WILLIAM WALKER, OF NICARAGUA.—[FROM A PHOTOGRAPH BY MEADE BROTHERS.]

FIGURE 4.1. "General William Walker, of Nicaragua." *Harper's Weekly* wrote that the general was "certainly one of the most remarkable men of the age" but was "effeminate in appearance." *Harper's Weekly* 1 (May 23, 1857): 332.

Both northern and southern newspapers expressed disappointment and dismay upon first seeing Walker, since, as the New York *Herald* reported, "General Walker does not look like the terrible man he seems to be. . . . When his features are in repose [he] does not look like a man of much energy." As an account in the New Orleans *Delta* titled "The Man of Destiny. A Lesson for Old and Young Fogies" put it, Walker "is a very ordinary-looking person, and cannot boast of any fine physical gifts. . . . He is considerably under the 'middle height,' standing barely five feet four in his boots, and nothing strikingly intellectual in his countenance can be said to counterbalance this serious deficiency in inches."[19] His appearance dismayed his own soldiers,

[19] *NYH*, June 17, 1857. See also F. H. Duffee, "Gen. William Walker, Commander in Chief of the Nicaraguan Forces," *The Philadelphia Sunday Mercury*, no date, in the Wheeler

one of whom noted upon meeting Walker, "There he sat! A little, white-haired, white-eyebrowed, boyish-looking man...."[20]

Even Walker's own filibustering allies had difficulty finding much to praise in his appearance. According to one supporter, "to the casual observer, his personal appearance, his mild imperfection of face, would not indicate the determined force of his character." Another close ally of Walker's, William Vincent Wells, agreed. "Few persons unacquainted with General Walker would imagine, from his personal appearance, that so much ability lay beneath so plain an exterior. In stature, little above five feet four, he presents the appearance of a rather dull, slow-moulded person." It was generally accepted that on Walker, "the mouth, that feature which usually expresses so much, indicates nothing of the real character of the man," and that his "thin, light-colored, and closely cut" hair also was cause for disappointment. James Carson Jamison, who fought for Walker, claimed that "his vital energy" was "surprisingly great" given his "small stature."[21]

In an age when phrenology promised to reveal an individual's character through a study of bumps on the head, observers looked to his face for the key to his personality. In many men the forehead was revealing, but this both Wells and the *Delta* dismissed as "broad and rounding," but without, the *Delta* remarked, "being unusually characteristic or remarkable." His nose was another disappointment. Walker's nose, according to the *Delta*, "belongs to the school which Nicholas Nickleby denominates the 'composite.'" Wells was more direct, commenting that Walker's nose was "by no means of that description which physiognomists declare belongs to men of genius. The remark of Napoleon, that a long nose and dilated nostrils always denote the ability to carry out any plan with vigor and promptitude, seems in this case to have gone astray." To make matters worse, according to Jamison, "a woman's voice was scarcely softer than Walker's."[22]

Deaderick had only a uniform to negotiate, but Walker's entire physical person inspired suspicion about his martial virtues. The difficulties of

Collection, Series I, #10, scrapbook; "The Hero of Nicaragua," New Orleans *Times*, July 19, 1857; "Biographical Sketch of General Walker" *NYH*, Dec. 26, 1855; "Who Walker Is" *Louisville Times*, January 15, 1856; "The Man of Destiny," New Orleans *Sunday Delta*, July 27, 1856.

[20] Stewart, *Last of the Fillibusters*, 11.

[21] John H. Wheeler, manuscript of "A new work on Nicaragua ..." Wheeler Collection, Series II, # 1: 85; Wells, *Walker's Expedition to Nicaragua*, 199–200; "The Man of Destiny," New Orleans *Sunday Delta*, July 27, 1856; "A letter from a Young Washingtonian on his travels" letter dated November 29, 1855, San Juan del Sud, to Messrs. Gales and Seaton. Unidentified paper, Wheeler Collection, Series 1, #21: 51; Jamison, *With Walker in Nicaragua*, 18.

[22] "The Man of Destiny," New Orleans *Sunday Delta*, July 27, 1856; Wells, *Walker's Expedition to Nicaragua*, 199–200; Jamison, *With Walker in Nicaragua*, 18. See Charles Colbert, *A Measure of Perfection; Phrenology and the Fine Arts in America* (Chapel Hill, 1998) on the difficulties of aligning the inward and outward man. On the gendered implications of phrenology, and especially the feminine associations of the small head, see Nancy Leys Stepan," "Race and Gender: The Role of Analogy in Science," *ISIS* 77 (June 1986): 269.

projecting a martial image with an appearance and voice like Walker's were obviously great. In Deaderick's account, however, Walker's character makes itself felt, regardless of his appearance. In the course of the story he faces down rebellious troops, "fierce, big-whiskered" officers, and the Costa Ricans, and he proves with the smallest acts that he is "no trifler." Amidst the squalor, General Walker alone maintains a reputation for "the iron will and reckless courage of the true man of destiny." That the soldiers do not sooner revolt against their condition Deaderick attributes entirely to "fear, though no love, of General Walker." Walker seems to provide evidence that outward appearance, even among martial men, is no key to character. As Deaderick writes, "though there was a nasal whine in the tone of the little General, and no great fire in his unmeaning eye, there was yet a quiet self-reliance about him extremely imposing, and which, as I thought, reached back of any temporary sufflation as tyrant of Rivas, and was passed upon perennial character."[23]

The men may fear Walker, but they also despise him. Deaderick quickly learns that "the hatred towards General Walker and the service seemed almost universal amongst the privates." Virtually all of the soldiers feel as though Walker enticed them to Nicaragua "under false pretenses." Not only does he deny them promised wages, and decent food and clothing, but he forces them to bear these indignities, since without a passport from Walker himself, fleeing the country is impossible. Once Costa Rica offers Walker's soldiers free transit back to the United States, desertion becomes an epidemic among the men. Begrudgingly, Deaderick deserts both Walker and his hopes of proving himself as he joins the exodus.[24]

Deaderick concludes his narrative with an attack on the romantic fiction that leads boys to war, and he returns to his alter ego for one last act of resistance, tellingly an attack on the very uniform he craved upon first landing in Central America. "Samuel Absalom tore the large, dirty canvas letters M.R., signifying Mounted Ranger, off from this blue flannel shirtbreast; and his experience as filibuster in Nicaragua closed." Deaderick begrudgingly acknowledges the importance of appearance when he ends his own "experience as filibuster" through a simple tear of clothing. Deaderick dramatizes the transparency of character by showing that the character of "Samuel Absalom, filibuster" can be reduced to a pair of letters on a uniform.[25]

Throughout "Samuel Absalom, Filibuster," Deaderick struggles to resolve the tension between the inward and outward man, between substance and trappings. Of the many failures of the war, it is the failure to display his "quality" that Deaderick most bemoans. Deaderick neither looks the part of the soldier nor is ever able to prove his martial virtues on the field. Walker

---

[23] "The Experience of Samuel Absalom, Filibuster," *Atlantic Monthly* IV, 660.
[24] Ibid.
[25] Ibid., 60.

does not look the part of the soldier either, and although he proves himself a man of will, he, too, ultimately fails as both a man, and as a filibuster, because he lacks so many other things – money, diplomacy, and, seemingly, human sympathy as well. For Deaderick, Nicaragua is a lost opportunity, not so much because the chance to bring democratic institutions to Nicaragua has failed (the ostensible purpose of the expedition), but because displaying his martial virtues through heroic acts and a good appearance proves just as difficult as it was in San Francisco.

The Promise of Regeneration

The cultural negotiations that shaped Deaderick's narrative – what it meant to be a man in a time of economic and social transformation, how to make manhood manifest, and the mutually constitutive nature of gender and American foreign relations – are central elements of most American writing on expansionism in the antebellum period. Political tracts, booster travelogues, and the journals and letters of ordinary travelers reveal the contested nature of the twin issues of manhood and success in America. Walker explicitly promised the "regeneration" of Central America, but he implicitly offered the chance for personal regeneration to the martial men who followed him.[26]

Or so Walker's supporters believed. *The Atlantic Monthly* was not alone in pondering the conditions that drove urban men to follow Walker. In the fictional 1857 story "Mr. Seedy," *Harper's Monthly* told the sad tale of a New Yorker who was raised a gentleman but left destitute by his father's untimely death. When the narrator of the tale meets Mr. Seedy in a New York boarding house he is indeed seedy looking, in "threadbare coat buttoned over invisible linen . . . in short the pervading evidences of one so young of gentility gone to seed."[27] Seedy is snubbed by other guests and condescended to by the servants, a condition that leaves him wild-eyed and suicidal. The narrator secretly follows him through town. At first he worries that Seedy, walking near the river, will drown himself, or that he will rob someone. But as Seedy turns onto Broadway, and enters a doorway,

in a moment, the terrible reality flashed across my mind. Up those stairs were the head-quarters of the Walker Relief Committee. Mr. Seedy was about to join the filibusters! Had I seen him attempt self-destruction, I should have endeavored to prevent it. Had I seen him commit a highway robbery, I should have deemed the act perilous, and a sad evidence of 'mental insanity.' But *this* made my blood run cold.[28]

---

[26] On Walker's promise to "regenerate" Central America see William Walker, *The War in Nicaragua* (Mobile, 1860); Horace Bell, "Confessions of a Filibuster," *The Golden Era*, July 23, 1876.

[27] "Mr. Seedy," *HNMM* 15 (September 1857): 529–33.

[28] Ibid., 530.

Seedy admits that he desired "only to end my miserable existence, and have chosen, rather than drown as a suicide, to be shot or hanged or starved as a hero." The narrator manages to dissuade Seedy from joining the fili-busters, and the story ends happily with a wealthy and well-dressed Seedy embraced by those who previously shunned him, most importantly his fi-ancé's once-dismissive parents.[29]

"Mr. Seedy" provides another view of the difficulties facing martial men in antebellum America. The force that leads Seedy to try to enlist in New York – an inability to compete in a world in which appearance is the primary measure of a man – is the same one that leads Deaderick to enlist in San Francisco. In Nicaragua, Seedy believes he can finally succeed as a hero, even if in death. But the story more directly condemns this impulse than does Deaderick's narrative. In what is clearly a cautionary tale written from a restrained perspective, Seedy proves himself a man not through martial action (indeed the author equates filibustering with the clearly unheroic act of suicide) but by regaining his fiancé. Seedy is unmanned when his wife's family rejects him, and he proves his manhood by regaining his patriarchal authority. In other words, Seedy's manhood is achieved when he takes his proper place in a nuclear family. *Harper's Monthly* places a clearly classed spin on this chain of events by emphasizing Seedy's "genteel" origins. It might be acceptable (if ultimately futile) for a working man to join Walker out of desperation, but for a man of quality there is only one possible route to masculine power, the embrace of, and by, family. Of course given the fact that Seedy only regains his fiancé through the sheer luck of an inheritance, *Harper's* never actually offers a solution to the problem that drove Deaderick, Seedy, and thousands of antebellum American men to filibustering excursions in the first place.

Men continued to be attracted to filibustering after Walker's banish-ment in 1857. This was primarily because territorial expansionism into Latin America promised immense rewards to its exponents. While these two stories focus on men who failed to achieve success and authority in antebellum America, and who turned to Walker out of desperation, it would be wrong to assume that only the desperate heeded his call. A wide variety of American men joined filibustering excursions – from Freemasons motivated by anti-Catholicism and the supposed brotherhood of man to U.S.-Mexico War soldiers who were having difficulty readjusting to civilian life. College students and European idealists fleeing the failed revolutions of 1848 joined Walker's army. Wealthy southern gentlemen like Roberdeau Wheat and John Quitman became highly visible symbols of the cross-class appeal of filibus-tering, which offered an exceptional opportunity for male camaraderie and close male friendship. As Robert May has illustrated, many filibusters lucky

---

[29] Ibid., 531.

enough to return alive from one failed venture actively searched out another to join.[30]

Filibustering offered special appeal to young urban men looking for a thrill. Members of the violent, homo-social, "sporting culture" that developed in America's cities thrilled to urban amusements from brothels, to cock fights, to the theater. The illegal excitement of filibustering offered another masculine diversion. James E. Kerrigan, a twenty-seven-year-old New York City councilman and U.S.-Mexico War veteran, who would later serve in the Union Army and U.S. Congress, apparently found his activities as elected official, Democratic Party political thug, and volunteer fire company member insufficiently exciting. Kerrigan put his promising political career on hold to follow Walker to Nicaragua in 1856, bragging to a reporter from the New York *Herald* that he was bringing fifty men with him. Gregarious, personable, and with a reputation as a "natural born fighter... as ready with his pistol as at fisticuffs," Kerrigan chose to put his skills to work on the new frontier.[31]

Most filibustering recruits, however, were, like David Deaderick, economic failures. Unsuccessful miners, apprentices dismissed from their trades, urban mechanics facing wage cuts, and unemployed immigrants all turned to filibustering for financial reasons. John Mack Faragher has written that Oregon Trail pioneers of the 1840s were "men with dreams of success, but most were not yet successful."[32] A close examination of the men who joined Walker's filibusters suggests that filibuster recruits were much the same. Typical of Walker's recruits was North Carolinian Charles Tayloe. Tayloe went to sea at age sixteen, and at age twenty-eight left the drudgery of the common sailor for the opportunity to become an officer in Walker's army, along with his younger brother John. The Tayloe boys came from a respectable family; their father was collector of customs in Okracoke Inlet and had served in the North Carolina State Senate, but when they joined Walker they had most likely not yet achieved any degree of stability in their economic or personal lives. Filibustering expeditions promised pay equal to or better than that provided by the U.S. Army, and it also promised golden opportunities

---

[30] Antonio Rafael de la Cova, "Filibusters and Freemasons: The Sworn Obligation," *Journal of the Early Republic* 17 (Spring 1997): 95–120; May, *Manifest Destiny's Underworld*, 93–101.

[31] *NYH*, January 10, 30, 1856; Tyler Anbinder, *Five Points: The Nineteenth-Century New York City Neighborhood That Invented Tap Dance, Stole Elections, and Became the World's Most Notorious Slum* (New York, 2001), 274–6; New York *Times*, August 8, 1887 (quotation). On urban sporting culture see Patricia Cline Cohen, *The Murder of Helen Jewett: The Life and Death of a Prostitute in Nineteenth-Century New York* (New York, 1998).

[32] John Mack Faragher, *Women and Men on the Overland Trail*. 2nd ed. (New Haven, 2000), 183. Faragher also sees gender as a motivating factor in westward migration. Pioneer men "Longed for a... test of their own masculinity. Thus they were driven to experiences such as the overland emigration, for on the trail they would be following, as it were, the blazes of previous masculine generations." 182–3.

in the new territory. Boosters represented Central America as a veritable paradise, offering success in love and business to the American who was willing to work, even men who, like Deaderick, clearly had not succeeded in America.[33] A poem in the New York *Picayune* in 1856 put the charms of Nicaragua to the working man in an eloquent verse. Nicaragua was a place

> Where all things grow without the taming of a plough,
> Where men grow fat by feasting, sans the sweat of brow.
> Offers its steaming wealth to those who like to seek it,
> And own their masters, if they'll stick by and keep it.[34]

In the aggressive expansionist imagination, Central America offered easy living to white American men, and it also offered an opportunity to reassert the advantages of whiteness, regardless of income. The ability to assert racial dominance over non-white peoples was a crucial factor in the assimilation of immigrant groups like the Irish in the United States in the antebellum period, providing the means for the construction of a "white" American identity, but this identity of course excluded African-Americans. As economic transformations, including the decline of the apprentice system and independent artisanal workshop rendered the financial situation of working people increasingly precarious, racism against African-Americans became increasingly vehement. The message in the *Picayune* poem was that in Nicaragua, success is only a matter of endurance, and no white man need have a master, would have had a reassuring resonance for white men in both the North and the South.[35]

By the time Walker passed a decree reintroducing African slavery into Nicaragua in September of 1856, the assertion that in Nicaragua, people

---

[33] John H. Wheeler, *Reminiscences and Memoirs of North Carolina and Eminent North Carolinians* (Columbus, 1884), 20–2. Detailed information on Walker's soldiers can be found in Item 120, Register of the Army of the Republic of Nicaragua and Folder 85: Men and Stores sent to Caribbean Sea, 1860, both in the WWP. Based on a study of the Army of the Republic in 1857 conducted by Dr. Alejandro Bolaños G., Masaya, Nicaragua, 1972, and a study conducted by myself of "immigrants" to Nicaragua in 1860, the following observations can be made about the men who chose to follow Walker. Their average age was slightly over 26 years, the vast majority listed some form of skilled labor for their occupation, and very few listed an occupation that could be considered white collar. Between twenty-eight percent (in 1860) and fifty-nine percent (in 1857) of the men were born in northern states. Although the race of individuals was not listed, complexion was. Most were described as "fair." According to Robert May, fifty-five of the eighty-four López filibusters on one list were under the age of twenty-five. May, *Manifest Destiny's Underworld*, 94. On the occupations of filibusters see 96–101.

[34] "All about Walker," attributed to "Sarey's Hands," New York *Picayune*, January 19, 1856. This poem was published *before* Walker's slavery decree.

[35] Noel Ignatiev, *How the Irish Became White* (New York, 1996); David Roediger, *The Wages of Whiteness: Race and the Making of the American Working Class* (London, 1991); Streeby, *American Sensations*.

could "own their masters" took on a far more literal meaning. Walker reintroduced slavery to Nicaragua in the hopes of drawing southern partisans to his cause, despite the fact that he had welcomed African-American recruits to his army and African-American settlers to Nicaragua. The few African-Americans who followed Walker were understandably dismayed by this turn of events, and they quickly deserted him. But with the slavery decree, William Walker crystallized his reputation as a racial hero who could provide opportunities otherwise closed to white men. Walker became the agent of what Richard Slotkin has called "a reformulation of the Frontier project in terms of racial warfare." On the new Central American frontier, the martial man could prove his character through heroic acts against racial inferiors. Elevated by his uniform, military status, and Anglo-Saxon racial identity, the foot soldier of aggressive expansionism could participate in the regeneration, through violence, of both the new frontier and himself.[36]

"Are there not brave, adventuresome, enterprising young Americans in the United States who will come here and assist in the regeneration of . . . the whole of Central America," readers in New Orleans were asked by a correspondent from Walker's final foray to Honduras in 1860. The white men who joined Walker's army, and the armies of other filibusters, answered yes to this question. They came to Latin America with high expectations. Here they might find a comfortable life and the opportunity to achieve success through martial acts, at a time when a focus on the outward trappings of financial success held them back in the United States. But as debates at home illustrated, not even sustained success on Walker's part convinced restrained men that his actions were honorable.[37]

Restraint as a Virtue: Walker Condemned

William Walker attracted at least as many critics as he did supporters, especially after his hold on power in Nicaragua became shaky during the first months of 1857. A close examination of the critique laid out by Walker's opponents provides a clear view of the manly characteristics valued by restrained men. In an editorial highly critical of filibustering, *Harper's Monthly* made it clear that it was no abolitionist agenda that drove the paper to disavow aggressive expansionism on the eve of William Walker's first filibustering expedition to Sonora. *Harper's* instead argued that both filibusters

---

[36] Richard Slotkin, *The Fatal Environment: The Myth of the Frontier in the Age of Industrialization, 1800–1860* (New York, 1985), 250; Slotkin, *Regeneration Through Violence: The Mythology of the American Frontier, 1600–1860* (Middletown, CT, 1973). On Walker's reasons for reintroducing slavery, see Walker, *The War in Nicaragua*, 266.

[37] Squier, "Nicaragua: an Exploration From Ocean to Ocean," 744; "Our Special Correspondent at Truxillo, August 18, 1860," New Orleans *Delta*, September 4, 1860.

and abolitionists were unworthy of respect for exactly the same reasons: They both rejected the force of law but retreated to the protection of laws when threatened. Both filibusters and abolitionists lacked character then, for two reasons. They rejected the patriarchy of the legal system, and they were inconsistent in their behavior. "Ultra abolitionists will boldly preach disunion," *Harper's* wrote, but when threatened, "away to the Mayor run these consistent men, and demand the protection of the very laws they have been so ruthlessly assaulting." The same "beautiful consistency is manifested by their filibustering antipodes." Filibusters "get up a pirate war in contempt of the national sovereignty; they denounce all legal attempts to restrain them as interfering with the 'higher law' of their impressionable sympathies. The moment, however, they begin to experience personally some of the evils of their rash procedures, forthwith we hear them talking very learnedly and disinterestedly about the law of nations." Restrained men recognized the rule of law. Martial men, and abolitionists, appealed to a higher law. For filibusters that higher law was encoded in America's Manifest Destiny. But restrained men rightly pointed out that even on their own terms, filibusters and abolitionists were failures. By looking for protection from American law, they proved that they were not actually independent of that law. Both of these groups proved unmanly because they failed to resolutely face the implications of their beliefs.[38]

A later editorial in *Harper's Monthly*, "Cowards and Brave Men," returned to the question of manhood and filibustering in an oblique way. Acknowledging that some Americans might embrace filibusters as models of manhood, the magazine offered an opposing and clearly restrained model of masculinity grounded in Christian sacrifice. In the midst of Walker's Nicaraguan campaign, the magazine argued that true bravery is not revealed in battle. "The soldier fights because he must. He can not help himself." As examples of a "less doubtful heroism" *Harper's* offered several. "Pestilence is a more appalling calamity than War, and requires a stouter heart to meet it.... Still greater courage and firmness are required to remain poor, when there is a chance of becoming rich by means which most men do not scruple to employ.... But the most decisive proof of independence and courage is to be truly religious ... in a gay, and worldly, and proud society."[39]

While *Harper's Monthly* asserted that self-imposed poverty was a notable sign of Christian virtue, many critiques of the filibusters focused on the economic failures and shoddy work ethic of the recruits. The San Francisco *Alta California* contrasted filibusters with men who worked diligently at their profession. The paper claimed that most filibusters were men who had

---

[38] "Editor's Table," *HNMM* VI (January 1853): 266, 268. The claim that filibusters invoked the "law of nations" referred to the demand for United States protection made by filibusters in Cuba after capture by Spanish authorities.

[39] "Editor's Table: Cowards and Brave Men," *HNMM* XII (February 1856): 410–13.

FIGURE 4.2. "Retreat from Massaya," in "A Ranger's Life in Nicaragua," *Harper's Weekly* 1 (March 28, 1857): 201.

failed in "half a dozen different professions," and were "too good to work and too afraid to steal." Another critic bemoaned in 1857 that America had been "termed a nation of filibusters" because "of a few restless spirits in our midst, who, perhaps, even at home, would rather steal than work." A narrative of the war published in *Harper's Weekly* in 1857, "A Ranger's Life in Nicaragua," claimed that men were actually corrupted by filibustering. "It does not appear that fillibusterism improves the character," the ranger wrote. Even men of "a superior order" become shirkers and "slaves" under the tedium of the soldier's routine in Nicaragua. In the aftermath of Walker's slavery decree, this final critique carried a particularly clear message to pro-slavery and Free-Soil readers alike. Accompanying illustrations highlighted the wretched conditions of Walker's volunteers, illuminating their humiliation in front of the Central Americans (see Figure 4.2).[40]

In his memoirs of serving as an officer in Walker's army, Horace Bell, an Indianan who arrived in San Francisco during the gold rush, agreed that while there were some true believers in Manifest Destiny and "Central

---

[40] San Francisco *Alta California*, October 7, 1854; "Cincinnatus," (Marvin Wheat) *Travels on the Western Slope of the Mexican Cordillera in the form of Fifty-One Letters* (San Francisco, 1857), 432; "A Ranger's Life in Nicaragua," *Harper's Weekly* 1 (March 28, 1857): 202.

American regeneration" among the troops, most soldiers were drunken failures. "With few exceptions they were composed of men of desperate and broken fortunes, penniless gamblers, small-fry military adventurers, young men too lazy to work, too proud to beg, and too honest to steal, with a small sprinkling of United States army officers, whose dissipated habits had led to their retirement from the service ... men perfectly competent when sober, a rare thing." Restrained men, who overwhelmingly embraced temperance, would have read tales of heavy drinking in filibustering armies as further evidence of their degeneracy.[41]

Another critic accused Walker of neglecting his soldiers and destroying families by enlisting under-aged boys. The three ill soldiers that expansionist booster Thomas Francis Meagher met in a Costa Rican hospital a year after the war's end represented the geographic diversity of Walker's recruits – one was from Louisville, one was from New York, and one was from Quebec. The Canadian boy, "he would not be eighteen till June, and yet he had been in every battle the Fillibusters fought," had deserted his sick widowed mother for the excitement of war in Nicaragua. Walker tore boys from their mothers and could also be needlessly cruel to women as well. In June of 1857 a letter to the New York *Times* claimed that Walker refused rations to a sickly woman in his infirmary and also denied passage home to the widow of an army surgeon. The woman was later shot, and died while undergoing amputation.[42] Both of these stories offered examples of the domestic ruin wrought by aggressive expansionism. For supporters of restrained manhood who upheld the sanctity of the home, no critique was more damning than one focused on the domestic sphere.

The fact that an aggressive expansionist like Meagher condemned William Walker within a narrative that encouraged the annexation of Costa Rica suggests how polarizing a figure Walker had become by the end of the 1850s. Many supporters rejected Walker after he left Nicaragua, perhaps realizing the degree to which he had actually undermined American interests in the region. The rabidly expansionistic *Democratic Review*, which for a time supported Walker, continued to uphold the ideal of martial manhood while attributing the American failure in Nicaragua to the character of the soldiers and their leaders. The journal asserted its "firm conviction" that "the history of this war ... is still, with all its disgraces, a vindication of the American character" proving that "in no part of the world nor in any age, are the traits of a conquering and a dominant people to be found in greater perfection than among ourselves." But many of Walker's soldiers "were fugitives from justice" with "hands hardened by crime." Their weakness was clear from their appearance, in "faces made hideous by years of gambling, violence,

---

[41] Bell, "Confessions of a Filibuster."
[42] Thomas Francis Meagher, "Holidays in Costa Rica," *HNMM* 20 (January 1860): 162; Stewart, *Last of the Fillibusters*, 69.

FIGURE 4.3. "Nicaragua, – Fillibusters [*sic*] Reposing after the Battle in Their Quarters at the Convent," *Frank Leslie's Illustrated Newspaper* (May 3, 1856), 336. This wood engraving from one of the most popular periodicals of the day shows General William Walker's men relaxing after battle in the convent of San Francisco, during their entrance into Granada in 1855. Hardly the picture of "Anglo-Saxon" energy, several filibusters are shown drunk and unconscious, while others play cards and read newspapers (perhaps printed by Walker himself). The only Nicaraguan in the scene is a young, partially naked child who offers the filibusters cigars. Several filibusters recline on hammocks, smoking, in a perfect representation of the stereotypical "lazy" Nicaraguan man critiqued in U.S. travelogues to the region. Library of Congress, Prints and Photographs Division [LC-USZ62-108152].

and debauchery. . . . Despising all the conventions and formalities of life, they learned to neglect its higher obligations." In short, Walker's men lacked the character of the solders of earlier wars. "Whole masse [*sic*] drunk at the instant of attack . . . drunkards strolling about at night with loaded pistols, in hands that craved the excitement of some second murder. *It was not so in Mexico!*" (see Figure 4.3).[43]

But the *Democratic Review* hesitated from following this line of reasoning to its logical conclusion – the embrace of a restrained model of manhood. Walker's failure as a commander was, the journal argued, the result of his excessive restraint. "What availed his systematic method, useful to a closet barrister in the cross-questioning of a witness; or that extreme and cultivated

[43] "Central America – The Late War in Nicaragua," *USDR* 40 (July 1857): 10–11, 19, 20.

coolness, and aristocratic hauter – when the question was of controlling men of sympathy? . . ." Had Walker been more aggressive, perhaps he could have commanded his unruly band. "Temperance in a commander – and Walker was, perhaps, the most temperate man in the expedition – is only a virtue of the body, caused by prudence or disinclination, unless it rises to the dignity of heroism by compelling and exacting temperance in others."[44]

According to the *Democratic Review*, Walker's failure lay in an excess of restraint. Most critics thought differently and saw in Walker a dangerous combination of anachronistic and overly aggressive qualities. In December of 1857 Walker was arrested on Nicaraguan soil during a carefully planned return to the country where he still considered himself president. He was not arrested by Nicaraguans, but by an American naval officer, Commodore Hiram Paulding. Paulding justified his arrest of Walker on a reading of Walker's character, since at the time of arrest it was not clear that Walker had broken any laws. As *Harper's Monthly* reported, "the propriety of the course taken by Commodore Paulding in arresting Walker upon foreign soil has been questioned." But in his dispatch to the government Paulding explained, "I could not regard Walker and his followers in any other light than as outlaws who had escaped from the vigilance of the officers of the Government, and left our shores for the purpose of rapine and murder." By arresting Walker, Paulding hoped to "vindicate the law and redeem the honor of our country" he stated.[45]

Walker received extensive support in this affair, since even President Buchanan condemned Paulding for exceeding his rights in arresting Walker upon foreign soil. None the less, many politicians agreed with Paulding's assessment of the filibuster character. While criticizing Paulding, President Buchanan himself claimed that Walker's expedition was little more than "an invitation to reckless and lawless men to rob, plunder, and murder the unoffending citizens of neighboring States." The Whig senator James Pearce of Maryland agreed, and he summed up the importance of the underlying reading of gender and character to both positions in his statement to Congress. "Nothing surprises me more than the sympathy which is expressed for General Walker," he claimed. "In a few localities . . . he may be regarded as a hero; but the larger part of our countrymen view him as an offender against our laws, a violator of the laws of nations, and a cold, relentless oppressor of the people whom he ruled with military rigor." If Walker displayed manly characteristics, Pearce wrote, they were manly characteristics of a long-dead era. Walker, he stated "is an ambitious dreamer. The enterprise

---

[44] Ibid., 19–20.
[45] *HNMM* XVI (February 1858), 400; James R. Doolittle, *Justification of Commodore Paulding's Arrest of Walker and his Command at Puenta Arenas. Speech of James R. Doolittle, of Wisconsin. Delivered to the United States Senate, January 21, 1858* (Washington, DC, 1858), 13.

which he has undertaken is one that does not belong to the age, and is not in accordance with its spirit. . . . It belongs, rather to that dark period in the Christian era. . . . when the Vikings and Northmen went wherever they could, disregarding the obligations of national justice, making might right, and carrying rapacity and rapine wherever they went."[46]

Louisiana Democratic senator John Slidell, whose failed diplomacy helped precipitate the U.S. Mexico War, agreed with Pearce that although he might have been considered a hero in another age, Walker was an anachronism. Referring to "this new William the Conqueror" who "proceeded to dispossess the ancient proprietors of their domains, distributing them among his adherents," Slidell bemoaned the fact that Paulding had "succeeded, in the eyes of many of our people, in investing [Walker] with the martyr's crown; and pseudo-martyrs have, in all ages, found devotees to worship at their shrine."[47]

Paulding, in contrast, was a true man for the age, Pearce asserted. He used "no language disrespectful to General Walker. . . . no language . . . which could be considered disgraceful to that officer." But nonetheless, Paulding spoke, carried himself, and behaved with the manly display of true character. "We do not wish our officers when executing a stern duty to speak with bated breath, and accompany the act by apologetic flourishes. We want them to speak like men, like officers; to speak whatever is to be said, plainly, frankly, without apology and necessary qualification. This is what Commodore Paulding has done." In other words, Walker's (bad) character was evident from actions only considered manly in a long-dead age – an age of violence and aggression. Paulding's (good) character was revealed in his manly and forthright restraint from both undignified language and unnecessary violence, as well as in his prevention of Walker's violence against Central America. Paulding, a personification of restrained manhood, offered a model

---

[46] "Speech of Hon. J. A. Pearce, of Maryland, on the Presentation of a Medal to Commodore Paulding; delivered in the Senate of the United States, January 28, 1858." *Congressional Globe*, 34th Congress, 1st Sess., 1857–1858 (Washington, DC, 1858), 1538; *HNMM* XVI (March 1858): 544. Soon after this "grave error" Buchanan relieved Paulding of his command, although Robert May argues that this was not a case of cause and effect. Robert E. May, "James Buchanan, the Neutrality Laws, and American Invasions of Nicaragua," in *James Buchanan and the Political Crisis of the 1850s*, Michael J. Birkner, ed. (Selinsgrove, 1996): 123–45. For support of Walker over Paulding see the *Philadelphia Evening Argus*, December 19, 1857. The Baltimore *Sun*, the Washington *Evening Star*, the *States*, and the *NYH* also supported Walker over Paulding. Wheeler Collection, Series I, #12, scrapbook of clippings, LOC.

[47] "Speech of Hon. J. A. Pearce, of Maryland, 1538." Other southerners opposing Walker included Virginian John Letcher and the Texas fire-eater Louis Wigfall, who called Walker a pirate. May, *Southern Dream of a Caribbean Empire*, 194. Slidell also had personal reasons for opposing Walker. Once a supporter of filibustering, Slidell may have opposed Walker because of his personal enmity for the increasingly visible Walker ally (and similarly incompetent diplomat), Pierre Soulé.

of manly character sharply at odds with that of Walker. He upheld the law, his manners were good (and thus he could be judged a man of character by his appearance), and he commanded attention without resorting to violence.[48]

The Heroic Viking of Our Time: Walker Celebrated

Putnam's magazine clearly preferred Paulding's restrained manhood to the martial model offered by Walker and shared many of the assumptions about the lawless, unmanly character of the filibuster with critics like Senator Pearce. After listing "filibusteros" among the possible political factions available to a voter in its 1854 editorial "Our Parties and Politics," *Putnam's* condemned the "propagandists of the South" for their filibustering fantasies. "We know that schemes, open and secret, are prosecuted for the acquisition of Cuba...eager grasping eyes are set on Mexico...another senator has broached the recognition of the Dominican Republic, with an ulterior view to its annexation." The magazine condemned "eager grasping" and outright aggression as inappropriate. But what was the alternative?[49]

Just six months later, in the editorial "Men of Character," *Putnam's* provided a seeming justification of filibustering when answering this question. The assertion that "character is what involuntarily commands respect.... It is what makes itself felt," was one that an aggressive expansionist could embrace. "Pride and self-reliance almost always accompany" character, *Putnam's* claimed. "Its possessor is not easily moved by either censure or applause, and is utterly indifferent to what Mrs. Grundy will say." Seemingly predicting and justifying Walker's obsessive behavior, *Putnam's* stated that "the man who has character must be independent, fearless, and discriminating in his judgment. He is not influenced by the position a man holds, or the clothes he wears, in forming the estimate of him."[50]

Given that a magazine openly hostile to filibustering suggested that manly character expressed itself through fearlessness, self-reliance, and independence, it is perhaps not surprising that supporters of aggressive expansionism celebrated Walker and his fellow filibusters as the true men of the 1850s. The pro-filibustering position had several elements that illuminate the contours of the competing view of manhood in this period. Supporters of filibustering rejected Paulding's dignified restraint in favor of Walker's martial qualities.

Aggressive expansionists maintained that William Walker proved his masculinity through his heroic courage, aggressivity, and rejection of both physical and financial comfort. Many accounts of his heroism focused on his

---

[48] "Speech of Hon. J. A. Pearce, of Maryland." One has to question what sort of language Pearce considered insulting, given that Paulding called Walker an "outlaw" who intended "rapine and murder."

[49] "Our Parties and Politics," *PMM* (September 1854): 233, 244–5.

[50] "Men of Character," 267–9.

fearlessness. One of his soldiers marveled that although he was shot twice, "and knocked off his feet both times" he "remained on the field." *De Bow's Review* directly contrasted the manliness of the filibuster with the effeminacy of the anti-expansionist. A filibuster "sacrifices, very often, all the endearments of home and country, encounters privation and suffering, and perils health and life, to benefit country or mankind, and asks only reputation and fame as its pay and recompense." Anti-expansionists had none of these manly qualities. "Free Love is the latest and most vaunted of their schemes of benevolence, and they invite us to enter its sensual, enervating saloons, as a sort of panacea for all the ills that human flesh is heir to." A martial man embraced danger rather than sensuality, and those who criticized aggressive expansionism did so only from their own weakness. "The selfish love indolence, ease, and quietude too much, ever to become filibusters" *De Bow's* concluded.[51]

Heroicized accounts of Walker, such as "The Man of Destiny" in the New Orleans *Sunday Delta*, envisioned him as the antithesis of the restrained man, who focused his energy on domestic concerns and financial prosperity. Walker was a man of will, a man above pecuniary concerns, a man who offered the promise of salvation through manly action despite an unimpressive appearance. With a "strong substratum of Scotch common sense in his character," he boasted a fine genetic heritage, not unimportant, given the racial component of filibustering. He was gifted with a good education, but he was wise enough to see the limitations of book learning. Walker "discovered the law to be a very poor wet-nurse, and contemptuously dropped its nipple" in favor of filibustering. In other words, he became a man when he rejected the feminized virtues of learning for manly action. Walker's education was not as significant in his greatness as was his self-knowledge. While in college, he gained not only a knowledge of Latin but "a tolerable knowledge of himself... for self-knowledge is the basis of all daring thoughts and daring deeds." Indeed, this self-knowledge, identified in the definition of character in *Putnam's*, separates the brave men from cowards. Cowards will be recognized not only by the eyes of men of character but by a greater eye as well. "The coward does not know himself, but God knows him, and even if he buried his head in the sand, ostrich-like, the great eye would perceive and despise his meanness."[52]

---

[51] Jamison, *With Walker in Nicaragua*, 38; "Acquisition of Mexico-Filibustering," DBR 25 (December 1858): 616, 617. Sensuality also was seen as "contaminating" by another group of martial men, the German Freikorps, the volunteer army that became the core of Hitler's private army, the Sturm Abteilung. Klaus Theweleit, *Male Fantasies. Vol. 1. Women, Floods, Bodies, History*. Stephan Conway, translator. (Minneapolis, 1987), 63–79.

[52] "The Man of Destiny," New Orleans *Sunday Delta*, July 27, 1856. For some prime examples of Walker adulation see, for example, the New York *Sun*, January 2, 1856; "Who is General Walker," New York *Daily News*, February 8, 1856; "General Walker's Early Love," Baltimore *American Democrat*, February 7, 1856; Stewart, *Last of the Fillibusters*, 7. These

Walker's eye, as well, despised all meanness. Although his "blue-gray eye observed quietly.... without any demonstrativeness or unnecessary display," boosters noted that Walker never left his will in doubt. Playing up comparisons to the Democratic Party's greatest hero, Andrew Jackson, supporters attributed to Walker's "Jacksonian willingness to 'take the responsibility,'" the success that "the conqueror of Nicaragua" had achieved. "Assuredly, 'Danton! no weakness!' appears to be his motto." Walker was a man of "daring spirit, capable of great combinations, fitted with an iron will, resolute and just, wise and bold...a true Man of Destiny." One of Walker's men agreed: "With all his placidity of voice and demeanor, men leaped eagerly into the very cannon's mouth to obey his commands." One newspaper article claimed Walker was such a powerful figure that he frightened the less-manly Costa Ricans. "An American merchant" living in Costa Rica reported that "the Costa Rican soldiers are all terrified of 'Walker's demoniac power'...The superstitious dread of Walker's miraculous power and ubiquity is more in his favor than any real force he can command."[53]

The comparisons between Walker and Andrew Jackson – another physically frail man who proved himself through great military victory, expanded the territory of the nation, and was lauded for his iron will – are revealing. Filibustering was largely, although not exclusively, supported by the expansionist wing of the Democratic Party. Lawrence Frederick Kohl has argued that Democrats and Whigs differed primarily in terms of their relationship to the emergence of an individualistic social order. While wealthy and poor men could be found in both parties, Whigs had "internalized values and habits of behavior that guided their passage through life." They were relatively comfortable with economic transformation and generally optimistic about economic change in the future, but they also believed that law was necessary to maintain social stability. Democrats, on the other hand, relied "too much on social ties and a social order that no longer existed, they expressed

---

elements also appear in personal correspondence about Walker. See, for example, J. C. W. Brenan correspondence, Stockton, CA, October 31, 1860, BL. Even some critical sources admitted that Walker's will inspired respect and "an interest which none can help feeling in one who has manifested so much boldness, energy and resolution." One obituary of Walker noted that while he demonstrated "a disregard of national law and the common moralities of civilized nations" and had led the U.S. government to be viewed as "ambitious, deceitful, and treacherous by those who, before Gen. Walker visited them, looked upon our Republic as a model for imitation," none the less, the paper concluded, "his career exhibits...invincible firmness of character; a bravery unsurpassed and a confidence in his own ability impossible to be shaken." New Orleans *Picayune*, September 19, 1860.

53 "The Man of Destiny," New Orleans *Sunday Delta*, July 27, 1856; Jamison, *With Walker in Nicaragua*, 18; Unidentified newspaper articles on Walker, Folder 160a, WWP. While Walker was rarely compared to Andrew Jackson so directly as in this account, the elements of his personality celebrated by boosters are largely the same as those for which Jackson was venerated. On the elements of Jackson's myth, see John William Ward, *Andrew Jackson: Symbol for an Age* (New York, 1953).

frustration and anger with the impersonal and aggressive world they actually encountered." Unified by their shared belief that they were outside the main currents of power in society, Democrats longed for the past and distrusted the future. Democrats also viewed Whig attempts to ensure a stable society through law as oppressive.[54]

The characteristics that Kohl ascribes to the Whigs can easily be transferred to the restrained men who opposed filibustering, and not surprisingly, many of those men were or at one time had been Whigs. Likewise, the attributes Kohl ascribes to the Democrats fit well with those of the martial supporters of filibustering. Although Kohl does not take gender into account, and the national Whig party was dead by the time Walker came to power, his observations on the divisions between the parties are illuminating. An understanding of Democrats as nostalgic about the past, uncomfortable with the changing economic order, and suspicious about legal limitations to their actions helps contextualize the pro-Walker position expressed by his martial supporters.[55]

Walker's will, bravery, and pure motives were all recognized and praised in one of the key events in his career, the "Liberty and Nicaragua" meeting, held in New York's Central Park on a Friday evening in May of 1856. Attended by thousands of Walker's supporters in New York at the height of his success in Nicaragua, Walker and his efforts were lauded by an assortment of national politicians, all of whom were Democrats. Michigan senator Lewis Cass predicted that "the difficulties which General Walker has encountered and overcome will place his name high on the roll of the distinguished men of his age," words he would learn to regret when as secretary of state under James Buchanan he was forced to deal with Walker's continued flaunting of the neutrality laws. William Cazneau, a well-connected entrepreneur and veteran of the Texas independence movement and the U.S.-Mexico War, served as special agent to the Dominican Republic under President Pierce and unsuccessfully lobbied for the annexation of the Dominican Republic. He announced that "no true man" would dare cross Walker, for Walker was the "lion of Spanish-American regeneration." The San Francisco editor Edward A. Pollard was also effusive in his praise of Walker, and he lauded the man in terms that indicate the centrality of discourses of character to Walker's public persona. Pollard claimed to be speaking in order to "vindicate the personal

[54] Ward, *Andrew Jackson*; Lawrence Frederick Kohl, *The Politics of Individualism: Parties and the American Character in the Jacksonian Era* (New York, 1989), 228.

[55] Several authors have provided gendered analyses of the parties that fit well with both Kohl and the restrained/martial dichotomy explored here. Elizabeth R. Varon, *We Mean to Be Counted: White Women and Politics in Antebellum Virginia* (Chapel Hill, 1998); Ronald J. Zboray and Mary Saracino Zboray, "Gender Slurs in Boston's Partisan Press during the 1840s," *Journal of American Studies* 34 (2000): 413–46. On the collapse of the national Whig Party see Michael F. Holt, *The Rise and Fall of the American Whig Party: Jacksonian Politics and the Onset of the Civil War* (New York, 1999).

character and personal motives of General Walker." Walker was praisewor-
thy, according to Pollard, because he was not "animated ... by any purposes
of private aggrandizement, by any hope of public fame," nor was he driven
by "the passion of ambition." Walker was simply, in Pollard's words, "a
hero. ... not a man who courts applause, or who cares for public opinion."
Walker was a man of will, "who is bound to carry out his won ideas of
duty and right in the cause of progress." Pollard predicted lasting fame for
Walker, and received extensive "applause and cheers" for his words.[56]

De Bow's Review reiterated these points in 1858, when support for the
deposed leader had become more subdued. "The true character of William
Walker is, as we sincerely believe, but little known," *De Bow's* professed.
"He is a man incapable of sordid or selfish motives, and entirely destitute
of any thing like ambition, in the popular sense of the term. ... With all the
mild thoughtfulness and gentle manners of true decision of character ... the
regenerator of Central America might readily pass under hasty observation as
a very commonplace and unimportant individual. The secret of his character
lies in the suppressed enthusiasm of his heart."[57]

Thus William Walker was lauded as an incorruptible man, a man beyond
reach of money, a man of absolute will. Is it not to such men that America,
and indeed the Americas, should look? A correspondent to the New York
Tribune from Truxillo, Honduras, in 1860 stated that "[a] dead country is to
be resurrected; who will undertake the work if Americans refuse? It is a work
worthy of the age, and many will soon see the greatness of the enterprise
in which the band of Americans now here have embarked." Reinforcing the
connection to Manifest Destiny and the settling of the West, a letter to *El
Nicaraguense* from an "Amigo del Sud" made the point that those who were
anxious to emigrate to Nicaragua "are not fillibusters in the usual sense of
that word, but simply emigrants, worthy descendants or imitators of those
who penetrated the dense forests of the West and the plains of Texas, and
whose energy and industry made our country what it is."[58]

If men of the past created America, why reject as anachronistic the standards of valor that made those men heroes? Filibuster boosters refused to
do so. Walker was revered by many as the true offspring of American patriots. John H. Wheeler, who was serving as U.S. envoy to Nicaragua when
Walker took power, wrote in a manuscript draft on Walker's adventures in
Nicaragua that "like Lafayette, he has come to aid in the struggles for liberty;
like Washington he sought no imoulient or reward, except the gratitude of

---

[56] Speeches delivered at the "Liberty and Nicaragua" meeting, held in Central Park, Friday
evening, May 23rd, 1856, in Wells, *Walker's Expedition to Nicaragua*, 227–8, 236, 280–81
1; May, *Southern Dream of a Caribbean Empire*, 94; Brown, *Agents of Manifest Destiny*,
324.

[57] "The Walker Expedition, 1855," *DBR* 24 (February 1858): 150.

[58] "The Walker Expedition," *NYH*, September 1, 1860; letter from "Amigo del Sud" in New
Orleans, published in *El Nicaraguense*, Granada, Nicaragua, January 25, 1856.

the country and the liberation of its citizens." A report titled "Antiquity of Fillibusterism [*sic*]," signed by "A Soldier in Co. E." in *El Nicaraguense*, Walker's newspaper in Nicaragua, summed up this position. Comparing those who object to filibustering to "tottering crowned heads," the author offers an historical justification of the better model of manhood. "Was it the native Saxon or the fillibustering Norman who instilled vigor and energy into the English nation?" the author asked rhetorically. "Who fought for and gained American independence but adventurers?...I of Nicaragua am but a representative of the fillibusters of the past." Residents of New York City or Washington in 1858 could attend performances of the burlesque *Columbus El Filibustero*, which suggested another model of filibustering greatness.[59]

Some writers looked further afield for models of filibustering greatness. In one account he was "the heroic Viking of our times, the great nation-builder, the representative of Republican progress, Col. William Walker." An account in the *Pennsylvanian* took a different tack in its Viking analogy: "The intrepid soldier of freedom is held near in every liberty loving heart...The Dane was repelled as an invader, Walker was hailed as a savior.... The Dane was a destroyer, but the 'gray-eyed' man is a regenerator."[60]

While this justification turned Pearce's condemnation, that filibusters were men of the past, on its head, another justification for filibustering took a contrary tact. Filibusters were great men not because they upheld a fine historical model but rather because they fulfilled a modern ideal of manhood. The Oakland *Leader* reported that Walker "holds not his power by the hereditary sanction of the divine right of kings, but by the more modern and substantial tenure of conquest and force of arms.... Who shall say that...infusing into the breasts of its present degraded population a national ambition, is not worthy of some commendation." Another account praised Walker for learning a true Jacksonian history lesson: "The world shifts and changes.

---

59 John H. Wheeler, "A new work on Nicaragua, the centre of central America. Its past history, present position and future prospects," Wheeler Collection, Series II, #1: 85; "Antiquity of Fillibusterism," signed by "A Soldier in Co. E." *El Nicaraguense*, Granada, Nicaragua, January 25, 1856. This author had a point. As Robert May argues "Americans since the birth of the republic had been in the habit of conducting private military invasions into foreign lands, and they had been doing it despite a sequence of federal laws and prosecutions in federal courts designed to discourage that very behavior." May, "Manifest Destiny's Filibusters," in *Manifest Destiny and Empire: American Antebellum Expansionism*. Sam W. Haynes and Christopher Morris, eds. (College Station, TX, 1997), 150; See also May, *Manifest Destiny's Underworld*, 60.

60 "The Man of Destiny," New Orleans *Sunday Delta*, July 27, 1856; "Affairs in Nicaragua," The *Pennsylvanian*, n.d., Wheeler Collection, Series I, #12: 116; The Knights of the Golden Circle, another filibustering group that dreamed of founding a slaveholding empire centered in Mexico, also embraced the "men of the past." They revealed their enthusiasm for medieval manhood when they adopted a uniform resembling a medieval coat of mail. Fortunately, they never had the chance to wear it. May, *Manifest Destiny's Underworld*, 105.

What was true a century ago is not true to-day; what is true to-day will not be true in a century hence."[61]

The finest accounts managed to join the past and present in their celebration of Walker and to show that he was admirable both for his historical and modern qualities. As the New Orleans *Sunday Delta* reported in a review of Walker's book, *The War in Nicaragua*, Walker personified "American Viking Politics," and was himself a Viking for today's world. Walker, the paper wrote, "is a remarkable type of the representative men of the day of this country. It would be difficult to name another person who combines more closely and inseparably the worker and the thinker. His whole career...looks like incarnate thought in action." Indeed, the *Delta* declared, "It is hard to say whether he is more a man of the times or of the future." The paper expressed no doubt that a recent publication by Walker was "calculated to exert a peculiar charm alike over men of action and men of mediation."[62]

Even *Harper's Monthly* lauded Walker at the height of his success, declaring him a wonderful combination of old and new. "We have again and again called Walker a hero.... We are obliged to recognize a persistence, and endurance, a resolute heroism which merit a higher place in human esteem that can be ceded to all the knights errant of history and Faerydom.... The difference is that ours is a nineteenth century hero.... Who knows how soon he may replace the laurel of the hero with the diadem of a king?"[63]

Given that many Americans were uncomfortable with the present, and suspicious of the future, it is hardly surprising that they would embrace Walker precisely because he seemed to be out of step with the times. This was revealed to supporters not only because his actions represented a seemingly disappearing standard of manliness, but because, above all else, he appeared immune to the corrupting power of money that so disabled men in the current age. It was for this reason, his supporters claimed, that Walker made his fatal decision to cross Vanderbilt and his Accessory Transit Company after Vanderbilt's support had helped him gain power. "Walker was not made of the material that would bow the suppliant knee to wrong in any quarter," claimed a supporter, "much less to an arrogant corporation."[64]

Supporters, north and south, agreed. According to a letter writer to the Boston *Herald*, "General Walker, purely unselfish, has only the ambition...of having his name placed high among those who have been the benefactors of mankind." That the spirit of filibustering was above the petty interests of the businessman was clear to the New Orleans *Sunday*

---

[61] Oakland *Leader* quoted in *El Nicaraguense*, Granada, Nicaragua, January 25, 1856; "The Man of Destiny," New Orleans *Sunday Delta*, July 27, 1856.

[62] "General Walker's Book," New Orleans *Sunday Delta*, April 8, 1860.

[63] *HNMM* XIV (January 1857), quoted in Carr, *The World and William Walker*, 113.

[64] Jamison, *With Walker in Nicaragua*, 56.

Delta: "It is a strange thing in this age of dollars and dotage, of huckstering and bargaining, and universal buying and selling...to see the Kinghood of the old Scandinavian sailors, with its lofty hopes, its inexhaustible daring, its almost arrogant self-reliance, reappearing suddenly in our midst. Wall Street can not understand it." Walker's good friend, William Vincent Wells, praised his "utter disregard of personal ease or luxury, and an indifference to wealth. His motives are pure and honorable, and his aspirations *beyond riches*. This is a difficult statement for the money-worshipping crowd to believe, but his whole life demonstrates the fact." An 1857 ad for a southern competitor to Vanderbilt's Central American steamship line also celebrated Walker for not succumbing "to Wall Street influence" while the New Orleans *Times* agreed that "in an age wedded too much to mean and sordid pursuit," Walker was "one of the most distinguished men of his generation." For men who feared that an appearance of wealth had grown more important than manly character in antebellum America and who longed for the social ties of an earlier time, Walker provided the reassurance of a largely fictional past when different values prevailed. What William Walker promised was that even an "effeminate" looking man could prove his value, and his masculinity, through martial acts. Or could he?[65]

The Gray-Eyed Man Has Come

For Americans like Deaderick, uncomfortable with the increasing importance of appearance in America, Walker seemed to provide an ideal model. Above the sordid interests of personal wealth, and constantly proving his character through martial acts, Walker's model of manhood was understandably seductive, especially to men who had failed to find success in America. Even after his defeat, many of his soldiers maintained that their "chief was a hero" and "probably the greatest of all the soldiers of fortune."[66] But Walker found himself trapped in the same quandary as did Deaderick. In a country increasingly focused on the external, Walker might reject the siren song of wealth, but he could not, finally, overcome the problem of his appearance.

   Like Deaderick, Walker's followers wanted it both ways. What they desired was that character make itself "felt" as *Putnam's* put it. They demanded that true character reveal itself on the outside at the same time that they rejected the idea that character was transparent, that money could buy an

---

[65] "Letter on Nicaragua," Boston *Herald*, January 18, 1856; "The Man of Destiny," New Orleans *Sunday Delta*, July 27, 1856; Wells, *Walker's Expedition to Nicaragua*, 199–200; W. Alvin Lloyd's *Steamboat and Railroad Guide*, Published by W. Alvin Lloyd, (New Orleans, 1857), xi; "The Hero of Nicaragua," The New Orleans *Times*, July 19, 1857. See also "Our New York Correspondence," Lancaster, PA, *Public Register*, January 19, 1856 for another Pro-Walker letter along the same lines.

[66] Lucas, *Nicaragua, War of the Filibusters*, 17.

appearance that signified character. It is for this reason that Deaderick focuses so much attention on the soldier's uniform. His clothes never measure
up to the inward picture he carries of himself. While Deaderick resents being
judged by his appearance, he feels, and believes, that character should reveal
itself outwardly.

Walker was forced to resolve this same problem. The trouble with Walker,
the most dedicated booster admitted, was his extremely unprepossessing
appearance. Short, fair, and slim of build, his appearance belied his character,
or so boosters claimed. Even his voice was nearly as soft as a woman's.
Was it possible that Walker's character could be both silent, and entirely
invisible?

The answer, of course, was no. Since there was no returning to an earlier
social order, when a man was known for his actions, it was impossible that
character could remain invisible. Deaderick hoped that a uniform would reflect his character, but a uniform was not enough to fix Walker's problems.
Walker's character was revealed, finally, in his eye. As the lone outward sign
of his character, a description of his gray eyes became a central aspect of
accounts of the great filibuster. As "a letter from a Young Washingtonian
on his travels" reported to the press in late 1855, "we could hardly believe
that the little insignificant looking person before us was the man who had
shown such great talents as a military leader. . . . The only thing remarkable
in his appearance are his eyes, which are large, of a light gray, and project in
such a way that they look almost pointed." In other accounts, his eyes were
"almost hypnotic in their power" and shone with "the glint of broken steel."
William Wells went to great lengths to explain that "numerous descriptions
have been attempted by newspaper correspondents to do justice to this 'gray
eye,' but they convey a faint picture of the original; nor has the true expression ever been obtained by the daguerreotype." Only the true believer can
attempt to describe such a signifying eye. About "the principle feature of his
countenance," the *Delta* described an eye "of a blue-gray color, large, intelligent, occasionally dreamy, it has a thousand different expressions. Like the
relentless eye of Chatham, which held his rivals in constant check, it never
loses sight of an enemy for a moment; and its possessor holds you, as the
Ancient Mariner held the wedding guest, by its mysterious and glittering
power."[67]

Wells's account adds that it "would be difficult, in any written description, to convey an adequate idea" of this eye. Still he tries. "It is a deep and

[67] "A letter from a Young Washingtonian on his travels" letter dated November 29, 1855,
San Juan del Sud, to Messrs. Gales and Seaton. Unidentified paper, Wheeler Collection,
Series I, #21: 51; Jamison, *With Walker in Nicaragua*, 18; Lucas, *Nicaragua, War of the
Filibusters*, 116; Wells, *Walker's Expedition to Nicaragua*, 199–200. "The Man of Destiny,"
New Orleans *Sunday Delta*, July 27, 1856.

intensely brilliant *blue-gray*, large and intelligent, and the calm unimpassioned manner with which he fixes this upon whoever he comes in contact with, seems to penetrate the inmost thoughts. That he is highly educated, appears at the first glance." Walker's pale and intense eye, so central to physical accounts of the man, made it possible that a "small-sized and rather unattractive man," could be embraced as the Anglo-Saxon regenerator of Central America, a masculine race hero for the insecure at home. Walker's eye was the outward sign of his character.[68]

To a man of character, of course, this equation of an eye and a man would be wholly unacceptable. Walker himself was quite uncomfortable with the relationship between character and appearance that the wide circulation of his own likeness implied. As he wrote to a close supporter from New York on March 5, 1860 about his coming publication, *The War in Nicaragua*, "the publisher intends on putting an approved likeness of the Author in the book; and although it offends my sense of propriety I have to submit to it as a part of the 'hunting' of the trader" (see Figure 4.4).[69]

Yet Walker also allowed his own paper in Nicaragua, *El Nicaraguense*, to manufacture the legend that the indigenous peoples of Nicaragua believed they would be delivered from Spanish oppression by a "gray-eyed man" of the Anglo Saxon race. Admitting mid-story that "there is in these facts a tincture of romance almost too charming to reveal," *El Nicaraguense* none the less maintained that "the prophecy is deemed by the Indians as fulfilled" when visiting natives "hailed" Walker "as the 'gray eyed man,' so long and anxiously waited for by them and their fathers." American publications quickly picked up the story, reporting the fulfillment of "the superstitious old tradition, that a fair man, with 'eyes the color of the heavens,' would come across the sea and restore to the Indians the peace and abundance of their ancient days."[70]

When *El Nicaraguense* concluded its fabricated story of prophesy fulfilled by stating that "the Gray-eyed man has come," it unwittingly revealed more

[68] Wells, *Walker's Expedition to Nicaragua*, 199–200. For more on Walker's gray eye, see T. Robinson Warren, *Dust and Foam; or, Three Oceans and Two Continents* (New York, 1859), 184, 211–4; the *Daily States*, Washington, June 12, 1857; unidentified clipping from a London paper, Wheeler Collection, Series I, #11: 225; Richard Miller Devens, *Our First Century: Being a Popular Descriptive Portraiture of the One Hundred Great and Memorable Events of Perpetual Interest in the History of our Country* (Springfield, MA, 1877), 744; Stewart, *Last of the Fillibusters*, 5, 11.

[69] Letter from Walker to Fayssoux, March 5, 1860. Folder 68, WWP.

[70] "Additional from Central America, State of Affairs in Nicaragua," unidentified clipping, Wheeler Collection, series I, #11; *El Nicaraguense*, December 8, 1856. Walker's complicity in the story is reported in Brown, *Agents of Manifest Destiny*, 308. See also New York *Daily News* clipping, n.d., Wheeler Collection, Series I, #11: 19. His identification as the "gray-eyed man," Richard Slotkin points out, constantly reinforced the vision of Walker as race hero. Slotkin, *Fatal Environment*, 252.

FIGURE 4.4. Portrait of William Walker. Publisher S. H. Goetzel requested a da-
guerreotype of Walker to reproduce in Walker's history of his Nicaragua filibuster.
Perhaps it "offended" Walker's sensibilities to provide one because the etchings of
Walker that had appeared earlier in popular periodicals, like the one shown in Figure
4.1, tended to be more flattering than this "approved likeness." *The War in Nicaragua*
(Mobile, 1860).

than just the lengths to which Walker was willing to go to justify his presence
in Nicaragua. It also revealed the victory of appearance in the battle over
manhood in America. William Walker's lasting identification as the "gray-
eyed man of destiny" is a final irony. Walker's appeal to martial men rested
on their vision of him as a man whose character was proven through action,
not appearance, and whose filibustering excursions seemingly offered the

opportunity for other men to prove their character in a similar manner, even if they failed to achieve the markers of success at work and in the home that mattered to restrained men. Walker was the personification of the martial ideal that manhood could be made manifest through territorial expansionism. But even General Walker was forced to display his character externally. Perhaps *El Nicaraguense* was correct in stating that "the Gray-eyed man has come," but it was clearly Americans, and not the Nicaraguans, who had been waiting.

5

The Irresistible Pirate

Narciso López and the Public Meeting

> The Americans are a warlike people. . . . Separate the American from his laws, his religion, and his Constitution, and who more harsh and inexorable; his native energy, converted into a destroying power, directed *against* humanity, makes him the most irresistible of pirates and the most unscrupulous of oppressors. He is the only man that dares, in defiance of all the world, proclaim doctrines particularly harsh and aggressive, and with his native insolence mock Heaven itself, claim evil for his good, and instinct for his God.
>
> – John C. Calhoun, 1848.

John C. Calhoun, the South Carolina senator and slavery apologist, also was a leading congressional opponent of the war against Mexico. His scruples against an unjust war were buttressed by his fear of the impact the war (and subsequent addition of territory) would have on slavery and by presidential ambitions that he believed a principled stand against the war would assist. His strongest critique of the war, in a speech to the Senate in 1848, took the form of an extended discourse on American manhood. When Calhoun spoke against the conquest of Mexico, he offered a strong indictment of the "warlike" nature of his countrymen. Constrained only by laws and religion, the American man, Calhoun suggested, was in essence a vicious beast. Or so, he argued, Americans were behaving in Mexico. The Constitution betrayed, Americans were rampaging through the country, proclaiming "doctrines particularly harsh and aggressive" and substituting evil for good.[1]

Yet there was an ambivalence to Calhoun's critique of American manhood – the American might be, in essence, an aggressive bully, but he was a very successful bully. He alone dared defy the world because he alone had no fear of the world. The American, Calhoun argued, was "the most irresistible

---

[1] "Calhoun's Speech against the Conquest of Mexico," *The American Whig Review* 7 (March 1848), 218; John H. Schroeder, *Mr. Polk's War: American Opposition and Dissent, 1846–1848* (Madison, 1973); Carol and Thomas Christensen, *The U.S.-Mexican War* (San Francisco, 1998), 75.

of pirates," but as such, he could lay claim to being irresistible. Calhoun's critique was only utterable because his indictment of the American character was a form of backhanded flattery. Whatever else he might be, the American was still successful, and to American men in the 1840s and 1850s, the essence of success within Calhoun's critique made it quite palatable. The American man might be a pirate, but at least he was good at it.

Many Americans might not even understand Calhoun's assessment as criticism. Certainly American men would not wish to mock heaven or to claim ill for good, but mid-century success guides suggested that both harshness and aggression were qualities necessary to the man who hoped to win in the "battle of life." Even restrained men had to internalize a high degree of competitiveness in order to succeed in the business world.[2] Nor was it necessarily a bad thing to be an unscrupulous oppressor when one's higher goal was a noble one, as most Americans agreed America's was in Mexico. Indeed, some might argue, American men needed to embrace their martial qualities in order to succeed in the world, as individuals facing a tough business environment and as a nation of men standing together. As John Slidell, minster to Mexico, wrote to President Polk in late 1845 on the eve of war: "Depend on it: We can never get along with [the Mexicans] until we have given them a drubbing."[3] Calhoun's pirate was immoral, yes, but not lacking in appeal in 1840s America. The pirate's victims were not the only ones to find him irresistible in antebellum America, some American men found his very image difficult to resist as well.

Calhoun was not the only opponent of the U.S.-Mexico War to find fuel in the image of the pirate. Thomas Corwin, Calhoun's Senate colleague from Ohio, denounced President Polk in 1847 as no better than a pirate when he seized Mexico by force. Popular interest in pirates increased after 1848 when filibusterers (the very word derived from the Dutch term for pirate) began to capture headlines.[4] One 1699 history of piracy, reprinted twice in the 1850s, would most likely have induced déjà vu with its inquiry into the "recent" increase in piracy. "We shall not examine how it came to pass that our Buccaneers in the West Indies have continually increased till of late. This is an inquiry which belongs to the legislature." Pirates also haunted the historical imagination of travelers to Central America. The Pennsylvania doctor Charles Ross Parke noted in his diary in 1850 that Realejo was the "home or headquarters of the Pirate Morgan." Theodore Johnson explained in his guide for gold-rush travelers that the pirate Morgan was responsible

---

[2] Judy Hilkey, *Character Is Capital: Success Manuals and Manhood in Gilded Age America* (Chapel Hill, 1997), 74–85.

[3] Quoted in Christensen, *The U.S.-Mexican War*, 50.

[4] *Congressional Globe*, 29th Congress, 2nd. Sess., 1847, Appendix, 215–21. Speech delivered February 7, 1847; rise in popular interest based on my examination of popular literature from 1848–1860. The term *filibuster* or *freebooter* was derived from *vrijbuiter* (*vrij*, free + *buit*, booty).

for the bad appearance of the city of Panama. Johnson reminded readers that Morgan sacked the town in 1670, and he claimed that "From this calamity it never recovered."[5]

The question of whether the filibuster was anything more, or anything less, than a pirate was debated at some length in the antebellum press. At heart, the image of the pirate was a gendered one, as was made evident in the debates over William Walker and his followers. On the one hand, it seemed obvious to the enemies of filibustering that an army operating without government sanction could only be piratical. As the *New Englander and Yale Review* put it, the "outside world is unable to recognize any difference between a filibuster expedition sailing from Mobile or New Orleans for the lofty purpose of giving some more tropical country the full benefit and glory of American institutions, and an expedition for piratical purposes."[6]

Many supporters of filibustering strenuously objected to this position. During the early 1850s, as England and America attempted to work out a Latin American policy, The *Democratic Review* enjoyed pointing out that the British could hardly fault American expansion in the region given their historical support of piracy in the West Indies and Central America. "The English of Jamaica . . . were either pirates or the abettors of pirates," the *Democratic Review* noted in 1852. The following year the journal elaborated on the theme, describing the "renowned philanthropists and fillibusters [*sic*], known as the Buccaneers of America" as "outlaws, pirates, and cut-throats" who "were never restrained or punished" by Great Britain but "sailed under the flag of England from a British port" and were "notoriously winked at by the British Government, if not absolutely encouraged in their depredations and murders."[7]

As late as 1859, journalist Edward A. Pollard, writing in *De Bow's Review*, maintained that misunderstood William Walker was "assumed, without reason, to be an arrant filibuster." Great Britain, on the other hand, while "shaming our government to all Europe, for alleged complicity with Walker . . . was herself rendering homage at home to that celebrated

---

[5] Oliver L. Perkins, *The History of the Buccaneers of America: Containing detailed accounts of those bold and daring freebooters; chiefly along the Spanish Main, in the West Indies, and in the Great South Sea, succeeding the civil wars in England*, 2nd ed. (Boston, 1856), 12; Charles Ross Parke, November 8, 1850, in *Dreams to Dust: A Diary of the California Gold Rush, 1849–1850*, James E. Davis, ed. (Lincoln, 1989), 117; Theodore Taylor Johnson, *Sights in the Gold Region, and Scenes by the Way* (New York, 1849), 76.

[6] "The Moral of Harper's Ferry," *NEYR* 17 (November 1859), 1073–4. U.S. Representative John Letcher of Virginia also believed Walker to be "no better than a Pirate," and was disgusted by wide-spread public support Walker found in Washington, DC, in 1858. Robert E. May, *Manifest Destiny's Underworld: Filibustering in Antebellum America* (Chapel Hill, 2002), 76.

[7] "The Islands of the Gulf of Honduras: Their Seizure and Organization as a British Colony," *USDR* 31 (November–December 1852), 545; "The Valedictory of the Whig Administration," *USDR* 32 (May 1853), 463; see also Philadelphia *Public Ledger*, November 29, 1855; "The Amicable and the Amiable in English Policy," *USDR* 28 (March 1851), 248.

Anglo-Indian filibuster, Lord Dalhousie, for having added 'four kingdoms, besides lesser territories,' to her Indian empire.... It is too notorious that, for a century and a half, Great Britain has been engaged in extending her territory by corrupt arts and open violence." The real pirates were British or were supported by Britain.[8]

While Pollard assumed that piracy was wicked, and that even the term *filibuster* was one of opprobrium, the masculine character of piracy also held a powerful allure in the eyes of many American men. Indiana native Horace Bell, for example, recalled adopting the persona of "pirate" for himself when he joined Walker's army at the age of twenty-three. Recruits to Narciso López's 1849 filibustering expedition (which was stopped by the authorities on Round Island just off the coast of Mississippi) were explicitly enticed with the promise of "plunder, drink, women, and tobacco," suggesting the degree to which filibusters actually embraced piracy. Bell's enjoyment of filibustering for the opportunity it provided to play pirate was probably not unusual.[9]

New Yorker John L. O'Sullivan, the editor of the *Democratic Review*, was known as both the "father" of the term *Manifest Destiny* and the son of a man accused of piracy. In the summer of 1849, while López attempted to attract his troops with plunder and women, O'Sullivan lobbied Senator Calhoun to support the filibuster. Another prominent pro-slavery ideologue and politician, the U.S.-Mexico War hero John Quitman, had already thrown his support behind López; O'Sullivan though perhaps that Calhoun would come to the same conclusion, but Calhoun evidently found this pirate entirely resistible. Given his stated position on piracy, Calhoun declined O'Sullivan's request. But given the ambivalence Calhoun expressed in his evaluation of the pirate's character, it is perhaps predictable that he expressed some private admiration for López. Calhoun's decision was a wise one, since O'Sullivan, along with López, Quitman, and thirteen co-conspirators, was indicted for violating the Neutrality Act in the wake of the failed Round Island expedition. Calhoun died in March of 1850, just before López's troops left New Orleans in another attempted invasion of Cuba.[10]

[8] Edward A. Pollard, "The Central American Question," *DBR* 27 (November 1859), 580. See also "The Fate of Mexico," *USDR* 41 (May 1858), 342; George Fitzhugh, "Acquisition of Mexico- Filibustering," *DBR* 2514 (December 1858), 618.

[9] Horace Bell, "Confessions of a Filibuster," *Golden Era*, May 7, 1876; Tom Chaffin, *Fatal Glory, Narciso López and the First Clandestine U.S. War against Cuba* (Charlottesville, VA, 1996), 91.

[10] Chaffin, *Fatal Glory*, 81, 161; Stephen John Hartnett, *Democratic Dissent and the Cultural Fictions of Antebellum America* (Urbana, 2002), 98, (ftnt. 11) 205. It was "Cora Montgomery" (Jane McManus Storm Cazneau) rather than O'Sullivan who actually coined the term, as Linda Hudson has shown. Linda S. Hudson, *Mistress of Manifest Destiny: A Biography of Jane McManus Storm Cazneau, 1807–1878* (Austin, 2001), 46–8, 205–10. On the appeal of the pirate, see also "Affairs in Nicaragua," *The Pennsylvanian*, n.d., Wheeler Collection, LOC, Series I, #12, 116.

At the heart of the debate over piracy, of course, was the issue of what were the most notable parts of the pirate's character: his daring and bravery or his bloodthirsty lack of ethics. The treatment of the Caribbean's most famous pirate, Captain Henry Morgan, in *Harper's Monthly Magazine* illustrates the range of associations provoked by the idea of the pirate in the decade before the Civil War. Morgan's metamorphosis, from masculine hero to degenerate thug, not only reflects the range of antebellum perspectives on aggressive expansionism, but also the ongoing debate over manhood back home.

In September of 1855, *Harper's* published "Buccaneers of the Spanish Main," a quasi-historical account of piracy in the Americas, situating Captain Morgan's daring assault on Panama in 1670 within a larger context of piracy in the region. At the same time that Walker was making his own assault on Nicaragua, *Harper's* presented a highly romanticized vision of piracy. Pirates were fearless, strong, and wildly successful. In an expedition that is described as "the prototype of all the subsequent ones" (including, most likely, William Walker's), the Dutch pirate Davis loots Grenada, Nicaragua, without losing a single man, and then he makes his men rich with an equitable division of the booty. The buccaneers of the Spanish Main were a successful bunch. "Partly from their superior address and strength, and partly from the terror of their name, they managed, whatever the odds, not only to effect their purpose, but to throw almost the entire loss on the Spaniards." Rather than focus on what the author vaguely termed the "debauchery" of the buccaneer, *Harper's* pictured the pirates engaging in consensual sex with free-thinking Spanish and Indian women. Pirates "lived in princely style after a streak of good luck" and "the ladies who were superior to conventional rules, and agreed to share the homes of the lords of the sea, reaped abundant harvests."[11]

Not only was "a buccaneer's life...not so disagreeable," but it proved to be a healthy occupation as well: "By dint of exercise, the buccaneers had brought their bodies into such a healthy condition, that their flesh closed on a wound like an elastic substance, and diseases were unknown among them." The "excesses" committed by the pirates, including needless torture (but not rape), are blamed on the "astonishing tenacity" of the Spanish, who refuse to bow to the Protestant invaders. In this view, piracy, while unethical (although the Spanish brought it on themselves), was also fun, profitable, and healthy, offering men the opportunity for both sexual and military adventure, as well as the chance to vindicate Protestantism. Given William Walker's emergence in Central America at the time and the recent political victories of the anti-Catholic Know-Nothing Party, readers would have had difficulty missing the contemporary relevance of this celebration of piracy.[12]

---

[11] "Buccaneers of the Spanish Main," *HNMM* 11 (September 1855), 514–23.
[12] Ibid., 517, 522.

Later portraits of buccaneers in *Harper's* were not as flattering. In 1858, the magazine offered readers the romantic tale of a seventeenth-century French pirate, "An Old Filibuster," featuring pirates leading dissipated lives in Nicaragua.[13] In 1858 and 1859, *Harper's* published a multi-part travelogue titled "Tropical Journeyings" that repeatedly touched on the "bloodthirsty corsairs" of the region, focusing on the "diabolical wantonness" of the "heartless criminals." Composed of "refugees from all nations ... headed by some giant of crime" it was only the efforts of an "anti-piratical squadron" from the United States that finally brought peace to the Caribbean in the 1820s. As a multi-national band, these pirates were racially suspect, under the sway of an evil leader, and the enemies of the forces of good in America. Morgan's assault on Panama, described in great detail, is less daring than foolhardy, but above all, it is vicious. The buccaneers commit "brutalities too hideous to be told. Neither age nor sex was spared. The whole city was given over to rapine and murder." Nor does *Harper's* shy away from the question of the contemporary comparison, referring to Morgan's men as "ruthless filibusters." The only ambivalence in this condemnation of filibustering was offered by the accompanying illustration, "Buccaneers' Rendezvous," in which the pirates relax in the tropical splendor of Central America, ministered to by a shirtless dark-skinned woman (see Figure 5.1).[14]

The conversion of pirate from a model of manliness to its opposite is completed in "Morgan, the Buccaneer," of 1859. In a self-described "living poem, revealing woman's purity and constancy," *Harper's* names the "brutalities too hideous to be told" in a lurid manner, and it presents Morgan as unethical, savage, and ultimately unmanly.[15]

The author of "Morgan the Buccaneer" starts out on a familiar note, reporting that Morgan was known to be "a bold and successful cruiser" and that the Spanish refused to surrender to his army. But the behavior of Morgan's troops is wildly out of proportion to any offence of the Spaniards of Panama, and *Harper's* does not shy away from describing a scene that "beggars description. Wives were violated in presence of their husbands; daughters before their mothers. Lust and debauchery of every kind ran riot through the place. Some were inhumanly tortured. . . ." Other details offered to the reader included men "roasted alive," the "first women of the place" gang-raped, a church "turned into a place of prostitution," and other examples of the inhumanity of the pirates. Nor is it only a small group of rogue pirates who are responsible for these excesses; Morgan personally orders and carries out rapes, and he tortures a priest to death. In case any reader were still unsure about the depravity of the bunch, a description of the starving

---

[13] "An Old Filibuster," *HNMM* 18 (December 1858), 18–32.
[14] Oran, "Tropical Journeyings," *HNMM* 16 (April 1858), 486, 17 (June 1858), 28, and 19 (September 1859), 434–7.
[15] "Morgan the Buccaneer," *HNMM* 19 (June 1859), 20–37.

FIGURE 5.1. "Buccaneers' Rendezvous," from "Tropical Journeyings," *Harper's New Monthly Magazine* 16 (April 1858): 586.

pirates coming across a herd of cattle highlights their degradation: "The blood soaking their huge beards and dropping off upon their breasts, they presented altogether a most wild and savage appearance." While the pirates in the 1855 *Harper's* story are the picture of good health, these pirates become "deadly sick" from the "vile trash they had been compelled to eat."[16]

There is little ambiguity in this portrait of a very bad man. Morgan is savage, Morgan has no pity, and Morgan is not much of a leader either.

[16] Ibid., 23, 32, 28, 30.

Morgan tries the patience of men recruited through "false representations" by leading them on "fruitless marches" (reminiscent of those described by Walker's men). He fails to keep his men in line, thus missing the opportunity to capture a Spanish galleon, and he burns down Panama City, "for what purpose no one knew." (Walker burned down Granada during his retreat from Nicaragua for similarly obscure reasons.) In the climax of the tale, Morgan loses the respect of many of his men by jailing the story's heroine, the wife of a Peruvian merchant, after failing to "ring a consent from her." (That Morgan even looked for her consent is attributed only to the "atmosphere of purity" that surrounds her. "He felt abashed and uneasy in her presence, and powerless to play the brute with her.") Although Morgan finally frees the angelic heroine, it is due to no change of heart. Several of his men who "were moved to pity" and entranced by the "gentle manners, her surpassing beauty" and "that nameless charm that surrounds angelic purity" appeal to Morgan on her behalf, and he acts "governed by policy rather than feeling." Heartless to the end, Morgan betrays even his own men by keeping virtually all the booty for himself.[17]

It is not surprising that Morgan's truly depraved character is ultimately illustrated through his treatment of a woman, a woman unmoved by Morgan's offer of riches and so beyond reproach that she tells her captor, "Sir, my life is in your hands; but as to my body, my soul shall sooner be separated from it through the violence of your arms than I shall condescend to your request." Woman's purity and goodness, the self-proclaimed theme of the piece, was repeatedly mobilized by supporters of restrained manhood to undermine the appeal of piracy and aggression in American expansionist culture. Domesticity, female purity, and the sanctity of the family were among the most potent weapons that restrained men could draw on to critique martial manhood. Morgan may have gained fame and riches in his sway over Latin America, but few men would dream of modeling themselves on a man so heartless as to ignore the appeal of True Womanhood. It is not sufficient that his men despise him and that he acts like a brute, this "freebooter's" true character is revealed in his response to woman's purity.[18]

What accounts for the transformation of Captain Morgan from uninhibited manly man to loathsome savage in the narratives of *Harper's*? It is worth noting that privateering (the contemporary version of piracy) only

---

[17] Ibid., 30, 33, 35, 36.

[18] Ibid., 35, 36. Horace Bell reported a similar story involving William Walker. According to Bell, Walker imprisoned Donna Encarnacon, an immensely rich Nicaraguan who opposed his government, and he demanded a large "fine" for her speeches against his regime. Contrary to his expectations, Encarnacon refused to leave jail, embarrassing Walker. Still hoping to extort money from her, Walker offered to move her to the home of one of his officers, but she refused because the officer's wife was "disreputable." Finally, Walker was forced to free her, leaving him "beaten" by the experience in the eyes of his men. Horace Bell, "Confessions of a Filibuster," *The Golden Era*, August 27, 1876.

became illegal in 1856, when it was banned in the Declaration of Paris. It also seems likely that the increasingly chilly press coverage of William Walker and the proliferating reports of excesses committed by his troops in Nicaragua (including reports published in *Harper's*) played at least some part in the journal's waning enthusiasm for piracy. As Walker's single-minded dedication to conquer Central America appeared more and more unbalanced, the pirate may have lost some of his luster as a model for American manhood, at least among readers of *Harper's*.[19]

But this chronological account of the "fall" of the pirate more likely than not misrepresents the variety of reactions to aggressive manhood held by different Americans during the antebellum period. Ideologies of manhood were actively contested in antebellum America. Some Americans throughout the period saw the pirate as a loathsome creature absolutely lacking in the higher virtues and in respect for women who was happy to exercise unjust power over those weaker than himself. Others idealized the pirate as the aggressive, physically strong, and successful hero who rightly dominated those undeserving of respect. Both visions of manhood were celebrated in antebellum America, and both, it should seem clear, were defined in relationship to others – to both white and Latin American women, to African-Americans, and to racially and religiously tainted Latin American men.

This chapter investigates another aspect of the mutually constitutive nature of martial manhood and the foreign encounter by focusing on some of those men who found piracy irresistible – the urban working men who attended meetings in support of filibustering. Aggressive expansionists embraced the imperial encounter in the late 1840s and 1850s as an opportunity to assert the advantages of whiteness on a new frontier. By traveling through Latin America and by reading the accounts of travelers in the region, martial men formulated a racialized practice of manhood based on the domination of Latin American men and the objectification of Latin American women. Back home in the United States, men took advantage of urban public meetings held in support of filibusters like William Walker and Narciso López to celebrate and authorize their masculinity, to prove that their masculinity, and not that of restrained men, deserved public adulation. By the late 1850s, privateering had become as illegal as filibustering, but the pirate's allure was still alive and well in some circles.

Martial Manhood Comes Home

The contested nature of manhood in the United States in the antebellum era helped shape the aggressive expansionist encounter with Latin America by suggesting that aggression against an unworthy foe was virtuous and by

---

[19] Donald Chidsey, *The American Privateers* (New York, 1962), 145–6. On the appeal of privateering in antebellum America see Paul Gilje, *Liberty on the Waterfront: American Maritime Culture in the Age of Revolution* (Philadelphia, 2004), 172–5.

imagining Latin America as a place where brave, hard-working American men could succeed when their opportunities back home had been limited by increased competition and economic change. In their interactions with Latin American men and women, travelers from the United States reinforced their faith in their own courage, work ethic, and enlightenment, and they provided grounds for asserting that a martial aggressive manhood was the best manhood for the domination of the hemisphere. The frontier continued to be a place where a masculine practice organized around dominance made more sense than a masculine practice organized around expertise. Restrained masculinity was marginalized on the frontier at the same time that martial masculinity, in the eyes of men like David Deaderick, seemed to be marginalized at home.

The Latin American encounter not only provided an antidote to the rise of restrained manhood in the United States, it also shaped the contest over masculinity back home. It did so by providing new currency for the aggressive practices of marital masculinity in the person of heroic aggressive individuals. As R. M. Connell has suggested, the violence of the Latin American encounter was a predictable outgrowth of the "gendered enterprise" of empire. "Loss of control at the frontier is a recurring theme in the history of empires, and is closely connected with the making of masculine exemplars." In the 1850s, the masculine exemplars emerging from the violent encounters on the new frontier were, by and large, filibusters.[20]

William Walker was not the only filibuster to be heroized by urban working men. Urban Americans held memorial processions for completely inept filibusters like Henry Crabb. On the first two anniversaries of Crabb's execution in Sonora, San Franciscans held requiems for Crabb and his followers. They held benefits, balls, and serenades in honor of William Walker and composed and performed music to celebrate his success in Nicaragua. Urban residents could thrill to the manly exploits of the filibusters in theatrical performances from San Francisco and Sacramento to New York and New Orleans. Urban Americans voyeuristically packed federal courtrooms when filibusters went on trial for violating neutrality laws, and their support made gaining convictions nearly impossible. Urban residents also were the primary audience for an emerging sensational literature, including dime novels and city mysteries, which glorified an expansionist agenda after 1848. So great was enthusiasm for filibustering in urban America that Robert May has claimed it "deserves remembrance as a phenomenon of America's urban environment."[21]

---

[20] R. W. Connell, *Masculinities* (Berkeley, 1995), 187.

[21] *Daily Alta California*, April 7, 8, 1858; May, *Manifest Destiny's Underworld*, 71–5, 94 (quotation), 165; Frederic Rosengarten Jr., *Freebooters Must Die! The Life and Death of William Walker, the Most Notorious Filibuster of the Nineteenth Century* (Wayne, PA, 1976), 145, 160–2; NYT, May 27, 1850; Philadelphia *Public Ledger*, April 30, 1855; Streeby, *American Sensations: Class, Empire, and the Production of Popular Culture* (Berkeley, 2002).

One place where men openly proclaimed their martial vision of manhood was at the public meeting, an important feature of urban political culture in the antebellum era. Mary Ryan has described the political meeting as a cornerstone of urban political culture, holding "sacred status" in the 1830s and 1840s. By the 1850s, however, the political meeting was on the decline as "segmented spaces, parade culture, and public meetings" were no longer "capacious enough to accommodate all the newcomers." While certain types of public meetings were less inclusive in the 1850s than they had been in previous decades, at least one type of meeting thrived in the years before the Civil War – the meeting dedicated to celebrating aggressive expansionist activities, especially by filibusters. While these meetings, which occurred in cities across the country, were not openly partisan in nature, they were expressly political, and they brought together a broad assortment of urban residents in solidarity with a common violent masculine practice.[22]

Meetings in support of the U.S.-Mexico War, like the "Great War Meeting" held at Tammany Hall in New York City in January of 1848, drew thousands of male spectators and offered an opportunity for urban men to assert their support for both aggressive expansionism and martial manhood.[23] Speakers at the Tammany Hall meeting mixed gendered metaphor with a strong sense of Manifest Destiny: "The Americans regard this continent as their birth-right. The seed of all their settlements has been sown in blood and watered by blood." Sam Houston asserted that "assuredly as to-morrow's sun will rise and pursue its bright course along the firmament of heaven, so certain it appears to my mind, must the Anglo Saxon race pervade the whole Southern extremity of this vast continent, and the people whom God has placed here in this land, spread, prevail and pervade throughout the whole rich empire of this great hemisphere." He was met with "great cheers" and cries of "annex it all" from the audience. Democratic senator Henry S. Foote of Mississippi asserted the absolute authority of aggression when he compared Americans in Mexico to the "children of Israel," who "under the direction of Jehovah himself, acquired what was deemed a good and valid title to all the territory included in the promised land, by force of arms alone."[24]

While audience members at the Great War Meeting retired to a bar at the conclusion of the meeting, opponents of martial manhood, or at least

---

[22] Mary Ryan, *Civic Wars: Democracy and Public Life in the American City during the Nineteenth Century* (Berkeley, 1997), 138, 157. The most significant work about the filibuster meetings has been done by Tom Chaffin in *Fatal Glory* and "Sons of Washington: Narciso López, Filibustering, and U.S. Nationalism, 1848–1851," *Journal of the Early Republic* 15 (Spring 1995): 79–108, although Chaffin fails to describe the meetings themselves or their significance in great detail.

[23] "The Great War Meeting," *NYH*, January 30, 1848; "The War Meeting," *NYT*, January 31, 1848.

[24] "The Great War Meeting," *NYH*, January 30, 1848.

of the Democratic Party in New York, were composing a condemnation of the proceeding that placed the entire event in its gendered context. The New York *Tribune* excoriated the speakers of the meeting as "advocates of more Butchery and Subjugation among us" who employed "lies and liquor" to keep the working men of New York from their proper place – home with their families. The meeting occurred, sadly enough, on "a Saturday evening, when the tired laborer wends his way wearily homeward, hoping to enjoy for a brief season the delights and affections of home – when the Christian's thoughts turn naturally to the coming day of worship as well as rest, and to the Prince of Peace. . . . "[25] The contrast between the two visions of manhood, one religious, sober, family centered, and mindful of the value of peace, the other violent and more interested in male camaraderie than the domesticated household, was clear.

The public meeting in favor of aggressive expansionism did not end with the Treaty of Guadalupe Hidalgo – it was central to buttressing support for William Walker and other filibusters.[26] Narciso López was one of the most prominent filibusters of the era. He made three separate attempts to liberate Cuba in the late 1840s and early 1850s. His campaigns were financed by American money, made by American volunteers, and undertaken with both the acknowledged and unacknowledged political support of high-ranking U.S. officials. López's recruiting agents were active in Baltimore, Washington DC, New York, and Philadelphia, as well as in the rural South in 1849, the year that O'Sullivan unsuccessfully lobbied Calhoun and ended up indicted for violating the Neutrality Act. That summer, between 450 and 600 of López's troops were blockaded by U.S. naval officers on tiny Round Island. The Taylor Administration's handling of the Round Island blockade was mocked by some as overkill, but it prevented the Round Island troops from meeting up with similarly sized forces from New York in an intended two-pronged filibuster on Cuba (see Figure 5.2).[27]

Although López spoke of liberating Cuba, he indicated to his American supporters that annexation to the United States was the ultimate goal of his filibustering attempts.[28] A charismatic figure, he was quite popular among

---

[25] "The War Meeting," *NYT*, January 31, 1848.

[26] The "Liberty and Nicaragua" meeting was held in New York's City Hall Park on a Friday evening in May of 1856 at the height of Walker's success. Attended by thousands of his New York supporters, Walker and his efforts were lauded by an assortment of national politicians. "The Great Walker Meeting in the Park at New York." New York *Evening Mirror*, May 24, 1856.

[27] Antonio Rafael de la Cova, *Cuban Confederate Colonel: The Life of Ambrosio José Gonzales* (Columbia, 2003), 8–10; May, *Manifest Destiny's Underworld*, 22–3; *NYT*, August 25, 29, 30, September 1, 1849; Antonio Rafael de la Cova, "The Taylor Administration versus Mississippi Sovereignty: The Round Island Expedition of 1849," *Journal of Mississippi History* 62 (Winter 2000): 325–6.

[28] Richard Tansey, "Southern Expansionism: Urban Interests in the Cuban Filibusters," *Plantation Society* 1 (June 1979): 228.

THE GREAT NAVAL BLOCKADE OF ROUND ISLAND.

FIGURE 5.2. "The Great Naval Blockade of Round Island. Showing the Immense Importance of Having an Efficient 'Right Arm of the National Defence [*sic*]'" (1849). This cartoon satirizes both the Taylor administration's anti-filibustering efforts and the elaborate dreams of aggressive expansionists. In September of 1849 Narciso López planned a two-prong attack on Cuba from New York and Round Island in the Gulf of Mexico off the coast of Mississippi. A naval blockade of Round Island prevented the attack, but López was only temporarily dissuaded. Although the artist is critical of the current Spanish regime in Cuba, he represents the filibusters (shown on the shore of Round Island) as infantile and ineffectual. The artist mocks the naval blockade as both unnecessary and beneath the dignity of the Navy, since the filibusters are too busy playing games and banqueting to pose a threat to anyone. One sailor announces that "this is as safe and more glorious than Tampico," contrasting the blockade with the heroic naval actions of the U.S.-Mexico War. The filibusters may not be men of action in this cartoon, but they dream big. Kites in the shape of stars (or new states on a flag) read "Canada" and "Cuba" while diners toast other potential new territories, including Venezuela, Santo Domingo, the Yucatan, and the Republic of Sierra Madre. An official from the Taylor administration admonishes the filibusters, "You should thank us ye Pirates and Robbers of Cuba for saving you from [Spanish governor of Cuba Federico] Roncali's Garrote." Predictably, a filibuster responds "We are no Pirates!" and points to the actions of the Spanish to reveal the identity of the true buccaneers. The official's warning proved prescient – López and fifty-one American recruits would be executed in Cuba less than two years later. Library of Congress, Prints and Photographs Division [LC-USZ62-16000].

expansionists like John L. O'Sullivan, despite the potentially problematic issue of his nationality. As we have seen, American travelers viewed Latin American men with a disdain based on both racial and religious grounds. Given that they were especially dismissive of Latin American soldiers after the U.S.-Mexico War, one might expect that they would hesitate before embracing a Latin American general.

López, who was born in Venezuela, was swarthy, dark eyed, and relied on a translator to help him with his limited English. But his supporters proved willing to overlook his racial difference. Popular representations of him "whitened" him to a great degree, both figuratively (he was often described as Spanish or as Creole) and literally, as in the woodcut print of a pale López that appeared in the New Orleans *Delta* in 1850. The author regretted that the print "is far from doing justice to his fine features and noble expression" (see Figure 5.3). As with William Walker, supporters focused on López's eyes as a way of resolving the conflict between his appearance and his stature as an "American" filibuster. Varina Davis, wife of the future Confederate president, was typical in describing López's "glowing eyes and silvery hair" rather than his skin color. Another account described his "glorious falcon eyes, darker than a starless night, yet burning with all the fire of a southern sun, how they drew you with mystic influence to trust the great heart which beamed in their depths." To a certain extent, López supporters had an easier time than did Walker supporters in resolving his crisis of appearance because, as travelers through Latin America discovered, racial categories in Latin America did not conform to those in the United States. The fact that Cuba was a slaveholding society also may have encouraged Southerners, especially, to identify with the Creole slaveholding elite that made up the bulk of López's supporters.[29]

General López was not dissuaded by Round Island. He invaded Cuba in May of 1850 but was repulsed by Spanish forces. Back in the United States he was greeted as a hero, and he began organizing another invasion. López became a sensation during his final filibustering foray in August of 1851. Late at night on August 21, news reached New York that fifty-one American volunteers had been executed by the Spanish after their capture in Cuba. Among them was a young New Orleans customhouse employee, Colonel William Crittenden, who was also the nephew of U.S. attorney general John J. Crittenden.[30]

---

[29] May, *Manifest Destiny's Underworld*, 21; New Orleans *Daily Delta*, May 26, 1850; Chaffin, *Fatal Glory*, 47; Lucy Holcombe noted that López "was dark, with the passionate splendor of a southern clime... his eyes flashed with patriotic enthusiasm" but also emphasized his European origins, comparing him at another point to "those grand old Italian pictures artists so much love." Lucy Holcombe Pickens, *The Free Flag of Cuba: The Lost Novel of Lucy Holcombe Pickens*. Orville Vernon Burton and Georganne B. Burton, eds. (Baton Rouge, 2002), 57, 120.

[30] Tansey, "Southern Expansionism," 233, 241.

GENERAL NARCISO LOPEZ,

COMMANDER OF THE LIBERATING ARMY OF CUBA.

In presenting our readers the above wood-cut of the gallant chief at the head of the Cuban revolutionary movement, we feel bound to remark, that owing to the haste with which it has been prepared, it is far from doing justice to his fine features and noble expression. A very good full length lithograph of the General, represented in the act of unfurling the standard of the Cuban Republic, may be seen on the walls of our office.

SHIELDS. SC.

Engraved expressly for the "Delta," by Shields & Collins.

FIGURE 5.3. "General Narciso Lopez, Commander of the Liberating Army of Cuba." New Orleans *Daily Delta*, May 26, 1850.

Young Crittenden had attracted young urban clerks and sons of southern planters to join his company with promises of large cash bonuses and Cuban sugar plantations. But the filibusters were greatly outnumbered, and a predicted rebellion among Cuban Creoles in their support failed to materialize. As the *Democratic Review* put it, the soldiers were "captured when incapable of resistance, shot down without trial, like dogs without owners, and buried like dogs." One newspaper reported that a Havana waiter "showed to everybody as a proof of the glorious act he had performed, the testicles of one of the victims, which he had cut," literalizing the symbolic destruction of the manhood of the American volunteers. Although López was widely believed to be marching through Cuba on the way to victory he was executed on September 1. For about a week, until positive news of the general's defeat reached New Orleans, public meetings were held across America to protest the execution and rumored desecration of the bodies of the American volunteers and to support López.[31] At least twenty-five public meetings in support of López were held across the country in late August of 1851.[32]

López had a severe and damaging effect on relations between the United States and both Spain and Cuba. Richard Henry Dana, who traveled to Cuba in the late 1850s, was "surprised to find what an impression the López expedition made in Cuba – a far greater impression than is commonly supposed in the United States." Dana then recounted the "massacre" that prompted so many public meetings. "The fears of the government and hopes of the sympathizers exaggerated the force, and the whole military power of the government was stirred against them. Their little force of a few hundred broken-down men and lads, deceived and deserted, fought a body eight times their number and kept them at bay, causing great slaughter." While López and his men failed in their efforts, the popular account of the event heroized

[31] "Narcisso [sic] Lopez and His Companions," *Democratic Review* 29 (October 1851): 292; Tansey, "Southern Expansionism," 241 ftnt. 42. Although López was killed September 1, 1851, and rumors of his demise circulated as early as August 30 via the *National Intelligencer*, it was not until September 6 that the New York *Daily Tribune* confirmed his death and the end of the "independence movement." The *Herald* confirmed it September 7. Coverage of the López expedition was extremely unreliable in general. Both reform papers and the penny press reported virtually any rumor they received, sometimes running wildly optimistic reports on the same page as completely contradictory testimony.

[32] Meetings for which I have extensive descriptions include New York City meetings, August 22, 23, 26 (*NYH, NYT, New York Post, Philadelphia Public Ledger*); Jersey City, August 27, (*NYH*); Philadelphia, August 22, 25 (*Public Ledger, NYH, NYT*); Pittsburgh, August 28 (Pittsburgh *Daily Morning Post*). Meetings with short descriptions include Memphis, August 12 (in the Memphis *Enquirer*, August 13, reprinted in the *NYH*), Montgomery, Alabama, August 17 (Montgomery *Journal*, August 18, reprinted in the *NYH*), Belleville, Georgia, July 26, 1851 (Savannah *News*, August 23, reprinted in the *NYH*), Raymond, Mississippi, August 7, 1851 (New Orleans *Delta*, August 8, reprinted in the *NYH*), Mobile, August 22 (Mobile *Herald*, August 23, reprinted in the *NYH*), Jeffersonville, Indiana, August 24 (Jeffersonville *Banner*, August 25, reprinted in the *NYH*), Louisville, August 27, (Louisville *Democrat*, August 29, 1851, reprinted in the *NYH*), St. Louis, August 24 (St. Louis *Intelligencer*, August 28, reprinted in the *NYH*), Nashville, August 24 (or 23?), Savannah, August 22, New Orleans, August 21, Memphis, August 29, Washington, DC, September 1 (all in the *NYH*), Boston, August 23, Washington, DC, August 27, Louisville, August 28, Cincinnati, August 28 (the *Tribune* predicted that it "does not promise to amount to much"), Baltimore, August 27, and September 5 (all in the *NYT*). According to the *Herald* on August 27, "before long there will not be a city or town in the whole country" without a public meeting. All meetings were held in 1851.

PLACE WHERE LOPEZ LANDED.

FIGURE 5.4. "Place Where Lopez Landed." Images related to Narciso López's final disastrous filibustering foray in 1851 were deemed noteworthy in later years, even in articles that were not primarily about López, like this 1853 travel narrative, "Three Weeks in Cuba." López did not choose an ideal landing spot in 1851. El Morrillo was sparsely inhabited and "the timid inhabitants had fled into the hills." *Harper's New Monthly Magazine* 6 (January 1853): 174.

them as victims of overwhelming force and the underhanded treachery of the Spanish (see Figure 5.4).[33]

The López meetings were remarkable not because of the thousands of men that gathered for them, since large public meetings were somewhat common occurrences, but because due to their subject matter, they merited detailed descriptions in those largely Democratic penny papers sympathetic to expansionism. At the same time López and his cause transcended party politics by appealing to national issues – American honor, the treatment of American soldiers, and territorial expansionism. As Tom Chaffin has shown, Narciso López inspired great nationalist sentiment within America. As a result, these meetings were reported in nonpartisan papers as well as in the

[33] Richard Henry Dana, *To Cuba and Back: A Vacation Voyage* (Boston, 1859), 223. Tom Chaffin found that the López expedition is still vivid in the historical imagination of Cubans today. *Fatal Glory*, xi–xii.

Democratic press, a useful consideration when trying to evaluate attendance at these meetings. The López meetings, the focus of the remainder of this chapter, provide an unparalleled lens on the culture of aggressive expansionism within the United States. It was at the moment of López's horrific failure, and the slaughter of American troops, that the largely underground world of filibustering and the masculine culture that supported it became most public.[34]

The López meetings were often described as spontaneous by supporters, but they were almost always advertised through the posting of handbills around the city, or in certain neighborhoods, listing the time, location, and reason for the meeting, either the same or following day. A meeting for the following night also might be announced at a meeting. López meetings were held in central, urban public spaces capacious enough to hold an enormous crowd of people, the premier location for meetings in New York City being City Hall Park. In Memphis, Savannah, and Philadelphia, López meetings originally planned for indoor spaces were forced to move to the largest outdoor public spaces in the city due to the size of the crowds. These meetings were held in the evening, scheduled to begin between 5 and 7 PM, although none of them seem to have started on time. The nineteenth-century popular historian Joel Tyler Headley claimed that evening meetings were by definition "ominous" and were designed for purposes of more than "mere speech-making," but most likely these public meetings were held when they were to allow working men to attend in large numbers. The Headley quote underscores the fact, however, that the very nature and audience of these meetings threatened some urban dwellers.[35]

Meeting organizers constructed stages from which speakers could address the crowd.[36] Often there was room on the stage specifically set aside for reporters. In the early López meetings in both Philadelphia and New York City, no press area was provided, resulting in disgruntled reporters and limited coverage of the meeting in the paper.[37] Since one of the premier purposes of these meetings was to widen and strengthen support for an expansionist agenda, in which the press was crucial, meetings later in the week were more solicitous of the needs of friendly reporters. The most media savvy

---

[34] Tom Chaffin, "Sons of Washington."

[35] Joel Tyler Headley. *The Great Riots of New York, 1712–1873.* 1873 (Indianapolis, 1970), 103.

[36] Stages were not always competently constructed. *NYT*, August 23, 1851.

[37] The *Herald* reported that even at the second New York meeting, on August 23, "there were no arrangements whatever made for the press, and our reporter was compelled to take his place in the midst of the crowd, jostled about, and unable to take notes, or even hear, except at intervals" (*NYH*, August 24, 1851). At the August 26 meeting in New York, "the arrangements made for the press were tolerably good, but the reporters were crushed and crowded by men who had no particular right to be on the platform... One man so interfered with one of the reporters that it was found necessary to eject him from the platform" (*NYH*, August 27, 1851).

organizers not only set aside a secure press area but also provided torches by which reporters could take notes.[38]

A series of speakers, local political or military figures, addressed the crowd over the course of a few hours, well into the darkness even in the summer months. Speakers tended to refer to national political and military figures as a way of validating their own positions, by either reading selections from the writings of these men or, ideally, reading a letter from the figure prepared especially for the event. Quite often, in the case of these filibustering meetings, speakers would tell the crowd that a significant figure was expected to appear but through bad luck or illness was unavailable at the last minute. An ex-mayor presided over one of the Philadelphia meetings, and two meetings in New Orleans featured elected officials, but for the most part speakers at the López meetings were not significant political figures.[39]

The order of the speakers appears to have been fixed ahead of time, but could change during the meeting itself, according to the spirit of the crowd. Meetings could be abbreviated due to bad weather or an unsupportive crowd.[40] They always ended with the adoption of resolutions. In the case of the Cuba meetings, these resolutions were similar enough to suggest that López supporters had either adopted wholesale the resolutions of a previous meeting in another city, or that there was a common committee helping coordinate meetings around the country. The similarity of the resolutions, and the fact that some speakers directly referred to events or speeches in other cities as if the audience would be familiar with them, point to a shared urban culture and experience of the expansionist public meeting that unified Americans, North and South, during the decade before the Civil War. In some cities, including Nashville and New York, "grand processions," including inflammatory signs and banners (calling for "revenge" and "vengeance"),

[38] At the first López meeting in New York, "a temporary stand was erected late in the afternoon, but was totally insufficient for the officers" (*NYH*, August 23, 1851).

[39] The *National Intelligencer* of August 26, 1851 claimed that "no man of any mark has made his appearance at the meetings which have been held." The Boston *Courier* joked that the "Fillibusters" were all taken ill, given that they didn't show up for their own meetings. Boston *Courier*, August 25, reprinted in the *NYT*, August 26, 1851; Robert G. Caldwell, *The López Expeditions to Cuba, 1848–1851* (Princeton, 1915), 115. The former U.S. commissioner for Louisiana, M. M. Cohen, presided over a pro-López meeting in July in New Orleans, and M. M. Reynolds, district attorney, presided over the August 21, New Orleans meeting. Chester S. Urban, "New Orleans and the Cuba Question during the López Expeditions of 1849–1851: A Local Study in 'Manifest Destiny'," *Louisiana Historical Quarterly* 22 (1939): 1143, 1160.

[40] The Boston meeting was cut short by heckling from the audience, and when it began to rain in New York, some audience members suggested breaking up the meeting. Boston *Courier*, August 25, reprinted in the *Tribune*, August 26, 1851. At the New York meeting of August 22 "a slight sprinkle of rain came down, and some one proposed an adjournment to Tammany Hall, but Mr. R said 'No! If it were not for the rain, the earth would not produce the bountiful fruits on which we live. If the Almighty sees it to send down the rain, let us welcome it.' The rain was welcomed with three cheers" (*NYT*, August 23, 1851).

marked the conclusion of the meeting. Occasionally parades led to meetings as well. In Savannah, Georgia, rockets and bonfires illuminated the square where the López meeting was held, while other meetings featured bands playing patriotic songs.[41]

The López meetings, like meetings held in support of the U.S.-Mexico War, attracted big crowds. The New York *Herald* reported that at least 15,000 attended the first López meeting in City Hall Park and claimed that 25,000 to 30,000 men were at a Philadelphia meeting a few days later, while the more critical *Tribune* claimed that an earlier Philadelphia meeting attracted "no less than 15,000." Thousands of men also attended López meetings in even smaller cities like Memphis, while the López meeting in Pittsburgh may have been the largest public meeting held in that city up to that time. In sheer numbers of attendees, the López meetings attracted more supporters than did meetings that would be held at the height of William Walker's success.[42]

While female participation in partisan activities was welcomed in the 1840s and 1850s, especially by the Whig Party, urban public meetings were events for men only.[43] Although they drew men from across the economic spectrum, working men made up the majority of attendees. Both the words of speakers and the reporting of the meetings highlighted the importance of working men in the crowds. The New York *Herald* reported that "about five thousand persons, chiefly of the hard fisted working class" were at a meeting in Jersey City. At the López meetings in New York, speakers directed comments straight to the "working men" in the audience, as did speakers at the Jersey City meeting who critiqued "silk stocking aristocrats" who would "starve to death by their own laziness." A reporter at a Washington, DC, meeting noted the strong presence of "b'hoys" in the audience, a favored slang term for the young urban "sporting men" who were active in volunteer fire companies and urban amusements.[44]

---

[41] The New York meeting of August 26 and Jersey City meeting of August 27 adopted the resolutions of the Philadelphia meeting of August 25. On parades see *NYH*, August 23, 24, 26, 1851. Savannah, *NYH*, August 27, 1851.

[42] Philadelphia attendance reported in *NYH*, August 27, 1851; *NYT*, August 26, 1851. There were 8,000 men reported at the New York August 26 meeting. The *NYT* claimed that more than 1,000 attended the Baltimore August 27 meeting (*NYT*, August 30, 1851); Pittsburgh *Daily Morning Post*, August 28, 1851. Altschuler and Blumin claim that turnout at political rallies was generally exaggerated, but the fact that papers with conflicting agendas would both claim large numbers at this meeting seems to support a large turnout. Glen Altschuler and Stuart Blumin, *Rude Republic: Americans and their Politics in the Nineteenth Century* (Princeton, 2000), 61–9.

[43] Ryan, *Women in Public*, 130–6; Ryan, *Civic Wars*, 120–1; David Grimsted, *American Mobbing, 1828–1861: Toward Civil War* (New York, 1998), 183.

[44] *NYH*, August 28, 1851; *NYT*, August 30, 1851; On firefighting b'hoys see Amy S. Greenberg, *Cause for Alarm: The Volunteer Fire Department in the Nineteenth-Century City* (Princeton, 1998).

The primary purposes of meeting organizers appear to have been, first of all, to support America's Manifest Destiny, and America's honor, and to make it clear that participants were ready to fight for both. It was this aspect that was highlighted in the posted handbills calling men to the meeting, which essentially asked anyone who cared about America's honor to attend. With Cuba, calls for revenge for the deaths of the American volunteers, and for Cuban independence, were subsumed within a heavy rhetoric of Manifest Destiny. A typical comment (to "great applause" as the reporter noted) was, "Cuba will be one of the United States.... God himself has decreed that Cuba shall be free, and that she shall be a state of this glorious confederacy, and human power cannot prevent it." Another speaker revealed how slippery Manifest Destiny's slope was with his comments, "Nor shall this movement cease with the independence of Cuba. What is begun there will extend to Mexico, and in less than two years the American continent clear to Patagonia will be part and parcel of the United States." His words were met with "[g]reat cheering, and cries of 'that's the talk.'" Cuban independence was thinly veiled code for the annexation of Cuba, and of much of the rest of the Western Hemisphere. Lest anyone doubt the extent of this fantasy of territorial expansionism, consider the words of Enoch Camp at the August 26 meeting in New York City: "I should like to see the British government preventing us from taking possession of Canada tomorrow, if we were so disposed. I mean Cuba, not Canada! Yet, though when the time comes to do so, we should like to see them prevent us." [45]

The second objective of these meetings was to raise money. Without exception, at least one speaker at each meeting made a direct plea for funds for support of the filibusters, and most sets of resolutions also included a resolution to collect funds. Here we can see the way meetings brought together different classes. A speaker at a New York meeting asked that "rich men" in the audience "come forward with the sinews of war" otherwise it was "useless for the working classes, who are the bone and sinew of the country, to assemble and take part in public meetings." At a Jersey City meeting,

[45] The only full description of a handbill I have from the Cuba meetings was in Jersey City, for the August 27 meeting. *NYH*, August 28, 1851; Cuba comment in *NYH*, August 23, 1851; camp quote, *NYH*, August 27, 1851. Other examples of great Manifest Destiny speech include Tom Carr at the New York City meeting, August 22, 1851: "I love to look upon you. There is an American spirit in you – a spirit that cannot be stayed – a spirit that will pervade this continent and its adjacent islands, and will one day encircle the earth itself." The following day Carr announced that, "By God! America belongs to us." The audience responded with "loud cheers and reiterated cries" (New York *Post*, reprinted in the Philadelphia *Public Ledger*, August 25, 1851). A letter proposing the cession of the Hawaiian Islands to the United States ran on the same page of the *Public Ledger*, and in Jersey City on August 27, General Wright stated that, "It is well known that a feeling has long existed in the United States for the acquisition of Cuba" (*NYH*, August 28, 1851).

speakers appealed directly to the self-respect of the working men themselves in order to raise money.[46]

The third objective of these meetings was to provoke violence abroad. The audience was directed to join with like-minded men and "support" the filibusters, preferably by becoming filibusters themselves, but also by demanding political support for the filibusters by elected officials. Both of these objectives were tricky to verbalize. Filibustering, and joining a filibustering army, were and had always been against the law. This fact was blatantly obvious to the audience despite the ridiculous lengths orators went to in their attempts to refute it. Speakers frequently quoted Secretary of State Daniel Webster completely out of context on the rights of Americans to support foreign wars, despite Webster's open and unmitigated hostility to filibustering. They did so in order to suggest that Webster would be unlikely to reign in further attempts on Cuba, despite the precedent set by the Taylor administration at Round Island and the blunt statement of neutrality by his successor, Millard Fillmore. Speakers also suggested that Washington, Lafayette, and Franklin were spiritual kin to the filibuster. None of these feints was very convincing. "There is only a hair's difference between the pirate and the patriot," concluded one speaker after unsuccessfully finessing that hair. To a certain extent the failure to collapse that space didn't matter. One purpose of the meeting, after all, was to assert that a man could be both pirate and patriot, that martial manhood could also be the most patriotic vision of manhood.[47]

The political aspect of the filibustering meeting also presented difficulties. Politicians ran these meetings and clearly looked to gain political capital from them. Yet the topic demanded a certain nonpartisan tone, however transparent. The extent of Walker and López's support in northern cities makes it obvious that filibustering supporters did not see filibustering in sectional terms, despite the claims of many historians otherwise.[48] López

---

[46] *NYH*, August 24, 1851. New York *Evening Mirror*, May 24, 1856. The *NYH* also commented on wealthier men in the movement, reporting that in Savannah, "clerks (many of them from opulent families) are leaving their employers by scores, and are exchanging their yardsticks for swords, bayonets, &c" (*NYH*, September 4, 1851).

[47] *NYH*, August 23, 1851. Quote from Major Maynard, *NYH* August 24, 1851. President Fillmore issued a proclamation on April 25, 1851 clarifying the fact that filibustering was illegal, and setting a penalty for filibustering of a fine of not more than three thousand dollars and jail term of not more than three years. This was similar to a proclamation made by President Taylor in August of 1849. James D. Richardson, ed. *A Compilation of the Messages and Papers of the Presidents, 1789–1902*, (Washington, DC, 1903), III:7. On the clear and recognized illegality of filibustering see *NYT*, August 23, 1851; Lucy Holcombe's filibustering novel, *The Free Flag of Cuba*, written in 1854 repeatedly compared the Cuba filibusters to Lafayette and Washington in an attempt to redeem their reputation. Pickens, *The Free Flag of Cuba*.

[48] According to Michael A. Morrison, Northerners "were less concerned with peace and honor than with the motives and character of the filibusters. López's supporters, a northern

also attracted bipartisan support, since the annexation of Cuba promised to improve the fortunes of real estate speculators and many businessmen, especially in port cities. One journalist asserted before the 1851 invasion that the American annexation of Cuba would increase annual trade in New Orleans by $25 million. Not surprisingly, support for López in New Orleans was wide spread, and one historian has estimated that thirty percent of members of López annexation committees in that city were Whigs. Several prominent southern Whigs, like J. A. Kelly, president of the New Orleans chapter of the Winfield Scott Association, sailed with López to Cuba. For the most part, Whigs who supported López were unified in their opposition to the foreign policy of Whig president Millard Fillmore.[49]

A close examination of the orators at the August 1851 meetings, however, as well as of the identities of the many men appointed to honorary positions at the meetings (there were seventy separate vice presidents at the August 22 New York López meeting, many of whom were politicians), proves that by 1851 filibustering had become a movement supported and encouraged by, and identified with, the Democratic Party, despite the fact that some filibusters, like Henry Crabb and Sam Houston, were not Democrats. Politicians in other parties continued to find political capital in less criminal expressions of Manifest Destiny, but the Democrats claimed filibustering as their own.[50] The *Democratic Review* minced no words on the issue. The "silly" Whig administration was directly responsible for López's death, a crime made worse by their continued slander of the filibuster. The Whigs "take pleasure

---

Democrat chided, were the 'ignorant, conceited young men of the South, knowing little beyond their plantations and courthouses, and inflated through their habit of commanding Negroes with inordinate self importance'" (*Knoxville* [Tenn.] *Whig*, June 1, 1850). Morrison also claims that the López's pro-slavery agenda turned Northerners against him. Morrison quotes the Philadelphia *Public Ledger*, which opposed the filibusterer: "For this purpose they would invade Cuba, rescue it from that oppressive Spanish rule which looks forward to the extinction of slavery, and make it a bright star in the Southern confederacy, brilliant with the lustre of that peculiar institution which secures universal freedom by interminable bondage" (*Public Ledger*, April 28, 1851, May 27, 1850). But other Philadelphia papers supported López, as reports of the public meetings there make clear. Michael A. Morrison, *Slavery and the American West: The Eclipse of Manifest Destiny and the Coming of the Civil War* (Chapel Hill, 1997), 132–3.

[49] Richard Tansey identified sixty-nine Democrats and thirty Whigs among members of López annexation committees. Tansey, "Southern Expansionism," 238, 233, 240.

[50] The Whig Party was not truly anti-expansionist, but it tended to be anti-aggressive expansionism and anti-annexation. Even the partisan *Whig Review* was an original supporter of the colonization of Nicaragua for the purposes of building a canal and keeping the region out of the hands of the British. In 1852 the journal wrongly predicted that "Nicaragua, already a natural and necessary dependency of the United States, is not likely to become a slave state, and will not consequently excite the kind of interest that was awakened in behalf of Texas. Are we to have a second 'Canadas' at the South, for the convenience of Birmingham and Manchester? The Whigs alone can decide that point." "Nicaragua and the Interoceanic Canal," *American Whig Review* 15 (March 1852): 265.

in stigmatizing them as common freebooters, cut-throats and pirates" Cora Montgomery wrote in the journal. Only "time will decide whether they were pirates and cutthroats, or heroes and patriots."[51]

Speakers at the public meetings held for López were less open about their political affiliation. When a speaker at the Jersey City meeting referred to his audience as "you, the hard fisted democracy" he was quick to add "I do not mean it in a party sense." The fact that both audience and speaker knew that the "party sense" was exactly what was meant was highlighted in exchanges like the following, at an August 23 meeting in New York. When the Tammany politician Isaiah Rynders made the typical gesture to the "highest legal authority in the United States, the authority of Daniel Webster" the *Herald* reported that "voices" cried out, "To h-ll with Webster," and "He is Whig."[52] Horace Greeley's New York *Tribune* saw through the obfuscation immediately, condemning the "park gas-pipes" who called for support of López. "The Park demonstrations have primarily and mainly a groveling party purpose. The Rynderses, Tom Carrs and Lije [Elijah] Purdys of our city have been some time out of office, and are ravenous for spoils."[53]

These public meetings supported not just the Democratic Party but also the ideal of martial manhood. Within descriptions of these meetings it is easy to see the contours of a violent masculine culture, in the North and the South, where honor could only be redeemed through aggression, and where every man needed to be ready to fight. Banners at several meetings announced

---

[51] "Narcisso [*sic*] Lopez," *USDR* 29 (October 1851): 293, 300.

[52] Rynders responded: "No matter whether he is a whig or a democrat, he speaks the truth, and party prejudice must not put him down (when he is right)" (*NYH*, August 24, 1851). Jersey City: *NYH*, August 28, 1851). At the August 26 meeting in New York, the party rhetoric was quite direct as speaker Enoch Camp heaped opprobrium on the "faction" that opposed "this movement" and also "the Mexican war, and yet brought forward one General, who conquered in that war as a candidate for presidential office" (*NYH*, August 27, 1851). Rynders also tried to remove the partisan angle when he claimed he was reminded of "a meeting which took place on the same spot a few years ago, when the people of New York assembled, without distinction of party, to take action in relation to the Mexican War" (*NYH*, August 23, 1851). There were forty vice presidents and twelve secretaries at the Philadelphia meeting of August 25, mostly Democrats. *NYH*, August 26, 1851.

[53] *NYT*, August 25, 1851. The insults escalated quickly. At a meeting of six to eight thousand people Rynders called Greeley "a craven-hearted dastard and base liar," and claimed that "I degraded my manhood by striking a white livered coward that dared not resent it." He then threatened Greeley's life, most likely all in response to Greeley's insults against the "gas pipe" in the *Tribune*. *NYT*, August 24, 1851. About the park orators in general Greeley wrote: "Those who do so take their lives in their hands and must look well to the edge of their weapons, for behind these they have nothing to fall back on." On Rynders in particular he said "he greatly preferred gassing in New York to fighting in Mexico. So with the lot.... These are the very lads to foment a war, but a very different class will be required to prosecute it" (*NYH*, August 25, 1851). For more on Rynders and filibustering as "just another cut of Democratic patronage," see Chaffin, "Sons of Washington," 96.

"The blood of Americans cries for revenge," while resolutions stated that "the present is a crisis when energetic action, rather than tardy diplomatic intervention, is required." Speakers in Baltimore, New York, and other cities advertised and promoted filibustering expeditions by stating that they were being prepared at that very moment in that very city, by some of the very men in the audience. Speakers challenged the masculinity of listeners. Tammany politician Isaiah Rynders claimed that Andrew Jackson himself would "upbraid the American people with imbecility and cowardice, for submitting quietly to such indignity." Others described insults to America in dramatic terms. Even within the agonal conventions of antebellum political speech, calls to violence at the López meetings stand out. The rhetoric of the orators, their inflammatory language, and appeals to the manhood of listeners all worked to provoke men to risk their lives in overthrowing the government of a friendly nation without sanction of their own government. The rhetoric of the expansionist public meeting also marginalized the masculinity of the restrained man as impotent in the context of the present crisis.[54]

Whether these meetings inspired violence at home as well was much debated among reform-minded commentators who considered "the whole spirit of the revolutionists as dangerous and unjustifiable." The wealthy New York Whig diarist George Templeton Strong referred to López supporters as "self-consecrated missionaries of Republican scum."[55] The López rallies, in particular, brought together men of different occupations in support of a hyper-masculine nationalistic agenda, provoking fantasies of disorder among some observers. At rallies in New York, Jersey City, Washington, DC, and Philadelphia commentators remarked on the "unmistakable aspect of rowdyism" or otherwise expressed worries about the young working men gathered in large numbers late at night in their cities. The *Tribune* reported that Washington, DC, filibusters had been "on a bender again" but "discordant yells, 'making night hideous,' and disturbing the peaceable and quiet inhabitants of the vicinity" were the extent of the disorder. The August 22 meeting in New York was described as "particularly exciting" at the conclusion of the evening with "cries of 'revenge,' 'liberty to Cuba,' &c, resounded

---

54 *NYH*, August 23, 1851; New York *Post*, reprinted in the Philadelphia *Public Ledger*, August 25, 1851. Energetic action quote from Philadelphia meeting, August 15, 1851. Filibustering underway quote, *NYH*, August 24, 1851; Montgomery (Alabama) *Journal*, August 18, 1851, also in *NYH*, August 24, 1851, Baltimore August 27 meeting (*NYT*, August 30, 1851). Rynders quote, *NYH*, August 23, 1851. Rynders struck a similar note at a public meeting in support of William Walker in 1856, when he told the crowd that Nicaragua needed an injection of American "vitality." Rynders joined the New York branch of the "quasi-filibustering" organization, the Order of the Lone Star, formed soon after López's death. May, *Manifest Destiny's Underworld*, 33–4, 129. On agonal language in antebellum America, see Kenneth Cmiel, *Democratic Eloquence: The Fight over Popular Speech in Nineteenth-Century America* (New York, 1990), 64–5.

55 *NYH*, August 27, 1851; George Templeton Strong, *The Diary of George Templeton Strong*, Allan Nevins and Milton Halsey Thomas, eds. (New York, 1952), vol. 2:65.

through the air." The "hard fisted working men" at the Jersey City meeting were "fired with the contagious enthusiasm that seems spreading all over the land." Strong noted in his diary on August 28 that Isaiah Rynders had "tried to raise" a row in New York, "but without success."[56]

In New Orleans, rioters destroyed Spanish-owned businesses and threatened the lives of Spanish officials upon learning of the execution of the Americans. In reports of the New Orleans riot in northern newspapers, the López meeting and riot were linked together, suggesting that those attending the meeting made good on the threats of revenge common to orators at all the Cuba meetings. In fact, the speakers at the New Orleans meeting universally appealed to order, attempting to calm rioters after most of the damage was done. With the possible exception of the New Orleans riot, there are no examples of domestic violence resulting from any of these meetings, and a lot of the worry occasioned by these meetings seems to have been a reflection of the mixed nature of the gatherings, more that any real threat posed by them.[57]

The fact that violent rhetoric did not result in riots raises the question of the extent to which one can extrapolate the beliefs of the audience from the speeches made at these meetings. Speakers clearly spoke to the martial manhood of the audience, but were audiences listening?[58] The fact that fund raising for filibustering expeditions was always difficult suggests that perhaps listeners were not completely in tune with the spirit of their orators, an opinion expressed by the *National Intelligencer*: "It is a consoling circumstance that the people have not responded to the call of those gentry. They understand the matter." The *Tribune* also claimed that there "was very little evidence of enthusiasm" at the August 22 meeting in New York. At the same time, however, the *Tribune* was quick to raise an alarm about the "number of persons" in a "high state of enthusiasm" who wandered the streets after that meeting. The Boston *Courier* also seemed to want to have it both ways. The paper claimed that a meeting in Boston was made of "quite combustible materials" but that the listeners were essentially uninterested in the question of Cuba. According to the *Courier*, the speaker asked his audience if they

---

56 Washington, DC, quotes, *NYT*, August 30, 1851, September 2, 1851; the New York meeting of August 22, *NYH*, August 23, 1851; Jersey City, *NYH*, August 28, 1851; Strong, *Diary*, vol. 2:63. Although Strong was strongly opposed to filibustering in general, and to the López expeditions in particular, he concluded on August 24 that "[a]nyhow, Cuba will be annexed – or independent of Spain in ten years." *Diary*, vol. 2:62.

57 On New Orleans see *NYH*, August 26, September 1, 1851 and New Orleans *Crescent*, August 22, 1851, New Orleans *Bee*, reprinted in the *NYH*, September 1, 1851. The New Orleans press "universally exonerated the filibusters and the permanent population, and attributed the disorders to the lower and more ignorant classes." Urban, "New Orleans and the Cuba Question," 1158, 1160.

58 Were listeners really paying attention, or would Glen Altschuler and Stuart Blumin identify this as just another example of a few motivated party regulars attempting, unsuccessfully, to motivate an apathetic public? Altschuler and Blumin, *Rude Republic*.

were "ready to go to Cuba now, when some person on the balcony answered, that he was 'ready to go to– drink.' This interruption entirely disconcerted the orator."[59]

Certainly the attendees of these meetings were ready to go drink, as were the attendees of the "Great War Meeting" in favor of the annexation of Mexico. But that was not all they were interested in. In the detailed descriptions of these meetings it is possible to hear the voices of at least some audience members, like the thirsty Bostonian, who spoke back to the stage. A few cursed Daniel Webster, some encouraged talk of the annexation of the entire continent, but almost all expressed enthusiasm for an expansionist agenda and cheered the loudest when the most aggressive actions were espoused. If meeting attendees were not themselves ready to ship out to Cuba, certainly they were willing to threaten to do so. As speakers attempted to finesse that "fine line between pirate and patriot" at the urban public meeting, manifest manhood came full circle. White men of different economic statuses were able to affirm a gendered, violent culture, both abroad in their interactions with Latin American men, and at home at urban public meetings. Travelers and politicians alike turned to Latin America in order to provide authority to masculine practices that were increasingly marginalized at home. The aggressive expansionist encounter provided support to a vision of America that was hard fisted, honorable, and ever expanding, as martial men believed God wished it.[60]

---

[59] *National Intelligencer*, August 26, 1851; *NYT*, August 23, 1851. Quote about Boston from Boston *Courier*, August 25, reprinted in the *NYT*, August 26, 1851. Filibusters were constantly complaining about the difficulty of raising funds. For an analysis of this problem in New Orleans see Urban, "New Orleans and the Cuba Question," 1162; on filibuster fundraising in general see May, *Manifest Destiny's Underworld*, 169–82.

[60] According to Charles H. Brown, "There was no shortage of men eager to sail to Cuba." *Agents of Manifest Destiny: The Lives and Times of the Filibusters* (Chapel Hill, 1980), 91. There were Cuban men at some of the meetings, but if African-Americans were there, no reporters took note of it.

6

American Women Abroad

> I showed him your picture, he said, bonito, which means pretty, I think if you
> were here you could make a bargain with him, you would have nothing to do
> but go to mass, a slave to carry a mat for you to kneel upon, and swing in
> your hammock the remainder of the day, he is very pretty and dresses in good
> taste....
>
> – Letter from Mary Jane Megquier to Angie Megquier, Panama, 1849

Mary Jane Megquier was a wife and mother in southern Maine when she
made the unusual choice in 1848 of accompanying her husband to the gold
fields of California. During her three trips across Central America over the
next eight years she wrote frequently to the children she left behind in Maine,
especially her growing daughter, Angie. The only woman among 200 passengers on a steamship from New York to Chagres in 1849, she attracted
a great deal of attention both at sea and in Panama, where she and her
fellow travelers waited anxiously for transport on to California. "A white
lady was such a rare sight they were coming in to see me until we found we
could get no sleep" she complained. When Megquier wrote to Angie from
the Isthmus, she adopted a playful tone on the subject of Panamanian gender
relations. She had shown Angie's picture to a "young Spaniard" she had seen
"a number of times," she claimed, and the man seemed interested.[1]

The vision she sketched, of a potential life of languid ease in the tropics,
no doubt amused her daughter greatly, and not only because it suggested
that Angie agree to a marriage to a Catholic Panamanian she had never
met. Megquier's imagining of Angie's married life also derived its humor

---

[1] Quoted in JoAnn Levy, "The Panama Trail: Short Cut to California," *Overland Journal* 10
(Fall 1992): 29; Mary Jane Megquier, *Apron Full of Gold: The Letters of Mary Jane Megquier
from San Francisco, 1849–1856*, 2nd ed., Polly Welts Kaufman, ed. (Albuquerque, 1994), 27.
On Megquier's life see Megquier, 1–10, and Levy, 28–9. On women in the gold rush see Brian
Roberts, *American Alchemy: The California Gold Rush and Middle-Class Culture* (Chapel
Hill, 2000).

from the incongruity of its gender relations – the vision of an American woman laying about in a hammock was as laughable as that of a woman from southern Maine ministered to by a slave. In fact, Megquier's suggestion that there was a place for an American woman in the fantasy of Central American "personal annexation," as Sam Houston termed it, was in itself comical. White American men had no trouble visualizing themselves at work, and in love, in the region. As this study has argued, that visualization was a central theme of the Latin American encounter, and one supporting aggressive expansionism. But white American women were notably absent from this aggressive expansionist fantasy. Megquier's vision was remarkably similar to that formulated dozens of times in the travelogues of American men, but it functioned only as a joke for this American woman. Indeed, even Megquier's physical description of the "pretty" suitor, so tastefully dressed, evokes male descriptions of coquettish Latin American women (see Figure 6.1).

Megquier's joking engagement with the fantasy of personal annexation reveals the marginalized position of white American women within the reigning conventions of the Latin American encounter in the antebellum era. This is not to say that white women were unimportant to the encounter. As audiences for published travelogues and the letters written by male travelers, they helped negotiate the meaning of aggressive expansionism. As models of womanhood, they shaped the vision of Latin American women in the lands being considered for takeover. Although filibustering was an enterprise deeply bound up with masculine ideologies, including the opportunity to escape from the increasing authority of American women, and was supported at all-male public meetings, white American women were not unified in their opposition to it. Jane McManus Storm (later Jane Cazneau), writing under the pseudonym Cora Montgomery, first coined the phrase *Manifest Destiny*, and she was one of the preeminent national journalistic voices supporting Narciso López.[2]

But a close examination of the writings of American women on the issue of Manifest Destiny between the U.S.-Mexico and Civil wars, from the letters of travelers to published writings on aggressive expansionism, indicates some profound differences between many of them and their male peers. Female travelers were divided by sectional affiliation, personal experiences, and wealth. But in general, ordinary women appear to have encountered Central America with far less of a sense that the region was the next step in America's Manifest Destiny then did male travelers, and, as Mary Jane Megquier's correspondence with her daughter makes clear, they did not engage in the same fantasy of personal and national conquest in the region. Although Cora Montgomery was one of the most vocal proponents of

---

[2] On the role of women as an audience negotiating the meaning of the gold rush, see Roberts, *American Alchemy*, 8.

FIGURE 6.1. Mary Jane and Angie Megquier with family members in 1853. Mary Jane Megquier is seated to the left between her sons, Arthur and John. To the right Angie Megquier Gilson is seated with her daughter Jennie in her lap and husband Charles Gilson standing to her right. Angie clearly made a different marriage choice than that jokingly suggested by her mother in 1849. Courtesy of the Huntington Library, San Marino, CA.

territorial expansionism, her writings were notably less martial than those of leading male expansionists in the same period.

This chapter will explore the role of women in the extension of Manifest Destiny to the new Latin American frontier by looking at the experiences of female travelers in Central America, the marginalization of white American women in booster accounts of the region, and female-authored accounts in support of filibustering. Although historians have argued that white women, and the ideology of domesticity, were crucial actors in the unfolding of Manifest Destiny in western expansion before the U.S.-Mexico War, on the new frontier of Latin America, they were deliberately excluded. Aggressive expansionism in the 1850s was explicitly, and exclusively, about manifesting manhood without white American women.

Manifest Domesticity in Latin America

Catharine Beecher, probably the antebellum era's leading exponent of domestic ideology, declared in her 1841 *Treatise on Domestic Economy* that "the Disposer of events" designed that America "shall go forth as the cynosure of nations, to guide them to the light...."[3] Territorial expansionism, as a political issue intimately connected to war, was theoretically deemed outside the purview of domesticated womanhood in the middle of the nineteenth century. Yet domesticity was not as limiting or limited an ideology as the vision of antebellum America divided into separate male and female spheres of influence might suggest. Historians of European imperialism have long asserted that empire, in Britain especially, "was intimately wedded to the Western reinvention of domesticity."[4] In the United States, elite women were central to the construction and practice of politics in the nineteenth century, through their work as hostesses and informal agents of networking in Washington, DC, in the Early Republic to their roles as partisans in the Second Party System. By the 1840s, Elizabeth Varon has shown, politicians realized that "women were indispensable as allies," and "by the 1850s, Virginians across the political spectrum agreed that women could play a role in electoral politics complementary to that of men." Until the late 1850s, southern women, whose domestic virtues endowed them with superior patriotism, were expected to use their political power in support of national unity. It was

[3] Catharine Beecher, *A Treatise on Domestic Economy for the Use of Young Ladies at Home and at School* (Boston, 1841), 12. On Beecher's role in formulating and promoting domesticity see Kathryn Kish Sklar, *Catharine Beecher: A Study in American Domesticity* (New Haven, 1973).
[4] See Anne McClintock, *Imperial Leather: Race, Gender, and Sexuality in the Colonial Context* (New York, 1995), 17; see also Karen Tranberg Hansen, ed., *African Encounters with Domesticity* (New Brunswick, NJ, 1992); Rosemary Marangoly George, "Homes in the Empire, Empires in the Home." *Cultural Critique* 26 (1993–1994): 95–127.

only in the final years of the decade that women became outspoken southern partisans.[5]

Manifest Destiny before the U.S.-Mexico War certainly heroized masculine exemplars, from the trapper, to the scout, to the lone frontiersman.[6] But women were far from peripheral presences on the frontier. Women were central to the practice and legitimation of the Second Party System, and they were likewise central to the success of one of the most politicized of issues, westward expansion. Lynnea Magnuson has explored the manner in which women's domesticating force legitimated territorial expansionism in the years before the U.S.-Mexico War, justifying violence against Native Americans in the name of protecting white womanhood and allowing Americans to cast western settlement as a civilizing venture. Middle-class women from the North who settled the West envisioned their actions as patriotic and understood themselves as agents of American "civilization," while politicians utilized images of female settlement to promote Manifest Destiny. "There was a symbiotic gender relationship between male and female agents of Manifest Destiny expansion on the frontier: women could not carry out the nation's civilizing mission alone, but men also needed women. The discourse of Manifest Destiny wrote 'civilizing' into the expansion mandate, and domesticity was the ideal of civilized society."[7]

Magnuson's findings support Amy Kaplan's contention that domesticity and Manifest Destiny were mutually constitutive in the 1840s. The two ideologies developed simultaneously, and both relied on "a vocabulary that turns imperial conquest into spiritual regeneration in order to efface internal conflict or external resistance in visions of geopolitical domination as global harmony."[8] Domesticity was employed to justify national expansion, while Manifest Destiny also supported domesticity, despite the fact that most antebellum women's periodicals did not generally address "political" topics, and female-authored travel narratives pointedly separated themselves from narratives by men. Catherine Maria Sedgwick, one of the most popular writers of the period, made this explicitly clear in an 1841 travelogue. "Do not fear that I am about to give you a particular description" of business matters, she

[5] Catherine Allgor, *Parlor Politics: In Which the Ladies of Washington Help Build a City and a Government* (Charlottesville, 2000); Elizabeth Varon, *We Mean to be Counted: White Women and Politics in Antebellum Virginia* (Chapel Hill, 1998), 3, 5.

[6] Richard Slotkin, *The Fatal Environment: The Myth of the Frontier in the Age of Industrialization, 1800–1860* (New York, 1985), 161–207.

[7] Lynnea Magnuson, "In the Service of Columbia: Gendered Politics and Manifest Destiny Expansion" (Ph.D. Diss., University of Illinois at Urbana-Champaign, 2000), 129.

[8] Amy Kaplan, *The Anarchy of Empire in the Making of U.S. Culture* (Cambridge, MA, 2002), 23–50, quote page 31; for an earlier version of this essay see Kaplan, "Manifest Domesticity," *American Literature* 70 (September 1998): 581–606; see also Karen Sánchez-Eppler, "Raising Empires like Children: Race, Nation, and Religious Education," *American Literary History* 8 (1996): 399–425; Vicente L. Rafael, "Colonial Domesticity: White Women and United States Rule in the Philippines," *American Literature* 67 (December 1995): 639–66.

reassured her readers. "Our 'woman's sphere,' the boundaries of which some of our sex are making rather indefinite, does not extend to that subject."[9]

As Sedgwick's aside suggests, the boundaries of the 'woman's sphere' were quite malleable. Antebellum female writers often invoked the domestic in order to sanction political commentary.[10] Representations of domesticity in women's novels in the antebellum period contributed to and enabled narratives of nation building, and a vision of "traveling domesticity" conceptualized the home as a mobile space that could encompass other lands while simultaneously expelling the foreign within it. In their guide for new housewives, *American Woman's Home*, Catharine Beecher and her sister Harriett Beecher Stowe advocated settlements of Christian families around the globe in order to share the blessings of American beliefs and institutions. *Godey's Lady's Book*, the most popular women's magazine of the era, likewise ran a travel narrative titled "Life on the Rio Grande" in 1847 that equated the domesticating power of the white American woman with increasing civilization in new states and territories. Without once mentioning the war that at that very moment engrossed the attention of both Mexico and the United States, *Godey's* argued that adherence to the woman's sphere was the key to successful expansionism.[11]

Magnuson and Kaplan's insights into the mutually supportive nature of domesticity and Manifest Destiny significantly undermine the increasingly tenuous ideology of separate spheres,[12] and they convincingly account for territorial expansionism in areas where family migration was the norm: on the Oregon Trail, in the upper Midwest, and to Mexican Texas. But what role might women, or domesticity, play in sex-segregated migrations like the gold rush or, especially, in filibustering? "Traveling domesticity," not surprisingly, seems to have been limited to areas where women were traveling.[13] It was

---

[9] Catherine Sedgwick, *Letters from Abroad to Kindred at Home* (New York, 1841), 52–3. Periodicals directed to female abolitionists were of course highly political in content.

[10] As Mary Suzanne Schriber has explored, "nineteenth-century rhetoric to the contrary, all subjects were women's subjects." *Writing Home: American Women Abroad, 1830–1920* (Charlottesville, 1997), 8.

[11] Catharine Beecher and Harriet Beecher Stowe, *The American Woman's Home* (New York, 1869), 458–9; "Life on the Rio Grande," *Godey's Lady's Book* 32 (April 1847): 177–8; Kaplan, *Anarchy of Empire*, 23–50.

[12] The vision of separate spheres is conceptually flawed because "the world of women is part of the world of men, created in and by it." Joan Scott, "Gender: A Useful Category for Historical Analysis," *American Historical Review* 91 (December 1986): 1056. The ideology of separate spheres has been under attack for at least a decade. See, for example, the special issue of *American Literature* on the subject. Cathy Davidson, ed. "No More Separate Spheres!" *American Literature* 70 (September 1998): 443–668.

[13] John Mack Faragher has shown that family groups were the norm in overland travel to Oregon. Among overland travelers in 1846 (before the gold rush), 40.6% were adult men, 20.3% were adult women, and 39.1% were children. Sixty-three percent of all adults traveling were married. There were slightly more adult women traveling to Oregon in 1853, and slightly fewer children, but virtually the same percentage of married migrants to Oregon in

not unknown in male writings on the new frontier of Latin America. Aggressive expansionists occasionally legitimated their presence in Latin America on the basis of the mistreatment of local women by local men. Three years before William Walker invaded the country, John Letts encouraged an American presence in Nicaragua by critiquing the incessant labor of the "lovely" women of Nicaragua. "[F]emales are toiling, day after day, for life, in the service of inhuman masters," he wrote. The common assessment that men in the region were lazy, and that women did all the work, could lead American men to the same conclusion. But expansionists in Latin America were far less likely to make this argument than were European colonial powers.[14]

The supposed threat that "savage" Native Americans posed to white womanhood was a key justification for American westward expansionism from the colonial period forward. It occasionally makes an appearance in the literature of aggressive expansionism in northern Mexico, where marauding bands of Native Americans posed ongoing difficulties for Mexican settlers and authorities. None other than William Walker attempted to justify his first filibuster to Sonora by claiming that Sonoran women asked him to "bring down enough Americans to keep off the Apaches" soon after an Apache attack on a nearby town resulted in several women being taken into captivity and a number of men and women being killed. But there is very little evidence that the "respectability" of white women played the same role in legitimating an imperialist presence in Latin America as it did in European colonies or in westward expansionism. As the following chapter will explore, female respectability was central to discourses of religious and commercial expansionism in the Pacific. But it was marginalized in the masculine discourse of aggressive expansionism that reigned in Latin America.[15]

1853. Among migrants heading to California in 1853, however, only 30.6% were married, 70.4% were male, 12.7% were female, and 16.9% were children. Family groups were not the norm among gold-rush travelers by land or sea. Filibustering invasions, of course, were accompanied by virtually 100% male armies. *Women and Men on the Overland Trail.* 2nd ed. (New Haven, 2000), 195.

[14] Scholars of the British Empire have long noted how domesticity supported colonialism. British officers in India, for instance, created the myth of the "effeminate Bengali" who did not sufficiently revere women in order to justify their own presence in the country. Mrinalini Sinha, *Colonial Masculinity: The 'Manly Englishman' and the 'Effeminate Bengali' in the Late Nineteenth Century* (Manchester, UK, 1995). "Ladylike behavior was a mainstay of imperialist civilization" in the late nineteenth century but not in the antebellum American encounter with Latin America. Cynthia Enloe, *Bananas, Beaches, and Bases: Making Feminist Sense of International Politics* (Berkeley, CA, 1990), 181; John M. Letts, *A pictorial view of California: Including a description of the Panama and Nicaragua routes, with information and advice interesting to all, particularly those who intend to visit the gold region, by a returned Californian* (New York, 1853), 157.

[15] William Walker, *The War in Nicaragua* (Mobile, 1860), 21. On the captivity narrative as justification for expansionism, see Slotkin, *The Fatal Environment*, 63–8; Carroll Smith-Rosenberg, "Dis-Covering the Subject of the 'Great Constitutional Discussion,' 1786–1789," *JAH* 79 (December 1992): 841–73.

White women may not have been present in large enough numbers to shape the Latin American encounter through the discourse of domesticity, but they were not completely absent from the region. Some women, like Mary Jane Megquier, made the onerous sea-route journey to California. Given antebellum America's "gendering of geography," female travelers to a not-yet-annexed region occupied a tenuous space. "Traveling domesticity" allowed Americans in the western territories of the United States to envision the area as part of a national "home," even if the existence of Native-American tribes as "domestic dependent nations" (as the Supreme Court deemed them in the 1831 case, *Cherokee Nation v. State of Georgia*) troubled the easy distinction between foreign and domestic.[16] Female travelers to Latin America were not only outside the home, but wholly outside the United States. White American women in the streets of Panama or San Juan were even more problematic to the "public" man than were women in the streets of urban America. Given the centrality of the vision of Latin American women to the fantasy of Central American annexation as conceptualized by aggressive expansionists and regular men alike, what interest could heterosexual white American women share in aggressive expansionist fantasies?[17]

An examination of the writings of female travelers suggests some answers to this question. In general, the middle-class American women who left records of their travels through Central America on the way to California (the high cost of the voyage insured that virtually all female travelers were middling or above) did not share the same expansionist vision of Latin America as did male shipmates. Male travelers perceived Central America as within the reach of America's Manifest Destiny, both worthy of, and in need of, American intervention. If American women thought about Central America in these terms, they kept these thoughts to themselves.[18]

Women, like men, found the Central American landscape lovely. Alfred DeWitt wrote to his brother that "my wife seemed to enjoy the scenery very much [on the Chagres river] the appearance of the banks on the narrow river is beautiful covered with a luxuriant growth of trees and shrubs.... the

---

[16] Priscilla Wald, *Constituting Americans: Cultural Anxiety and Narrative Form* (Durham, 1995), 23–35.

[17] Susan Scheckel, *The Insistence of the Indian: Race and Nationalism in Nineteenth-Century American Culture* (Princeton, 1998), 74. On the "gendering of geography" see Mary Ryan, *Women in Public: Between Banners and Ballots, 1825–1880* (Baltimore, 1990), 58–94; Schriber, *Writing Home*, 12–45; Glenna Matthews, *Rise of Public Woman: Woman's Power and Woman's Place in the United States, 1630–1970* (New York, 1992), 93–171; Magnuson, "In the Service of Columbia," 128.

[18] The difference between men's and women's accounts of Central America may in part be due to the different circumstances of both groups. Most women who left accounts of their journeys were married and traveling with husbands or other male escorts. Most men who left accounts were either unmarried or, if married, had left their wives at home. The men may have been more adventurous to begin with, although any woman who voluntarily traveled through Central America in 1850 could hardly be deemed unadventurous. On the gold rush as a middle-class event, see Roberts, *American Alchemy*.

ladies were delighted with the scene, the singing of different birds, perfume of the air and beauty of the shores made it appear like an enchanted place." New Jersey native Lucilla Linn Brown was "perfectly delighted" by the "luxuriant growth of tropical trees, shrubs and flowers" along the river as well.[19]

Women, like men, occasionally commented on the laziness of locals and their lack of initiative. Brown wrote to her family in 1849 that "[c]ows are by no means scarce on the Isthmus, but the inhabitants make no use of milk when they want to make cheese – whether owing to laziness or ignorance, I know not." Mary Jane Megquier also suggested that the Panamanians were "too indolent" to milk their cows and complained that although the country offered the "finest soil in the world," no vegetables were cultivated. Part of the fault, however, she lay at the feet of American adventurers, specifically William Walker. She wrote to her daughter Angie in November of 1855 that there were no eggs or chickens in Nicaragua because "the country was invaded by fillibusters."[20] But women virtually never compared Central America to the United States directly or suggested the role American industry might play in the region. In general, women appeared far less interested in the ultimate fate of Central American sovereignty than did men.[21] And of course, with the exception of Megquier's humorous aside to Angie, women did not construct fantasies of "annexing" themselves to Central American men.

However, although female travelers do not seem to have entered Central America with the intention of remaking the region in their image, as they did on the Oregon Trail and as men did in Central America, there was certainly the possibility that Central American travel might remake them. Isthmus travel was challenging to both men and women, and it may have offered American women a means of denaturalizing gender norms at home.

Female travelers virtually never discussed the fandango or female sexuality, topics of wide-spread discussion among their male companions. Lucilla Linn Brown was one of the few who commented on Latin American cultural expression at all. "Their dancing was rude, and simple as their music – still there was grace in their movements."[22] Women also rarely discussed the appearance of either women or men, although certainly they had as much

---

[19] Typescript of letter from Alfred DeWitt to his brother George, from San Francisco, August 28, 1849. DeWitt Family Papers, BL; Levy, "The Panama Trail," 31; see also Glenda Riley, "Women on the Panama Trail to California 1849–1869," *Pacific Historical Review* 55 (November 1986): 531–48.

[20] Gaylord A. Beaman, "Pioneer Letters," *The Quarterly of the Historical Society of Southern California* 21 (March 1939): 22; Megquier, *Apron Full of Gold*, 15, 140.

[21] The only exception I found to this rule was Mallie Stafford, who claimed that in Aspenwall buildings are "essentially modern and American." Stafford did not write her account until the 1880s, however, and her account is colored by the political and social context of the Gilded Age. Mrs. Mallie Stafford, *The March of Empire* (San Francisco, 1884), 19.

[22] Beaman, "Pioneer Letters," 22.

opportunity to observe the appearances of Central Americans as did their male companions. Emeline Hubbard Day commented in her journal that "[t]he females were dressed quite fancifully. Their dresses are mostly a thick white gauze, with a great many flounces trimmed with lace.... very low in the neck and short sleeves. Their white clothing is very clean and beautiful." Day's primary interest, however, was the manner in which this clothing remained so clean and beautiful. "We saw some dressed in the cleanest white trimmed with costly lace and seated flat on the ground in dust several inches deep – we saw several washing. They go to a river or rivulet and sit down in the water which is quite warm and wash them on the gravel bottoms until they are perfectly clean and white."[23]

Day was unusual in that she devoted almost a quarter of her description of Central America to women's laundry practices, but like many female travelers, she expressed an intense interest in women's work in Central America. Mary Ballou, whose 1851 account of Panama lacks any description of the scenery or of the physical appearance of Central Americans, focused almost exclusively on the labor of the "Spanish Ladies" she saw. She was particularly interested in a meat market where the saleswomen displayed eggs and potatoes, and "they cut their meat in strips and hung it up on trees and poles." Mallie Stafford noted that native women "carrying immense baskets of fruit on their heads" stood in contrast to the "Castilian ladies of the upper classes, who might be seen on balconies and verandahs, reclining in easy chairs and hammocks."[24]

Tortilla making also was a subject of some interest to female travelers, as it was to female readers at home. The Cincinnati *Ladies' Repository* devoted a long article to the practice in 1857 and concluded that women in Costa Rica were overworked by the need for fresh tortillas at every meal. The reviewer of a Costa Rican travelogue informed readers that the preparation of tortillas demanded that "15,000 women, or one-tenth of the entire population," labor "regularly fourteen hours a day. The moral deduced from this calculation is, that if the Costa Ricans would use fewer tortillas, and more animal food, their women would find time for other, and perhaps more congenial employments." The radical proposal that Central American women be freed from their tortilla-making duties was beyond that voiced by ordinary women traveling through the region. None the less, the exposure to an alternative norm of female labor may have led women to question the naturalness of women's work at home.[25]

More challenging to gender norms was the nudity, or near nudity, that female travelers were regularly exposed to in the Isthmus. A dearth of sleeping

[23] Emeline Hubbard Day journal 1853–1856, March 31, 1853, BL.
[24] Mary B. Ballou, *"I Hear the Hogs in My Kitchen," A Woman's View of the Gold Rush*, Archibald Hanna, ed. (New Haven, 1962), 7; Stafford, *The March of Empire*, 19.
[25] "A Central American Paradise," *Ladies' Repository* 17 (July 1857): 429.

quarters in Central America forced both men and women to loosen some of their standards of propriety. New Englander Annie Esther Walton wrote to her sister in Connecticut that "[w]e all slept in one room on separate cots, and we all *undressed*. First the ladies went to bed, then the gentlemen put out the light and did the same." J. Goldsborough Bruff relayed a similar scene: "On awakening, and sitting up in my cot, I was astonished to see a young woman sitting up also in the next cot to me, and fastening the back of her dress, while all around were upwards of a hundred men perhaps, in every stage of rising and dressing." Upon questioning, she told Bruff that she was used to it.[26]

Of course many native inhabitants of the region never dressed in the first place. Like most women, Mary Jane Megquier simply noted on her first trip through the region that she was surrounded by native people, "most of them naked." Emeline Hubbard Day also noted without comment that "the natives are about half-dressed generally but many there are who are entirely naked." A few women associated nudity with a more general critique of the region. Writing to her sister from Panama, Annie Esther Walton expressed her disgust at the "horrid place" by adding "so very dirty. Most all go naked with a *small* apron. The children wear only hats."[27]

Male nudity, in particular, troubled standards of propriety for female travelers. Sarah Merriam Brooks, who traveled across the Isthmus in 1852 with her three-year old daughter, recalled difficulties with their boatmen, "big, black fellows, almost naked" who refused to keep any of their clothes on unless given breakfast by their white travelers. "Desperately ugly in looks, they proved equally so in character" she concluded. In general, however, men seem to have expressed more anxiety on the part of white women on this score than did the women themselves. Milo Goss wrote with horror to his cousin Catherine that "I have seen many of the boatmen entirely naked, and ladies from the States sitting within six feet of where the men were standing." In their own accounts, even "refined" women seem to have taken nudity in stride. Wealthy and politically connected Jessie Benton Frémont laughingly recalled predictions that she would be "a Washington fine lady, and make objections to the Indians having no clothes on," during her travels through the Isthmus. Upon reaching Chagres, Frémont, as predicted, found herself surrounded by "naked, screaming, barbarous negroes and Indians," but she did not appear overly disturbed by the scene. Mary Crocker found Nicaragua "new and strange, particularly the *naked* natives" but also "soon became accustomed to [it] as to many other unpleasant things." Although gender codes in the United States suggested that women should find naked men highly disturbing in general, women devoted far less space in their letters

---

[26] Beaman, "Pioneer Letters," 27; Bruff, *Gold Rush*, 513.
[27] Megquier, *Apron Full of Gold*, 14; Day journal, 1853–1856, 1853 entry, no date, BL; Beaman, "Pioneer Letters," 27.

and diaries to descriptions of nude Central Americans than did their male travelling companions.[28]

Male nudity was threatening to American women, and to American male observers, because of the association of nudity with sexuality and the looming specter in the antebellum period of interracial sex. Although the sexual exploitation of slave women by white men was a fact of life in the South, it was the supposedly innate laviciousness of the black man, and his desire for white women, that haunted the imaginations of Southerners. In his 1787 *Notes on the State of Virginia*, Thomas Jefferson compared the "uniform" preference of African-Americans for whites to "the preference of the Oranootan for the black woman over those of his own species." By the early nineteenth century, the assertion that "lust" was the "strongest passion" of black men, "and hence, rape is an offense of too frequent occurrence," as one southern lawyer wrote in 1858, had become one of the key tenants of pro-slavery discourse.[29]

When men were naked, the "danger to sexual integrity" became "the likely issue in the encounter of a woman with indigenous males." Nor could women simply avert their eyes. Steamship travelers often were transported between ship and shore on the backs of Panamanian men. The necessity of physical contact between white women and Panamanian men heightened the anxiety of some travelers. Theodore Johnson imagined that "the dark and yellow natives came wading out in high glee, especially to get the ladies." Sarah Brooks "wanted to scream" when "all at once, without a word of warning, I was grabbed from behind. One black arm was around my waist, another under my knees, and I was lifted up and carried straight out into the water."[30]

Notably however, Brooks presents this incident as an example of how travel forced her to test her assumptions and capabilities. She reports that her fear melted away when she heard the laughter of her three-year-old

---

[28] Sarah Merriam Brooks, *Across the Isthmus to California in '52* (San Francisco, 1894), 35, 37; Milo Goss Letter to "Cousin Catherine," Galgona, New Granada, May 19, 1850, Goss Family Letter Collection, 1849–1853, BL; Jessie Benton Frémont, *A Year of American Travel: Narrative of Personal Experience*. 1878 (San Francisco, 1960), 27; Crocker quoted in JoAnn Levy, *They Saw the Elephant: Women in the California Gold Rush* (Hamden, CT, 1990), 50. Crocker's husband was soon-to-be railroad magnate Charles Crocker.

[29] Paul Finkelman, *Defending Slavery: Proslavery Thought in the Old South* (Boston, 2003), 49, 154. Martha Hodes, *White Women, Black Men: Illicit Sex in the Nineteenth-Century South* (New Haven, 1997).

[30] Theodore Taylor Johnson, *Sights in the Gold Region, and Scenes by the Way* (New York, 1849), 306; Brooks, *Across the Isthmus to California*, 63. Mary Suzanne Schriber has pointed out that in travel literature written by American women in the nineteenth century, indigenous men are always represented as respectful of white female propriety. There is little evidence that this dynamic is at work in the letters and diaries considered here, but nor is there a great deal of obvious anxiety on the part of American women about their safety. Schriber, *Writing Home*, 79–80.

daughter and their male traveling companion, both of whom accepted their own "rides" as great fun. Mrs. D. B. Bates of Kingston, Massachusetts, also described riding "post-back," as she called it. In Bates's account, the event provided an opportunity to critique the strength of Panama's men, and the weight of some of her fellow travelers. "The natives being so submerged, one could not judge well of their muscular developments; and some of the more corpulent ladies were afraid to trust their immense proportions on the back of a slender native, for fear of being dropped." After landing, she recalled, "more than a dozen natives surrounded me, all holding their hands for a bit, (ten cents,) each claiming the honor of having carried me on his back to the shore." Even when surrounded by nude men, Bates maintained her equanimity: "They all bore such a striking resemblance to one another, and having no garments by which they could be distinguished, I was sorely troubled to know to whom I was indebted for my novel ride."[31]

As these stories reveal, travel in Central America could have a destabilizing effect on women's expectations about proper female behavior. In her study of western expansion, Julie Roy Jeffrey has argued against the idea that "the frontier liberated women from conventional gender roles and made them nearly equal to men." There is nothing in the accounts of female travelers that suggests that the Central American passage made women nearly equal to men, but just as the western frontier challenged both women and expectations about women, so, too, did travel through Central America. It may be wrong to describe Central American travel as liberating, but women's accounts suggest that they often experienced it that way.[32]

Travel through Central America temporarily freed women from many of the normal and onerous responsibilities of housework. They were able to write in great detail about the tortilla making and clothes washing of Latin American women because they were not engaged in such "drudgery" themselves. Some women understandably suggested that travel was actually a pleasure. Although there are few surviving records of the reactions of servant women to Isthmus travel, they may have especially appreciated this aspect of their travels. Alfred DeWitt told his mother that "our woman Elizabeth said it was no trouble at all to go over the isthmus, and it was only a bit of a pleasure party." His wife Margaret did just as well, making "no complaint

---

[31] Mrs. D. B. Bates, *Incidents on Land and Water, or Four Years on the Pacific Coast* (New York, 1858), 285.

[32] Julie Roy Jeffrey, *Frontier Women: Civilizing the West? 1840–1880*, Rev. ed. (New York, 1998), 227. John Mack Faragher also has dismissed the idea that women were more liberated in the West. "The move west called upon people not to change but to transfer old sexual roles to a new but altogether familiar environment." Faragher, *Women and Men on the Overland Trail*, 187. Two historians who have argued that women had more equality in the West are Page Smith, *Daughters of a Promised Land: Women in American History* (Boston, 1970), 221; Caroline Bird, *Born Female: The High Cost of Keeping Women Down* (New York, 1968), 22.

THE WAY THEY CROSS "THE ISTHMUS".

of fatigue" while crossing the Isthmus of Panama. Margaret also avoided sea sickness on the steamer to Panama. "Capt. Stoddard said that when he visited California he intended to have the first gold he procured made in a medal for her, certifying that she was the best lady sailor that he had met with" Alfred wrote proudly.[33]

Travel freed women from some housework but little about the Isthmus passage was easy. Heat, disease, the difficulty of procuring provisions, and the unreliability of transport from one point to another made this a grueling trip for all travelers. The rigorous nature of Central American travel posed a dramatic challenge to contemporary gender norms. Before the completion of the Panamanian railroad in 1855, travelers had to cross the mountainous interior of the country over unimproved paths on mule back. Nicaraguan passengers also were forced to ride mules for a portion of their journey. As Nathaniel Currier wittily illustrated in "The Way They Cross the Isthmus," this was a difficult task under the best of circumstances (see Figure 6.2). Female dress rendered it nearly impossible, since side saddles were unavailable in either Panama or in Nicaragua, as Mary Durant discovered. "To demure at this style of equipage would be of no use" she wrote, and so she attempted the three hour or longer journey mounted sideways on a man's saddle. While she was lucky, she noted that other "ladies fell from their mules – one more than once." The treacherous conditions demanded that women straddle their mules, but in order to do so, they had to first don appropriate clothing. In addition to all the other disruptive aspects of Isthmus travel, female travelers were forced to wear pants.[34]

[33] Alfred DeWitt to his mother from Panama, December 30, 1850; Alfred DeWitt to his parents from Panama, May 15, 1849. DeWitt Family Papers, BL. It would be wonderful to hear what Elizabeth or other working women thought of the crossing in their own words, but there are virtually no extant descriptions of Central America from American working women in this period. Riley, "Women on the Panama Trail to California," 531–48.

[34] Durant quoted in Levy, *They Saw the Elephant*, 49. A few women, including Mary Jane Megquier, brought their own side saddles. Riley, "Women on the Panama Trail to California," 536.

FIGURE 6.2. "The Way They Cross 'The Isthmus'" (New York, Nathaniel Currier, 1849). This Nathaniel Currier lithograph represents the travails of the Isthmus crossing (including cholera and crocodiles), as well as the tensions between local residents and travelers. Shirtless laborers row the boats, while hapless Americans swoon with illness and fall off their mules. An obsequious Panamanian offers to sell a mule for $1,500 while a traveler insults him. "Behold the Isthmus!! I think I smell gold already," declares one passenger, to which another replies "I rather guess it's the Guinea Nigger from the Gold Coast he smells." U.S. travelers often compared the mixed-race Latin Americans they encountered on the Isthmus with African-American slaves, but they rarely confused them in the manner represented here. Note that there are no female travelers. Library of Congress, Prints and Photographs Division [LC-USZ62–26405].

Given the other difficulties travelers faced, the amount of attention both women and men paid to the issue of women's clothing is notable. But female dress reform, and especially the "bloomer costume" advocated by some ante-bellum health reformers, was widely contested in the antebellum era. Critics mocked the "bloomer costume" for "unsexing" women, and they equated bloomers with gender role reversal. Supporters of dress reform reversed the accusation by labeling men who mocked the bloomer unchivalrous. At the height of gold-rush travel, this debate raged in popular periodicals. In the summer of 1851, *Harper's Monthly Magazine* pictured bloomer-clad women smoking cigars in public, while the author of "Bloomer Rights" in the *Democratic Review* condemned "the men, degenerate cases/With ladies now have changed their places/And gentle dames once served so true/By many courtly squires and knights/Their own campaigning now must do/To win the cause of Bloomer Rights" (see Figure 6.3). Traveling women had earlier rec-ognized the practical advantages of short split skirts, but the idea of women wearing pants was so disruptive to gendered expectations that dress reform won few converts on the Oregon Trail in the 1840s. Few, if any of the women traveling through Central America in the 1850s seem to have packed these costumes. Because they rejected "manly" women's clothes before leaving, they were, ironically, forced to wear actual men's clothes on the Isthmus.[35]

The open-minded journalist Bayard Taylor reported without much com-ment that "some ladies who had ridden over from Cruces in male attire, a short time previous, were obliged to sport their jackets and pantaloons several days before receiving their dresses." But most men and women were amazed at the scene. South Carolinian Daniel Horn marveled when "a day or so ago I saw a lady dressed in man's clothes a straddle a mule, a child in front, and her husband and another child walking. She seemed quite cheer-ful and I thought was quite amused at her own appearance and the notice she attracted." One astounded woman recalled that "I shall never forget my feelings when I found myself seated astride my mule, arrayed in boots and pants ... ready for any emergency."[36] Male clothing not only changed the appearance of a woman, it also, in this case at least, changed her perception of herself. The cross-dressed traveler was "ready for any emergency."

---

[35] *HNMM* 3 (August 1851): 424; *USDR* 29 (September 1851): 216; see also "Frippery," *PMM* 9 (May 1857): 466; and *The Living Age* 31 (December 13, 1851): 526–7. On the controversy over bloomers see Patricia A. Cunningham, *Reforming Women's Fashion: 1850–1920, Poli-tics, Health, and Art* (Kent, Ohio, 2003), 31–74; Faragher, *Women and Men on the Overland Trail*, 106.

[36] Bayard Taylor, *Eldorado: Adventures in the Path of Empire.* 1850 (Santa Clara, CA, 2000), 24; James P. Jones and William Warren Rogers, "Across the Isthmus in 1850: The Journey of Daniel A. Horn," *Hispanic American Historical Review* 41 (November 1961): 545; Sandra L. Myres, ed. *Ho for California! Women's Overland Diaries from the Huntington Library* (San Marino, CA, 1980), 27, ftnt. 30.

FIGURE 6.3. Bloomers and Cigars. *Harper's Monthly Magazine* reprinted this 1851 *Punch* illustration of the "manly and independent" bloomer costume along with a satirical letter from "Theodossa Eudoxia Bang, of Boston, U.S., Principal of the Homeopathic and Collegiate Thomsonian Institute for developing the female mind in that intellectual city" encouraging British women to adopt American dress reform. Both letter and illustration mock American gender and democracy, indeed the bloomer is cited as evidence of "the progressional [*sic*] influence" of "democratic institutions." They also reflect the discomfort many American men felt about women's changing roles in the antebellum period by suggesting that there was a slippery slope between dress reform and sexual inversion: "The American female delivers lectures, edits newspapers.... With man's functions, we have asserted our right to his garb, and especially to that part of it which invests the lower extremities. With this great symbol, we have adopted others – the hat, the cigar...." Dress reform was actively contested in Central America as well. *Harper's New Monthly Magazine* 3 (August 1851): 424.

The vision of women in men's clothing on the Isthmus was highly unsettling to both women and men, not only because it upset gender norms, but because it seemed to some observers that female travelers actually enjoyed the gender subversion. Mary Seacole, the Jamaican hotel manager in Cruces, Panama, repeatedly condemned cross-dressing, a behavior she identified specifically with American women. Some women chose to wear men's clothing to protect themselves from complements, she claimed, while others, especially women traveling back from California, seemed to take an unnatural pleasure in the male garb. They "appeared in no hurry to resume the dress or obligations of their sex," she groused.[37]

Male-authored travel narratives openly disavowed this reading of their wives' cross-dressing. In the account of an early steamship pioneer, the inauguration of the cross-dressing mule ride emerged out of desperate conditions. The extreme danger of Cholera in Chagres, he wrote, "gave rise to one of those bold steps, illustrative of the superior moral heroism of the fair sex over that of the sterner." Yet his narrative emphasizes not female but male heroism, since it is daring husbands who are brave enough to broach the subject. Faced with the dilemma of how to transport their wives across the Isthmus, the Reverend O. C. Wheeler tells a Mr. Whitney, "My wife has agreed to wear a suit of my clothes and ride as I do. If your wife will do so with yours, I will take her, otherwise I can not, for I think it is the only safe way." Both parties agreeing to the proposition, "the whole population, both native and foreign, was assembled to see the novel sight. The three left at once, amid the most exciting cheers." After a harrowing ten and a half hour journey, the party was met with "shouts of applause and pealing cheers, an exercise that continually increased, until they reached the hotel, where Mrs. Wheeler was taken from her horse, and carried by enthusiastic army officers and gentlemen pioneers, to her room." The officers and pioneers declared that "'these are the only two sensible ladies among us,' 'that is the only *rational* way for a lady to attempt the trip,' and others of similar import were repeated for the hundredth time."

By repeatedly emphasizing the public nature of the spectacle, and public support for the innovation, the steamship pioneer justifies what he clearly found to be an unsettling event. Both the representatives of martial manhood, the "officers," as well as "the whole population, both native and foreign," openly acknowledge the "rational" nature of cross-dressing. It may be the innovation of certain brave husbands, but it is an innovation that, the author makes clear, is publicly sanctioned. In his conclusion he also undermines the suggestion that, as Mary Seacole put it, cross-dressed women were in no hurry to resume the "obligations" of their sex. These women are quickly returned to their rightful clothes, and heroism is returned to the men involved. "This act inaugurated, and those noble men sanctioned and gave character and honorable repute, to an innovation adapted to the circumstances."[38]

---

[37] Mary Seacole, *Wonderful Adventures of Mrs. Seacole in Many Lands*. 1857. (New York, 1988), 18, 20.

[38] Society of First Steamship Pioneers, *First Steamship Pioneers* (San Francisco, CA, 1874), 86–7. The steamship pioneers are typical in their response to female masculinity, according to Judith Halberstam. "The way the dominant culture contained the threat that the mannish woman represented to hegemonic masculinity was to absorb female masculinity into the dominant structures." Judith Halberstam, *Female Masculinity* (Durham, 1998), 49.

As much as the steamship pioneer would like the reader to accept that "noble men" sanctioned their wives' cross-dressing, the spectacle of women in men's clothing remained an object of wonder to observers. The San Francisco *Alta California* offered an 1850 description of "Charley," "an individual whose sex would certainly never have been satisfactorily ascertained from outward appearance." Having "recently arrived here from Panama.... the lady (as she soon confessed herself to be)...boldly and practically proclaimed the right to 'wear the breeches....'" The newspaper reported that "Charley" displayed "a formidable brace of pistols and dazzling bowie knife, defied insult, declaring it to be her 'holy mission' to pursue and demolish a traitorous escort." Freed from her petticoats, "Charley" was not only renamed, but reborn as a martial man, retaining only her feminine desire for "vengeance" against an unfaithful lover.[39]

The story of "Charley" brings into relief the opportunities Central American travel offered white American women. Female travelers may not have envisioned themselves as the agents of Manifest Destiny in the region, as men did, but travel in the region offered women many opportunities. Central American travel was full of adventure for American women. They could observe women's labor without laboring themselves, ride on the backs of naked men, test their physical strength and endurance, and dress like men. Perhaps they could even behave like men for a short time.

But the story of "Charley" reveals that cross-dressing could have dangerous effects on American manhood. Cross-dressing could turn gender upside down, and turn a domesticated American woman into an armed and aggressive foe. Cross-dressing threatened to bring the vengeance of American womanhood down on unfaithful men. While the *Alta California* article doesn't suggest that "Charley's" escort left her for a Latin American woman, the implication for unfaithful male travelers was clear. Bringing a white American woman into Latin America could cause trouble. Given the opportunities for success in love and work the region offered, perhaps American men would be better off leaving American women at home.

Removing White American Women from Latin America

The gendered narrative of manifest manhood promised work, women, and worldly success to the American man who would cast his lot in Latin America, but there was little room for American women in this aggressive expansionist fantasy. In the United States, "traveling domesticity" empowered women to make "it their duty to 'civilize' the frontier" by supporting moral causes and reform movements there.[40] Women were undesirable in Latin America precisely because their presence, and domesticating force,

---

[39] *Alta California*, January 21, 1850, quoted in Levy, "The Panama Trail," 31.
[40] Magnuson, "In the Service of Columbia," 20.

undermined the much vaunted opportunity of the region, and especially the possibility for white men to "annex" themselves to Latin American women. Sarah Brooks explicitly warned men against flirting with "a pair of bright eyes and rosy cheeks" in Central America in her travel narrative. One American she knew did, and he was nearly waylaid by a "peon" attempting his life. In her story Brooks alerts the man, thus saving his life, and she warns both him and the reader to "save his complements for some one besides Spanish women."[41]

One indication that "traveling domesticity" did not extend to the gold rush, at least in the 1850s, is the near total absence of white women or their needs in gold-rush travel guides. As this study has noted, descriptions of Latin American women in the guides indicate that men were the intended audience. Although small numbers of women traveled through the Isthmus between 1849 and 1860, (there were thirteen women on the very first steamship voyage from Panama and San Francisco in 1849, and increasingly greater numbers through the 1850s), the needs of female travelers were almost never addressed, although, as the bloomer controversy makes clear, they could certainly have used advice. White American women also rarely appear in booster narratives encouraging annexation in Latin America or in accompanying illustrations (see Figure 6.4).[42]

Men's desire to remove white women from Latin America is especially evident in texts supporting annexation and filibustering. The reigning equations of sex and expansionism in "Gaston, the Little Wolf" and "The Story of Blannerhassett," the two tales of filibustering as seduction discussed in the first chapter of this study, offer an explanation for this absence. Those in favor of filibustering and annexation visualized aggressive expansionism as offering the opportunity for white American men (in this case the Americanized Frenchman, Gaston de Raoussett-Boulbon) to find adventure and love in a foreign context freed from the domesticated constraints of convention and propriety. Opponents of filibustering, on the other hand, suggested that aggressive expansionism would undermine domestic tranquility and bring ruin to the family home. When Harman Blennerhassett follows the bad martial model of Burr, his wife suffers the indignity of watching drunken militia members don her clothes, and the family's domestic bliss is destroyed. For aggressive expansionists, martial manhood can only bloom when freed from the constraints of domesticity, while for restrained men, aggressive expansionism is unacceptable in part because it disables women from fulfilling their domestic role.

In her study of citizenship in antebellum America, Nancy Isenberg has suggested that the aggressive "language of chivalry" that supported expansionism was opposed by antebellum feminists because it "accentuated physical

---

[41] Brooks, *Across the Isthmus to California*, 50–1, 58; see also Richard Henry Dana, *Two Years Before the Mast*. 1840 (New York, 1945), 82–4.

[42] Levy, *They Saw the Elephant*, 44.

ENTRANCE TO A COFFEE ESTATE.

FIGURE 6.4. "Entrance to a Coffee Estate." Expansionist travelogues focused on the opportunities open to American men on the "new frontier" but left American women at home. The 1853 *Harper's Monthly* travelogue, "Three Weeks in Cuba," was unusual in that it pictured the island populated by happy American families. "American coffee planters in this district" lived in comfort with their "highly intelligent families" in "mansions...comfortably situated near running streams and in the midst of fruit-trees and flower gardens." The presence of upper-class women in this illustration is notable for its rarity. *Harper's New Monthly Magazine* 6 (January 1853): 172.

prowess and bodily strength" as prerequisites of citizenship. "Even before the [U.S.-Mexico] war," she writes, "the language of chivalry already had foreshadowed the internal dangers that American women posed through resisting the march of conquest." Many women used their powers both within and outside the household to fight against territorial expansionism. The well-known writer and abolitionist Lydia Maria Child loudly protested against the "insane rage for annexation in this country" and directed much of her political energy against seizing "the territory of our neighbors by fraud or force." At one point she wrote in exasperation, "I do believe if we could annex the whole world we should try to get a quarrel with Saturn in order to snatch his ring from him."[43]

Women who spoke out against expansionism were clearly a threat to the continued march of Manifest Destiny. But the mere presence of those who

---

[43] Isenberg, *Sex and Citizenship*, 141; Edward P. Crapol, "Lydia Maria Child: Abolitionist Critic of American Foreign Policy," *Women and American Foreign Policy: Lobbyists, Critics, and Insiders*, Edward P. Crapol, ed. (New York, 1987), 2, 15.

remained silent also posed a problem to an expansionist fantasy based on the personal annexation of Latin American women. Not surprisingly then, both male-authored travelogues and male travelers suggested that white American women had best avoid Central America altogether.[44]

American men agreed that Central American travel was arduous, in part to highlight their success in surviving it.[45] The presence of American women traveling on the same routes tended to undermine that narrative. Travelers like Francis Edward Prevaux reported the difficulties of American women with some relish. "Mrs Tuck is a maiden lady and a *lettle* [sic] too *nice* to cross the Isthmus comfortably. Her fine *feelings* were frequently shocked by the nude statuary which every where presented itself to view." Daniel Horn wrote home about "one lady who took it in her head to walk over" the Isthmus, rather than ride, "and succeeded, but think [how] she paid for it, as I saw her a few days afterwards and she was quite feeble and appeared to be quite sick. She did not get much credit for her feat from sensible men." The "sensible men" would never have considered walking over the Isthmus when it was possible to ride, and if they were forced to walk, would hardly like to have acknowledged that a woman also could complete such a heroic feat.[46]

But men were not the only ones to emphasize the difficulties women faced when traveling. For every woman who took the challenges of travel in stride, another complained bitterly. Mary B. Ballou experienced frequent discomfort in Panama. While Mrs. D. B. Bates sometimes downplayed the arduous nature of her travel experiences, other women in her narrative faint and die. Jessie Benton Frémont devoted a good portion of her travel account to her near death by fever, while Margaret DeWitt admitted that she expected to "suffer a great deal" from heat during her passage.[47]

Not surprisingly, the narrative of expansionism as "travelling domesticity" was somewhat compromised by the dangers that travel in the territories in question posed to female health. Nor was it simply the rigorous nature of

[44] Caren J. Deming has described a similar process in Western fiction where the "domestication of the wilderness – the task of white women" undermined any chance for "guilt-free liaisons with Indian women." Caren J. Deming, "Miscegenation in Popular Western History and Fiction," in *Women and Western American Literature*, Helen Winter Stauffer and Susan J. Rosowski, eds. (Troy, NY, 1982), 96.

[45] G. J. Barker-Benfield points out that reformers also wished to keep women out of the West for similar reasons. "It is possible" he writes about the Reverend John Todd, "that his desire to prevent women from entering not just the male sphere but its roughest, hairiest sector was to prevent himself from being left even further behind that sector himself, and even behind the point where the social spheres just touched." *The Horrors of the Half-Known Life: Male Attitudes Toward Women and Sexuality in Nineteenth-Century America*, 2nd ed. (New York, 2000), 192.

[46] Prevaux letter to parents, from Panama, June 29, 1850, BL; Jones and Rogers, eds., "Across the Isthmus in 1850," 545.

[47] Ballou, "*I Hear the Hogs in My Kitchen*"; Bates, *Incidents on Land and Water*; Frémont, *A Year of American Travel*; Margaret DeWitt letter, April 1849, DeWitt Family Papers, BL.

the Isthmus crossing that raised problems for white women in Latin America; the dangers of Central America's tropical climate posed a real challenge to boosters who wanted to promote annexation and settlement in the region. Male travelers asserted that women suffered more from the climate than did men, and some female travelers agreed. Lydia Prevaux wrote to her in-laws that "there is a something in this climate which makes one so weak and lazy that the slightest exertion is a burden."[48]

Travelogues reinforced the idea that the climate of Central America was unsuitable for white American women. Although William Wells went to great lengths to achieve the annexation of Nicaragua in the mid 1850s, he also warned against the emigration of white women. In San Juan del Sur, he wrote, "languor and debility" were common, "the effects of which are sure to mark themselves upon the female visitor who remains under the enervating influence of the tropical sun." Marvin Wheat expressed similar concerns about Mexico in his 1857 annexationist travelogue. The Philadelphia-born wife of one settler, Mrs. Collier, becomes "rather ill, suffering from neuralgia, and also the paralysis in her arms" in his account. Not even Creole women of European descent were immune from the climactic horror of Central America, some travelogues claimed. T. Robinson Warren suggested that Mexico's climate was to blame for the premature death from consumption of Margarita, "a blonde among brunettes, with the most prodigious flow of animal spirits."[49] The conclusion a careful reader would have to draw from these expansionist narratives was that however delightful the region might be to an American man, for a white American woman it was dangerous ground.

Pro-filibustering fiction by both men and women suggested that there was little room for American women in the fantasy of Manifest Destiny – indeed that American women were incompatible with aggressive expansionism altogether. The popular writer of city mysteries, Ned Buntline, capitalized on the furor over the final López expedition to Cuba in his 1851 novel, *The Mysteries and Miseries of New Orleans*. In his usual formulaic narrative about a wealthy rake and the honest girl he misleads, Buntline attributes the failure of López's last filibuster to a vengeful wife. In the second of the novel's story lines, an alcoholic gambler, Charles Gardner, drives his beautiful wife Fanny into the arms of another man through his neglect. After Gardner kills his wife's seducer, Fanny vows vengeance against him. Gardner decides to join López's filibustering troops but is followed to Cuba by Fanny, who reveals the whereabouts of the troops to the Spanish authorities of the island.

---

[48] Prevaux letter to parents, from Panama, June 29, 1850, BL.

[49] William V. Wells, *Explorations and Adventures in Honduras, comprising sketches of travel in the gold regions of Olancho, and a review of the history and general resources of Central America. With original maps, and numerous illustrations* (New York, 1857), 28; "Cincinnatus" (Marvin Wheat), *Travels on the Western Slope of the Mexican Cordillera in the form of Fifty-One Letters* (San Francisco, 1857), 133; T. Robinson Warren, *Dust and Foam; or, Three Oceans and Two Continents* (New York, 1859), 179.

The death of the attorney general's nephew, William Crittenden, and his fifty American soldiers is thus directly attributed to the wholly fictional Fanny.[50]

Buntline, a clear supporter of aggressive expansionism writing for an equally expansionist urban audience, plays the defeat of Crittenden and López for its maximum effect. At the moment of his death, William Crittenden cries out, "There is a word in the lexicon of life more infamous than *coward*; that word is – *Spaniard*!" Buntline reinforces the image of the cruel Spaniard when "dastardly soldiers" mutilate the American corpses and utter "wild, inhuman yells." The filibusters, on the other hand, are "gallant," and while the troops were small in number, "each was a *man*" Buntline asserts. The men wander for days without food and water, and they demonstrate their extreme valor in battle. Even the dastardly Fanny ultimately recognizes that they are "brave men," and models of martial manhood.[51]

Fanny Gardner, in contrast, is decidedly unwomanly. Indeed, the Spanish authority is so horrified by her betrayal that for a moment it appears that gender might trump filibustering – the filibuster and Spaniard come together against the unwomanly woman who causes the downfall of López. As the Spaniard tells Fanny, "Nature erred in making you a woman, lady! You should have been a man." This is not entirely her fault, Buntline argues. Gardner holds at least some responsibility for ignoring his wife. "Had you given me your society," she tells him, "I would have been pure and happy – you, prosperous and contented!" His failures as a husband, she suggests, are responsible for her murderous rage. But since Gardner also deserts his wife for the thrill of aggressive expansionism, her critique of his absence could just as easily apply to sober and attentive filibusterers.[52]

Buntline's narratives are not known for their realism, but the fact that he attributes the fall of López's American troops to a white American woman should give the reader pause. Fanny Gardner becomes, in this story, the personification of the missing American woman in the aggressive expansionist narrative – a controlling and destructive force that martial men were wise

---

[50] In my discussion of antebellum novels I will be following their own conventions of referring to female characters by their first names and to male characters by their surnames. Ned Buntline, *The Mysteries and Miseries of New Orleans* (New York, 1851). On the popularity of city mystery novels see Michael Denning, *Mechanic Accents: Dime Novels and Working-Class Culture in America*. Rev. ed. (London, 1987), 13, 85. Shelly Streeby has argued that Buntline fits into an entire story paper genre in which "scenes of empire-building in the Americas" become "perilous but possibly redemptive sites where damaged urban masculinities might be rehabilitated and where urban class conflicts might give way to cross-class homosocial bonds between white brothers forged at the expense of people of color." I would add to this that it does so at the cost of white American women as well. Shelly Streeby, *American Sensations: Class, Empire, and the Production of Popular Culture* (Berkeley, 2002), 155.

[51] Buntline, *Mysteries and Miseries of New Orleans*, 85, 65, 62, 99.

[52] Ibid., 74, 99. Whether there was such a thing as a sober filibuster was questioned by some who had taken part in these expeditions. See Horace Bell, "Confessions of a Filibuster," *The Golden Era*, July 25, 1876.

to try to escape, and foolish to allow into the sanctum of the new frontier. While women on the western frontier made use of the rhetoric of domesticity to support expansionism, men in Latin America made use of the rhetoric of Manifest Destiny to undermine domesticity. In the "annexationist" fantasy of American man and Latin American woman, the American woman is necessarily absent. Buntline's *The Mysteries and Miseries of New Orleans* suggests the trouble that can emerge if she is reintroduced to that narrative.

Female Filibusters? Lucy Holcombe and Cora Montgomery

Although filibustering was bound up in the formation of masculine identity in a number of ways, female supporters of filibustering were not unknown. Know-Nothing Party supporter Anna Ella Carroll of Maryland was fiercely devoted to American expansionism, and she wrote that God intended that "the wings of the American eagle" spread the "Protestant Bible and their American Constitution. . . . over the countries of the world" so that "our own strength shall increase, our own resources expand, and an additional impetus be given our moral, commercial and political greatness." Although Carroll opposed slavery, she employed the language of Republican motherhood to laud a not-yet proslavery William Walker in 1856 in decidedly different terms than did most of his supporters. Walker was not notable for his martial virtues so much as for the fact that he had "a *good* mother" for whom he "supplied the place of a daughter" with the "amiability of his disposition, and the sweetness of his temper."[53]

Although filibustering armies were almost exclusively male, a number of William Walker's officers brought their wives to Nicaragua. Families also were attracted to Nicaragua by Walker's liberal land policies. Some southern women openly supported Narciso López. The women of New Orleans sewed a flag, for a "free Cuba," and presented it to López on the eve of one of his filibustering excursions. The wealthy and well-connected Washington resident, Rose Greenhow, who would later become the Confederacy's most illustrious female spy, unsuccessfully lobbied her close friend John C. Calhoun to support López only five days after John L. O'Sullivan had failed in the same enterprise.[54]

---

[53] Janet L. Coryell, "Duty with Delicacy: Anna Ella Carroll of Maryland," *Women and American Foreign Policy: Lobbyists, Critics, and Insiders*, Edward P. Crapol, ed. (New York, 1987), 17, 60. The American eagle of course, was an easily recognized symbol of empire and was included in the great seal of the United States to picture the imperial ambitions of the young American empire. Carroll Smith-Rosenberg, "Dis-Covering the Subject of the 'Great Constitutional Discussion,' 1786–1789," *JAH* 79 (December 1992): 842; Anna Ella Carroll, *The Star of the West: or, National Men and National Measures*, 3rd ed. (Boston, 1857), 349–50.

[54] Robert E. May, *Manifest Destiny's Underworld: Filibustering in Antebellum America* (Chapel Hill, 2002), 23, 197–9; New Orleans *Daily Delta*, May 26, 1850.

Greenhow was not the only elite and politically connected southern woman to embrace López's cause. Lucy Holcombe was a Tennessee-born southern belle of renowned beauty and a liberal northern education. Under the evocative pseudonym H. M. Hardimann, a twenty-two-year-old Holcombe wrote what one historian has called the "first filibustering novel about Cuba," in 1854.[55] *The Free Flag of Cuba* does not fit the conventions of "women's fiction" as defined by Nina Baym. Holcombe wrote in a distinctly political vain for a primarily male audience, with the twin goals of changing U.S. policy toward Cuba and vindicating Narciso López and his disastrous 1851 expedition. As the one-time fiancé of William Crittenden, Holcombe had a personal interest in redeeming the reputation of the Cuba filibusters.[56]

The Free Flag of Cuba is a celebration and vindication of martial manhood. Worthy male characters in the novel support López, and Holcombe equates opposition to filibustering with female weakness. President Fillmore's neutrality proclamation, "a mere piece of coquetry with Spain," reveals his unmanliness. Using the same language of chivalry that would be exploited by William Walker's supporters, Hardimann, or Holcombe, repeatedly compares the filibusters to knights. She highlights their heroism by asserting that they filibustered out of the purest motives – love of liberty, and not a desire for personal gain, drive the volunteers to Cuba. While the actual volunteers to López's raids were drawn with promises of "plunder" and wrote ditties about making money in Cuba, the protagonist of Holcombe's novel, Ralph Dudley, actually dedicates his ample fortune to López's cause. In a notable reversal of the chain of events that brought David Deaderick and other filibusters to the "new frontier," Dudley goes to California to find a fortune *after* failing as a filibuster.[57]

Holcombe repeatedly describes Cuba as a beautiful woman in the grip of an evil man. "With false promises on their lips, they encircled in their dark, treacherous arms the fairest child of southern waters." But the noble men of America will come to her rescue: "What wonder then that young America, the nation-knight, who loves liberty no less than beauty,

---

55 *The Mysteries and Miseries of New Orleans* would seem to deserve that title. Lucy Holcombe Pickens, *The Free Flag of Cuba: The Lost Novel of Lucy Holcombe Pickens.* Orville Vernon Burton and Georganne B. Burton, eds. (Baton Rouge, 2002), 3. I will refer to the author by her maiden name, Holcombe, since she was single at the time of publication.

56 Nina Baym, *Women's Fiction: A Guide to Novels by and about Women in America, 1820–1870* (Ithaca, 1973), xvi–xvii; Pickens, *Free Flag of Cuba*, 5–7.

57 Pickens, *The Free Flag of Cuba*, 60. Several prominent New Orleans individuals lost their fortunes in López's invasions, but they invested in the filibusters in the hopes of making huge profits on real estate and trade once Cuba was annexed to the United States. Laurence J. Sigur, for example, sold his New Orleans newspaper to raise $40,000 for a ship for López in 1851. Richard Tansey, "Southern Expansionism: Urban Interests in the Cuban Filibusters," *Plantation Society* 1 (June 1979): 233.

should brave the dangers of war, wave, and garotte, to release the fair thrall."[58]

Ralph Dudley is admirable, according to Holcombe, because he rejects the comforts of home for the honor of the field of battle. His fiancé, Genevieve Clifton, is the model of the demure southern belle. She is adamantly opposed to Dudley's filibustering plans and presents a series of coherent arguments against filibustering in an attempt to change his mind. She even goes so far as to call López a pirate, an accusation that understandably infuriates Dudley, although another character in the novel notes jokingly that in his outrage, Dudley himself wanted only "a belted sword and black feather, to represent the pirate completely." Resisting Genevieve's entreaties, Dudley dismisses her scruples as nothing more than predictable female weakness. "She was a woman, and this expedition was bringing danger to her lover."[59]

Genevieve's arguments are logical. At one point she suggests that a small band of Americans could have little chance against Spain, to which her fiancé replies, "Think you so little of American prowess that five hundred of our strong, brave men, with the addition of the armed natives, would fail to snatch from the poor crumbling power of Spain that bright child of the waves . . . ?" The failure of the invasion, of course, vindicates Genevieve entirely. Yet Holcombe clearly intends the reader to agree with Dudley and dismiss her arguments. This is because male honor, Holcombe suggests, is the most important consideration for a man, and it should matter to a woman just as much. When a secondary character, Eugene de France, yields to the entreaties of the women in his family and stays home, he is shamed.

"I wish to heaven I had gone with Colonel Dudley, as a man would have done. Who but a coward would yield to tears when brave men beckoned him to follow to a generous strife?"

The hot flush of shame and anger burned on his cheek.[60]

When offered a second opportunity to join López, de France jumps at the chance, and although his death leaves the family without a single male member, he is remembered as a hero.

In her own way, Holcombe makes as strong an argument against the involvement of white women in filibustering as does Buntline. Genevieve accuses Dudley of loving Cuba more than her. Cuba is a "Spanish beauty," and "it is for her that you leave me miserable." The only literal Cuban woman in the novel, the "fair" daughter of a New Orleans mother and Cuban father, is executed after refusing to give up secrets about the filibusters to the evil Spanish officer. Women, Holcombe argues, are by and large "silver

[58] Pickens, *The Free Flag of Cuba*, 130, 210. The garotte was the preferred method of execution in nineteenth-century Spain. Victims, including Narciso López, were slowly strangled with a metal wire.

[59] Pickens, *The Free Flag of Cuba*, 108, 32.

[60] Ibid., 67, 87.

chains" that "bind" men. Women are the main obstacle preventing men from achieving their destiny on the field of battle. What the filibusters in this novel were after, above all, was, "'Fame!' the noble bride of statesmen, of warriors, and kings! Is he not over-bold to bend his boy brow at such a shrine!" Dudley ignores Genevieve's tears, arguing that "he must not be thwarted even by those he loved, least of all by a woman."[61]

But not all women stand in the way of male honor. Mabel Royal, a visiting northern schoolmate of Genevieve's, suggests an alternative and proper model of American womanhood, one that nurtures and supports martial manhood by upholding both honor and filibustering, even at the expense of domestic bliss. Mabel is as strongly pro-filibustering as any man in the novel, and she makes it clear that only the most risk-taking filibuster could win her heart. Mabel professes that she has no unladylike political opinions but also suggests that if American women appeared to be growing too strong minded, it was the fault of overly weak men. "I think, if man were truer to his duties, woman would not seek to assist him in his legitimate sphere." Mabel embraces the idea of separate spheres and the opportunity to exert influence over her husband from within the home. "Woman has great power, if she would realize and accept it," she tells Genevieve.[62]

But the model Mabel presents of the manner of womanly encouragement for aggressive expansionism is far from that of the "traveling domesticity" that buttressed less martial forms of Manifest Destiny. The women in *The Free Flag of Cuba* must, like its anonymous author, be content to stay at home, while the men prove their masculine virtues in Cuba. By making Mabel a Northerner, and giving her a southern love interest, Holcombe fulfilled her role as a southern woman in the mid 1850s by promoting sectional harmony, even if she did not write under a female name. But with her portrayal of Mabel, Holcombe also advocated a self-sacrificing ideal of female patriotism that would gain wide acceptance as the model of Confederate womanhood. When her paramour dies in Cuba, Mabel swallows her sorrow and marries another. Lucy Holcombe, who lost William Crittenden in Cuba, likewise chose to marry. She became the wife of wealthy planter and politician Francis W. Pickens, who later became South Carolina's secessionist governor. As Lucy Holcombe Pickens, she gained renown as a one of the first women of the Confederacy, and she was the only woman ever pictured on Confederate currency.[63]

Holcombe's novel proves that women could and did support both aggressive expansionism and martial manhood, even if it was at the expense of domesticity in Latin America. But there was ambivalence in Holcombe's

---

[61] Ibid., 73, 145, 91, 76.
[62] Ibid., 108, 105.
[63] Varon, *We Mean to be Counted*, 138; Pickens, *The Free Flag of Cuba*, 1–2.

account, since the very men she heroicized were actually killed in Cuba in a poorly planned invasion that not only brought dishonor on them and the United States but also damaged American interests in the region. A similar ambivalence marks the writings of the other major female supporter of filibustering, who, not coincidently, also wrote under a pen name. The most significant author, male or female, on the topic of Manifest Destiny in the 1840s was arguably Jane McManus Storm (after 1848, Jane McManus Storm Cazneau), popularly known at the time as Cora Montgomery, or simply Montgomery.[64]

Jane McManus was born in upstate New York in 1807 and lived an entirely unconventional life. She spent her first decades in the Northeast before investing in and eventually moving to Texas in the 1830s. McManus was married twice, and she was named as mistress of that destroyer of domestic bliss, Aaron Burr, in an 1834 court case. She converted from Protestantism to Catholicism, spoke fluent Spanish, and was active in the Texas independence and statehood movements. A talented and prolific journalist, Montgomery (as she was most often publicly known) served as the political editor in the mid to late 1840s of both the *United States Magazine and Democratic Review*, and the New York *Sun*, at the time the most widely circulated newspaper in the world, while also raising a son from her first, short marriage.[65]

Like many leading boosters during the period, Montgomery had personal as well as political interests in the Americanization of Latin America. She invested widely in the region and actively pushed for the annexation of not only Texas, but also Nicaragua, Cuba, the Dominican Republic, and the Yucatan. She knew and supported both López and William Walker, and she served on diplomatic missions for the United States, most significantly a failed secret peace mission to Mexico from November 1846 to April of 1847. Her diligence in Mexico led General Winfield Scott to label her, not entirely flatteringly, "a plenipotentiary in petticoats." She wrote a number of widely read travelogues to the region, which she usually published anonymously. It was Montgomery who created the phrase "Manifest Destiny" as author of essays widely attributed to John L. O'Sullivan, her boss at the *Democratic Review*. It was Montgomery, rather than O'Sullivan who penned "The Great Nation of Futurity" in 1839, where the phrase first appeared. It was Montgomery

---

[64] The best study of Jane McManus Storm Cazneau (who went by the names Jane McManus, Jane Storm, and Jane Storms before marrying William Cazneau in 1848 1849) is Linda S. Hudson, *Mistress of Manifest Destiny: A Biography of Jane McManus Storm Cazneau, 1807–1878* (Austin, 2001). See also Anna Kasten Nelson, "Jane Storms Cazneau: Disciple of Manifest Destiny," *Prologue: The Journal of the National Archives* 18 (Spring, 1986): 25–40.

[65] Hudson, *Mistress of Manifest Destiny*. When discussing Jane McManus Storm Cazneau's writings I will refer to her as Montgomery for the sake of clarity.

who in the 1845 essay "Annexation" described continental expansion as "the fulfillment of our Manifest Destiny."[66]

While O'Sullivan has been called the father of Manifest Destiny, it is Montgomery who is the phrase's rightful mother. That title, however, is not a perfect fit. Given the fact that Montgomery's entire career stands in stark contrast to the ideology of separate spheres, perhaps it is more appropriate to label her the "mistress" of Manifest Destiny, as her biographer has, rather than as its mother. Although men took credit for many of her most significant essays and books, Montgomery was a well-known public figure who was accepted as an equal in the elite journalist circles and who was deferred to by leading political figures of the day. The fact that, until recently, researchers failed to consider whether Montgomery was the author of the anonymous expansionist essays in the *Democratic Review*, suggests another level upon which Manifest Destiny has continued to be a gendered narrative.[67]

From her positions at the *Sun* and *Democratic Review*, and as the editor of *La Verdad*, a newspaper for Cuban exiles in New York, Montgomery was "the voice of Young America," the Democratic Party faction in support of territorial expansionism, trade, commerce, and national unity. Under the pen name Montgomery, Cazneau published so extensively on the issue of Cuba that her name became "synonymous with the Cuban Independence faction in New York" between 1847 and 1850. Yet while Montgomery fervently advocated America's Manifest Destiny, a close examination of her writings indicates important differences between her understanding of Manifest Destiny and that of aggressive expansionists writing after the U.S.-Mexico War.[68]

Missouri senator Thomas Hart Benton, father of Jessie Benton Frémont, believed that Montgomery had a particularly "masculine stomach for war and politics." As the only female correspondent in the U.S.-Mexico War, she repeatedly demonstrated that she would not be constrained by gendered conventions of the era. But Montgomery also understood the power of "traveling domesticity" to advance Manifest Destiny. Her 1852 travelogue *Eagle Pass; or, Life on the Border* employed domestic imagery in order to combat Mexican debt peonage. Much as Harriet Beecher Stowe mobilized visions of family life and household interiors to condemn slavery in *Uncle Tom's Cabin*, Montgomery focused on the horrors that debt peonage wrought on families. In chapters focusing on aspects of her home on the Mexican

---

[66] Moses S. Beach, "A Secret Mission to Mexico," *Scribner's Monthly* 18 (May 1879): 139–40. The failure in Mexico was not hers alone; "Annexation, *USDR* 16 (July–August, 1845): 5–10. With the use of a grammar-check program, Hudson has persuasively revealed that Montgomery was the author of many crucial expansionist texts previously attributed to her editor, John O'Sullivan, including the essay in which the phrase was first used, "The Great Nation of Futurity," *USDR* 6 (November 1839): 426–30; Hudson, *Mistress of Manifest Destiny*, 46–8, 205–10.

[67] Hudson, *Mistress of Manifest Destiny*, 48.

[68] Ibid., 96, 115, 117.

border ("My New Family," "Gardening") and on gender relations ("The False Wife"), Cora Montgomery expressly adopted the position of a woman upholding the sanctity of the household. She also suggested the role that white American women could play fighting the inequity of Mexican laws from within the household by protecting the mistreated Mexican peasants who worked for them.[69]

Montgomery's anonymous essays for the *Democratic Review* contain nothing comparable, suggesting that there was nothing "natural" about women envisioning Manifest Destiny in domestic terms. Women could participate in the political realm in this era, but only on a limited basis. When they overstepped the bounds of their sphere, they became an object of ridicule. When writing as a woman (as in *Eagle Pass*) Montgomery invoked "traveling domesticity" because it was the most powerful trope at a woman's disposal, if she did not wish to incur the wrath of readers. When writing in a male persona, as an anonymous journalist, she had a far wider range of arguments at her disposal.

But while her essays in the *Democratic Review* and the New York *Sun* make little use of domestic imagery, they also avoided the worst excesses of martial discourse that turned to aggression as a means to prove American manhood. An opponent of the U.S.-Mexico War (but supporter of the All-Mexico movement) who believed the United States could eventually control all of Latin America through the judicious use of trade and commerce, "Montgomery" warned in 1846 in the *Sun* that "I would not see our eagle merely a bird of prey!" In "Annexation" she described Mexico as "impotent" and "weak," but she asserted that Mexico's weakness "should have constituted her best defense" against war. Aggressive expansionists, of course, claimed that weakness was itself a justification for war. In the 1851 essay "Narcisso [sic] Lopez and his Companions" she suggested that the filibuster and his men were heroes rather than pirates, not based on their martial virtues, but because they acted out of patriotic and disinterested motives. The patriotic and religious content of the letters they wrote at gunpoint, she maintained, "show they were of the stuff of which heroes are made."[70]

Montgomery was a Democratic Party stalwart and "negrophobe" who doubted for most of her life whether the two races could peacefully coexist in

---

[69] Benton quote in Hudson, *Mistress of Manifest Destiny*, 69; Cora Montgomery, *Eagle Pass; or, Life on the Border* (New York, 1852); Harriet Beecher Stowe, *Uncle Tom's Cabin* (London, 1852); Lori Merish, *Sentimental Materialism: Gender, Commodity Culture, and Nineteenth-Century American Literature* (Durham, 2000).

[70] "Correspondence," New York *Sun*, July 7, 1846; see also "Correspondence," New York *Sun*, July 17, 1846; Hudson, *Mistress of Manifest Destiny*, 71–6; "Annexation," *USDR* 16 (July–August, 1845): 9, 7; "Narcisso [sic] Lopez and His Companions," *USDR* 29 (October 1851): 293. Lynnea Magnuson argues that Cazneau used her status as a woman to critique the morality of the war. Magnuson, "In the Service of Columbia," 87.

the United States.[71] But she was also a proponent of both the gradual emancipation of slaves and the emigration of African-Americans to the Caribbean. She argued that the annexation of Texas would help funnel slaves out of the upper South, and into the Caribbean. She wrote in favor of annexing Texas that "every new slave state in Texas will make at least one free state from among those in which the institution now exists, to say nothing of those portions of Texas on which slavery can not spring and grow." In the 1848 essay "Principles Not Men" she stated that "the evil of slavery has been deplored by all parties, north and south since the formation of the government," a position certainly not accepted by most Southerners at the time.[72]

She also asserted throughout her career that Manifest Destiny would be accomplished through the voluntary action of neighboring peoples drawn through networks of trade and commerce to the shining example of America. In part, this was possible because the United States was so potent, a "hale, hearty youth in the prime of his vigor" in contrast to "old superannuated" Great Britain. But Manifest Destiny would be driven primarily by America's social institutions rather than by individual masculine enterprise. As she described in the 1845 essay "Annexation," Anglo-Saxon emigrants had already poured into California with "the plough and the rifle . . . marking its trail with schools and colleges, courts and representative halls, mills and meeting houses."[73] Montgomery may have been America's premier exponent in the late 1840s of a vision of Manifest Destiny that was gradual, inevitable, and, if not particularly domestic, not notably martial, either. While it would be wrong to identify her as an advocate of restrained manhood, the centrality of commerce to her vision of Manifest Destiny was more compatible with that of restrained than martial men.

Montgomery's gradualist ideology stands in stark contrast to the aggressive expansionists who "twisted her words" and "borrowed her phrases" after she moved away from New York and her editorial duties in the early 1850s to join her second husband, the entrepreneur and diplomat William Cazneau, in the Dominican Republic. Montgomery warned against the American eagle becoming a bird of prey, while James De Bow, editor of

---

[71] On "negrophobia" and the Democratic Party see Thomas Hietala, *Manifest Design: Anxious Aggrandizement in Late Jacksonian America* (Ithaca, 1985), 10–54, 167–72. For a contemporary statement of the position see Robert J. Walker, "Letter of Mr. Walker, of Mississippi, Relative to the Annexation of Texas," (Washington, DC, January 8, 1844), in Frederick Merk, *Fruits of Propaganda in the Tyler Administration* (Cambridge, MA, 1971), 221–52.

[72] "Annexation," *USDR* 16 (July–August, 1845): 7. Montgomery developed these ideas further in "The King of Rivers," *Democratic Review* 25 (December 1849): 506–15; "Principles, Not Men," *Democratic Review* (July 1848), 6.

[73] Robert E. May, "Lobbyists for Commercial Empire: Jane Cazneau, William Cazneau, and U.S. Caribbean Policy, 1846–1878," *Pacific Historical Review* 48 (August, 1979): 383–412; Hudson, *Mistress of Manifest Destiny*, 115–6; "Narcisso [sic] Lopez and His Companions," *Democratic Review* 29 (October 1851): 297; "Annexation," *Democratic Review* 16 (July–August, 1845): 9.

De Bow's Review, predicted in the 1850s that "the Eagle of the republic shall pass over...and...by war conquer...." While Montgomery looked to Latin America for a means to end slavery in the United States, expansionists like De Bow turned to the region to expand slavery. There was no reason why Montgomery, as a woman, needed to place the interests of the Union first, although by doing so she conformed to gendered expectations that political women would serve as sectional mediators. After all, she wrote anonymously. Montgomery was neither a representative journalist nor a representative woman in the nineteenth century, but as the greatest female journalist of the era, her restrained vision of Manifest Destiny provides a notable contrast to the discourse of aggressive expansionism that followed her.[74]

The fact that the most significant female supporter of filibustering had a "masculine stomach," and the only woman to write a pro-filibustering novel wrote in the persona of a "Hardimann," suggests that while "traveling domesticity" shaped westward expansionism, something quite different was going on in Latin America. Rather than domesticity shaping and justifying expansionism, what could be called "traveling masculinity" appears to have been at work in the 1850s. Men left for Latin America in order to redeem martial practices of manhood. Whether they succeeded or failed, martial manhood traveled back to the United States and was disseminated at public meetings and through novels like *The Free Flag of Cuba*.

Although white American women were in the minority among female travelers in Central America, women and domesticity were not marginal to the construction of the Latin American antebellum encounter. Letters and diaries of female gold-rush travelers reveal that they entered Central America with less of a sense of American's Manifest Destiny in the region than did their male traveling companions. They did not imagine an American presence in the area redeeming womanhood in the same manner that men imagined an American Central America could redeem manhood.

But Central American travel held the potential of transforming gender norms at home none the less. Traveling women watched other women labor and considered the meaning of their work. Women were forced to test themselves in the Isthmus, to engage in behavior that would have been socially unacceptable in the United States, from encounters with naked men, to cross-dressing and riding astride a saddle. The subversive potential of the journey was great, even if, as in westward expansion, women may not actually have been liberated by the experience.

That fact that Central American travel could empower women was problematic for men, but it was not the only reason why men expressed ambivalence about the presence of white women on the new Latin American

---

[74] Hudson, *Mistress of Manifest Destiny*, 116; De Bow quoted in Basil Rauch, *American Interest in Cuba, 1848–1855* (New York, 1948), 187–90.

frontier. By meeting the challenges of travel, women undermined the claims male travelers made for the heroic nature of the journey. As socially sanctioned agents of domesticity and civilization on the western frontier, there was a precedent for white women to use their powers to reform unseemly male behavior in ways that may not have been appealing to the martial exponents of aggressive expansionism. The chance for American men to fight, drink to excess, and seduce Latin American women was circumscribed by the presence of white American women. Proponents of filibustering, especially, made it clear that these women had best stay out of Latin America.

Cora Montgomery was one woman who refused to stay home. Her anonymity allowed her the freedom to employ arguments in favor of the spread of Manifest Destiny in Latin America that other women, constrained by popular expectations about the political limitations of female activism, did not have access to. Yet she maintained an allegiance to the Union, and an unwillingness to advocate the worst excesses of aggression and warfare in the name of Manifest Destiny, that set her apart from fiercer advocates for martial expansionism. By the middle of the 1850s, Montgomery had embraced commercial expansionism as the best means for achieving America's destiny abroad, and she was advocating a vision of expansionism that restrained men were more likely to embrace than martial men. Martial manhood and its "traveling masculinity" drove expansionism in Latin America. But in the islands of the Pacific, the restrained man's vision of religious and commercial expansionism would have its hour in the sun.

7

Manifest Destiny and Manly Missionaries

Expansionism in the Pacific

> The whole enterprise of this nation, which is not an upward, but a westward one, toward Oregon, California, Japan, etc.... is perfectly heathenish, – a filibustering toward heaven by the great western route.... What end do they propose to themselves beyond Japan? What aims more lofty have they than the prairie dogs?
>
> – Henry David Thoreau, 1853

In May of 1853, *Putnam's Monthly Magazine* published a short article, "Reminiscences of Honolulu: The Feast of Lanterns." After first remarking that descriptions of Hawaii had become "so ordinary, so commonplace" that another tale of the islands might not automatically engage the interest of the reader, the author recalled not the landscape or history of the islands but rather the drunken events of one exciting evening in Honolulu. Spurred on by a "boyish exhilaration" resulting from the "bracing and invigorating" climate of Oahu, the author and a gathering of "Californians, very nice but very 'fast' young men" decided to stage a "serenade" with "a large invoice of Chinese lanterns" that "had that day been offered for sale." Dressed in Chinese costume, the drunken "fast young men" paraded about Honolulu, singing songs, and repairing into private homes for further libations. Eventually the "feast of lanterns" degenerated into "dismal howls," "insane and frantic war dances," and "pranks innumerable which had been perpetrated in the small hours" to the "terror and dismay of the good citizens, toward the winding up of that impromptu affair." In the punch line to his tale, the author recounts that the following morning, "many were the rumors abroad of a well-disguised attempt at revolution by Californian filibusters, and the resident Chinese," which had "only been put down by the strong and energetic measures of the government."[1]

---

[1] "Reminiscences of Honolulu," *PMM* 1 (May 1853): 558–61.

Antebellum urban working men frequently dressed up in costume before parading. Historians have argued that by appropriating the costumes of African-Americans and Native Americans, working men of European extraction, especially the Irish, were able to simultaneously assert their own whiteness and to justify behaving in an unseemly, disorderly, or even criminal manner. That a costumed gathering of "fast young men" would degenerate into something like a riot would hardly merit notice in the urban centers of the United States. But in Honolulu in the early 1850s, this gathering took on a dramatically different meaning than it would have in New York, Philadelphia, or San Francisco.[2] To the people of Honolulu "the feast of lanterns" had metamorphosed into an "attempt at revolution by California filibusters." Clearly, the author meant to mock the fears of Hawaiians and perhaps also to mock the "energetic measures of the government" that proved unable to control even a small disorderly crowd in its streets.

What "Reminiscences of Honolulu" brings into focus is the uneasy position of sovereign countries within filibustering range of the United States in the 1850s and the continuing health of Manifest Destiny in the decade after the U.S.-Mexico War. As this chapter will explore, expansionist lust reached far into the Pacific in the antebellum era. Commodore Perry's expedition to Japan proved that the expansionist imagination could travel beyond the bounds of the Western Hemisphere. The kingdom of Hawaii, (also known as the Sandwich Islands at the time), was never actually invaded by American mercenaries but was subject to repeated filibustering scares. Indeed, "Reminiscences of Honolulu" was based on an actual event – the arrival of "fast young men" from California who many in San Francisco and Hawaii believed were intent on "revolution" in Honolulu. This chapter will consider how the events and discourse of Pacific expansionism differed from those in Central America and the Caribbean. In the Pacific, anti-annexationists promoted a vision of Manifest Destiny that was at once restrained, and at the same time as sweeping as any filibuster's. As in Latin America, gendered expectations, hopes, and fantasies proved central to the unfolding of aggressive expansionism, but in the Pacific it was the manly Christian, rather than the martial filibuster, who had the upper hand.

The *Game Cock*

In November of 1851, only three months after Narciso López and his men were executed in Cuba, the kingdom of Hawaii prepared for attack. Word of an invasion from California had circulated around the islands for months,

---

[2] On blackface, costume, and rioting see David R. Roediger, *The Wages of Whiteness: Race and the Making of the American Working Class* (London, 1991), 104–11; Susan Davis, *Parades and Power: Street Theater in Nineteenth-Century Philadelphia* (Philadelphia, 1986), 77–111; Philip J. Deloria, *Playing Indian* (New Haven, 1998).

but by October mere rumors had solidified around seemingly tangible evidence. A ship was on its way to Hawaii. According to a confidential letter from San Francisco received by Hawaii's minister of foreign affairs, 200 armed men, "carrying with them a ready-made Constitution," intended to debark soon in the Sandwich Islands. Their supposed intention: to establish in Hawaii "a Republican government, peaceably if they can – forcibly if they must. The plot is intended to be kept a profound secret."[3]

Someone was not particularly good at keeping a secret, since the plan was widely commented on in the press. The San Francisco *Daily Evening Picayune* reported on October 15 that "a party of restless young bloods numbering about 160, are about sailing from this Port for the Sandwich Islands for the purpose, it is said, of revolutionizing the government of his Kanaka majesty." The *Picayune* was unable to say "whether they go really with revolutionary purposes." The California *Daily Courier* noted, however, that the passengers on the ship *Game Cock* were "well armed, and are of that peculiar temperament that prefers a row of any kind, to order and quiet, and that leads them to commit an act first and determine the object of their actions afterwards." News of the voyage was reported as far afield as Philadelphia. Of course the news made it back to Hawaii. The *Polynesian* reprinted a number of the articles that had "naturally excited considerable attention and some alarm here."[4]

Contemporary readers would have understood immediately that the threatened "act" alluded to by the *Courier* was an armed uprising and that the *Game Cock* was supposed to be full of filibusters. López's recent career ensured that. Aggressive expansionism was flourishing at the start of the decade. According to one Californian, opposition to filibustering in 1850 was as unpopular a position to hold as opposition to slavery in some parts of the country.[5]

San Francisco was one place where slavery was decidedly less popular than filibustering. By the time the *Game Cock* left San Francisco Bay, a shipload of men planning to invade Ecuador had already sailed under the direction of Juan José Flores, the exiled president of the country. Those who survived the failed mission returned to California by the end of 1851. The first of the decade's six filibustering expeditions to Sonora, Mexico, had also already

---

3 William Ladd to Robert Crichton Wyllie, October 28, 1851. AH Foreign Office Letter Book, Vol. 13A, Foreign Officals in Hawaii File, September 1847–January 1852, 1408.
4 *Daily Evening Picayune*, October 15, 1851, quoted in letter from Wyllie to Severence, November 3 1851. AH, Foreign Office Letter Book, Vol. 13A, 1410; California *Daily Courier*, October 29, 1851, and Philadelphia *Public Ledger*, January 12, 1852, in Wyllie to Severance, November 3, 1851. Ibid., 1707; Andrew F. Rolle, "California Filibustering and the Hawaiian Kingdom," *Pacific Historical Review* 19 (1950): 251–63; *Report of the Minister of Foreign Relations, read 14 April, 1852* (Honolulu, 1852), 17; *The Polynesian*, November 22, 1851.
5 Horace Bell, *Reminiscences of a Ranger: Early Times in Southern California* (Santa Barbara, 1927), 214, cited in Rolle, "California Filibustering and the Hawaiian Kingdom," 253.

been launched from the city. Quartermaster general Joseph C. Morehead landed in La Paz in June after planning a two-pronged attack on Sonora, but he was forced to return to the United States in defeat. Just after the *Game Cock* set sail, the French filibuster Charles de Pindray sailed to Guaymas, Mexico, with 150 eager adventurers and hopes of forming a settlement in the gold-rich territory. Pindray died under mysterious circumstances in Mexico, but this did not dissuade other filibusters, nor did it prevent the local press from reporting, often encouragingly, on these excursions.[6] California's very origins as a territory free from rule by Mexico had a filibustering flavor, as John C. Frémont's "Bear Flag" revolt against Mexico's government in 1846 was carried on without the explicit support of U.S. military commanders, earning Frémont the label of "filibuster" in some quarters. In short, the possibility that ordinary men could travel to Hawaii in the hopes of taking it over would not have seemed implausible to San Franciscans. In the context of America's Manifest Destiny, and especially the activities of other gold-rush San Franciscans, it might have seemed only too likely.[7]

Clearly this was how Hawaii's minister of foreign affairs, Robert Crichton Wyllie, saw matters. In public, Wyllie drew up a plan for a 5,000-man army, and he encouraged the legislature to levy a military tax on the citizenry. In private, he dispatched emotional letters to allies in both the islands and the United States. To the Hawaiian chief justice, William L. Lee, Wyllie wrote, "Our political days are numbered.... We will fall without one feeling of pity or sympathy from anyone.... Personally I have only one life to throw away, and that a very worthless one." To another friend he reported that "we are threatened with great dangers." Despite conflicting accounts, that "1000 passengers (Gentlemen and Ladies) are coming...merely to pass the Winter" and that "the Chief Capitalists are coming to make specific overtures to the King and Government to give up the country voluntarily in terms all cut and dry," Wyllie admitted to Lee that "what I believe is there is mischief brewing." He warned officials on all six of Hawaii's islands to gather armed forces and to await the arrival of the *Game Cock* from San Francisco.[8]

---

[6] Charles H. Brown, *Agents of Manifest Destiny: The Lives and Times of the Filibusters* (Chapel Hill, 1980), 159–73; Helen B. Metcalf, "The California French Filibusters in Sonora," *California Historical Society Quarterly* 18 (1939): 3–21; Robert E. May, "Manifest Destiny's Filibusters," in *Manifest Destiny and Empire: American Antebellum Expansionism.* Sam W. Haynes and Christopher Morris, eds. (College Station, TX, 1997): 146–79.

[7] Brown, *Agents of Manifest Destiny*, 217; Edward P. Crapol, "Lydia Maria Child: Abolitionist Critic of American Foreign Policy," *Women and American Foreign Policy: Lobbyists, Critics, and Insiders*, Edward P. Crapol, ed. (New York, 1987), 11. One historian, at least, would disagree with pinning the label of filibuster on Frémont, since he led American troops and had the implicit support of the U.S. government. May, "Manifest Destiny's Filibusters," 149.

[8] Wyllie to Lee, November 5, 1851, AH, Foreign Office and Executive File (FO & EX File), November 1851; *Report of the Minister of Foreign Relations*, 84–7. The Privy Council financed 100 trained men in Oahu, 750 infantrymen on Oahu, and 50 soldiers on Maui and the Island of Hawaii. By March of 1852 these numbers had been reduced considerably so that

To his close friend Lee he was openly pessimistic about the odds of a Hawaiian victory. "[I]f we can not beat back the invaders," he stated, the armed forces "might at least... prevent the natives from joining" the fili-busters. Wyllie had "no confidence" in the natives' "loyalty to the chiefs" or in King Kamehameha, who was often drunk. Wyllie wrote Lee that in his present dissipated state, "anything is better than to leave the King at the mercy of any 50 determined men." The king, paying little heed to his minister's warnings, left the seat of government in Honolulu for a visit to the island of Maui on the eve of the invasion. Wyllie begged him to return, but he warned the king to travel under disguise, lest the filibusters attempt a sneak attack on the king's vessel.[9]

The *Game Cock* arrived in Honolulu on November 15, with 32 or 33 passengers, rather than the originally reported 160. Foremost among them was Samuel Brannan, a leading San Francisco citizen. Brannan, an original forty-niner, head of a prestigious San Francisco volunteer fire company, and Mormon missionary, was a man of action. He published the first newspaper in the California territory, erected buildings in San Francisco, stood trial for fraud, and may have started the gold rush by reportedly displaying a bottle of dust from Sutter's mill in the San Francisco streets. His very presence on the *Game Cock* gave credence to the most elaborate tales of intended colonization and filibustering. It was entirely within his character to attempt such a thing.[10]

Brannan was a recognized leader of San Francisco's sporting subculture and a clear expositor of martial manhood. His fellow passengers on the *Game Cock* were likely the sort of men that Brannan associated with in San Francisco, young men, members of volunteer fire companies, gold miners, or those who catered to the gold trade. But the wealthy Brannan was no mere merchant or miner, and the male culture he personified was not simply a brawling, working-class barroom culture. Volunteer firemen, especially in San Francisco, were often men of means, but they chose not to conform to the

---

only 60 men on Oahu were still being paid; Wyllie to Chief Justice, November 7, 1851, AH, Local Officials File; Wyllie to Charles Gordon Hopkins, November 20, 1851, AH, Foreign Office Letter Book, 5, January 1850–December 1854, 82; Wyllie to Lee, November 5, 1851, AH, FO & EX File, November 1851.

9 Wyllie to Lee, November 5, 1851, AH, FO & EX File, November 1851; Wyllie to King Kame-hameha, November 20, 1851, AH, FO & EX File, XV, 1415; Rolle, "California Filibuster-ing," 258; Wyllie quote from Wyllie to Lee, November 5, 1851, AH, FO & EX File, November 1851; Sally Engle Merry, *Colonizing Hawaii: The Cultural Power of Law* (Princeton, 2000), 79; Wyllie to Charles Gordon Hopkins, November 20, 1851. AH, Foreign Office Letter Book, vol. 5, January 1850–December 1854, 83. The king's intemperance was a long-standing prob-lem, and especially disturbing to temperate Americans living in Hawaii. In 1843, the first U.S. commissioner to Hawaii, George Brown, ended his first presentation to the king with "a tirade on the evils of intemperance, and an effort to secure a pledge of total abstinence." Sylvester Stevens, *American Expansion in Hawaii, 1842–1898* (Harrisburg, PA, 1945), 13.

10 On Brannan see Louis J. Stellman, *Sam Brannan: Builder of San Francisco* (New York, 1953).

emerging middle-class standards of decorum and propriety that would mark members of this class in the late nineteenth century. They exerted themselves physically with acts of daring, but they also distinguished themselves in the public sphere with acts of bravery and philanthropy. Urban volunteer fire companies provided fire service and an active social life for young men. They were highly visible organizations that earned praise from urban residents, especially in combustible San Francisco during the 1850s. Volunteer firemen, like Brannan, were recognized and praised for their initiative and lack of fear, and they personified a martial ideal of manhood that was perhaps more admired in gold-rush San Francisco, a city with few women and no established class structure, than it was in most other cities before the Civil War.[11]

When San Francisco's newspapers referred to the passengers on the *Game Cock* as "restless young bloods" it gestured toward this prominent martial subculture. Their ship was aptly named, since these young bloods might patronize a cock fight in any of the many San Francisco saloons that offered this entertainment. Men, lured by gold, entered San Francisco Bay with fantastic plans every day. But men also left San Francisco Bay with fantastic plans. The city was full of ambitious men, and it rewarded the daring and hearty for their fearless actions, whether on the gold fields, in fire companies, or on filibustering expeditions. These men might be impetuous, but they were also deserving of respect. To "prefer a row of any kind, to order and quiet," as one paper put it, was not necessarily a condemnation in gold-rush era San Francisco. Nor would it have been a condemnation in 1850s New Orleans or New York, other centers of expansionist activity. In short, the very fact that these particular men, members of a subculture who were rewarded and praised for their acts of daring, were aboard the vessel, itself supported the idea that they might attempt to wrest control of Hawaii from the king. Fifteen of the ship's passengers, in fact, had previously been involved in vigilante activity in San Francisco. Certainly these "men of action" must have been up to something dramatic. Both natives and police were on guard as the *Game Cock* arrived in port.[12]

Brannan hoped for a meeting with Kamehameha, but if he was disgruntled that the king did not acknowledge his arrival, he gave little sign of it. He

[11] On volunteer fire companies in San Francisco see Amy S. Greenberg, *Cause for Alarm: The Volunteer Fire Department in the Nineteenth-Century City* (Princeton, 1998). The best portrait of the sporting subculture is Patricia Cline Cohen, *The Murder of Helen Jewett: The Life and Death of a Prostitute in Nineteenth-Century New York* (New York, 1998). On society in gold-rush San Francisco see Brian Roberts, *American Alchemy: The California Gold Rush and Middle-Class Culture* (Chapel Hill, 2000); Philip J. Ethington, *The Public City: The Political Construction of Urban Life in San Francisco, 1850–1900* (New York, 1994); Peter R. Decker, *Fortunes and Failures: White-Collar Mobility in Nineteenth-Century San Francisco* (Cambridge, 1978); Robert M. Senkewicz, *Vigilantes in Gold Rush San Francisco* (Stanford, 1985).

[12] Brown, *Agents of Manifest Destiny*, 163; May, "Manifest Destiny's Filibusters," 169.

and his men refused to give up their personal firearms to the local authorities, but despite one arrest for "furious riding" the first day in port, they caused little trouble at first and gave no sign of violent intentions. Brannan bought some property in Honolulu, and he attempted for several days to meet with the king in Maui. Trouble broke out between Brannan's men and some whalers in the harbor over supposed looting of mail bags on the *Game Cock*. Brannan was accused by one of his own men of removing letters from the mail bags informing the authorities of his illicit plans in Hawaii. Later, some of his men got into a barroom brawl in the French Hotel. No insurrection was attempted. No illicit intentions were discussed publicly by the *Game Cock's* passengers. Wyllie's fears were put to rest, for the time being, while Brannan's dreams of empire, if he had any, were dashed. The *Game Cock* came and went, with no more disturbance than might be expected from any visiting boatload of "restless young bloods," and certainly less than that produced by the fictional participants of the "feast of lanterns."[13]

By New Year's Day, 1852, Brannan and his companions were back in San Francisco. Whatever their intentions upon sailing, their failure at filibustering earned them ridicule at home. One of Wyllie's correspondents reported to him that the ship was greeted in port by cries of "Well, have you taken the Islands? Who's the King? Is it you?" The *Daily Alta California* facetiously reported that despite their "extravagant notions relative to a change in the Hawaiian government," their only booty was twenty-two barrels of whale oil.[14] Clearly San Franciscans expected more from their "young bloods" then oil importation. Failed filibusters like Walker were greeted with praise, but the men who traveled to Hawaii were met with derision. In the martial subculture that supported aggressive expansionism, it was these men's lack of aggression that was mocked. The failure of the Hawaiian visitors to raise arms against Hawaii, no matter how foolish and doomed to disappointment their filibustering scheme might be, was seen by some as a greater dishonor then the criminal nature of a real filibustering expedition. In an era of aggressive expansionism, and a subculture of daring, the real loser was the man unable or unwilling to go through with his plan of attack.

---

[13] James H. Tanner Broadside, March 15, 1852, AH, FO & EX File, 1852; Stellman, *Sam Brannan*, 141, 145. These accusations were never investigated by the Hawaiian authorities, perhaps because, as the American commissioner to Hawaii put it, "so great is the number of American seamen here...and so prone are they to have difficulties with their officers and with the police, that it requires much patience, discretion and good temper to manage all these disputes.... These seamen heretofore have been in the habit of appealing to the consul on very trivial causes of complaint." Severance to Edward Everett, February 10, 1853. *Publications of the Historical Commission of the Territory of Hawaii*, vol. 1 (4) 1927 (Honolulu, 1927), 21.

[14] Henry Heap to Wyllie, January 10, 1852, AH, Miscellaneous Foreign File, January–March, 1852. *Daily Alta California*, January 2, 1852; Hitchcock to Wyllie, January 8, 1852, AH, Miscellaneous Foreign File, January–March 1852.

Thus ended America's most notable antebellum filibustering episode in the Hawaiian kingdom. Many in Hawaii and in San Francisco expected armed insurrection, and depending on their perspectives they were either relieved or disappointed by the decidedly anticlimactic outcome.[15] Uneventful as it was, the visit of the *Game Cock* to Hawaii lived on in the memory of Hawaiians. In his speech to the 1852 legislature, Kamehameha bemoaned that "the peace of my Kingdom has been threatened with an invasion of private adventurers from California," and outlined efforts he was making to "protect, efficiently, the lives and property of all who live under my dominion." In fact, at the time of the *Game Cock's* voyage, the U.S. Navy already kept a ship of war in port in Hawaii at the request of the Hawaiian government and had trained native troops. This was in keeping with an 1849 treaty between the two governments agreeing to restrain and apprehend filibusters, or in the words of the treaty, "all persons being charged with the crimes of murder, and piracy." Any filibuster rash enough to take on Hawaii would have faced certain hostility from the governments of France, England, and the United States, all of which had an interest in maintaining the sovereignty of Hawaii.[16]

Nonetheless, Wyllie continued to believe that the visitors had come with evil intentions, and filibustering scares continued to plague Hawaii. According to one historian, Hawaii abolished its feudalistic land system at this time in order to discourage filibustering schemes. In 1854, however, Wyllie insisted that he had received "very credible reports" of an invasion of 350 "dangerous men here, from California, armed with revolvers and other weapons." U.S. commissioner David Gregg reported that fear of filibustering was so great by 1854 that "the King and Chiefs, as well as the Prince are almost afraid of their own shadows. The very sound of the word 'filibusters' makes them

---

[15] Brannan's true intentions will probably never be known, but there is little evidence that he had any intentions of wresting control of Hawaii from the king. Robert May concluded that Brannan "may have had a vague takeover scheme in mind" but that the passengers seem to have been motivated by the unrealistic desire to buy up land cheaply. May, "Manifest Destiny's Filibusters," 169, fn. 2; see also, William Cooper Parke, *Personal Reminiscences of William Cooper Parke* (Cambridge, 1891), 27–8; *Daily Evening Picayune*, October 30, 1851.

[16] Island resident Elizabeth Parker noted that "[c]onsiderable excitement was caused at Honolulu and all the island ports by the arrival of so many Californians as have visited them the present winter, and great military preparations were made to destroy them, if anything like revolution was attempted." Mrs. E. M. Wills Parker (Elizabeth Parker), *The Sandwich Islands as They Are, Not as They Should Be* (San Francisco, 1852), 13; Robert Colfax Lydecker, *Roster, Legislatures of Hawaii 1841–1918: Constitutions of Monarchy and Republic, Speeches of Sovereigns and Presidents* (Honolulu, 1918), 33. Whether Brannan was aware of this treaty is not known, but as a filibuster, he would have been thwarting the will of the United States, in the face of a warship, highly unprepared himself, and with a newly signed treaty providing for his arrest. United States Congress, "Hawaiian Islands," *Senate Exec. Doc.* No. 45 (Washington, DC, 1894), 1416; Rolle, "California Filibustering," 253; Wyllie to King Kamehameha, November 20, 1851. AH, FO & EX file, XV, 1415. Merry, *Colonizing Hawaii*, 4–5, 76–7, 84–5.

quake...." That Hawaii barely escaped the grasp of the Americans in the early 1850s was an opinion shared by many up to the time the monarchy was overthrown and Hawaii ceded sovereignty to the United States in 1898.[17]

Hawaiians had good reason to fear aggressive expansionists in the 1850s. Hawaii was a vulnerable independent kingdom of strategic importance in the Pacific trade and to the international whaling industry, the lynchpin of an emerging Pacific Basin Frontier. Between 1843 and 1860, Honolulu, and Lahaina (on the island of Maui) received visits of an average of 425 whaling vessels a year. Although France, England, and other countries had a significant financial interest in the islands, by the 1840s, the foreign trade of Hawaii had begun a steady shift to the west coast of the United States. In the early 1850s it was primarily Americans who were taking advantage of the newly opened right of foreigners to purchase Hawaiian lands. The French repeatedly threatened Hawaiian sovereignty well into the 1850s, although that threat was limited by the competing interests of the United States and England. King Kamehameha was an extremely weak sovereign who left Hawaii highly vulnerable before his early death in 1854. It is not surprising that a group of martial men might think that this ruler would, as one letter writer accused, "voluntarily come into the arrangement" whereby he would surrender rule."[18]

Even before the U.S.-Mexico War, American periodicals asserted that the island chain was both a desirable commercial acquisition and ideal location for American settlement. In 1843, the *Merchants' Magazine* enumerated the value of the Hawaiian trade and encouraged the United States to prevent European encroachment in the area. An 1845 article in the *National Intelligencer* offered a highly detailed description of trade between America's Pacific outpost in Oregon and Hawaii in order to reveal that "the Anglo-Saxon

---

[17] Stevens, *American Expansion in Hawaii*, 41; Ralph S. Kuykendall, *The Hawaiian Kingdom 1778–1854, Foundation and Transformation* (Honolulu, 1957), 291; Wyllie quote from Wyllie to M. Kekuanaoa, the governor of Oahu, November 17, 1854, AH, FO & EX Local Officials File, 1854; Gregg quote from David Gregg to G. W. Ryckman, July 21, 1854, in the David L. Gregg letterbook, AH, 204–206. See also letter to W. H. Richardson, August 16, 1854. Richard Hammond Letterbook, 1854–1855, 95, HL; Wyllie to John Ricord, December 1, 1854, AH, FO & EX Miscellaneous Foreign File, July–December 1854. In the 1890s, historians and journalists referred back to the 1851 "filibustering" episode in their efforts to contextualize contemporary annexation efforts. See D. B. Walker, "California Filibusters Planned to Take Hawaii from Kamehameha III," Honolulu *Star-Bulletin*, February 24, 1934; Parke, *Personal Reminiscences*; A. P. Taylor, "The Mobilization for the Defense of Hawaii," Honolulu *Advertiser*, January 19, 1913; "Foiled Filibusters, A Tale of the Early 'Fifties,'" *Paradise of the Pacific*, March 1892.

[18] Thomas Schoonover, *Uncle Sam's War of 1898 and the Origins of Globalization* (Lexington, KY, 2003), 13, 20–21; Merry, *Colonizing Hawai'i*, 90; Hiram Bingham, *Residence of Twenty-One Years in the Sandwich Islands* (Hartford, CT, 1847), 586–613; quote in William Ladd to Robert Crichton Wyllie, October 28, 1851, AH, Foreign Office Letter Book, Vol. 13A, Foreign Officials in Hawaii, September 1847–January 1852, 1408.

or Anglo-American race are bettering the world with their language, their laws, their literature, and their religion. . . . In Polynesia, our present article will show that its march has been and is rapidly onward." After its own enumeration of the value of trade passing though the islands, *The Living Age* reported in 1845 that while "civilization" was "rapidly advancing" among the native peoples, immigrants didn't need to be particularly civilized (or hard working) themselves. This, the paper suggested, "would be a strong inducement to certain of the 'loafing' population of this city to emigrate at once. How delightful it would be . . . to lie at full length in the sunshine of that beautiful climate, and have enough to eat all the year round, at the expense of one cent a day!"[19]

Many heeded the call. Between 1840 and 1850, the foreign population of Hawaii increased from one thousand to fifteen hundred people, most of whom were American. Hawaii's growing and powerful expatriate community, increasingly frustrated with the sovereign, made no secret of their interest in closer ties to the United States. According to Sally Engle Merry, the independence the Hawaiian kingdom managed to maintain in the 1840s came at a heavy price. It was purchased at the expense of Hawaii's religious and secular laws, via claims of "civilization" enforced by an Anglo-American political system, largely administered by foreigners. Nonetheless, Hawaiian sovereignty was fragile, and "threats of takeover by imperial powers and challenges by resident foreigners remained strong and imminent."[20]

After the U.S.-Mexico War, American enthusiasm for Hawaii dramatically increased. Wyllie dated the first reports of "machinations contrary to the peace and order of this kingdom," to "soon after the peace between Mexico and the United States, whereby California became part of the later." As one California newspaper described the appeal of the Islands, "the spirit of enterprise and adventure has for centuries been pursuing its course westward, and now . . . when American progress on our continent has been stayed by

---

[19] James Jackson Jarvis, "The Sandwich or Hawaiian Islands," *Hunt's Merchant Magazine* 9 (August 1843): 111–36; "The Sandwich Islands," reprinted from the *National Intelligencer* in *The Living Age* 5 (April 26, 1845): 165–7; "The Sandwich Islands," *The Living Age* 4 (February 8, 1845): 339. The city referred to in the quote is New York.

[20] Whatever vocal support for annexation might have existed among the expatriates at this time did not constitute a consensus on the issue. As Luther Severance put it in 1851, Americans in Hawaii "may not like to substitute the American tariff for the Hawaiian." Quoted in Stevens, *American Expansion in Hawaii*, 57; Merry, *Colonizing Hawaii*, 86–90. Merry claims that competition between England, the United States, and France "impeded all of them from taking the islands," 90. On the same point see William Pencak, "Social and Legal Change in Hawaii before 1860: Parallel Development with the United States," in *The Law in America 1607–1861*, William Pencak and Wythe W. Holt Jr., eds. (New York, 1989), 269–304. The struggle of the Hawaiian monarchy for international recognition is painfully evident in Hiram Bingham's narrative of missionary efforts in Hawaii, *Residence of Twenty-One Years in the Sandwich Islands*.

the waves of the Pacific . . . the eye of the adventurer is looking far off into the ocean." Some gold-rush pioneers continued their journey west when the promises of the gold fields did not pan out. A number of these men, upon reaching Hawaii, "were not hesitant to proclaim their dissatisfaction with the established authority and to threaten revolution and a republican Hawaii," according to one historian of the period.[21]

To expansionists at home, this was as it should be. Borrowing one of the preeminent metaphors of expansionist discourse, the *Alta California* wrote of the islands in April of 1851,

The native population are fast fading away, the foreign fast increasing. The inevitable destiny of the islands is to pass into the possession of another power. That power is just as inevitably our own. . . . The pear is nearly ripe; we have scarcely to shake the tree in order to bring the luscious fruit readily into our lap.[22]

Nor were San Franciscans alone in coveting the ripe fruit of Hawaii, or rather the ripe fruit that was Hawaii. In 1849 a Whig newspaper in Lowville, New York, published a lengthy editorial advocating the annexation of Hawaii. Only days after the *Game Cock's* arrival in Honolulu, the *Oregon Statesman* declared that "where our countrymen migrate, they sow seeds of self-government, which naturally find root in the hearts of men and causes a longing for the free institutions of America; nor will they rest satisfied until they become incorporated into the glorious union . . . it is the inevitable destiny of the Sandwich Islands." A year later the same paper claimed "that those islands will ultimately form a part of the American Union, we regard as inevitable." The *California Courier* agreed, reporting in late 1851 that "our opinion is that those Islands will soon be under the dominion of the Star-spangled banner." And at a Democratic festival in Albany, New York, in 1852, one of the toasts offered was to "Cuba and the Sandwich Isles – may they soon be added to the galaxy of States."[23]

Politicians expressed the same sentiment. In his annual message in 1851, President Fillmore pointed out that the Hawaiian Islands "lie in the course of the great trade which must at no distant day be carried on" between the United States and Asia. The Senate twice requested information from the

---

[21] *Report of the Minister of Foreign Relations*, April 14, 1852, 17; *Alta California*, October 26, 1851, quoted in *The Polynesian*, November 22, 1851; Stevens, *American Expansion in Hawaii*, 42.

[22] San Francisco *Alta California*, April 22, 1851. Quoted in Kuykendall, *The Hawaiian Kingdom 1778–1854*, 408. The metaphor of Hawaii as fruit was too appetizing for later historians to pass by. In his history of United States relations with Hawaii, Sylvester Stevens concluded that Hawaii, "fruit of American frontier expansion," was finally "ripe for harvesting." Stevens, *American Expansion in Hawaii*, 299.

[23] Kuykendall, *Hawaiian Kingdom, 1778–1854*, 383–384, 410; *Oregon Statesman*, November 18, 1851, November 3, 1852, quoted in Stevens, *American Expansion in Hawaii*, 43; *California Courier*, October 24, 1851, quoted in *The Polynesian*, November 22, 1851.

president on a supposed proposition by the king to transfer sovereignty of the islands to the United States, and twice the Senate was denied. In response, California Democrat Joseph McCorkle made an inflammatory speech in Congress in August of 1852 demanding the immediate annexation of the islands, a proposition that met with widespread approval on the Pacific coast. A proposal from a group of New York investors to purchase the island chain for $5 million was submitted to the king around the same time, and the possibility of annexing the islands was again discussed in the House of Representatives in early 1853.[24]

President Pierce hoped to annex Hawaii – and for a period in early 1854 the U.S. commissioner, David L. Gregg, believed that the monarchy would seek annexation as a way to guard against filibustering. Hawaii's growing and powerful expatriate community made no secret of their interest in closer ties to the United States. On July 4, 1854, American residents paraded through the streets of Honolulu in support of annexation: "Thirty-two girls of American parentage, dressed in white, wreathed in flowers, each baring the name of a state on her sash, in large gold letters," were followed by "'Young America,' a company of very young men in uniform." Commissioner Gregg gained King Kamehameha's agreement to draft a treaty of annexation, but by the end of 1854 he had become convinced that rumors of proposed filibustering excursions had turned much of the local population firmly against the United States. Historians have argued that it was threats of filibustering missions that ultimately undermined official efforts to annex Hawaii in the 1850s.[25]

The anxiety about filibustering that pervaded Honolulu in the early 1850s was simultaneously captured and mocked in the article "Life in Hawaii," published by *Putnam's Magazine* in 1853. While visiting Honolulu in 1852, the narrator and his friends at first laughed at the "many rumors afloat . . . of the fillibustering intentions of some of the San Francisco visitors." But after noting the strange behavior of some Hawaiians, the visitors came to believe that the rumors "were *not* as groundless as we had imagined." The narrator and his friends "dashed through the town" to "the headquarters of our California acquaintances" where they overheard "the bloodthirsty exclamations from within of 'I'll take the *King* with a club.'" Only later did they realize that the Californians had been playing chess. While many in the United States fervently wished for the annexation of Hawaii, "Life in Hawaii" reveals the destructive affect of aggressive expansionism on

---

[24] Stevens, *American Expansion in Hawaii*, 43–5; speech by Representative McCorkle, August 30, 1852, in the *Congressional Globe*, 32nd Congress, 1st Sess., Appendix 1081; Kuykendall, *Hawaiian Kingdom, 1778–1854*, 409–10.

[25] David L. Gregg to William Marcy, January 5, November 14, 1854, Dispatches from U.S. ministers in Hawaii, T30, Roll 5, National Archives; Gerrit P. Judd IV, *Hawaii: An Informal History* (New York, 1961), 81; Proclamation of King Kamehameha, December 8, 1854, Official Dispatches, Hawaii (reel 6); May, "Manifest Destiny's Filibusters," 146–8, 168.

American diplomacy. Even visiting Americans were infected with the fear of filibustering.[26]

Health and Hula: Annexationists Consider Hawaii

"Reminiscences of Honolulu" and "Life in Hawaii" are just two examples of Hawaiian travelogues that proliferated in the antebellum era. So many of these narratives were published after the gold rush that the author of *Putnam's* "Reminiscences of Honolulu" could bemoan the fact that "a visit to the Sandwich Islands" by 1853 was "so commonplace an affair, that a trip to Newport scarcely excites more attention." But there is ample evidence that Americans maintained a healthy appetite for Hawaii travel narratives in both periodical and book form. According to a review of one such narrative in 1857, "many volumes, some of them confessed to be the most attractive in the whole range of romance and adventure, have been written in reference to these seas and islands." Reviews of at least six Hawaiian Islands travel narratives appeared in American periodicals between 1849 and 1857. American readers did not have to purchase the Reverend Henry T. Cheever's best-selling 1851 publications *The Island World of the Pacific* or *Life in the Sandwich Islands* in order to appreciate his openly expansionist views, they could read reviews of and excerpts from his books in a number of periodicals. The October 1851 issue of the *International Magazine of Literature, Art, and Science* praised Cheever's "judicious" account and quoted Cheever at length on the "providential plan of the world's great Ruler, that the Sandwich Islands should yet be adopted into the Great American Confederacy."[27]

Annexationists like Cheever employed many of the same arguments to gain that Pacific outpost as were used to further Manifest Destiny in the West in the 1840s and in Latin America in the 1850s. Hawaiians were not entitled to their land because they refused to work it. As an article in *Putnam's Magazine* put it, the natives "turn a deaf ear to applications for their lands, which have been waste and untilled since the creation." Cheever asserted that annexation was the surest means for America to help oppressed people. In his preface to *Life in the Sandwich Islands* he argued that only America could save the Hawaiians, since "the Islanders" had "a

[26] "Life in Hawaii," *PMM* 2 (July 1853): 17–23.

[27] "Reminiscences of Honolulu," *PMM* 2 (May 1853): 558; "The Islands of the Pacific," *PMM* 8 (August 1856): 156; Henry T. Cheever, *The Island World of the Pacific* (New York, 1851); "The Sandwich Islands Today," *International Magazine of Literature, Art, and Science*, vol. 4 (October, 1851): 298; see also "Life in the Sandwich Islands," *USDR* 30 (May 1852): 477. For reviews of other books see "Sandwich Island Notes," the *NEYR* 13 (February 1855): 1–19; "Kiana: A Tradition of Hawaii. James J. Jarvis," *The North American Review* 85 (October 1857): 573. On the rise of the travel narrative in writings on Hawaii see W. Patrick Strauss, *Americans in Polynesia, 1783–1842* (East Lansing, MI, 1963), 163–4.

moral claim upon the American nation for protection. In no way can this be more efficiently bestowed than by receiving them into the family of this great republic."[28]

Boosters of the annexation of Hawaii argued that it was a necessary acquisition for the United States because it was, like Central America, on a natural route of trade. Given the "present policy, which is opening the ports of Japan, laying out a railroad across the continent, and wisely contemplating the future value of American traffic with the East," *Putnam's* concluded, it would be "forgetful" to "overlook the important position of this group." Hawaii was "precisely in the track of that coming trade, and . . . commands the outlets of Oregon and California." In 1852 *De Bow's Review* argued that "The Hawaiian Islands, and the Pacific States and Territories of the United States, are naturally and indissoluble allied to each other, in respect to their relative geographical position, as well as their respective interchangeable productions." In 1855 the journal reiterated that "[i]f Cuba be necessary as a key to the gulf and western valleys, why not these islands, with their admirable harbors, as half-way houses of refuge for our whalemen – points of security in the voyages of our Californian and Oregonian marine?"[29]

As in Latin America, annexationists mobilized American fears of foreign encroachment. If the United States didn't claim Hawaii, another foreign power would. If Hawaii "not be speedily transferred by quiet negotiation to the United States, it will end in a *catastrophe* or pass into the keeping of England or of France." *Putnam's Magazine* stated "Now, the evil of foreign powers having strongholds on the Atlantic and Gulf borders, has been made so manifest that the wisdom of preventing its *growth* here cannot be questioned."[30]

Annexationists pointed to the ongoing Americanization of Hawaii to press for an outcome that residents of the Islands would supposedly warmly welcome. *De Bow's Review*, the pro-slavery journal that encouraged the conquest of Latin America through force of arms, was a fervent supporter of the annexation of the Sandwich Islands. The periodical ran regular and enthusiastic pieces on Hawaii through the late 1850s, extolling the climate, productivity, strategic importance, and beauty of the island chain, and almost always concluding with the author's firm belief that Hawaii "will be annexed." Among the "many and cogent" arguments in favor of annexation,

---

[28] "The Hawaiian Islands," *PMM* 5 (March 1855): 243; Henry T. Cheever, *Life in the Sandwich Islands: or, The Heart of the Pacific, as It Was and Is* (New York, 1851), 5.

[29] "The Question of Annexation," *PMM* 5 (March 1855): 246; "The Islands of the Pacific," *DBR* 13 (November 1852): 458; Dr. Wood, "Our Island Neighbors," *DBR* 22 (March 1855): 288–98.

[30] "The Question of Annexation," *PMM* 5 (March 1855): 246.

De Bow's pointed out that "the Hawaiians themselves, king and all," call for it, that "by their long association with the Americans they have become, to a great extent, assimilated in feelings and principles to ourselves," and that annexation would be "peaceful" and "bloodless."[31]

Putnam's Magazine agreed that an Americanized Hawaii called out for annexation. The "good citizens of the United States" residing in Hawaii have a "earnest and yearning desire for annexation" because they are held back by the native peoples, the journal wrote. "The residence here of the American mission for a generation; the commerce and business of the islands in all time past, as well as now, almost entirely in American hands; the capital invested in the group mainly American; the majority of the white population Americans; the laws, courts, schools and churches generally framed by Americans, after American models, have each and all in their way contributed to form the public sentiment as American also." After a visit to the Islands, T. Robinson Warren concluded that "essentially American in feeling and institutions, these islands must, necessarily, eventually fall under the rule of the Americans, in spite of English intrigue, or French bravado." By 1855 *Putnam's Magazine* could firmly assert that annexation was a matter of when – not if. "When the 'Territory of Hawaii,' shall become a portion of the Union, there will be ways and means in abundance for immigrants by the thousands." It also reported that "every newcomer from the United States" to the islands "becomes an *annexationist,* on finding himself so surrounded by American influences, that he feels as if he were already within an inchoate portion of his great Republic."[32]

Hawaii, like Latin America, offered opportunities for American men in health, work, and love. Henry Cheever described "seabathing" as a "tonic" and surfing an "exhilarating" activity that promised to cure the "dyspepsia from many a bather at Rockaway or Easthampton... The missionaries at these islands, and foreigners generally, are greatly at fault in that they do not avail themselves more of this easy and unequalled means of retaining health or of restoring it when enfeebled." *Putnam's Magazine* claimed that there were neither "hurricanes, tornadoes, nor typhoons" in Hawaii, and that it was "singularly free from all those elements of disease that are usually the fatal inheritance of warm latitudes. A vigorous old age

---

[31] "Central America, Usury Laws, Sandwich Islands," *DBR* 18 (January 1855): 69; A. W. Ely, "The Islands of the Pacific," *DBR* 18 (February 1855): 214. See also, Dr. Wood, "Our Island Neighbors," 22 (March 1855): 288–98; "The Islands of the Pacific," November 1852, January 1855, June 1847; "New Fields for American Commerce," December 1847; "The Sandwich Islands," February 1858; "The Hawaiian Islands," May 1858. All in *DBR.*

[32] "The Hawaiian Islands," *PMM* 5 (March 1855): 244, 243, 26; T. Robinson Warren, *Dust and Foam; or Three Oceans and Two Continents* (New York, 1859), 260; "The Question of Annexation," *PMM* 5 (March 1855): 247.

can be attained and enjoyed by those who would not survive the middle period of life amidst the rigors of the north." Even livestock fared well in Hawaii. "Veterinary professors would starve in Hawaii, for horses are never sick. . . ."[33]

Hawaii was as good a place to prosper financially as to gain health. T. Robinson Warren noted that "with a climate of unprecedented salubrity, and a soil bearing almost spontaneously all the products of temperate and tropic clime, these islands possess advantages for military and naval depots, such a combination of which are not to be found in the world." As *Harper's Monthly* described it in an article published a few months before the *Game Cock* incident, Hawaii was a land not only of "enchanting beauty" but also of "luxurious production." Other sources particularly extolled the business climate. The author of *Putnam's* "Reminiscences of Honolulu" repeatedly pointed out that Honolulu was a "large, thriving, and handsome *American* town, with wealthy merchants." The exuberance of trade was illustrated by the fact that those Chinese lanterns, the prop that inspires the Californians' spree, are newly arrived and offered for sale that day.[34]

Hawaii was a sensual land, annexationists agreed. "The fascination of the easy out-of-door life common at the Islands" was "a charm that wins upon one from day to day, and weds him to the spot, as to a bride." The women of the country naturally expressed Hawaii's sensuality. T. Robinson Warren summarized the general position that in Hawaii, "the girls are grace personi-fied, and the very perfection of physical beauty, and although copper-colored, still that is lost in their full expressive eye and animated features." Women adorn their "red-skinned" but "erect and beautiful" necks with tastefully constructed flower-wreaths in Cheever's account, and while many eventu-ally become "gross, sensual creatures," from the ages of "ten to fourteen" they are lovely, "with bright, sparkling eyes, faces full of sportiveness and glee, and their forms expanding like rose-buds."[35]

The athletic ability of the Hawaiian woman was much commented on, and descriptions of women surfing, swimming, and riding horses fill travel-ogues. According to one source, female riders attracted attention not only for their ability at their "ruling passion" but for their appearance on horseback. "The riding costume of these tawny Dianas is *unique*" one author wrote. "Low silk or velvet hats, gay with feathers and flowers, and scarfs [*sic*] and ponchos of gaudy hues, complete this novel attire, which presents an original

---

[33] Reverend Henry T. Cheever, *Life in the Sandwich Islands* (New York, 1851), 66–8; see also "Life in the Sandwich Islands," *The International Magazine of Literature, Art, and Science* 4 (3): 298–9; "The Hawaiian Islands," *PMM* 5 (March 1855): 241, 243.

[34] Warren, *Dust and Foam*, 261; "The Last Priestess of Pele," *HNMM* 3 (August 1851): 354; "Reminiscences of Honolulu," *PMM* 1 (May 1853): 558.

[35] "The Hawaiian Islands," *PMM* 5 (March 1855): 241; Warren, *Dust and Foam*, 245; Cheever, *Life in the Sandwich Islands*, 108, 171–2.

The "Hula-hula."

FIGURE 7.1. "The Hula-hula," from "Life in Hawaii," *Putnam's Monthly Magazine* 2 (July 1853): 21.

and picturesque combination of garments, exceedingly pleasing to the foreign eye."[36]

Like the women of Latin America, Hawaiian women were often seen in a state of undress that annexationists found highly noteworthy. "These damsels dismount and unrobe [*sic*]...in public, in the twinkling of an eye they disengage themselves from the mystic folds of their flowing skirts" explained the narrator of a *Putnam's* piece. The "hula-hula" dance offered the vision of scantily clad women engaged in movements "singularly striking and graceful," and understandably merited a great deal of attention (see Figure 7.1). That "unfaithful wives" were "a class disagreeably numerous in the South Seas Islands" was emphasized by anti-annexationists more often than by annexationists, although the widespread perception of female promiscuity offered its own appeal. The fact that Hawaiian women could make devoted wives was suggested by one story recounted by Warren, in which a Hawaiian woman swam thirty miles through high seas, dragging her

---

[36] "The Hawaiian Islands," *PMM* 5 (March 1855): 242. See also Warren, *Dust and Foam*, 246; Cheever, *Life in the Sandwich Islands*, 67; Edward T. Perkins, *Na Motu: or Reef Rovings in the South Seas* (New York, 1854), 116.

unconscious white husband after a boat accident. She survived, but sadly, he did not.[37]

For the most part, however, annexationist fantasies of Hawaii were less dependent on Hawaiian women than were similar fantasies about Latin America. In large part this was because observers agreed that the native Hawaiian was dying out. When Captain Cook first arrived in Hawaii in 1778 the native population numbered 300,000. By the 1850s that number had been reduced by more than two-thirds. The rapid decline of the native Hawaiian population seemed to support annexation to some by providing proof of America's destiny. After describing the great advances made by Americans in agriculture and trade in Hawaii, *Putnam's Magazine* pointed out in 1855 that "while all these attributes of a civilized community are thus establishing a foothold in Hawaii, the native race, now reduced to 70,000 souls, is verging towards extinction." The *Democratic Review* had reached the same conclusion in 1849: "The Kanaka race is disappearing, as every race must disappear that comes in contact with the whites . . . their breed has deteriorated." *De Bow's Review* directly compared the Hawaiians to the rapidly dwindling tribes of North America: "The race must soon become extinct. . . . The experience of the Polynesians and of the American Indians has proved that the aboriginal races, under the present philanthropic system of Christianization, can no more change their habits of life, as required by present Christian systems, than the leopard can change his spots." As a minister, Cheever saw God's hand in the process, and believed that it argued "of Providence and destiny" that the Hawaiians "should so soon give out." God had evidently decreed that "their days are numbered, and the end of their existence as a nation is near." Cheever rejoiced that at least they had the good fortune of Christian conversion before their demise.[38]

---

37 "The Hawaiian Islands," *PMM* 5 (March 1855): 242; "Life in Hawaii," *PMM* 2 (July 1853): 21; "Last Priestess of Pele," *HNMM* 3 (August 1851): 354–9. See "Sandwich Island Notes," in the *NEYR* 13 (February 1855): 1–19 for a negative assessment of the hula in particular and the influence of Hawaiian women on American men; "*Scenes and Scenery in the Sandwich Islands, and a trip through Central America. By James J. Jarves Moxon.*" Reprinted from the *Athenaeum. The Living Age* 1 (June 29, 1844): 390; see also Cheever, *Life in the Sandwich Islands*, 106–7, 172; Warren, *Dust and Foam*, 246.

38 "The Question of Annexation," *PMM* 5 (March 1855): 244–5. On the decrease in population see also Rufus Anderson, *The Hawaiian Islands: Their Progress and Condition under Missionary Labors* (Boston, 1864), 269–78; "A Residence of Twenty-One Years in the Sandwich Islands," *USDR* 24 (April, 1849): 382; A. W. Ely, "The Islands of the Pacific," *DBR* 18 (February 1855): 213. See also Warren, *Dust and Foam*, 260. While much of the population decline was due to disease, critics also attributed it to the poor gender relations in Hawaii. After examining five recent British publications on Polynesian society, the *Edinburgh Review* concluded that the diminishing population of Polynesians was primarily the result of female promiscuity and the "deplorable condition of women," including overwork during pregnancy and female infanticide. "Whether the downward tendency of the Polynesian race will be stopped . . . is something more than human foresight can determine. This much, however, we are entitled to assert; this desirable end can never be accomplished but on one

Perhaps because Hawaiians appeared to be a fleeting presence, pro-annexation authors employed a vision of white American women happily transported to the islands. While aggressive expansionist literature suggested that white women were unwelcome in Latin America, in Hawaii they thrived. Henry Cheever advised the construction of beach bathhouses so that white women could surf. He advised "both sexes" to gain the healthy benefits of the sport he termed "this great luxury of a life within the tropics." *Putnam's Magazine* suggested that white women surpassed even Hawaiian women in the use of their mellifluous language. "Aloha. Never harsh, even when uttered by the husky-voiced Kanaka, charming when lisped by the native girl, it becomes music itself on the lips of a pretty New Englander."[39]

The precipitous decline of the native population also provides an explanation for the relative absence of hostile representations of Hawaiian men in aggressive expansionist travelogues, compared with Latin American travelogues. In the antebellum period, idealized portraits of Native Americans in art, fiction, and theater served to simultaneously distance New Englanders from the corruption of Europe and to justify Andrew Jackson's policy of Indian removal as inevitable. Americans thrilled to the tragic fate of the Wampanoag King Philip in the theatrical sensation, *Metamora*, and they embraced fictional accounts of Pocahantas as an idealized "American" woman because Native Americans had been successfully displaced to make way for white settlement, and their fate appeared to be sealed.[40]

Descriptions of native Hawaiian men in pro-annexation literature were likewise more likely to be governed by an "imperialist nostalgia" for a lost age when Hawaiian men were warriors than by a critique of their manhood and character in the present. While the author of the *Putnam's Magazine* article, "Life in Hawaii," described natives as "careless and lazy" and joked that "it always takes two natives to carry a pig, even if it be only a week old," the magazine also bemoaned the effects of "civilization" on the Islanders. "As I looked at the stately figures of some of the men, and pictured to myself the Islander as he appeared in 1772, I could not help contrasting his manly

condition – that of softening the lot and improving the condition of the women...." "The Polynesians; and New Zealand," *Edinburgh Review*, reprinted in *The Living Age* 25 (June 15, 1850): 497–508, quote page 507; Cheever, *Life in the Sandwich Islands*, 80. Cheever added that "it will remain to be remarked that the date of their depopulation and decay, like that of all the other islanders of the Pacific, and the tribes of North and South America, synchronizes with their discovery and the official intell of the Gospel," 80–1. Unaware of the role of disease in the decimation of native populations in the New World, Cheever seems to attribute this process to God's work.

[39] Cheever, *Life in the Sandwich Islands*, 68; "Life in Hawaii," *PMM* 2 (July 1853): 18.

[40] Jill Lepore, *The Name of War: King Philip's War and the Origins of American Identity* (New York, 1998), 191–26; Lynnea Magnuson, "In the Service of Columbia: Gendered Politics and Manifest Destiny Expansion" (Ph.D. Diss., University of Illinois at Urbana-Champaign, 2000), 179.

FIGURE 7.2. "1772" from "Life in Hawaii," *Putnam's Monthly Magazine* 2 (July 1853): 22.

bearing then, with the spectacle he so often presents *now* that he is 'civilized,' (?) and has been made a really useful member of society." Accompanying illustrations offer the image of a brave warrior standing alone in native dress, and another bent over to pull a carriage (see Figures 7.2 and 7.3). Another travelogue described a Hawaiian man as "entirely fearless of danger, quick in his movements, careless of fatigue, and an excellent caterer," but "at intervals crazy." The author also suggested that despite his admirable characteristics, he and his race were unsuited to "civilized life." The Hawaiian's "whole conduct was a complete explication of savage eccentricity," he concluded.[41]

In his widely read *Two Years Before the Mast*, Richard Henry Dana repeatedly contrasted dissipated and idle Mexicans with the "well formed and active" and "intelligent" Hawaiians he met and worked with in the hide trade in California. One "fine specimen of manly beauty" in particular drew

[41] Renato Rosaldo, "Imperialist Nostalgia," *Representations* 26 (Spring 1989): 107–22. For an exploration of how this nostalgia functioned in Mark Twain's Hawaii writings see Amy Kaplan, *The Anarchy of Empire in the Making of U.S. Culture* (Cambridge, MA, 2002), 51–91; "Life in Hawaii," *PMM* 2 (July 1853): 17, 20, 21; "Scenes and Scenery in the Sandwich Islands," *The Living Age* 1 (June 29, 1844): 392.

FIGURE 7.3. "1852" from "Life in Hawaii," *Putnam's Monthly Magazine* 2 (July 1853): 22.

Dana's rapturous praise. A "perfect seaman" who loved to read, Dana's Hawaiian companion sported "one of the pleasantest smiles I ever saw" and "eyes he might have sold to a duchess at the price of diamonds for their brilliancy. As for their color, every change of position and light seemed to give them a new hue...." Yet Dana also suggested that his Hawaiian Adonis was an anachronism, bemoaning the fact that the Hawaiians "seem to be a doomed people." He blamed missionaries for their fate. "The curse of a people calling themselves Christians seems to follow them everywhere."[42]

Dana's description of the noble and manly Hawaiian functions in his narrative primarily to highlight the dissipated unmanliness of the Mexican. But the vision of "doomed" Hawaiians also justified annexation because imperial nostalgia for a race seemingly already "lost" served, in Hawaii as in the United States, to justify the displacement of the remaining "fallen" members of the race. As Brian Dipple has suggested in the case of Native Americans, "The belief in the Vanishing Indian was the ultimate cause of the Indian's vanishing."[43]

[42] Richard Henry Dana, *Two Years Before the Mast*. 1840 (New York, 1945), 87–8, 259.
[43] Brian W. Dipple, *The Vanishing American: White Attitudes and U.S. Indian Policy* (Middletown, CT, 1982), 71.

While some expansionists drew on the beauty of Hawaii's women as a means of selling the islands, Elizabeth Parker made her own appeal for the annexation of the island chain with a very different gender argument. In her 1852 publication, *The Sandwich Islands as They Are, Not as They Should Be*, Parker, a Hawaiian resident, flatly rejected the romantic vision of Pacific Islanders popularized by Herman Melville in his 1846 best-seller *Typee: A Glimpse of Polynesian Life*. "I have looked in vain for his noble warriors, or graceful Fayaway, in the wide-mouthed, flat-nosed creatures around me, whose only beauty is grossness, and only expression, sensuality" she wrote. The "totally depraved" Hawaiians lived in "perfect and most filthy harmony." While male expansionists suggested that the Hawaiian language was at its finest when uttered by white American women, Parker claimed that white women were terrified to teach their children the language lest they be corrupted by the native Hawaiians. The natives sing "songs of so indecent a character, and dances, performed naked, so horrible, that they are not even named by foreign ladies."

In her portrait of life in Hawaii, the "foreign ladies" are constantly accosted by the obscene spectacle of female sexuality. Lest this representation attract some unscrupulous men, Parker underlined the danger of interaction with Hawaii's women in a description of native dining practices. A "flat-nosed young beauty of sixteen seized a horrible cuttle-fish, and, striking her white, sharp teeth into it, was in an instant deluged in the blood and black juice of the creature, which wreathed its long tentaculae about her head and face, till she almost petrified us into stone, as did her prototype, the Gorgon of old." Merely looking at such sights could prove fatal to the moral, if not to the physical life.[44]

Like Richard Henry Dana and other expansionists, Parker lay the fault for the decline of the native Hawaiian at the feet of the missionaries, who, she claimed, kept "native slaves" in their households, and who had corrupted what was once a "fine athletic race" knowing only innocent pleasures. The fact that the natives were dying off at a rate of twenty percent Parker took as a blessing. Yet Hawaii was otherwise a paradise on earth, with idyllic weather, fine agricultural prospects, and a stunning landscape. The clear solution to the problems of Hawaii, including the difficulties "foreign women" faced in having to witness the depravity of native women, was American annexation. "The Kanakas look up to the whites with great reverence and admiration, and they fully believe, that if they had a government like that of the United States, their country would start forward in the race of civilization as rapidly as California has done.... There is not a shadow of a doubt but, if a few wise and resolute men were found to guide and lead them, that the entire people, with the king at their head, would joyfully aid in the overthrow of the present, and the creation of a new form of government." Parker also argued that because the natives were "excessively indolent" and practiced

---

[44] Parker, *The Sandwich Islands as They Are*, 7, 8, 6.

infanticide, "whether, eventually, these Islands should be annexed to the United States, or become an independent republic, the introduction of slavery is indispensable to their value."[45]

Parker's suggestion that slavery be introduced into Hawaii was a radical one, and it raises the issue of the pro-slavery character of antebellum aggressive expansionism. This book has emphasized that American men from both sides of the Mason-Dixon line internalized the ideology of Manifest Destiny and believed that destiny was yet unfulfilled in the decade before the Civil War. Other historians have persuasively argued that the most active supporters of filibustering by the late 1850s were those looking to expand slave territory. While both pro-slave and anti-slavery men imagined foreign territories as potentially American in character before the Civil War, those willing to act on those hopes were a more select bunch. Most filibusters or intended filibusters in the last years of the 1850s were encouraged by dreams of new slave states and territories. While support for William Walker continued to be strong in urban America in the late 1850s, the new filibustering plots were being hatched in the South by pro-slavery activists.[46]

While native Hawaiians were harshly exploited laborers, there was no slavery in nineteenth-century Hawaii. Nor did Hawaii naturally lend itself to the expansion of slavery, not only because slavery was illegal in the kingdom, but also because no American territory or state on the Pacific Coast allowed slavery once the Compromise of 1850 brought California into the Union as a "free" state. According to the geographic vision that allowed expansionists to imagine island or non-contiguous territories as an integral part of the United States, the Hawaiian Islands would extend the culture and practices of California and the Oregon territory, not those of the South. Therefore, the introduction of slavery was highly inappropriate. Given the fact that most American residents of the island chain were of New England or California origin, African slavery in Hawaii was a highly unlikely prospect.[47]

Parker's modest proposal notwithstanding, those in favor of Hawaiian annexation recognized that they needed to make a special appeal to Southerners who recognized the limits of slave expansion in the Pacific. William Henry Trescot suggested annexing both a free Hawaii and a slave Cuba for the purposes of balance in his 1849 Charleston, South Carolina, publication *A Few Thoughts on the Foreign Policy of the United States*, since both were necessary for the protection of American trade.[48]

Even the pro-slavery advocate Francis Poe, writing for *De Bow's Review* in 1858, was unwilling to openly advocate the introduction of African slavery

---

[45] Ibid., 8, 11. 17. The term *kanaka* refers to native Hawaiians.

[46] Robert E. May, *Manifest Destiny's Underworld: Filibustering in Antebellum America* (Chapel Hill, 2002), 249–79.

[47] Ernest S. Dodge, *New England and the South Seas* (Cambridge, 1965), 138–59.

[48] William Henry Trescot, *A Few Thoughts on the Foreign Policy of the United States* (Charleston, 1849) reviewed in "Our Foreign Policy," *DBR* 16 (January 1850): 1–6.

to the island chain, although he strongly hinted that it might solve the "labor problem" resulting from the declining native population. The fact that Hawaii was an inappropriate outpost for African slavery suggests one reason why, despite the many filibustering scares in the region, Hawaii never actually faced an invasion of armed Americans in the antebellum period. Urban men from eastern states had limited exposure to the remote chain beyond what they read in popular periodicals, filibustering Californians were kept busy harassing Mexico, and Southerners looking to gain new slave territories had much better prospects in Latin American than they did in the Pacific Ocean.[49]

Missionary Work as (Anti) Expansionism: Restrained Manhood in Hawaii

What *Harper's Monthly* travel narrative would be complete without a climb up the flank of a volcano? In the 1854 aggressive expansionist travelogue, "San Juan," the Nicaraguan guide hired to escort a party of American adventurers up a volcano faints from the exertion, highlighting both the vigor of the Americans and general feeble nature of Nicaraguan manhood. The successful mountain climbers are rewarded with the smiles of Nicaragua's women, who, it is suggested, are thrilled to finally bestow their affections on some manly men. "San Juan," and the other travel narratives of Latin America that were published in the 1850s provided a justification for aggressive expansionism in the region by promising success in both work and love to the American man willing to climb the actual or metaphorical volcano.[50]

Manhood in Hawaii fares somewhat differently in "The Last Priestess of Pele," published in *Harper's* in 1851. This affirmation of restrained manhood and the healing powers of Christianity provides a dramatic contrast to the gendered images that encouraged aggressive expansionism in Latin America. "The Last Priestess of Pele" offers an expansionist fantasy of restrained manhood that upholds missionary work, rather than armed conquest, as the proper method for Americanization abroad. Tohelo, a young Hawaiian chief who offers to escort a party of Americans up the volcano Kiranea not only successfully completes the climb, but he manages to hold up his end of a conversation despite the fact that the American narrator was "nearly overcome with heat and fatigue." The Christian Tohelo is described as having a "superior mind" and "a soul susceptible of the sublime and beautiful." He is engaged to be married to Oani, "the last Priestess of Pele," but is forced by her father to choose between the woman he loves and his

---

[49] Francis Poe, Esq. "The Hawaiian Islands," *DBR* 24 (May 1858): 347–51.

[50] As William Stowe writes in *Going Abroad*, climbing was a favored method for a traveler to establish his authority and prove himself a "centered, ordering perceiver and knower." By assuming "a central and usually superior position in relation to one's surroundings," the traveler forces "the slovenly wilderness of the 'foreign' world to surround it. The most obvious way to do this is to climb a hill or a tower." *Going Abroad: European Travel in Nineteenth-Century American Culture* (Princeton, 1994), 50; E. G. Squier (as anon.), "San Juan," *HNMM* X (December 1854): 52.

Christianity, a religion her father judges incompatible with that of Pele, the Volcano Goddess.

Tohelo reveals his true manhood by sacrificing his personal happiness (with Oani) to the greater Christian Truth. "A convulsive motion passed over his manly features; his strong frame trembled; and, in a voice half-choked by contending feelings, he said, 'Oani, I must – I must leave you. There is but one God, and Him only will I serve.'" When the distraught Oani attempts to jump to her death into the volcano, Tohelo saves her life though his "wonderful presence of mind and activity." Tohelo's manliness, never in doubt in this story, is illustrated not only by his physical strength, endurance, and "manly" features but, above all, by his Christian belief. Tohelo is strong and brave, but his manhood is ultimately proven by his willingness to sacrifice personal happiness for God. While aggressive expansionists argued that missionary work had corrupted Hawaiians, this story offers a corrective that places Christianity at the heart of true manliness and missionary activity at the center of Americanization abroad.

Hawaiian "true" womanhood is also redeemed in "The Last Priestess of Pele." Oani eventually becomes a Christian herself and is reunited with Tohelo, since, as the narrator comments, although women might be "inferior in other things" they "surpass us in depth and unchangeableness of affection." At the close of the story they are a "loving and happy pair." Oani has, in effect, given up her career as Priestess of Pele in exchange for a life of domestic bliss, a baby, and a snug Christian home (complete with sitting room). A stronger argument for missionary work could hardly be imagined.

That the household of the Priestess of Pele now resembles an American Christian home can be attributed to the example set by missionary wives who worked with their husbands to Christianize Hawaii. The American Board of Missionaries insisted that only married missionaries settle in Hawaii, and missionary wives played a crucial role in winning the respect of Hawaiians and of fostering religious and social reform in the antebellum era. The first company of missionaries to Hawaii were instructed by the Prudential Committee of the American Board to "aim at nothing short of covering those islands with fruitful fields and pleasant dwellings, and schools and churches; of raising up the whole people to an elevated state of Christian civilization."[51]

---

[51] "The Last Priestess of Pele," *HNMM* 3 (August 1851): 354–9; Kuykendall, *Hawaiian Kingdom 1778–1854*, vol. 1: 71; Judd, *Hawaii*, 41–4. Attempts by missionary wives to impose American domestic standards in Hawaii were problematic and of limited success. "Mission wives created unease and sometimes outright pain in the objects chosen for their charity, as they created unease and pain, frustration and unhappiness, for themselves. . . . Mission wives attacked and undermined those very aspects of Hawaiian culture which offered Hawaiian women some measure of autonomy in their own system. Meanwhile they were powerless to recreate for Hawaiians the conditions which gave American women the degree of informal power which they themselves knew." Patricia Grimshaw, *Paths of Duty: American Missionary Wives in Nineteenth-Century Hawaii* (Honolulu, 1989), 156.

Missionary wives, like other female proponents of the "woman's sphere" pulled off the trick of elevating the position of women within the home by working outside it. As Richard Henry Dana reported to the New York *Herald* in 1860 after visiting the Islands, "The missionaries to the Sandwich Islands went out in families, and planted themselves in households, carrying with them, and exhibiting to the natives, the customs, manners, comforts, discipline, and order of civilized society. Each house was a centre and source of civilizing influences...."[52] Missionary wives were clear agents of "manifest domesticity" in Hawaii who promoted Americanization via reform and "civilization" in the same manner as did middle-class women on the western frontier.

Interestingly, the labor of female missionaries in "The Last Priestess of Pele" is left invisible, and it is the restrained manhood of Tohelo, rather than the womanhood of Oani, that is foregrounded. While it is unclear whether Tohelo's model manhood was the result or cause of his Christian conversion, Christianity has worked to remake the social order into an appropriately patriarchal form, taking women out of the public sphere and putting them back into the domestic sphere. The American narrator, generally a passive witness to this tale, manages to affirm his own restrained manhood, although he admits to exhaustion on his climb. By encouraging Tohelo, by visiting his family's home, and above all by praising Oani's housekeeping skills, the narrator offers the model of a Christian, forthright manhood that venerates domesticity abroad as well as at home.[53]

James Jackson Jarves's widely reviewed 1857 novel *Kiana: A Tradition of Hawaii* also featured a manly Hawaiian. The chief, Kiana, although six foot six inches tall, otherwise conforms to the masculine physical ideal of the era. He is "finely proportioned, with round elastic limbs, not over muscular or too sinewy, like the North American Indian, but full.... His face was strikingly handsome, being, like his body, of that happy medium between womanly softness and the more rugged development of manly strength, which indicates a well harmonized physical structure." He is remarkably strong and brave, and he rules by "moral influence, rather than by force" because "all felt safer and better under his rule." Like Tohelo, he personifies a restrained masculine ideal as well, despite the fact that he can be a fierce warrior. "There were in all his actions a pervading manliness and generosity, joined to a winning demeanor, which stamped him as one of nature's gentlemen." Kiana is nominally Christianized in the course of the story, and he spurns heathen

[52] Richard Henry Dana quoted in Anderson, *The Hawaiian Islands*, 100. On the work of promoting the "woman's sphere" see Kathryn Kish Sklar, *Catharine Beecher: A Study in American Domesticity* (New Haven, 1973).

[53] "Last Priestess of Pele," *HNMM* 3 (August 1851): 354–9. This story resonates with (but does not directly reference) the abolishment of kapus (religious behavioral bans) in the 1820s, and particularly the famed example of Christianized Chiefless Kapiolani defying Pele by standing at the mouth of an active volcano. Pencak, "Social and Legal Change," 288.

Hawaiian women after exposure to an example of "true womanhood," in this case a Spanish castaway. It is notable that the villain in this story is a Mexican of "Aztec" blood, who despises the Spanish for their treatment of his "race." The story thus contrasts the good Hawaiian with the bad Mexican, and it also contrasts the bad and violent territorial expansionism of the Spaniard with the good and peaceful efforts of missionaries.[54]

Both "The Last Priestess of Pele" and *Kiana* suggest that America's influence was best exercised in Hawaii through missionary work rather than annexation, a position shared by most religious reformers in the Northeast. Of course, not all missionaries opposed Hawaiian annexation. The Reverend Henry Cheever supported annexation as "indispensable for the protection of these Islands against the insults and aggressions of the French," but he imagined an American Hawaii still "moulded to a great degree by American missionaries." Most aggressive expansionists, however, looked forward to the decline of missionary influence as a positive result of annexation.[55]

Although the annexation of Hawaii promised to bring a new free state into the Union, most anti-slavery forces also rejected Hawaiian annexation efforts. The anti-slavery *New Englander and Yale Review* was no friend to expansionist ventures into potential slave territories in Latin America and the Caribbean, but, as the journal made evident in its review of the 1854 travel narrative, *Sandwich Island Notes*, it was equally hostile to the notion of annexing the Hawaiian kingdom. After rejecting the book as "slovenly," "unmitigated slipshod," and "dressed up in . . . pompous inanities," the *New Englander* proceeded to devote nineteen pages to a critique of further territorial expansionism that echoed the racial discourse of the Free-Soil movement.

George Washington Bates, the anonymous author of *Sandwich Island Notes*, strongly supported the annexation of the Hawaiian Islands. His arguments were predictable: annexation would be a great boon to American trade, the fertile soil could be made fabulously productive with American ingenuity, and the native people would better prosper under an American system of law than under the current missionary-led regime. Like other annexationists, he condemned the missionaries for corrupting and exploiting the Hawaiian people: "The Missionary policy has evidently been to keep the natives in a state of vassalage and tutelage – to make them pay the expense of their tuition by a species of religious serfdom. Religious freedom and emancipation are their only hope, and this they will secure by the free laws of an American state."[56]

---

[54] James Jackson Jarves, *Kiana: A Tradition of Hawaii* (Boston, 1857), 55–6, 23, 208–9.
[55] Cheever, *Life in the Sandwich Islands*, 209.
[56] "Sandwich Island Notes," the *NEYR* 13 (February 1855): 1–19; *Sandwich Island Notes*, by "a Haolé" (George Washington Bates) (New York 1854), quoted in "Sandwich Island Notes," 18.

The pro-missionary *New Englander* called this final argument "unblushing hypocrisy" since "it is one of the grounds of annexation, that the Hawaiian race is doomed to speedy extinction." The journal asserted that "with annexation comes ... the extinction of the race." But the fate of the Hawaiian people was secondary in its critique to the fate of another race, the American Anglo-Saxon. Quoting *Sandwich Island Notes* back at itself, the *New Englander* argued that intercourse between the native Hawaiians and "foreigners" was almost always disastrous for both parties. That "the white man, severed from the civilizing influences of society, is capable of becoming a more debased wretch than the savages or aborigines among whom he lives," was immediately evident in Hawaii. Examples like a "complete savage" who "was once a white man" before a "four years' intercourse with the most debased and wretched of the natives" were "numerous on the islands."[57]

The fault for the inevitable debasement of American men in Hawaii lay with Hawaii's women. While "The Last Priestess of Pele" suggested that a strong Christian man could overcome the Hawaiian woman's innate weakness, could Christianize her, and could turn her into a "true woman," critics of Hawaiian annexation based their argument in the image of the American man inevitably corrupted by association with the immoral Hawaiian woman. In doing so, of course, anti-annexationists revealed their veneration of the Christian home and belief in the power of women to shape the characters of their families.

This conceptualization of women's moral influence stands in clear contrast to that held by martial men. In the view of supporters of aggressive expansionism, the women of the future territories, whether in Latin America or Hawaii, were like mirrors, passive beings who reflected back their own martial manhood rather than shaped their character. Thus even an immoral woman could not adversely effect her husband. As the *New Englander* reviewer argued, however, intermarriage between American men and Hawaiian women was "more commonly a source of evil than good." While one might conclude that "when a foreigner marries a native woman, he will exert almost every effort to raise her in the scale of civilization," such "is not the case." "Almost, as a general thing, this union is but a license to indiscriminate sensual indulgence and horrible brutality.... In a very brief period their masculine tyrants commence their brutality, force their unjust exactions, and become unfaithful to the conjugal vows."

While Bates attributed the decline of foreign virtue in the Hawaiian context to the already debased character of the "low class of foreigners" in Hawaii, the *New Englander* drew another conclusion all together. Because only missionaries were strict enough in their morality to withstand the

---

[57] On this point, see also "Sandwich Island Notes," *The Living Age* 42 (September 23, 1854): 593.

temptations to vice offered in Hawaii, annexation would lead to the corruption of both American and native in the Islands. "We know not of a more lamentable sight than is here presented," the *New Englander* claimed, than "the victims of civilized lands, the offscouring [*sic*] of Christanized nations, struggling by every species of temptation to sink them into still lower depths of pollution."[58]

The critique that intercourse with native Hawaiians was corrupting to Americans resonated with an argument commonly invoked by the Free-Soil Party, and its Republican Party descendants. Free Soilers claimed that "association with any black degraded the white race" and that therefore expansion should be limited to territories without slavery, and in which both slavery and the immigration of free African-Americans should be forbidden. But Hawaiians were neither enslaved, nor were they, of course, of African origin. How convincing this racial critique might have been is difficult to judge, but the fact that the *New Englander* employed it reveals the extent to which antebellum expansionism was stained in the anti-slavery mind by its association with the slave power, the growing perception among Northerners that slave-owning interests exerted an unnatural and corrupting degree of influence on the federal government. The *New Englander* suggested that Hawaii might become a slave state yet: "As all our annexations have been to open a wider area for the extension of slavery, we much fear that the Genius which has presided over the administration of our government, has been the Genius of Slavery, and we have no doubt but that the same evil genius will preside over the annexation of the Sandwich Islands."[59]

Of course, to describe anti-slavery forces as anti-expansionist is to miss the way in which they, too, had internalized the logic of America's Manifest Destiny. The *New Englander* envisioned annexation as a disaster for both Hawaiians and Americans but like the author of the "Last Priestess of Pele," embraced the expansionist activity of American missionaries. In a celebratory review of missionary activity, "A Half Century of Foreign Missions," in August of 1860, The *New Englander* suggested the extent to which ideas of Manifest Destiny shaped the views of even committed opponents of aggressive expansionism. While loudly opposed to the U.S.-Mexico War, to Hawaiian annexation, and to filibustering in general, the journal conceptualized the significance of American missionary activity in terms familiar to supporters of all those movements.

Missionary activity had brought "some sense of the superiority of a Christian manhood to the barbarous ideas of well-being and well doing" across

---

[58] "Sandwich Island Notes," the *NEYR* 13 (February 1855): 112–15, 18.
[59] Eric Foner, *Free Soil, Free Labor, Free Men: The Ideology of the Republican Party before the Civil War* (New York, 1970), 266; Eric Foner, "Racial Attitudes of the New York Free Soilers," *New York History* XLVI (October 1965), 311–29; "Sandwich Island Notes," *NEYR* 13 (February 1855): 18.

the globe. It had increased knowledge of other peoples: "What exploring expedition ... has done more, in this nineteenth century, to increase our knowledge of earth ... than has been done by missionaries?" It had opened up trade routes to American business and saved lands from falling into the expansionist hands of European nations. As an example of all of this, the author pointed to Hawaii, where, only fifty years earlier, the people "were almost literally slaves." Had it not been for the missionaries, "[l]ong ere this time, these islands, the most important group in Polynesia," would have become "a possession of some European power. ..." In some ways, missionary activity was better than annexation since, "the political and commercial result of the mission has been, that Hawaii is acknowledged as an independent sovereignty; that its relations to the American people could not become more favorable to our commercial and national interests if those islands were a recognized dependency of ours." Furthermore, the missionaries were doing the work of Americanization, creating "institutions of government, of popular education and of religion" that "as the old race gradually and peacefully recedes, will mold the character and secure the national independence of the more vigorous race that is already coming in." Catharine Beecher argued in her *Treatise on Domestic Economy* that in fact "the principles of Democracy, then, are identical to the principles of Christianity." The *New Englander* made the same point. Protestantism not only promoted Americanization, it was, in fact, "Americanism" itself, since it promoted "internal democracy, civil and religious," wherever it was introduced.[60]

In its optimistic assessment of the future of missionary activity, the *New Englander* embraced a vision of the expansion of American values as all encompassing as the most aggressive annexationist. "Think of this great Union of States, just now beginning to unfold its capacity of wealth and power and growth – just beginning to escape from the danger of impending barbarism, and to achieve its own predestined place in history" the author exclaimed. "Think how recently the dissevered parts of this terraqueous [*sic*] world have been brought into intimate connection with each other – all regions opening to peaceful commerce – the nations becoming conscious of their mutual dependence – steamships everywhere scorning the currents, puffing at the winds, and bringing the remotest shores into proximity."[61]

While opposed to annexation, the *New Englander* still celebrated the joining of the oceans, the growth of the nation, and its "predestined place in history." The waters meet in mutual and intimate embrace in this formulation; there is no violent forcing through of iron bands for the *New Englander*. But from the vantage point of this article, the aggressive expansionist future and

[60] "A Half Century of Foreign Missions," *NEYR* 18 (August 1860): 720–4; Catharine Beecher, *A Treatise on Domestic Economy for the Use of Young Ladies at Home and at School* (Boston, 1841), 1.

[61] "A Half Century of Foreign Missions," *NEYR* 18 (August 1860): 725.

the restrained expansionist vision of Americanization carried out through missionary activity and trade looked extremely similar. In both cases, the reach of the United States was predestined, and virtually unlimited. Missionaries in Hawaii and their religious reform supporters in the United States thus effectively fought annexation in the 1850s through a clever co-opting of Manifest Destiny. America's domination of the hemisphere, they argued, could best be achieved not through territorial expansionism but through the spread of American institutions, including Protestantism and trade.

"Inevitable Consequences": The Perry Expedition to Japan, 1852–1854

As Henry David Thoreau saw it, the "whole enterprise" of the nation in the early 1850s appeared to be directed towards the setting sun. Westward expansion, "whether performed on foot, or by a Pacific railroad," he wrote to a friend in 1853, was "totally devoid of interest to me."[62] Unfortunately for Thoreau, the enterprise was of a great deal of interest to his fellow Americans. While boosters of Hawaiian annexation touted the island chain as a proper western outpost for the nation, business interests had yet more ambitious goals – an American outpost on the far edge of the Pacific. The ideology of Manifest Destiny, combined with the desire to exploit emerging markets in Asia, provided the impetus for one of the most significant expansionist encounters of the era, Commodore Matthew C. Perry's 1852–1854 expedition to Japan.

The Whig administration of Millard Fillmore was firmly opposed to filibustering but equally committed to the peaceful expansionism of American trade. After the United States and China signed a commercial treaty in 1844, Pacific trade boomed. Fillmore and his secretary of state Daniel Webster hoped that the establishment of a line of Pacific steamships might increase the China trade and allow the United States to better compete with the British in Asia. Steamships, while fast, also were dependent on coal. Japan, shut to Americans and most Europeans for more than 200 years, seemed to offer a logical location for coaling bases but had previously rebuffed American overtures. Between 1790 and 1853, the Japanese turned away at least twenty-seven visiting U.S. vessels. Matthew Perry, a hero of the U.S.-Mexico War from a distinguished family of naval officers, was determined to change that. Perry arrived in Japan in July of 1853 armed with four heavily fortified ships, the well-known journalist Bayard Taylor, and a politely worded letter from President Fillmore to the Emperor of Japan requesting trade relations. In essence, Perry invaded Japan, and Japanese compliance was forced by America's display of strength. When Perry returned the following year, the Japanese conceded American demands within range of seven ships with

---

[62] Henry David Thoreau to Harrison Blake, February 27, 1853, in F. B. Sanborn, ed., *The Writings of Henry David Thoreau* (Boston, 1906), vol. 6: 210.

more than 200 American cannon and heavy guns. Although Perry failed to negotiate a commercial treaty at the time (leading the New York *Herald* to deem the entire expedition "an expensive failure"), his success in opening up communications between the United States and Japan was a major triumph.[63]

Perry was an aggressive expansionist and firm exponent of Manifest Destiny. His expedition was, as one historian has written, "heavily fortified ideologically and philosophically, its participants and instigators having little doubt that the...invasion of Japan was ultimately a divinely-inspired enterprise: noble, just, and within the global historical scheme, inevitable." Although he traveled to Japan with the limited goals of gaining a refueling port and a commercial treaty, his trip convinced him that the United States needed to emulate European nations and become a colonial empire, sooner rather than later. In his narrative of the expedition, published at government expense in 1856, Perry outlined his imperial vision for the United States. Colonies, he wrote, were a "positive necessity" for the protection of "our vast and rapidly growing commerce" and the "inevitable consequences of our own ambitious tendencies" in the East. "The annexation of one country or province, whether by conquest or purchase, will only tend to increase the desire to add another and another, and we, as a nation, would have no right to claim exemption from this universal vice."[64]

Although Perry described the acquisition of colonies as a "vice," there was no doubt in his mind that American territorial expansionism, in contrast to that practiced by European powers, would bring only blessings to the world, even if the United States withheld the privileges of citizenship from men in newly conquered territories. Perry was passionate about gaining an immediate hold in the region, and he advocated seizing the islands of Ryukyu, southwest of Japan, for that purpose. He suggested to the administration in Washington that control of the islands could be justified by the recent mistreatment of American captives by the Japanese, and that the annexation of Ryukyu could help pressure Japan into opening up trade relations. In his journal, Perry noted not only the great beauty of the islands, and their clear strategic importance in Pacific trade, but also that the "imperial government

[63] *NYH* quoted in Samuel Eliot Morison, *"Old Bruin": Commodore Matthew C. Perry, 1794–1858: The American Naval Officer Who Helped Found Liberia* (Boston, 1967), 417; Peter Wiley, *Yankees in the Land of the Gods: Commodore Perry and the Opening of Japan* (New York, 1990), 86, 466; Walter LaFeber, *The Clash: A History of US–Japan Relations* (New York, 1997), 9–10; Michael Frederick Rollin, "The Divine Invasion: Manifest Destiny and the Westernization of Japanese Nationalism in the Late Tokugawa and Meiji Periods 1853–1912" (Master's thesis, The University of Texas at San Antonio, 2002); Henry F. Graff, ed., *Bluejackets with Perry in Japan: A Day-by-Day Account Kept by Master's Mate John R. C. Lewis and Cabin Boy William B. Allen* (New York, 1952), 33, 67.

[64] Rollin, "The Divine Invasion," 31; Matthew Calbraith Perry, *Narrative of the Expedition of an American Squadron to the China Seas and Japan* (Washington, 1856), vol. 2: 175–6.

maintained very slight authority over the government and people" there. The financial benefit to the United States of annexing Ryukyu would only be exceeded by the great blessings the United States would bring to the Ryukyuans. Striking a familiar note, Perry could "conceive of no greater act of humanity than to protect these miserable people against the oppressions of their tyrannical rulers," he wrote. "It will be politic and just to continue to these people the protection which I shall give them so long as I have the power and the countenance of American authority." Perry, like other American expansionists, upheld Manifest Destiny as a win-win proposal for the parties concerned.[65]

Unfortunately for the commodore, even the expansionist Democrat Franklin Pierce was unwilling to "take and retain possession of an island in that distant country." As one Perry biographer has written, "distant places like China and Japan, which were so clearly apparent on the horizon when Perry left New York in 1852, were dissolving in the particulate mists" by the time of his return. In 1852 the Japan expedition had been "a matter of table talk and calculation," and interest in the island chain ran so high that a Presbyterian clergyman in San Francisco sent away to New York for books on Japan in order to lecture his congregation. Popular accounts of Japan in 1852 and 1853 envisioned Japan as the natural next stop in American progress, a frontier in the "far west," rather than the east.[66]

By 1854, interest had waned. Enthusiasm for a trans-Pacific steamship line faded as Congress focused on constructing a transcontinental railroad. The treaties that Perry negotiated with Japan and Okinawa were ratified only six weeks after the divisive Kansas-Nebraska Act, which allowed residents to determine for themselves whether or not to permit slavery in their territories, thus nullifying the 1820 Missouri Compromise prohibition on the extension of slavery above the 36° 30' parallel. Perry and his accomplishments were overshadowed by controversy over the Act, and his vision of an American empire with a strong presence in Asia was rejected by the Pierce administration.[67] In an 1856 review of the literature on Perry and Japan published since the expedition, the *North American Review* bemoaned the lack of acclaim

---

[65] Wiley, *Yankees in the Land of the Gods*, 451–69, 487–9; Alexander DeConde, *Presidential Machismo: Executive Authority, Military Intervention, and Foreign Relations* (Boston, 2000), 53; U.S. Congress. Senate. *Message of the President of the United States, Transmitting a Report of the Secretary of the Navy...Relative to the Naval Expedition to Japan.* Senate Executive Document 34 (Washington, DC, 1855), 108–16; Matthew Calbraith Perry, *The Japan Expedition, 1852–1854: The Personal Journal of Commodore Matthew C. Perry,* Roger Pineau, ed. (Washington, DC, 1968), 86.

[66] *A Report of the Secretary of the Navy*, 108–10; *Literary World* (1852), 232, quoted in Graff, *Bluejackets with Perry in Japan*, 63–4; Wiley, *Yankees in the Land of the Gods*, 451. On American progress into Japan see "Japan," USDR 30 (April 1852): 332; "Commodore Perry's Expedition to Japan," HNMM 12 (March 1856): 441; "Japan," PMM 1 (March 1853): 241; LaFeber, *The Clash*, 7.

[67] Wiley, *Yankees in the Land of the Gods*, 456, 471.

Perry had received, and in particular that "filibustering operations in the Gulf of Mexico" were of more interest to Americans than the opening of Japan. The journal attributed Perry's weak reception to both the change of administration and the American love of "novelty." In 1854, Latin America, and not Japan, was the focus of American attention.[68]

The literature of the Perry expedition suggests further reasons for the failure of expansionism into Japan. Despite his efforts, Perry was never able to produce a vision of American annexation in the region as natural and pre-ordained. While anxious to secure an American presence at the edge of the Pacific, he avoided the gendered images that helped support expansionism in the Western Hemisphere. In both his public and private writings, he acknowledged that the Japanese were "industrious and ingenious," but he seemed genuinely repulsed by Japanese women, who had "fat dumpy figures, their lips being painted, making their black teeth and corroded gums the more conspicuous. 'There is no accounting for taste,'" he concluded after a consideration of Japanese beauty rituals.[69] While Perry believed the Japanese to be essentially inferior to Europeans, he did not suggest that Japanese men were lazy, or that Americans could make the best use of the blessings bestowed on the Japanese people.

Other accounts of the expedition expressed a similar ambivalence about the possibilities for the Americanization of the region. In his narrative of the expedition, journalist Bayard Taylor mixed disdain for the "artful and dissimulating policy" of the Japanese, with a clear respect for the manhood, manners, and agricultural skill of Japanese men. Taylor declared that "outside of England there is nothing so green, so garden like, so full of tranquil beauty" as the Japanese landscape. Despite what he considered the "mild, effeminate features" of the Japanese face, he admired the boatmen he met, "tall, handsomely formed men, with vigorous and symmetrical bodies, and a hardy, manly expression of countenance."[70]

The Japanese provided a display of their own masculine prowess for the American invaders. They entertained Perry and his men with an exhibition of the strength and athletic skill of fifty sumo wrestlers, each weighing between 200 and 400 pounds. The men lifted and carried huge bales of rice,

---

[68] "The American Expedition to Japan," *North American Review* 83 (July 1856): 236.

[69] Perry, *Narrative of the Expedition*, 1: 47, 50; Perry, *The Japan Expedition*, 181. Upon Perry's arrival in 1853, the shocked Japanese *Bafuku* stalled for time by offering women to the American invaders. LaFeber, *The Clash*, 13.

[70] Bayard Taylor, *A Visit to India, China, and Japan, in the Year 1853* (New York, 1855), 418, 435, 429, 415–16, 434. When the *Living Age* published a review of Taylor's book in 1855 it deemed the Japanese material as having the "least interest of any" part of the book. It is not clear whether this was because Americans were generally bored by stories of Japan or because Taylor's prose was less compelling in this section (he wrote without the benefit of most of his journals, which had been confiscated by the Navy). "Taylor's Visit to India, China, and Japan," (from the *Spectator*) *The Living Age* 47 (December 1855): 513–76.

and engaged in sumo matches. In Perry's account, sumo wrestling seemed "barbaric" rather than athletic, but the Americans could hardly help being impressed by the "brute animal force" of the "stall-fed bulls." Certainly this was the Japanese view of the encounter, as a contemporary Japanese representation of the event, contrasting puny Americans with hulking sumo wrestlers, makes clear (see Figure 7.4). Not only were Japanese men physically imposing, but they also proved to be imposingly polite. The American officers agreed that their Japanese counterparts "were as perfect gentlemen as could be found in any part of the world."[71]

Master's Mate John R. C. Lewis, who also kept a journal of the expedition, was likewise impressed by the agricultural abilities of the Japanese and declared the people of Ryukyu "a fine stout, intelligent race, exceedingly cleanly in their persons and hardy and industrious in their manners." Lewis was also horrified by the women of Ryukyu, declaring that "on an average [they] are as fat, ugly, and repulsive a set of females as the world can produce."[72] Public nudity provoked expressions of disgust more often than titillation among American observers. Perry's interpreter, Rev. S. Wells Williams, was generally less judgmental about Japanese customs than other Americans. But even he declared that "lewd motions, pictures and talk seem to be the common expression of the viler acts and thoughts of the people, and this to such a degree as to disgust everybody." Popular periodicals disseminated these representations. *Harper's Monthly Magazine* admired the "considerable agricultural skill" of the Japanese, as well as their roads and bridges, but informed readers that the women of the country were "awfully ugly." The *North American Review* struck a similar note in expressing its own amazement at the "customs of this strange people, where black teeth are a beauty."[73]

---

[71] Perry, *The Japan Expedition*, 190–4; Perry, *Narrative of the Expedition*, 1: 369–72; Joseph M. Henning, *Outposts of Civilization: Race, Religion, and the Formative Years of American-Japanese Relations* (New York, 2000), 8–9.

[72] Graff, *Bluejackets with Perry in Japan*, 100. One of the very few travelers to express admiration for the women he encountered in Japan was William Heine, a German-American artist traveling with the expedition. When "tricked out in their most elegant" he wrote, some Japanese women were "so prepossessing that they would have been called lovely in different cultures and other lands." Heine wrote in German, however, and his narrative was published in Leipzig for a German audience. William Heine, *With Perry in Japan*, translated by Fredrick Trautmann (Honolulu, 1990), 137. Originally published as *Reise um die Erde nach Japan an Bord der Expeditions-Escadre unter Commodore M. C. Perry* (Leipzig, 1856). Japanese diplomats who arrived in the U.S. to ratify the historic trading agreement finally negotiated by U.S. consul Townsend Harris were not overly impressed by American women either. LaFeber, *The Clash*, 24–5. For a different view, Morison, "Old Bruin," 388.

[73] Samuel Wells Williams, "A Journal of the Perry Expedition to Japan, 1853–1854," ed. Frederick Wells Williams, *Transactions of the Asiatic Society of Japan* 37 (1910): 183–4; Gregory Smits, "Making Japanese by Putting on Clothes," in *Making Japanese*, available online at: http://www.personal.psu.edu/faculty/g/j/gjs4/mj/ch4.htm; Henning, *Outposts of Civilization*, 24–5; "Commodore Perry's Expedition to Japan," *HNMM* 12 (March 1856): 449, 451, 454; "The American Expedition to Japan," *North American Review* 83 (July 1856): 236.

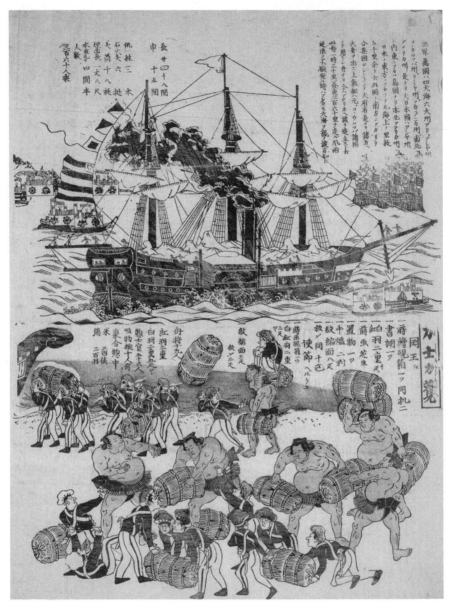

FIGURE 7.4. *Paddle Wheel Steamers and Sumo Wrestlers Carrying Rice Bales at Yokohama.* Japanese woodblock print, no date. Courtesy of the Mariners' Museum, Newport News, Virginia.

The manliness of Japanese men, the unattractiveness of the women of the region, and the obvious skill with which the Japanese made use of their land posed serious problems for aggressive expansionists. Americans in Japan encountered men of some substance, unattractive women, and a landscape so intensively cultivated that not even the most fervent annexationist could justify appropriation of those lands on the grounds that they were under-used. In addition, the Japanese were the "grossest idolaters and irreconcilable to Christianity," as Jedediah Morse noted in his children's geography text-book.[74] Given that the Catholicism of the Latin American made territorial expansionism in that region unpalatable to many Americans, the religion of the Japanese posed nearly insurmountable problems for anyone who hoped to see an American Ryukyu. Japan presented a fine realm for American trade, but ultimately was too foreign, and too distant, to foster and produce compelling annexationist fantasies.

Ironically, Perry's expedition helped "open up" Asia, not to the terri-torial annexation he desired but to female missionaries and the "traveling domesticity" that in Hawaii provided such a successful counter-narrative to annexationist propaganda. Virtually all female missionaries in the ante bellum period were missionary wives. Exponents of "manifest domesticity," they used their power as social reformers not to promote annexation but to promote the Americanization of Hawaii through the implementation of American religious and social forms. While exponents of annexation envi-sioned Hawaii as the perfect place for men to gain wealth, regain their health, and enjoy the "hula-hula," anti-annexationists countered that without the diligent attention of missionary wives and other proponents of restrained manhood, American manhood would sink into debauchery and degeneracy.

For a time in the 1850s, the annexation of Hawaii seemed possible, if not likely. But Hawaii was too peripheral to the interests of southern expansion-ists, and the expansionist vision of missionaries and their supporters, based in religion and commerce, proved more compelling then arguments in favor of annexation. The victory of restrained manhood and commercial expan-sionism in the battle over Hawaii would be repeated even further to the west. In the post-Civil War era, missionary women embarked on "woman's work for women" through separate female boards. In 1869, both the Congrega-tional and Methodist Churches set up women's boards for missions, and by 1900, there were forty-one American women's boards of varying sizes founded to send unmarried female missionaries to foreign lands, including

---

74 On American reactions to the "high cultivation" of the Japanese landscape in the later part of the century see Henning, *Outposts of Civilization*, 32–3; Jedediah Morse, *Geography Made Easy: Being a short but Comprehensive System of that very useful and agreeable Science* (New Haven, 1784), 201, quoted in Graff, *Bluejackets with Perry in Japan*, 25. Virtually every travelogue to Japan published in the United States in the antebellum era bemoaned the idolatry of the Japanese. See, for example, Graff, *Bluejackets with Perry in Japan*, 128, and "Commodore Perry's Expedition to Japan," *HNMM* 12 (March, 1856): 233–61.

Japan. Not long after the Chinese Exclusion Act of 1882 banned the Chinese from immigrating to the United States, a reverse migration was underway. By 1900, China had emerged as one of the key destinations for American missionaries.[75]

Female missionaries in China promoted a "domestic empire" in the late nineteenth century, further empowering restrained manhood and its reverence for the family home, and further undermining narratives that asserted that annexation, or imperial conquest, was the only, or even best, means of Americanization.[76] But the increased power of American women, represented in one part by their domination of missionary work, helped lead to a counter-insurgence of martial manhood. It would take more than forty years, and a war in the Philippines, before what Perry deemed the "inevitable consequences" of America's territorial ambitions in the Pacific would finally be revealed.

[75] Jane Hunter, *The Gospel of Gentility: American Women Missionaries in Turn-of-the-Century China* (New Haven, 1984), 11–13; Schoonover, *Uncle Sam's War*, 2–3, 38–40, 47–9.
[76] Hunter, *The Gospel of Gentility*, 128–73.

Conclusion

American Manhood and War, 1860 to the Present

> Were our ancestors better men and purer patriots than we, or has over-
> familiarity with the features of the monster, so hated and dreaded by them,
> glozed over their repulsiveness and converted their hideousness into beauties?
> – "The Story of Blannerhassett," *The Southern Literary Messenger*, 1858

Upon the death of Narciso López and his American volunteers in Cuba in
1851, Cora Montgomery stated that only "time will decide whether they
were pirates and cutthroats, or heroes and patriots."[1] During the 1850s,
there was ample debate but no consensus on the issue. Many men asserted
that filibustering was illegal, immoral, and expressed an antiquated ideal
of manhood, entirely inappropriate for nineteenth-century America. Others
celebrated filibusters for their fearlessness, skill in battle, and willingness to
die for a virtuous cause. In short, during the years between the U.S.-Mexico
War and the Civil War, the line between pirate and patriot was not well defined. While some men turned to religion, the family home, and success in
the business realm for self-definition, others insisted that success as a man
was defined by hyper-masculine virtues, including the ability to physically
dominate others and to act heroically in battle. During a period of national
peace, American men flocked to wars of their own making, aggression became a virtue in itself, and the entire hemisphere promised to bend to the
American will. Or so proponents of martial manhood imagined.

As economic and social transformations changed the conditions and practices of both manhood and womanhood at home, and as the appearance
of financial success increasingly replaced knowledge of a man's character
as the preeminent means of public evaluation, territories abroad glowed
with promise. Booster accounts of Latin America describe its fertile lands
as offering brilliant opportunities not only for the fulfillment of America's

[1] Cora Montgomery "Narcisso [*sic*] Lopez and His Companions," *Democratic Review* 29
(October 1851): 300.

Manifest Destiny but for the redemption of American manhood as well. Latin America offered opportunities for success in work and love that seemed increasingly inaccessible at home. Politicians and travelers alike linked national annexation to the personal annexation of Latin American woman to white American men as the best method of Latin American "regeneration" via Anglo-Saxon racial domination. Manifest Destiny promised a personal victory commensurate with providential intention to each and every man daring enough to venture to the "new frontier."

It was not only filibusterers, or their direct supporters, who believed that the United States was destined to expand exponentially after the U.S.-Mexico War. The private writings of men traveling through Central America and Mexico on the way to the gold fields in California reinforced the fact that their encounter was mediated by faith in Manifest Destiny and shaped by gender conventions. In Latin America it would be the martial virtues, as opposed to the restrained virtues that other men embraced at home, that promised to ensure success in both work and love. The new Latin American frontier seemed to offer a space where masculine practices organized around dominance, as opposed to expertise or technical knowledge, were still valued, during a period when large structural economic transformations rendered these practices increasingly marginalized at home.

For white American women, the foreign encounter often held different meanings. Central American travel could denaturalize American gender norms, allowing white women to watch and evaluate Latin American women's work and to undertake tasks that at home would have been considered inappropriate for or unachievable by their sex. Central American travel provided female travelers with excitement, adventure, and the chance to dress like men. Traveling on mule-back across the Isthmus may have been no more "liberating" for women than traveling by covered wagon on the Oregon Trail was, but the challenges of Central American travel may have posed more of a test to the limits of domesticity on an individual level because white women were so rare on the Isthmus. The discomfort men expressed about female travelers in Central America brought into question the very meanings of womanhood, and the suitability of American womanhood abroad.

Westward expansion proved that domesticity and Manifest Destiny could be mutually reinforcing. Some female supporters of aggressive expansionism utilized domesticity to support American territorial expansionism into Latin America, but others agreed with the vast majority of men that white women had best stay home. The fantasy of Latin America as expressed in the expansionist booster literature, and in the letters of male travelers, manifestly excluded white American women. While aggressive expansionists promised that Latin America was the perfect environment for bachelors to redeem their manhood, religious reformers in Hawaii offered the counter assertion that Hawaii promised bachelors a speedy decline into degeneracy. Debates over the destiny of Hawaii allowed for the exposition of a pointed critique of annexation by exponents of restrained manhood, and the use of "manifest domesticity" to *fight* annexation on the grounds that only missionaries, accompanied by wives, were virtuous enough to withstand the temptations of Hawaiian women.

It is in pro-missionary writings on Hawaii that the expansionist bent of restrained manhood is most obvious. Restrained men opposed the annexation of Hawaii on the same grounds that they opposed filibustering, the annexation of Cuba, and the U.S.-Mexico War. But their objections to territorial expansionism were based, in large part, in their faith that the United States could best exert control over the Western Hemisphere, and the world, through the propagation of its religious, social, and economic system. They did not disagree with annexationists that "every newcomer from the United States" to Hawaii "feels as if he were already within an inchoate portion of his great republic." They argued instead that Americanization would turn ever larger portions of the globe into similarly inchoate portions of the great republic, with none of the costs of territorial expansionism.[2]

Trade and Protestantism would go hand in hand in fulfilling America's Manifest Destiny. Restrained proponents of commercial expansionism opposed filibustering not only on legal and moral grounds but also because filibusters might actually inhibit American interests. *Harper's Weekly* expressed this opinion not long after William Walker was deposed in Nicaragua. "If we act fairly and generously with these people, their lands, cattle, corn, sugar, cochineal, chocolate, gold, silver, copper, all the precious marketable woods, guns, spices, drugs, and medicinal plants of their teeming volcanic soils, are at our service."[3] In their own way, restrained men were as convinced of the inevitable dominance of the United States as was any aggressive expansionist. Commodore Perry pushed President Pierce to annex Ryukyu, but aggressive expansionists never embraced the idea of an American outpost in Ryukyu. The Japanese-American encounter reveals the limits of manifest manhood in an alien culture and the necessity of a strong gender component to a convincing nineteenth-century expansionist narrative.

Historians of the American South have long maintained that antebellum southern society was ruled by a culture of male honor. Southern gentlemen, and the yeomen farmers who idealized them, embraced dueling long after Northerners had abolished the practice, upheld white supremacy and patriarchal authority, and internalized the need to maintain honor even at the cost of one's life. Southerners embraced militarism as the pinnacle of masculine virtue, showing strength, mastery, and self-control. This honor culture, some have argued, separated the South from the North, and greatly

---

[2] "The Hawaiian Islands," *PMM* 5 (March 1855): 246.
[3] *Harper's Weekly* (May 16, 1857), 312.

exacerbated sectional tensions. A "martial manhood" was mobilized by planters to gain yeoman support for the Civil War. As Bertram Wyatt-Brown has written, for many Southerners, "the Civil War was reduced to a simple test of manhood."[4]

While southern manhood was ruled by ideas of honor, this study has attempted to show how a culture of martial manhood bridged sectional divides through a vision of foreign territories and peoples as ripe for exploitation by fearless American men. As debates over the expansion of slavery led to increasingly acrimonious relations between the North and South, many men, ironically enough, believed American manhood could best be made manifest through further territorial expansionism. At the same time, even the limited victories for martial manhood that William Walker and Narciso López's invasions represented tended to reinforce the merit of martial virtues at home, further weakening the perception that the ability to compromise was, in fact, a virtue. The real irony is that the men who ignored sectional divisions in common support of filibustering did so in the name of equating manhood with the expression of violence.

The gendered culture of Manifest Destiny in the 1850s thus encouraged Northerners and Southerners to turn to violence as a solution to personal and national problems. Historians have long emphasized how debates over new territories enflamed sectional tensions by forcing the issue of slavery to the forefront of national debate. During the same years that the policy of popular sovereignty forced Americans to fight for control over Kansas, and the territories taken from Mexico in 1848, filibusters exacerbated the problem. Not only did filibustering present the specter of more territories to battle over, but the constant emphasis on gaining new lands helped convince Southerners that the Republican Party's free-soil platform really did spell the end of the South's "peculiar institutions." From their experiences with expansionism in the antebellum period, Southerners "understood the logic of empire: no growth implies death."[5] Indeed, had there been no filibustering one historian

---

[4] Stephanie McCurry, *Masters of Small Worlds: Yeoman Households, Gender Relations, and the Political Culture of the Antebellum South Carolina Low Country* (New York, 1995): 261; Bertram Wyatt-Brown, *Honor and Violence in the Old South* (New York, 1986), 28; Nicholas W. Proctor, *Bathed in Blood: Hunting and Mastery in the Old South* (Charlottesville VA, 2002), 72–73. Important works on honor in the Old South include Bertram Wyatt-Brown, *Southern Honor: Ethics and Behavior in the Old South* (New York, 1982); Kenneth S. Greenberg, *Honor and Slavery: Lies, Duels, Noses, Masks, Dressing as a Woman, Gifts, Strangers, Humanitarianism, Death, Slave Rebellions, the Proslavery Argument, Baseball, Hunting and Gambling in the Old South* (Princeton, 1996); Edward L. Ayers, *Vengeance and Justice: Crime and Punishment in the Nineteenth-Century American South* (New York, 1984); Dickson D. Bruce, *Violence and Culture in the Antebellum South* (Austin, 1979); Steven M. Stowe, *Intimacy and Power in the Old South: Ritual in the Lives of the Planters* (Baltimore, 1987); John Hope Franklin, *The Militant South, 1800–1860* (New York, 1956); McCurry, *Masters of Small Worlds.*

[5] William Appleman Williams, *Empire as a Way of Life* (New York, 1980), 91. For two differing views of the ill effects of Manifest Destiny on the Union see David M. Potter, *The Impending*

has suggested, both Southerners and Northerners would have been more open to compromise in 1860 and "the Union might have weathered the storm."[6]

But Manifest Destiny brought more than slavery to the public eye, it also lent support to an aggressive formulation of masculine identity. Westward expansionism in the 1840s was shaped by "traveling domesticity," but the Latin American encounter in the 1850s introduced the specter of "traveling masculinity" that brought martial virtues from the new frontier of Latin America back to the United States at urban public meetings and other celebrations of filibustering. In a period when what America needed, above all else, was men who valued compromise more than dominance and who eschewed violence in the name of peace, aggressive expansionism lent support to very different values.

The Southern Literary Messenger concluded its 1858 filibustering cautionary tale about Harman Blennerhassett and Aaron Burr with the question of who was the purer patriot, the ancestors of the past, who "stood erect as one man, to overthrow and crush the 'Treason'" of anyone who "proposed as one of the steps in a projected enterprise, anything which could be construed into a scheme for dismemberment of the Union" or the current generation, who "daily hear the value of the Union estimated, see its laws nullified, the decisions of its highest legal tribunal scoffed and derided by every fanatic or demagogue whose pet 'isms' they may interfere with, and we are not horrified." *The Southern Literary Messenger* clearly recognized the connection between the martial manhood that supported filibustering and the incipient collapse of the Union. "Over-familiarity with the features of the monster" of treason had "glozed over" the "repulsiveness" of its features, and even "converted their hideousness into beauties" for some advocates of aggression. It was easy for the author of "The Story of Blennerhassett" to identify Narciso López and his men, not as patriots, as Cora Montgomery suggested, but as pirates.[7]

Aggressive expansionism was ultimately a colossal failure. Martial manhood helped turn sectional differences into cause for war. Not only did filibustering enflame sectional feelings by introducing the specter of new slave territories at a time when the status of older territories was increasingly contentious, but it also failed to mediate emerging class distinctions, as proponents promised. The men who traveled to Latin America, Cuba, and Mexico failed to locate the magical path to success that eluded them at home. And of course, neither filibustering nor the martial attitudes of travelers helped American interests in Latin America.

Crisis, 1848–1861 (New York, 1976); Michael Paul Rogin, *Subversive Genealogy: The Politics and Art of Herman Melville* (New York, 1983), 106.

[6] On the effects of filibustering on the Civil War see Robert E. May, *Manifest Destiny's Underworld: Filibustering in Antebellum America* (Chapel Hill, 2002), 279.

[7] "The Story of Blennerhassett," *SLM* 27 (December 1858): 468.

On the contrary, aggressive expansionism can be said to have set American interests in Latin America back dramatically. From her job tending to traveling Americans in a Panama hotel, the Jamaican Mary Seacole had ample reason to bemoan the "crowds to California" who "were of the lowest sort, many of whom have since fertilized Cuban and Nicaraguan soil." She found it natural that the Central Americans "dreaded their schemes of annexation." The most recent historical studies of filibustering have reinforced Seacole's observations. In Mexico, Central America, the Caribbean, and even Hawaii, diplomatic efforts to annex new territories were undermined by filibusters and the hostility to the United States that they provoked.[8]

Filibustering also proved damaging to the interests of commercial expansionists, like Cora Montgomery, who imagined U.S. domination exercised through trade. The *Democratic Review*, once a staunch supporter of López and Walker, worried in print by 1857 that more filibustering expeditions would upset American trade efforts in the region. So long as the region was not "harassed by private military expeditions" like the "Walker system, which proved so disastrous to the interests of that ill-fated country, and to himself and others engaged in that military demonstration" Americans could make good use of the region. It "offers a field for commercial enterprise more valuable than that we can look for in Japan."[9] Given the damaging effects of filibustering on America's reputation abroad, and on the lives of its participants, it is hardly surprising that by the 1870s it had become an embarrassing memory; no part of the domesticated narrative of "American Progress" enshrined by John Gast.

But aggressive expansionism deserves to be remembered. Both the filibustering and diplomatic efforts to annex new lands in the Caribbean, Mexico, and Central America between 1848 and 1860 undermine the assertion that Manifest Destiny was conceptualized in strictly continental terms in the middle of the nineteenth century. Dreams of an overseas empire did not emerge with the Spanish-American War, they drove the actions of politicians who negotiated for Cuba, filibusters who met their deaths in Latin America, and gold-rush travelers who envisioned an American Central America alike. Nor were these dreams dramatically different from the visions of empire that motivated proponents of commercial expansion like Cora Montgomery. Although the idea that the United States was exceptional in terms of empire remains a prevailing paradigm, the history of aggressive expansionism should indicate that the United States took a contiguous continental form in the middle of the century due to luck far more than plan. Were it up to any of the men who hoped to filibuster or who attended a public meeting in support

---

[8] Mary Seacole, *Wonderful Adventures of Mrs. Seacole in Many Lands.* 1857. (New York, 1988), 51–2; May, *Manifest Destiny's Underworld*, 240–1; Joseph Stout Jr., *Schemers and Dreamers: Filibustering in Mexico, 1848–1921* (Fort Worth, TX, 2002).

[9] "Revolutions in Central America," *USDR* 40 (October 1857): 315, 329.

of Narciso López or voted with the Young America faction of the Democratic Party, by 1860 the United States might well have embraced Hawaii, Cuba, and portions of Central America and Mexico.[10]

The easy victory over Mexico in 1847 seemed to justify and empower martial men from 1848 to 1860. But the horrors of the Civil War drove Americans to very different conclusions about the relative merits of martial and restrained manhood by 1865. The experience of the Civil War led American soldiers to change their definition of courage from one of heroic individual exploits on the battlefield to simply surviving from day to day. The seemingly interminable tedium of camp routine, enormous loss of life due to communicable disease, and battlefield conditions radically altered by improved weaponry were factors for which enthusiastic recruits were unprepared. Like David Deaderick, the Walker recruit who failed to prove himself in Nicaragua, Civil War soldiers learned how wrong their romantic expectations about war were. The men who were lucky enough to return home to their families after the Civil War were far more likely to see restraint as a virtue than they had been when they first donned a uniform.[11]

At the same time that the reality of warfare seemed to mock the values of martial men, four years of war led to a centralization of the state and industrialization of the economy that greatly rewarded the masculine practices of restrained men. Romantic idealism gave way to bureaucratic pragmatism among intellectuals, and expertise and technical knowledge gained new currency as Americans embraced scientific pursuits, professionalization, and order. Class stratification further marginalized martial practices, which were increasingly limited to immigrant and working subcultures, while restrained practices became markers of middle- and upper-class membership. By the 1870s, when John Gast offered up his vision of Manifest Destiny as peaceful and domesticated, restrained practices of masculinity had become nearly hegemonic.[12]

Restrained manhood emerged triumphant from the Civil War and so, too, did the restrained vision of commercial expansionism. In the post-bellum years, Washington focused on creating a sphere of interest in the Western Hemisphere through economic relations, having realized that "with foresight and fortune, it might be possible to obtain the benefits of imperialism without assuming all its costs." James G. Blaine, who served as secretary of state under two Republican presidents in the 1880s, explained that the United

---

[10] Ann Laura Stoler, "Tense and Tender Ties: The Politics of Comparison in North American History and (Post) Colonial Studies," *JAH* 88 (December 2001): 829–65; Amy Kaplan, "'Left Alone with America': The Absence of Empire in the Study of American Culture," in *Cultures of United States Imperialism*, Amy Kaplan and Donald E. Pease, eds. (Durham, 1993): 3–21.

[11] Gerald Linderman, *Embattled Courage: The Experience of Combat in the American Civil War* (New York, 1987).

[12] George Fredrickson, *The Inner Civil War: Northern Intellectuals and the Crisis of the Union* (New York, 1965); R. W. Connell, *Masculinities* (Berkeley, 1995), 193.

FIGURE 8.1. "Commercial and geographical relation of New York to Europe and Asia, with views of Hong Kong, Honolulu, Aspinwall, Panama, and on the Pacific Railroad." This 1868 illustration of the United States at "the center of the commercial world" celebrated American commercial domination, and suggested that it might lead to further territorial expansion of "our own vast empire." *Harper's Weekly* 12 (May 30, 1868): 344–5. Library of Congress, Prints and Photographs Division, [LC-USZ62-117575].

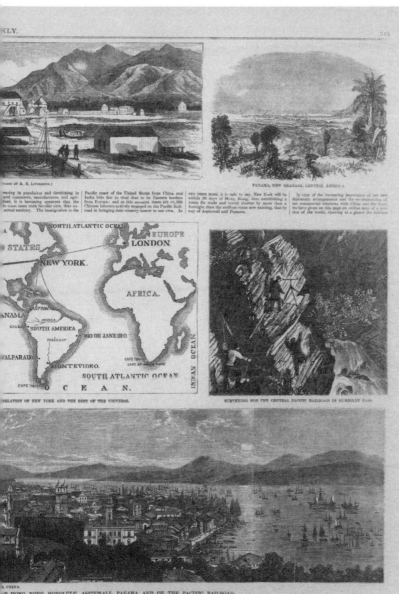

States sought "annexation of trade," not "the annexation of territory." But the United States also proved willing to defend that trade through force of arms, expending far more military resources to protect American investments in the Caribbean and in Latin America than it ever did to support filibusters. U.S. forces intervened in Panama alone three times between 1865 and 1873 in order to protect U.S. commercial ventures.[13]

The overwhelming success of commercial expansionism was celebrated as early as the 1860s, as in the *Harper's Weekly* 1868 visualization of the "Commercial and geographical relation of New York to Europe and Asia, with views of Hong Kong, Honolulu, Aspinwall, Panama, and on the Pacific Railroad" (see Figure 8.1). Anchored by a map placing the United States at "the center of the commercial world," *Harper's Weekly* dedicated two full pages to a visual depiction of the victory of American commercial domination over not only the Western Hemisphere but the whole world. A composite of seven illustrations offers views of American enterprise abroad, including, notably, Honolulu, and both Aspinwall and Panama in Central America, key sites of filibustering lust in the 1850s. A "map of the world on Mercator's projection" shows "the geographical relation of New York and the rest of the universe" in support of the claim that "the United States have become the great highway between Western Europe and Eastern Asia; and New York is rapidly becoming the 'world's great mart'." Although both map and scenes equated America's Manifest Destiny with trade, the accompanying text left the door open for further territorial acquisition. "Our own vast empire is rapidly increasing in population and developing in wealth, natural commerce, manufactures, and agriculture; indeed it is becoming apparent that the whole Pacific coast must soon become ours, thus extending our actual territory."[14]

While white American women were marginalized in the push for territorial expansionism in the 1850s, they were active participants in the commercial empire of the second half of the nineteenth century. Bourgeois American households avidly consumed the results of international trade, creating a "cosmopolitan domesticity" that at once "emerged from and promoted U.S. commercial expansion and empire."[15] For several decades, commercial

---

[13] Peter H. Smith, *Talons of the Eagle: Dynamics of U.S.-Latin American Relations* (New York, 2000), 25–9, quote page 25; Mary Ann Heiss, "The Evolution of the Imperial Idea and U.S. National Identity," *Diplomatic History* 26 (Fall 2002): 526; Brady Harrison, "The Young Americans," *American Studies* 40 (Fall 1999): 91.

[14] *Harper's Weekly* 12 (May 30, 1868): 344–5.

[15] Kristin Hoganson, "Cosmopolitan Domesticity: Importing the American Dream, 1865–1920," *AHR* 107 (February 2002): 55–82, quote page 60. Laura Wexler has shown that women also were active participants in the creation of empire at the turn of the century. Female photojournalists used gendered expectations about the female "innocent eye" to promote imperialism. "Their pictures helped to heighten regard for territorial acquisition in the Caribbean and the Pacific by erasing the violence of colonial encounters in the very act

empire flourished, and territorial expansionism stagnated. The United States purchased Alaska and Midway Island, more than one thousand miles west of Hawaii, in the 1860s, courtesy of William Seward, but President Ulysses S. Grant's attempts to annex the Dominican Republic in 1868 were rejected by the U.S. Senate. It wasn't until the United States conquered its own interior territory through the subjugation of Native-American tribes and the completion of transcontinental railroad that territorial expansion experienced a rebirth. In 1893, Frederick Jackson Turner declared that the continental frontier, "the meeting point between savagery and civilization," was gone, and with it one of the defining facts of the American character. Turner directly equated free land with democracy. Americans would need to find a new frontier that would allow them to develop their masculine virtues.[16]

Commodore Matthew Perry's vision of an American empire would finally be realized more than forty years after his return from Japan. Prior to the Civil War, most supporters of American annexation trusted that annexation would lead to the assimilation of conquered peoples. As Secretary of State John C. Calhoun had put it, expansionism was a process of "increase by growing and spreading out into unoccupied regions, assimilating all we incorporate." By the late nineteenth century, expansionists openly discarded the idea that newly absorbed peoples would be elevated to American citizenship.[17] The United States seized Cuba, Puerto Rico, Wake Island, and Guam in 1898. The 1899–1902 Philippine-American War resulted in an American occupation of the country, as well as the deaths of more than four thousand American soldiers, sixteen to twenty thousand Filipino soldiers, and perhaps two hundred thousand Filipino civilians. William McKinley's justification for the occupation had a familiar ring to those acquainted with the literature of antebellum expansionism – if the United States didn't occupy the region, it would fall pray to a European power. Hawaiian annexation, previously blocked by presidents who deemed it too controversial, easily passed through Congress during the Spanish-American War. President McKinley announced that Hawaiian annexation was "the inevitable consequence" of "three-quarters of a century" of American expansion in the Pacific. Nor was Central America forgotten. In 1903 President Theodore Roosevelt aided separatists against Colombia so that the Central American ship canal that in 1849 had so inspired Francis Lieber could finally be built through Panama.

of portraying them." Laura Wexler, *Tender Violence: Domestic Visions in an Age of U.S. Imperialism* (Chapel Hill, 2000), 7.

[16] Richard Drinnon, *Facing West: The Metaphysics of Indian Hating and Empire Building* (New York, 1990), 272, Turner quote page xiii.

[17] *Congressional Record*, 58th Congress, 1st Sess., 443; Frederick Merk, *Manifest Destiny and Mission in American History: A Reinterpretation* (New York, 1963), 256–7; Albert Weinberg, *Manifest Destiny: A Study of Nationalist Expansionism in American History*. 1935, reprint edition (Chicago, 1963), 160.

Between 1898 and 1934, the United States would launch more than thirty military interventions in Latin America.[18]

The near hegemony restrained manhood experienced after the Civil War proved to be short lived. The economic crisis of 1893–1897, along with an upsurge in immigration, an increase in women's power, and violent labor unrest, from the Haymarket massacre of 1884 through the Pullman strike of 1894, all provoked a new appreciation for martial practices among middle-class American men. Political leaders urged imperial policies to alleviate domestic discontent, and the engendering of American foreign policy bore bitter fruit.[19] As Kristin Hoganson has explored, concerns about the increasing effeminacy of American manhood, British arguments that "empire made men," and thirty years of romanticized memoirs of the Civil War produced a culture in which jingoes turned to war against Spain as a way to build character in American men.

By representing Cuba as an endangered woman, jingoes mobilized the ideal of male chivalry to build support for the Spanish-American War, while representing those opposed to war as "spineless cowards." Success in that war provided ammunition for the conquest and governance of the Philippines, which imperialists argued would reanimate American manhood, and which only "carping old women," as they called anti-imperialists, could object to. The Spanish-American conflict, and especially the heroic vision of Teddy Roosevelt's Rough Riders, a voluntary cavalry division made up of Harvard intellectuals and frontier cowboys, helped to energize a militant vision of masculinity that suggested that the easy life of the American middle class was emasculating its boys. Darwinian conceptions of struggle suggested that this process of emasculation, unless stopped, would eventually lead to the "suicide" of the white middle class in the face of more virile non-white and working men. At the same time, imperialists promoted a conservative role for white middle-class women, who could best serve the nation, they argued, through fruitful procreation rather than political engagement.[20]

No matter that Roosevelt, a small and sickly youth raised in an aristocratic family, was mocked for his fancy manners and clothes when he first

---

[18] Peter Booth Wiley, *Yankees in the Land of the Gods: Commodore Perry and the Opening of Japan* (New York, 1990), 489; Stanley Karnow, *In Our Image: America's Empire in the Philippines* (New York, 1989), 125; Kristin Hoganson, *Fighting for American Manhood: How Gender Politics Provoked the Spanish-American and Philippine-American Wars* (New Haven, 1998), 7; Anders Stephanson, *Manifest Destiny: American Expansion and the Empire of the Right* (New York, 1995), 75–8; Walter LaFeber, *The New Empire: An Interpretation of American Expansion, 1860–1898* (Ithaca, 1963), 5; Edmund Morris, *Theodore Rex* (New York, 2001), 271–97; Smith, *Talons of the Eagle*, 50.

[19] Thomas Schoonover, *Uncle Sam's War of 1898 and the Origins of Globalization* (Lexington, KY, 2003), 65.

[20] Hoganson, *Fighting for American Manhood*, 201, 202. On Darwinism and masculinity see Gail Bederman, *Manliness and Civilization: A Cultural History of Gender and Race in the United States, 1880–1917* (Chicago, 1995).

entered politics. By embracing what he called the "strenuous life" of out-door activities, blood sport, and physical competition, Roosevelt was able to remake himself in a military mode. He gave up his position as Assistant Secretary of the Navy at the beginning of the Spanish-American War, and he rode his military service all the way to the White House. At the Republican convention for the 1900 presidential election, one delegate proclaimed Roosevelt "an embodiment of those qualities which appeal everywhere to American manhood."[21]

Of course, as this study documents, gender ideology helped shape American foreign relations long before Theodore Roosevelt first reinvented himself. Manifest Destiny, in ideology and in practice, was grounded in ideas about manhood and womanhood. It flourished in the years between the U.S.-Mexico War and the Civil War because it seemed to offer a means for American men, especially those who had failed to find success in industrializing America, to redeem themselves and to affirm their practices of masculinity. Both letters from travelers in the region and the travelogues that proliferated in popular culture reveal an American image of Latin America as ripe for takeover. Latin America, in the expansionist view, was blessed by nature, a land where success was preordained. It was also a land where martial virtues were best exercised by white American men, full of easily overpowered, racially inferior men and of women ready for "annexation." The new frontier of Latin America seemed to offer the opportunity for personal and national regeneration. However counterproductive the martial activities of filibusters like William Walker and Narciso López ultimately were, the very fact that other men joined these quixotic missions in the first place, and that they were lauded even in failure, reveals the degree to which foreign relations and gender norms were linked in the antebellum era.

While the filibustering of the 1850s quickly faded from the national memory, at least among white Americans, the martial manhood of that period did not. In 1897, American readers thrilled to a best-selling romance that celebrated the ascendancy of the United States in the hemisphere and featured an American swashbuckler, Robert Clary, with clear martial virtues. One critic has claimed that *Soldiers of Fortune*, by Richard Harding Davis, "was so widely read that in some unquestionable way it doubtless helped prime the national psyche for the collective adventure in Cuba." The model for Davis's swashbuckler hero was none other than William Walker.[22]

---

[21] Quoted in Hoganson, *Fighting for American manhood*, 113; Amy S. Greenberg, "Manhood" in the *Encyclopedia of American Cultural and Intellectual History*, Mary Kupiec Cayton and Peter Williams, eds. (New York: Macmillan, 2001), vol. 1: 555–63; Edmund Morris, *The Rise of Theodore Roosevelt* (New York, 1979.)

[22] Richard Harding Davis, *Soldiers of Fortune* (New York, 1897). Richard Harding Davis also heroized Walker in his travelogue, *Three Gringos in Venezuela and Central America* (New York, 1896). As Brady Harrison has written, "Walker lurks in the spirit of adventurism

While considering the caustic effects of gender on foreign relations in the nineteenth century, it is difficult to avoid comparisons to the present. In the first years of the twenty-first century, America has a belligerent foreign policy that claims divine sanction for armed intervention abroad and political contests where even candidates with weak military experience go to great lengths to cover up their patrician upbringings and prove their martial virtues. Many Americans still believe that the superiority of their nation resides in its military power and the machismo of its leadership, while U.S. political leaders justify preemptive military strikes against foreign governments on the basis of the superiority of American culture, economics, and political forms.[23]

Of course manhood, womanhood, and ideology have changed in this country over the last one hundred and fifty years. Filibustering is dead, transformations in gender roles have brought significant shifts in the popular understanding of gender abroad as well as at home, and "annexationist" fantasies no longer drive foreign intervention, even if the fantasy of the willing Latina is still alive and well.[24] But however battered its premises, however far America progresses, martial manhood refuses to die. In the mid-nineteenth century, as today, gender and ideology mix into a potent cocktail. In 1850, Ralph Waldo Emerson, father of the "Young America" movement, predicted that "the reputations of the nineteenth century will one day be quoted, to prove its barbarism."[25] One hopes that future historians will reach a different conclusion about our own new century.

---

that officially called the American empire into being." Harrison, "The Young Americans," 91, 92.

[23] Alexander DeConde, *Presidential Machismo: Executive Authority, Military Intervention, and Foreign Relations* (Boston, 2000), 286–95.

[24] In his best-selling guide to relocating to Mexico, "Mexico" Mike Nelson addresses his male readers: "Just between us guys, let's be honest. **The reason a lot of you want to live in Latin America is so that you can meet and marry a *Latina*.** There's nothing wrong with that. There are some *Latinas* who would love to marry a gringo, some for true love and some because we have the reputations as good providers (if not as lovers). First of all, remember that **not all *Latinas* are interested in you.**" Mike Nelson, *Live Better South of the Border in Mexico: Practical Advice for Living and Working*, 3rd ed. (Golden, CO, 2000), 51.

[25] R. W. Emerson, *Representative Men: Seven Lectures* (Boston, 1850), 37.

Bibliography

PRIMARY SOURCES

Unpublished Manuscripts

Archives of Hawaii, Honolulu

David Gregg Letterbook
Foreign Office and Executive File
Foreign Office Letter Book
Foreign Officials in Hawaii File
Local Officials File
Miscellaneous Foreign File
Official Dispatches

The Bancroft Library, University of California at Berkeley

James S. Barnes correspondence, 1849–1857
J. C. W. Brenan correspondence
Emeline Hubbard Day journal, 1853–1856
DeWitt Family Papers
William Elder Correspondence
Goss Family Letter Collection, 1849–1853
Prevaux Family correspondence

The Beinecke Rare Books and Manuscripts Library, Yale University

William Prince diary

The Huntington Library, San Marino, CA

Journal of R. G. S. Ten Broock M.D. U.S. Army. 1854
Journal of J. A. Clarke, 1852
William Franklin Denniston, "Journal of a voyage from New York to San Francisco via Nicaragua ... ; mining near Mariposa, California; return via Panama. 1849–1850

Loyall Farragut, "Autobiography (1844–1872)" typescript
John Tracy Gaffey (Account of projected filibustering expedition into Nicaragua)
Richard Hammond Letterbook, 1854–1855
Diary of Alonzo Hubbard
Milton S(locum) Latham Letterbook, 1855–1857
Charles Parke journal
Ephraim George Squier, "Archeological notes on Nicaragua, Honduras, and San
    Salvador," A ms. 1 vol. c. 1853
Squier Collection, Honduras Interoceanic Railway, Topography and Level, books
    ms. 26 volumes (1858)
Squier Collection of Newspaper clippings on Central America, 1856–1860
Lucian Wolcott "Journal," vol. 2
Joseph Warren Wood diary (in 6 volumes). 1849–1852

Library of Congress, Manuscript Division

"The Diary or Register of David Anderson Deaderick, esq. Of Knoxville, Tennessee,
    born 1797, died 1873. Intimate family glimpses, natural phenomena, scourge of
    the civil war, customs of the times, 1824–July, 1872."
"The Stirring Adventures of a Lad from Knoxville, Tennessee, David Deaderick III,
    Who fought with Filibuster William Walker in Nicaragua. (With partial list of
    companions). Typewritten Notes presented the Library of Congress by George
    Magruder Battey III, Washington D.C. January. 23, 1940."
John H. Wheeler Collection

National Archives

Dispatches from United States Ministers in Hawaii, T30, Roll 5, microfilm

New York Public Library

Henry Hunter Peters diary (transcript)

Howard Tilton Library, Tulane University

Callender Fayassoux Collection of William Walker Papers

Newspapers

Daily Alta California (San Francisco, CA)
El Nicaraguense (Nicaragua)
Honolulu *Star-Bulletin*
National Intelligencer (Washington, DC)
New Orleans *Daily Delta*
New Orleans *Picayune*
New Orleans *Times*
New York *Herald*
New York *Picayune*

New York *Times*
New York *Times*
Philadelphia *Public Ledger*
Pittsburgh *Daily Morning Post*
The Polynesian (Honolulu)
San Francisco *Herald*

Journals

The American Whig Review
The Atlantic Monthly
Congressional Globe
De Bow's Review
Frank Leslie's Illustrated Newspaper
Godey's Lady's Book
Harper's New Monthly Magazine
Harper's Weekly
The International Magazine of Literature, Art and Science
The Knickerbocker
The Ladies' Repository
Littell's Living Age
The New Englander and Yale Review
North American Review
Putnam's Monthly Magazine
The Southern Literary Messenger
The Southern Quarterly Review
The United States Magazine and Democratic Review
Young Sam

Books and Other Miscellaneous Published Material

"An officer in the Service of Walker." *The Destiny of Nicaragua: Central America as it was, is, and may be.* Boston, 1856.

Anderson, Rufus. *The Hawaiian Islands: Their Progress and Condition under Missionary Labors.* Boston, 1864.

Averill, Charles. *The Secret Service Ship, or, the Fall of the Castle San Juan d'Ulloa.* Boston, 1848.

Baily, John, Esq., *Central America: Describing each of the States of Guatemala, Honduras, Salvador, Nicaragua, and Costa Rica.* London, 1850.

Ballou, Mary B. *"I Hear the Hogs in My Kitchen," A Woman's View of the Gold Rush.* Archibald Hanna, ed. New Haven, 1962.

Bartlett, John Russell. *Personal Narrative of Explorations and Incidents in Texas, New Mexico, California, Sonora, and Chihuahua.* New York, 1854.

Bates, George Washington (as "a Haolé"). *Sandwich Island Notes.* New York, 1854.

Bates, Mrs. D. B. *Incidents on Land and Water, or Four Years on the Pacific Coast.* 1858. New York, 1974.

Beecher, Catharine. *A Treatise on Domestic Economy for the Use of Young Ladies at Home and at School.* Boston, 1841.

———. and Harriet Beecher Stowe, *The American Woman's Home.* New York, 1869.

Beecher, Lyman. *A Plea for the West.* 1835. New York, 1977.

Bell, Horace. *Reminiscences of a Ranger: Early Times in Southern California.* Santa Barbara, 1927.

―――. "Confessions of a Filibuster," *The Golden Era* (San Francisco), May 7–August 27, 1876.

Bingham, Hiram. *Residence of Twenty-One Years in the Sandwich Islands.* Hartford, 1847.

Brooks, Sarah Merriam. *Across the Isthmus to California in '52.* San Francisco, 1894.

Bruff, J. Goldsborough. *Gold Rush: The Journals, Drawings, and Other Papers of J. Goldsborough Bruff, April 2, 1849–July 20, 1851.* Georgia Wills Read and Ruth Gaines, eds. New York, 1949.

Buntline, Ned. *The Mysteries and Miseries of New Orleans.* New York, 1851.

Capen, Nahum. *The Republic of the United States of America; Its Duties to Itself, and Its Responsible Relations to other Countries.* New York, 1848.

Carroll, Anna Ella. *The Star of the West: or, National Men and National Measures.* 3rd edition. Boston, 1857.

Cheever, Henry T. *Life in the Sandwich Islands: or, The Heart of the Pacific, as It Was and Is.* New York, 1851.

―――. *The Island World of the Pacific.* New York, 1851.

Clemens, Jeremiah. *The Rivals: A Tale of the Times of Aaron Burr and Alexander Hamilton.* Philadelphia, 1860.

Crofutt, George A. *Crofutt's New Overland Tourist and Pacific Coast Guide.* Chicago, 1887.

Dana, Richard Henry. *To Cuba and Back: A Vacation Voyage.* Boston, 1859.

―――. *Two Years Before the Mast.* 1840. New York, 1945.

Davis, Richard Harding. *Soldiers of Fortune.* New York, 1897.

―――. *Three Gringos in Venezuela and Central America.* New York, 1896.

Delany, Martin. *The Condition, Elevation, Emigration, and Destiny of the Colored People of the United States.* Philadelphia, 1852.

Devens, Richard Miller. *Our First Century: Being a Popular Descriptive Portraiture of the One Hundred Great and Memorable Events of Perpetual Interest in the History of our Country.* Springfield, MA, 1877.

Doolittle, James R. *Justification of Commodore Paulding's Arrest of Walker and his Command at Puenta Arenas. Speech of James R. Doolittle, of Wisconsin. Delivered to the United States Senate, January 21, 1858.* Washington, DC, 1858.

Doubleday, Charles W. *Reminiscences of the Filibuster War in Nicaragua.* New York, 1886.

Dunbar, Edward E. *The Romance of the Age; or, the Discovery of Gold in California.* New York, 1867.

Emerson, Ralph Waldo. *Essays and Lectures.* New York, 1983.

―――. *Representative Men: Seven Lectures.* Boston, 1850.

Emory, William H. *Report on the United States and Mexican Boundary Survey, made under the Direction of the Secretary of the Interior.* Washington, DC, 1857. 1859. 34th Congress, 1st Session, Ex. Doc. No. 135.

Fabens, Joseph Warren. *A Story of Life on the Isthmus.* New York, 1853.

Frémont, Jessie Benton. *A Year of American Travel: Narrative of Personal Experience.* 1878. San Francisco, 1960.

Gallatin, Albert. *Notes on the Semi-Civilized Nations of Mexico, Yucatan, and Central America.* New York, 1845.

Gilliam, Albert M. *Travels over the Table Lands and Cordilleras of Mexico.* Philadelphia, 1846.

Graff, Henry F., ed. *Bluejackets with Perry in Japan: A Day-by-Day Account kept by Master's Mate John R.C. Lewis and Cabin Boy William B. Allen.* New York, 1952.

Gregory, Joseph W. *Gregory's Guide for California Travelers; via the Isthmus of Panama.* New York, 1850.

Headley, Joel Tyler. *The Great Riots of New York, 1712–1873.* 1873. Indianapolis, 1970.

Heine, William. *With Perry in Japan.* Translated by Frederick Trautmann. Honolulu, 1990.

Hogan, William D. *High and Low Mass in the Roman Catholic Church; with Comments.* Nashua, 1846.

Jamison, James Carson. *With Walker in Nicaragua or Reminiscences of an Officer in the American Phalanx.* Columbia, MO, 1909.

Jarves, James Jackson. *Kiana: A Tradition of Hawaii.* Boston, 1857.

Johnson, Theodore Taylor. *Sights in the Gold Region, and Scenes by the Way.* New York, 1849.

Jones, James P., and William Warren Rogers. "Across the Isthmus in 1850: The Journey of Daniel A. Horn," *Hispanic American Historical Review* 41 (November, 1961): 533–54.

Kennedy, John P. *Memoirs of the Life of William Wirt.* Philadelphia, 1850.

Letts, John M. *A pictorial View of California: including a description of the Panama and Nicaragua routes, with information and advice interesting to all, particularly those who intend to visit the golden region.* New York, 1853.

Lloyd, W. Alvin. *W. Alvin Lloyd's Steamboat and Railroad Guide.* New Orleans, 1857.

Lowell, James Russell. *The Bigalow Papers.* Cambridge, MA, 1848.

Lucas, Daniel. *Nicaragua: War of the Filibusters.* Richmond, 1896.

Lydecker, Robert Colfax. *Roster, Legislatures of Hawaii 1841–1918: Constitutions of Monarchy and Republic, Speeches of Sovereigns and Presidents.* Honolulu, 1918.

Maury, Matthew F. *The Amazon, and Atlantic Slopes of South America.* Washington, DC, 1853.

McCollum, William, M.D. *California as I Saw it: Pencillings by the Way of its Gold and Gold Diggers! and Incidents of Travel by Land and Water.* Dale L. Morgan, ed. Los Gatos, CA, 1960.

Megquier, Mary Jane. *Apron Full of Gold: The Letters of Mary Jane Megquier From San Francisco, 1849–1856.* 2nd edition, Polly Welts Kaufman, ed. Albuquerque, 1994.

Miller, Joaquin. *The Complete Poetical Works of Joaquin Miller.* New York, 1972.

Monk, Maria. *Awful Disclosures of the Hotel Dieu Nunnery.* New York, 1836.

Montgomery, Cora (Jane McManus Storm Cazneau). *Eagle Pass; or, Life on the Border.* New York, 1852.

———. *The Queen of Islands and the King of Rivers.* New York, 1850.

Morse, Jedediah. *The American Geography.* 1789. New York, 1970.

Morse, Samuel F. B. *Foreign Conspiracy against the Liberties of the United States.* New York, 1835.

―――. *Imminent Dangers to the Free Institutions of the United States through Foreign Immigration, and the Present State of the Naturalization Laws. 1835.* New York, 1969.

Morton, Samuel George. *Catalogue of Skulls of Man and the Inferior Animals.* Philadelphia, 1849.

―――. *Crania Americana, or, A comparative view of the skulls of various aboriginal nations of North and South America.* Philadelphia, 1839.

Myres, Sandra L., ed. *Ho for California! Women's Overland Diaries from the Huntington Library.* San Marino, CA, 1980.

Nelson, Mike. *Live Better South of the Border in Mexico: Practical Advice for Living and Working.* 3rd edition. Golden, CO, 2000.

Parke, Charles Ross. *Dreams to Dust: A Diary of the California Gold Rush, 1849–1850.* James E. Davis, ed. Lincoln, NE, 1989.

Parke, William Cooper. *Personal Reminiscences of William Cooper Parke.* Cambridge, MA, 1891.

Parker, Mrs. E. M. Wills (Elizabeth Parker). *The Sandwich Islands as They Are, Not as They Should Be.* San Francisco, 1852.

Pearce, J. A. *Speech of Hon. J. A. Pearce, of Maryland, on the Presentation of a Medal to Commodore Paulding; delivered in the Senate of the United States, January 28, 1858.* Washington, DC, 1858.

Perkins, Edward T. *Na Motu: or Reef Rovings in the South Seas.* New York, 1854.

Perkins, Oliver L. *The History of the Buccaneers of America: Containing detailed accounts of those bold and daring freebooters; chiefly along the Spanish Main, in the West Indies, and in the Great South Sea, succeeding the civil wars in England.* 2nd edition. Boston, 1856.

Perry, Matthew Calbraith. *The Japan Expedition, 1852–1854: The Personal Journal of Commodore Matthew C. Perry,* Roger Pineau, ed. Washington, DC, 1968.

―――. *Narrative of the Expedition of an American Squadron to the China Seas and Japan.* Washington, DC, 1856.

Pickens, Lucy Holcombe. *The Free Flag of Cuba: The Lost Novel of Lucy Holcombe Pickens.* Orville Vernon Burton and Georganne B. Burton, eds. Baton Rouge, 2002.

Pierce, Hiram Dwight. *A Forty-Niner Speaks.* Sarah Wiswall Meyer, ed. Sacramento, 1978.

Poesche, Theodore, and Charles Goepp. *The New Rome; or, The United States and the World.* New York, 1853.

Prescott, William H. *History of the Conquest of Mexico.* Chicago, 1843.

Report of the Minister of Foreign Relations, read 14 April, 1852. Honolulu, 1852.

Richardson, James D., ed. *A Compilation of the Messages and Papers of the Presidents, 1789–1902.* Washington, DC, 1903.

Richmond, John L. *Mexico and Central America: The Problem and its Solution.* Washington, DC, 1858.

Roche, James Jeffrey. *The Story of the Filibusters.* New York, 1891.

Ruxton, George F. *Adventures in Mexico and the Rocky Mountains.* New York, 1848.

Safford, William H. *The Life of Harman Blennerhassett. Comprising an authentic narrative of the Burr expedition: and containing many additional facts not heretofore published.* Chillicothe, Ohio, 1850.

Seacole, Mary. *Wonderful Adventures of Mrs. Seacole in Many Lands.* 1857. New York, 1988.

Sedgwick, Catherine. *Letters from Abroad to Kindred at Home.* 2 vols. New York, 1841.

Sheldon, Henry Isaac. *Notes on the Nicaragua Canal.* 1897. Chicago, 1902.

Simmons, William E. *Uncle Sam's New Waterway.* New York, 1899.

Smith, Edmond Reuel. *The Araucanians: or, Notes of a Tour among the Indian Tribes of Southern Chili.* New York, 1855.

Society of First Steamship Pioneers. *First Steamship Pioneers.* San Francisco, 1874.

Squier, Ephraim George. *Adventures on the Mosquito Shore.* New York, 1891.

———. *Nicaragua: Its People, Scenery, Monuments, Resources, Condition and Proposed Canal.* 1852. New York, 1860.

———. *Notes on Central America: Particularly the States of Honduras and San Salvador.* New York, 1855.

———. *Observations on the Archaeology and Ethnology of Nicaragua.* 1853. Culver City, CA, 1990.

———. (as "Samuel A. Bard"). *Waikna: Adventures on the Mosquito Shore.* 1855. Gainesville, FL, 1965.

Squier, Ephraim G., and Edwin H. Davis. *Ancient Monuments of the Mississippi Valley.* 1848. Washington DC, 1998.

Stephens, John L. *Incidents of Travel in Central America, Chiapas, and Yucatan.* 1841. New Brunswick, 1949.

Stewart, William Frank. *Last of the Fillibusters.* Sacramento, 1857.

Stout, Peter F. *Nicaragua: Past, Present and Future; a Description of Its Inhabitants, Customs, Mines, Minerals, Early History, Modern Fillibusterism, Proposed Inter-Oceanic Canal and Manifest Destiny.* Philadelphia, 1859.

Stowe, Harriet Beecher. *Uncle Tom's Cabin, or Life Among the Lowly.* London, 1852.

Strong, George Templeton. *The Diary of George Templeton Strong.* Allan Nevins and Milton Halsey Thomas, eds. New York, 1952.

Sullivan, Edward Robert, Sir. *Rambles and Scrambles in North and South America.* London, 1853.

Taylor, Bayard. *Eldorado: Adventures in the Path of Empire.* 1850. Santa Clara, CA, 2000.

———. *A Visit to India, China, and Japan, in the Year 1853.* New York, 1855.

Taylor, John Glanville. *The United States and Cuba: Eight Years of Change and Travel.* London, 1851.

Thompson, Waddy. *Recollections of Mexico.* New York, 1846.

Thoreau, Henry David. *The Writings of Henry David Thoreau.* F. B. Sanborn, ed. Boston, 1906.

Tocqueville, Alexis de. *Democracy in America.* 1840. New York, 1981.

Tomes, Robert. *Panama in 1855. An Account of the Panama Rail-Road, of the Cities of Panama and Aspinwall, with Sketches of Life and Character on the Isthmus.* New York, 1855.

Trescot, William Henry. *A Few Thoughts on the Foreign Policy of the United States.* Charleston, 1849.

Tyson, James L. M.D. *Diary of a Physician in California: Being the Results of Actual Experiences Including Notes of the Journey by Land and Water, and*

Observations on the Climate, Soil, Resources of the Country, etc. 1850. Oakland, CA, 1955.

Udell, John. *Incidents of Travel to California, across the Great Plains; Together with the return trips through Central America and Jamaica; to which are added sketches of the Author's Life.* Jefferson, OH, 1856.

U.S. Congress. Senate. "Hawaiian Islands." Senate Executive Document 45. Washington, DC, 1894.

U.S. Congress. Senate. *Message of the President of the United States, Transmitting (a) Report of the Secretary of the Navy . . . Relative to the Naval Expedition to Japan.* Senate Executive Document 34. Washington, DC, 1855.

de Vattel, Emmerich. *The Law of Nations: or Principles of the Law of Nature Applied to the Conduct and Affairs of Nations and Sovereigns.* London, perhaps 1773.

Wagner, Moritz, and Carl Scherzer. *Die Republik Costa Rica in Central America.* Leipzig, 1856.

Walker, Robert J. *Letter of Mr. Walker, of Mississippi, Relative to the Reannexation of Texas: in Reply to the Call of the People of Carroll County, Kentucky, to Communicate his Views on that Subject.* Philadelphia, 1844.

Walker, William. *The War in Nicaragua.* Mobile, 1860.

Warren, T. Robinson. *Dust and Foam; or, Three Oceans and Two Continents.* New York, 1859.

Wells, William V. *Explorations and Adventures in Honduras, comprising sketches of travel in the gold regions of Olancho, and a review of the history and general resources of Central America. With original maps, and numerous illustrations.* New York, 1857.

————. *Walker's Expedition to Nicaragua: A history of the Central American War; and the Sonora and Kinney Expeditions, including all the recent Diplomatic Correspondence, together with a new and accurate map of Central America, and a Memoir and Portrait of General William Walker.* New York, 1856.

Wheat, Marvin (as "Cincinnatus"). *Travels on the Western Slope of the Mexican Cordillera in the form of Fifty-One Letters.* San Francisco, 1857.

Wheeler, John H. *Reminiscences and Memoirs of North Carolina and Eminent North Carolinians.* Columbus, 1884.

Williams, John J. *The Isthmus of Tehuantepec: Being the Results of a Survey for a Rail-road to Connect the Atlantic and Pacific Oceans, Made by the Scientific Commission under the direction of Maj. J. G. Barnard.* New York, 1852.

Williams, Samuel Wells. "A Journal of the Perry Expedition to Japan, 1853–1854." Frederick Wells Williams, ed. *Transactions of the Asiatic Society of Japan* 37. (1910): 1–261.

Woods, Daniel B. *Sixteen Months at the Gold Diggings.* New York, 1852.

SECONDARY SOURCES

Adler, Judith. "Origins of Sightseeing," *Annals of Tourism Research* 16 (1989): 7–29.

Allgor, Catherine. *Parlor Politics: In Which the Ladies of Washington Help Build a City and a Government.* Charlottesville, 2000.

Almond, Gabriel. *The American People and Foreign Policy.* 1950. New York, 1960.

Altschuler, Glen, and Stuart Blumin. *Rude Republic: Americans and Their Politics in the Nineteenth Century.* Princeton, 2000.

Anbinder, Tyler. *Five Points: The Nineteenth-Century New York City Neighborhood That Invented Tap Dance, Stole Elections, and Became the World's Most Notorious Slum.* New York, 2001.

―――. *Nativism and Slavery: the Northern Know Nothings and the Politics of the 1850's.* New York, 1992.

Anderson, Benedict. *Imagined Communities: Reflections on the Origin and Spread of Nationalism.* London, 1991.

Arendt, Hannah. "Imperialism, Nationalism, Chauvinism," *Review of Politics* 7 (Oct. 1945): 441–63.

Augst, Thomas. *The Clerk's Tale: Young Men and Moral Life in Nineteenth-Century America.* Chicago, 2003.

Ayers, Edward L. *Vengeance and Justice: Crime and Punishment in the Nineteenth Century American South.* New York, 1984.

Baker, Paula. "The Domestication of Politics: Women and American Political Society, 1780–1920," *The American Historical Review* 89 (June 1984): 620–47.

Barker-Benfield, G. J. *The Horrors of the Half-Known Life: Male Attitudes Toward Women and Sexuality in Nineteenth-Century America,* 2nd edition. New York, 2000.

Basch, Norma. *In the Eyes of the Law: Women, Marriage, and Property in Nineteenth-Century New York.* Ithaca, 1982.

Baym, Nina. *American Women Writers and the Work of History, 1790–1860.* New Brunswick, 1995.

―――. *Women's Fiction: A Guide to Novels by and about Women in America, 1820–1870.* Ithaca, 1873.

Beaman, Gaylord A. "Pioneer Letters," *The Quarterly of the Historical Society of Southern California* 21 (March 1939): 17–30.

Bederman, Gail. *Manliness and Civilization: A Cultural History of Gender and Race in the United States, 1880–1917.* Chicago, 1995.

Berger, Mark T. *Under Northern Eyes: Latin American Studies and U.S. Hegemony in the Americas, 1898–1990.* Bloomington, 1995.

Berkhofer, Robert F. Jr., *The White Man's Indian: Images of the American Indian from Columbus to the Present.* New York, 1978.

Bhahba, Homi K. *The Location of Culture.* London, 1994.

Billington, Ray Allen. *The Far Western Frontier, 1830–1860.* New York, 1956.

―――. *The Protestant Crusade, 1800–1860: A Study of the Origins of American Nativism.* 1938. New York, 1964.

Billington, Ray Allen, ed. *America's Frontier Heritage.* New York, 1966.

Bird, Caroline. *Born Female: The High Cost of Keeping Women Down.* New York, 1968.

Blaut, J. M. *The Colonizer's Model of the World: Geographical Diffusionism and Eurocentric History.* New York, 1993.

Blumin, Stuart M. *The Emergence of the Middle Class: Social Experience in the American City, 1760–1900.* Cambridge, UK, 1989.

Boydston, Jeanne. *Home & Work: Housework, Wages, and the Ideology of Labor in the Early Republic.* New York, 1990.

Boyer, Paul. *Urban Masses and Moral Order in America, 1820–1920.* Cambridge, MA, 1978.

Brown, Charles H. *Agents of Manifest Destiny: The Lives and Times of the Filibusters.* Chapel Hill, 1980.

Bruce, Dickson D. *Violence and Culture in the Antebellum South.* Austin, 1979.

Caldwell, Robert G. *The López Expeditions to Cuba, 1848–1851.* Princeton, 1915.

Campbell, Randolph B. *Sam Houston and the American Southwest.* New York, 1993.

Carnes, Mark C. *Secret Ritual and Manhood in Victorian America.* New Haven, 1989.

———. "Middle-Class Men and the Solace of Fraternal Ritual," in *Meanings for Manhood: Constructions of Masculinity in Victorian America.* Mark C. Carnes and Clyde Griffen, eds. Chicago, 1990, 37–52.

Carr, Albert Z. *The World and William Walker.* New York, 1963.

Castañeda, Antonia I. "The Political Economy of Nineteenth-Century Stereotypes of Californians," in *Between Borders: Essays on Mexicana/Chicana History*, Adelaida R. Del Castillo, ed. Encino, CA, 1990, 213–36.

Cayton, Mary Kupiec. "The Making of an American Prophet: Emerson, His Audiences, and the Rise of the Culture Industry in Nineteenth-Century America," *American Historical Review* 92 (June 1987): 597–620.

Chaffin, Tom. *Fatal Glory: Narciso López and the First Clandestine U.S. War against Cuba.* Charlottesville, VA, 1996.

———. "Sons of Washington: Narciso López, Filibustering, and U.S. Nationalism, 1848–1851," *Journal of the Early Republic* 15 (Spring 1995): 79–108.

Chidsey, Donald *The American Privateers.* New York, 1962.

Christensen, Carol and Thomas Christensen. *The U.S.-Mexican War.* San Francisco, 1998.

Clawson, Mary Ann. *Constructing Brotherhood: Class, Gender and Fraternalism.* Princeton, 1989.

Cmiel, Kenneth. *Democratic Eloquence: The Fight over Popular Speech in Nineteenth-Century America.* New York, 1990.

Cohen, Patricia Cline. *The Murder of Helen Jewett: The Life and Death of a Prostitute in Nineteenth-Century New York.* New York, 1998.

Colbert, Charles. *A Measure of Perfection; Phrenology and the Fine Arts in America.* Chapel Hill, 1998.

Connell, R. W. *Masculinities.* Berkeley, 1995.

Cooper, Frederick, and Ann Laura Stoler, eds. *Tensions of Empire: Colonial Cultures in a Bourgeois World.* Berkeley, 1997.

Coryell, Janet L. "Duty with Delicacy: Anna Ella Carroll of Maryland," in *Women and American Foreign Policy: Lobbyists, Critics, and Insiders*, Edward P. Crapol, ed. New York, 1987, 45–65.

Cott, Nancy F. *Bonds of Womanhood: "Woman's Sphere" in New England, 1780–1835.* 2nd edition. New Haven, 1997.

Crapol, Edward. "Lydia Maria Child: Abolitionist Critic of American Foreign Policy," in *Women and American Foreign Policy: Lobbyists, Critics, and Insiders*, Edward P. Crapol, ed. New York, 1987, 1–18.

———. "Coming to Terms with Empire: The Historiography of Late-Nineteenth-Century American Foreign Relations," *Diplomatic History* 16 (Fall 1992): 573–97.

Cunningham, Patricia A. *Reforming Women's Fashion: 1850–1920, Politics, Health, and Art.* Kent, OH, 2003.

Curti, Merle E. "Young America," *American Historical Review* 32 (Oct. 1926): 34–55.

Davidson, Cathy, ed. "No More Separate Spheres!" *American Literature* 70 (September 1998): 443–668.

Davis, Susan. *Parades and Power: Street Theater in Nineteenth-Century Philadelphia.* Philadelphia, 1986.

Decker, Peter R. *Fortunes and Failures: White-Collar Mobility in Nineteenth-Century San Francisco.* Cambridge, MA, 1978.

DeConde, Alexander. *Presidential Machismo: Executive Authority, Military Intervention, and Foreign Relations.* Boston, 2000.

De la Cova, Antonio Rafael. *Cuban Confederate Colonel: The Life of Ambrosio José Gonzales.* Columbia, SC, 2003.

———. "Filibusters and Freemasons: The Sworn Obligation," *Journal of the Early Republic* 17 (Spring 1997): 95–120.

———. "The Taylor Administration versus Mississippi Sovereignty: The Round Island Expedition of 1849," *Journal of Mississippi History* 62 (Winter 2000): 294–327.

De León, Arnoldo. *They Called Them Greasers: Anglo Attitudes Toward Mexicans in Texas, 1821–1900.* Austin, 1983.

Deloria, Philip J. *Playing Indian.* New Haven, 1998.

Deming, Caren J. "Miscegenation in Popular Western History and Fiction," in *Women and Western American Literature*, Helen Winter Stauffer and Susan J. Rosowski, eds. Troy, NY, 1982: 90–99.

Denning, Michael. *Mechanic Accents: Dime Novels and Working-Class Culture in America.* London, 1987.

Dipple, Brian W. *The Vanishing American: White Attitudes and U.S. Indian Policy.* Middletown, CT, 1982.

Dodge, Ernest S. *New England and the South Seas.* Cambridge, MA, 1965.

Dorsey, Bruce. *Reforming Men and Women: Gender in the Antebellum City.* Ithaca, 2002.

Douglas, Ann. *The Feminization of American Culture.* New York, 1977.

Doyle, Michael W. *Empires.* Ithaca, 1986.

Dozier, Craig. *Nicaragua's Mosquito Shore: The Years of British and American Presence.* Tuscaloosa, 1985.

Drinnon, Richard. *Facing West: The Metaphysics of Indian Hating and Empire Building.* New York, 1990.

Dubbert, Joe. "Progressivism and the Masculinity Crisis," in *The American Man*, Elizabeth Pleck and Joseph Pleck, eds. Englewood Cliffs, NJ, 1980, 303–20.

Dufour, Charles. *Gentle Tiger: The Gallant Life of Roberdeau Wheat.* Baton Rouge, 1957.

Enloe, Cynthia. *Bananas, Beaches, and Bases: Making Feminist Sense of International Politics.* Berkeley, 1990.

Ethington, Philip J. *The Public City: The Political Construction of Urban Life in San Francisco, 1850–1900.* New York, 1994.

Faragher, John Mack. *Women and Men on the Overland Trail.* 2nd edition. New Haven, 2000.

_____. "North, South, and West: Sectional Controversies and the U.S.-Mexico Boundary Survey," in *Drawing the Borderline: Artists-Explorers of the U.S.-Mexico Boundary Survey*, Dawn Hall, ed. Albuquerque, 1996: 1–11.

Feldberg, Michael. *The Turbulent Era: Riot and Disorder in Jacksonian America*. New York, 1980.

Ferrell, Robert H. *American Diplomacy: A History*. Revised and expanded edition. New York, 1969.

Finkelman, Paul. *Defending Slavery: Proslavery Thought in the Old South*. Boston, 2003.

Foley, Neil. *The White Scourge: Mexicans, Blacks, and Poor Whites in Texas Cotton Culture*. Berkeley, 1997.

Folkman, David I. Jr. *The Nicaragua Route*. Salt Lake City, 1972.

Foner, Eric. *Free Soil, Free Labor, Free Men: The Ideology of the Republican Party before the Civil War*. New York, 1970.

_____. "Racial Attitudes of the New York Free Soilers," *New York History* XLVI (October 1965): 311–29.

Foos, Paul. *A Short, Offhand, Killing Affair: Soldiers and Social Conflict during the Mexican-American War*. Chapel Hill, 2002.

Formisano, Ronald. *The Transformation of Political Culture: Massachusetts Parties, 1790s–1840s*. New York, 1983.

Franchot, Jenny. *Roads to Rome: The Antebellum Protestant Encounter with Catholicism*. Berkeley, 1994.

Franklin, John Hope. *The Militant South, 1800–1861*. Cambridge, MA, 1956.

Fredrickson, George. *The Black Image in the White Mind: The Debate on Afro-American Character and Destiny, 1817–1914*. New York, 1971.

_____. *The Inner Civil War: Northern Intellectuals and the Crisis of the Union*. New York, 1965.

Frenkel, Stephen. "Jungle Stories: North American Representations of Tropical Panama," *The Geographical Review* 86 (July 1996): 317–33.

Fuller, John Douglas Pitts. *The Movement for the Acquisition of All Mexico, 1846–1848*. Baltimore, 1936.

George, Rosemary Marangoly. "Homes in the Empire, Empires in the Home." *Cultural Critique* 26 (1993–1994): 95–127.

Gienapp, William E. "'Politics Seem to Enter into Everything': Political Culture in the North, 1840–1860," in Stephen E. Maizlish and John J. Kushma, eds. *Essays on American Antebellum Politics, 1840–1860*. College Station, TX, 1982, 15–69.

Gilfoyle, Timothy. *City of Eros: New York City, Prostitution, and the Commercialization of Sex, 1790–1920*. New York, 1992.

Gilje, Paul. *Liberty on the Waterfront: American Maritime Culture in the Age of Revolution*. Philadelphia, 2004.

_____. *Rioting In America*. Bloomington, 1996.

Ginzberg, Lori D. *Women and the Work of Benevolence: Morality, Politics, and Class in the Nineteenth-Century United States*. New Haven, 1990.

Goetzmann, William H. *Army Exploration in the American West, 1803–1863*. New Haven, 1959.

Goodman, David. *Gold Seeking: Victoria and California in the 1850s*. Stanford, CA, 1994.

Gordon Ann D., and Mari Jo Buhle. "Sex and Class in Colonial and Nineteenth-Century America," in *Liberating Women's History: Theoretical and Critical Essays*. Berenice A. Carroll, ed. Urbana, 1976, 278–300.

Gorn, Elliott J. *The Manly Art: Bare Knuckle Prize Fighting in America*. Ithaca, 1986.

——. " 'Gouge and Bite, Pull Hair and Scratch': The Social Significance of Fighting in the Southern Backcountry," *American Historical Review* 90 (February 1985): 18–43.

Graebner, Norman. *Empire on the Pacific: A Study in American Continental Expansion*. New York, 1955.

Greenberg, Amy S. *Cause for Alarm: The Volunteer Fire Department in the Nineteenth-Century City*. Princeton, 1998.

——. "Manhood" in the *Encyclopedia of American Cultural and Intellectual History*, Mary Kupiec Cayton and Peter Williams, eds. New York, 2001. vol. 1: 555–63.

Greenberg, Kenneth S. *Honor and Slavery: Lies, Duels, Noses, Masks, Dressing as a Woman, Gifts, Strangers, Humanitarianism, Death, Slave Rebellions, the Proslavery Argument, Baseball, Hunting and Gambling in the Old South*. Princeton, 1996.

Gregg, Robert. *Inside Out, Outside In: Essays in Comparative History*. New York, 2000.

Griffen, Clyde. "Reconstructing Masculinity from the Evangelical Revival to the Waning of Progressivism: A Speculative Synthesis," in *Meanings for Manhood: Constructions of Masculinity in Victorian America*, Mark C. Carnes and Clyde Griffen, eds. Chicago, 1990, 183–205.

Grimshaw, Patricia. *Paths of Duty: American Missionary Wives in Nineteenth-Century Hawaii*. Honolulu, 1989.

Grimsted, David. *American Mobbing, 1828–1861: Toward Civil War*. New York, 1998.

Griswold del Castillo, Richard. *The Treaty of Guadalupe Hidalgo: A Legacy of Conflict*. Norman, OK, 1990.

Grossberg, Michael. "Institutionalizing Masculinity: The Law as a Masculine Profession," in *Meanings for Manhood: Constructions of Masculinity in Victorian America*, Mark C. Carnes and Clyde Griffen, eds. Chicago, 1990, 131–51.

Halberstam, Judith. *Female Masculinity*. Durham, 1998.

Halttunen, Karen. *Confidence Men and Painted Women: A Study of Middle-Class Culture in America, 1830–1870*. New Haven, 1982.

Hammerton, A. James. *Cruelty and Companionship: Conflict in Nineteenth-Century Married Life*. London, 1992.

Hansen, Karen Tranberg, ed. *African Encounters with Domesticity*. New Brunswick, NJ, 1992.

Harris, Mark L. "The Meaning of Patriot: The Canadian Rebellion and American Republicanism, 1837–1839," *Michigan Historical Review* 23 (Spring 1997): 33–69.

Harrison, Brady. "The Young Americans," *American Studies* 40 (Fall 1999): 75–97.

Hartnett, Stephen John. *Democratic Dissent and the Cultural Fictions of Antebellum America*. Urbana, 2002.

Hartsock, Nancy C. M. "Masculinity, Heroism, and the Making of War," in *Rocking the Ship of State*, Adrienne Harris and Ynestra King, eds. Boulder, 1989: 133–52.

Harvey, Bruce Albert. *American Geographics: U.S. National Narratives and the Representation of the Non-European World, 1830–1865*. Stanford, CA, 2001.

————. "American Geographics: The Popular Reproduction of the Non-European World, 1830–1860." Ph.D. Dissertation, Stanford University, 1991.

Haynes, Sam W. "Anglophobia and the Annexation of Texas: The Quest for National Security," in *Manifest Destiny and Empire: American Antebellum Expansionism*, Sam W. Haynes and Christopher Morris, eds. 115–45.

Heiss, Mary Ann. "The Evolution of the Imperial Idea and U.S. National Identity," *Diplomatic History* 26 (Fall 2002): 511–40.

Henkin, David. *City Reading: Written Words and Public Spaces in Antebellum New York*. New York, 1998.

Henning, Joseph M. *Outposts of Civilization: Race, Religion, and the Formative Years of American-Japanese Relations*. New York, 2000.

Hewitt, Nancy A. *Women's Activism and Social Change: Rochester, New York, 1822–1872*. Ithaca, 1984.

Hietala, Thomas. *Manifest Design: Anxious Aggrandizement in Late Jacksonian America*. Ithaca, 1985.

Hilkey, Judy. *Character is Capital: Success Manuals and Manhood in Gilded Age America*. Chapel Hill, 1997.

Hodes, Martha. *White Women, Black Men: Illicit Sex in the Nineteenth-Century South*. New Haven, 1997.

Hofstadter, Richard. *The Paranoid Style in American Politics and Other Essays*. New York, 1965.

Hoganson, Kristin. *Fighting for American Manhood: How Gender Politics Provoked the Spanish-American and Philippine-American Wars*. New Haven, 1998.

————. "Cosmopolitan Domesticity: Importing the American Dream, 1865–1920," *American Historical Review* 107 (February 2002): 55–82.

Holden, Robert H. and Eric Zolov, eds. *Latin America and the United States: A Documentary History*. New York, 2000.

Holt, Michael F. *The Rise and Fall of the American Whig Party: Jacksonian Politics and the Onset of the Civil War*. New York, 1999.

Horsman, Reginald. *Race and Manifest Destiny: The Origins of American Racial Anglo-Saxonism*. Cambridge, MA, 1981.

Horton, James Oliver. "Freedom's Yoke: Gender Conventions among Antebellum Free Blacks," *Feminist Studies* 12 (Spring 1986): 51–76.

Horton, James Oliver and Lois E. Horton. *In Hope of Liberty: Culture, Community, and Protest Among Northern Free Blacks, 1700–1860*. New York, 1997.

Hudson, Frederic. *Journalism in the United States from 1690 to 1872*. New York, 1873.

Hudson, Linda S. *Mistress of Manifest Destiny: A Biography of Jane McManus Storm Cazneau, 1807–1878*. Austin, 2001.

Hunt, Michael. *Ideology and U.S. Foreign Policy*. New Haven, 1987.

Hunter, Jane. *The Gospel of Gentility: American Women Missionaries in Turn-of-the-Century China*. New Haven, 1984.

Ignatiev, Noel. *How the Irish Became White*. New York, 1996.

Isenberg, Nancy. *Sex and Citizenship in Antebellum America*. Chapel Hill, 1998.

_____. "The 'Little Emperor': Aaron Burr, Dandyism, and the Sexual Politics of Treason," in *Beyond the Founders: New Approaches to the Political History of the Early American Republic*. Jeffrey L. Pasley, Andrew W. Robertson, and David Waldstreicher, eds. Chapel Hill, 2004: 129–58.

Jeffrey, Julie Roy. *Frontier Women: Civilizing the West? 1840-1880*. Revised edition. New York, 1998.

Johannsen, Robert W. *To the Halls of the Montezumas: The Mexican War in the American Imagination*. New York, 1985.

_____. "The Meaning of Manifest Destiny," in *Manifest Destiny and Empire: American Antebellum Expansionism*, Sam W. Haynes and Christopher Morris, eds. College Station, TX, 1997: 7–20.

Johnson, John J. *Latin America in Caricature*. Austin, TX, 1980.

Johnson, Paul E. *A Shopkeeper's Millennium: Society and Revivals in Rochester, New York, 1815–1837*. New York, 1978.

Johnson, Paul E., and Sean Wilentz. *The Kingdom of Matthias: A Story of Sex and Salvation in 19th-Century America*. New York, 1994.

Johnson, Susan Lee. *Roaring Camp: The Social World of the California Gold Rush*. New York, 2000.

_____. "'A Memory Sweet to Soldiers': The Significance of Gender," in *A New Significance: Re-envisioning the History of the American West*, Clyde A. Milner, II, ed. New York, 1996: 255–278.

Joseph, Gilbert M., Catherine C. LeGrand, and Ricardo D. Salvatore, eds. *Close Encounters of Empire: Writing the Cultural History of U.S.-Latin American Relations*. Durham, 1998.

Judd, Gerrit P. IV. *Hawaii: An Informal History*. New York, 1961.

Kaplan, Amy. *The Anarchy of Empire in the Making of U.S. Culture*. Cambridge, MA, 2002.

_____. "'Left Alone with America': The Absence of Empire in the Study of American Culture," in *Cultures of United States Imperialism*, Amy Kaplan and Donald E. Pease, eds. Durham, 1993: 3–21.

Kaplan, Amy, and Donald Pease, eds. *Cultures of United States Imperialism*. Durham, 1993.

Karnow, Stanley. *In Our Image: America's Empire in the Philippines*. New York, 1989.

Kasson, John. *Rudeness and Civility: Manners in Nineteenth Century Urban America*. New York, 1990.

Kemble, John H. *The Panama Route, 1848–1869*. Berkeley, 1943.

Kerber, Linda. *Women of the Republic: Intellect and Ideology in Revolutionary America*. Chapel Hill, 1980.

Kimmel, Michael S. "The Contemporary 'Crisis' of Masculinity in Historical Perspective," in *The Making of Masculinities: The New Men's Studies*, Harry Brod, ed. Boston, 1987, 121–53.

Klunder, Willard Carl. *Lewis Cass and the Politics of Moderation*. Kent, OH, 1996.

Kohl, Lawrence Frederick. *The Politics of Individualism: Parties and the American Character in the Jacksonian Era*. New York, 1989.

Kolodny, Annette. *The Lay of the Land: Metaphor as Experience and History in American Life and Letters*. Chapel Hill, 1975.

———. "Letting Go Our Grand Obsessions: Notes Toward a New Literary History of the American Frontiers," *American Literature* 64 (March 1992): 1–18.

Kreneck, Thomas. "Houston, Samuel," in *The Handbook of Texas Online*. Available online at: http://www.tsha.utexas.edu/handbook/online/articles/view/HH/fho73.html.

Kuykendall, Ralph S. *The Hawaiian Kingdom 1778–1854, Foundation and Transformation*. Honolulu, 1957.

LaFeber, Walter. *The Clash: A History of US–Japan Relations*. New York, 1997.

———. *The New Empire: An Interpretation of American Expansion, 1860–1898*. Ithaca, 1963.

Langley, Lester D. *America and the Americas: The United States in the Western Hemisphere*. Athens, GA, 1989.

Lepore, Jill. *The Name of War: King Philip's War and the Origins of American Identity*. New York, 1998.

Leverenz, David. *Manhood and the American Renaissance*. Ithaca, 1989.

Levy, JoAnn. *They Saw the Elephant: Women in the California Gold Rush*. Hamden, CT, 1990.

———. "The Panama Trail: Short Cut to California," *Overland Journal* 10 (Fall 1992): 27–34.

Lewis, Jan. *The Pursuit of Happiness: Family and Values in Jeffersonian Virginia*. New York, 1983.

Lewis, Oscar. *Sea Routes to the Gold Fields: The Migration by Water to California in 1849–1852*. New York, 1949.

Linderman, Gerald. *Embattled Courage: The Experience of Combat in the American Civil War*. New York, 1987.

Livingstone, David. *The Geographical Tradition*. New York, 1992.

———. "The Moral Discourse of Climate: Historical Considerations on Race, Place, and Virtue," *Journal of Historical Geography* 17 (October 1991): 413–34.

Lott, Eric. *Love and Theft: Blackface Minstrelsy and the American Working Class*. New York, 1993.

Lucas, Daniel B. *Nicaragua: War of the Filibusters*. Richmond, VA, 1896.

MacCannell, Dean. *The Tourist: A New Theory of the Leisure Class*. New York, 1976.

Magnuson, Lynnea. "In the Service of Columbia: Gendered Politics and Manifest Destiny Expansion." Ph.D. Dissertation, University of Illinois at Urbana-Champaign, 2000.

Mallon, Florencia E. "The Promise and Dilemma of Subaltern Studies: Perspectives from Latin American History," *American Historical Review* 99 (December 1994): 1491–1515.

Mangan, J. A., and James Walvin, eds. *Manliness and Morality: Middle Class Masculinity in Britain and America, 1800–1940*. Manchester, UK, 1987.

Manning, William R., ed. *Diplomatic Correspondence of the United States concerning the independence of the Latin American Nations*. New York, 1925.

Manthorne, Katherine. *Tropical Renaissance: North American Artists Exploring Latin America, 1839–1879*. Washington, DC, 1989.

Matthews, Glenna. *The Rise of Public Woman: Woman's Power and Woman's Place in the United States, 1630–1970.* New York, 1992.

May, Ernest R. *American Imperialism: A Speculative Essay.* New York, 1968.

May, Robert E. *Manifest Destiny's Underworld: Filibustering in Antebellum America.* Chapel Hill, 2002.

———. *The Southern Dream of a Caribbean Empire, 1854–1861.* Baton Rouge, 1973.

———. "James Buchanan, the Neutrality Laws, and American Invasions of Nicaragua," in *James Buchanan and the Political Crisis of the 1850s,* Michael J. Birkner, ed. Selinsgrove, PA, 1996, 123–45.

———. "Manifest Destiny's Filibusters," in *Manifest Destiny and Empire: American Antebellum Expansionism.* Sam W. Haynes and Christopher Morris, eds. College Station, TX, 1997, 146–79.

———. "Lobbyists for Commercial Empire: Jane Cazneau, William Cazneau, and U.S. Caribbean Policy, 1846–1878," *Pacific Historical Review* 48 (August 1979): 383–412.

McAlister, Melani. *Epic Encounters: Culture, Media, and U.S. Interests in the Middle East, 1945–2000.* Berkeley, 2001.

McClintock, Anne. *Imperial Leather: Race, Gender, and Sexuality in the Colonial Context.* New York, 1995.

McCurry, Stephanie. *Masters of Small Worlds: Yeoman Households, Gender Relations, and the Political Culture of the Antebellum South Carolina Low Country.* New York, 1995.

Melish, Joanne Pope. *Disowning Slavery: Gradual Emancipation and "Race" in New England, 1780–1860.* Ithaca, 1998.

Merish, Lori. *Sentimental Materialism: Gender, Commodity Culture, and Nineteenth-Century American Literature.* Durham, 2000.

Merk, Frederick. *Fruits of Propaganda in the Tyler Administration.* Cambridge, MA, 1971.

———. *Manifest Destiny and Mission in American History: A Reinterpretation.* New York, 1963.

Merry, Sally Engle. *Colonizing Hawai'i: The Cultural Power of Law.* Princeton, 2000.

Metcalf, Helen B. "The California French Filibusters in Sonora," *California Historical Society Quarterly* 18 (1939): 3–21.

Meyer, Doris L. "Early Mexican-American Responses to Negative Stereotyping," *New Mexico Historical Review,* 53 (1978): 75–91.

Miller, David C. *Dark Eden: The Swamp in Nineteenth-Century American Culture.* New York, 1989.

Moore, Earl E. "The Panama Rail Road Company," *Manuscripts* 52 (Summer 2000): 209–18.

Morison, Samuel Eliot. "Old Bruin": Commodore Matthew C. Perry, 1794–1858: The American Naval Officer Who Helped Found Liberia. Boston, 1967.

Morris, Edmund. *The Rise of Theodore Roosevelt.* New York, 1979.

———. *Theodore Rex.* New York, 2001.

Morrison, Michael A. *Slavery and the American West: The Eclipse of Manifest Destiny and the Coming of the Civil War.* Chapel Hill, 1997.

Morrissey, Katherine G. "Engendering the West," in *Under an Open Sky: Rethinking America's Western Past*, William Cronon, George Miles, and Jay Gitlin, eds. New York, 1992: 132–44.

Moses, Wilson, ed. *Liberian Dreams: Back-to-Africa Narratives from the 1850s.* University Park, PA, 1998.

Mott, Frank Luther. *A History of American Magazines, Vol. II, 1850–1865.* Cambridge, MA. 1938.

Nelson, Anna Kasten. "Jane Storms Cazneau: Disciple of Manifest Destiny," *Prologue: The Journal of the National Archives* 18 (Spring 1986): 25–40.

Nelson, Dana D. *National Manhood: Capitalist Citizenship and the Imagined Fraternity of White Men.* Durham, 1998.

Olien, Michael D. "E. G. Squier and the Miskito: Anthropological Scholarship and Political Propaganda," *Ethnohistory* 32 (1985): 111–33.

Onuf, Peter S. *Jefferson's Empire: the Language of American Nationhood.* Charlottesville, VA, 2000.

Paludan, Philip S. *A Covenant with Death: The Constitution, Law, and Equality in the Civil War Era.* Urbana, 1975.

Paredes, Raymund A. "The Mexican Image in American Travel Literature, 1831–1869," *New Mexico Historical Review* LII (January 1977): 5–29.

Park, James William. *Latin American Underdevelopment: A History of Perspectives in the United States, 1870–1965.* Baton Rouge, 1995.

Park, Roberta J. "Biological Thought, Athletics, and the Formation of the 'Man of Character': 1830–1900," in *Manliness and Morality: Middle Class Masculinity in Britain and America, 1800–1940* J. A. Mangan and James Walvin, eds. Manchester, UK, 1987: 7–33.

Pattullo, Polly. *Last Resorts: The Cost of Tourism in the Caribbean.* London, 1996.

Pemble, John. *The Mediterranean Passion: Victorians and Edwardians in the South.* New York, 1987.

Pencak, William. "Social and Legal Change in Hawaii Before 1860: Parallel Development with the United States," in *The Law in America 1607–1861*, William Pencak and Wythe W. Holt Jr., eds. New York, 1989, 269–304.

Pike, Frederick B. *The United States and Latin America: Myths and Stereotypes of Civilization and Nature.* Austin, TX, 1992.

Pinheiro, John C. "'On Their Knees to Jesuits': Nativist Conspiracy Theories and the War with Mexico, 1846–1848." Unpublished paper presented at the annual meeting of the Organization of American Historians, April 3, 2003.

Pletcher, David M. *The Diplomacy of Annexation: Texas, Oregon, and the Mexican War.* Columbia, MO, 1973.

Poole, Deborah. "Landscape and the Imperial Subject: U.S. Images of the Andes, 1859–1930," in *Close Encounters of Empire: Writing the Cultural History of U.S.-Latin American Relations.* Gilbert M. Joseph, Catherine C. LeGrand, and Ricardo Salvatore, eds. Durham, 1998: 107–38.

Potter, David M. *The Impending Crisis, 1848–1861.* New York, 1976.

Powell, Philip Wayne. *Tree of Hate: Propaganda and Prejudices Affecting United States Relations with the Hispanic World.* New York, 1971.

Pozas, María del Carmen Suescun. "From Reading to Seeing: Doing and Undoing Imperialism in the Visual Arts," in Gilbert M. Joseph, Catherine C. LeGrand,

and Ricardo D. Salvatore, eds., *Close Encounters of Empire: Writing the Cultural History of U.S.-Latin American Relations*. Durham, 1998: 525–56.

Pratt, Mary Louise. *Imperial Eyes: Travel Writing and Transculturation*. New York, 1992.

Proctor, Nicholas W. *Bathed in Blood: Hunting and Mastery in the Old South*. Charlottesville, 2002.

Publications of the Historical Commission of the Territory of Hawaii, vol. 1 (4) 1927. Honolulu, 1927.

Pybus, Cassandra, and Hamish Maxwell-Stewart. *American Citizens: British Slaves: Yankee Political Prisoners in an Australian Penal Colony, 1839–1850*. East Lansing, MI, 2002.

Rafael, Vicente L. "Colonial Domesticity: White Women and United States Rule in the Philippines," *American Literature* 67 (December 1995): 639–66.

Ramirez Cabañas, Joaquin. *Gaston de Raousset: Conquistador de Sonora*. Mexico D.F., 1941.

Rauch, Basil. *American Interest in Cuba, 1848–1855*. New York, 1948.

Reynolds, David. *Beneath the American Renaissance: The Subversive Imagination in the Age of Emerson and Melville*. New York, 1988.

Riley, Glenda. "Women on the Panama Trail to California 1849–1869," *Pacific Historical Review* 55 (November 1986): 531–48.

Roberts, Brian. *American Alchemy: The California Gold Rush and Middle-Class Culture*. Chapel Hill, 2000.

Robinson, Cecil. *With the Ears of Strangers: The Mexican in American Literature*. Tucson, 1963.

Rodgers, Daniel T. *The Work Ethic in Industrial America, 1850–1920*. Chicago, 1974.

Rodríguez O., Jaime E., and Kathryn Vincent, eds. *Myths, Misdeeds, and Misunderstandings: The Roots of Conflict in U.S.–Mexican Relations*. Wilmington, 1997.

Roediger, David. *The Wages of Whiteness: Race and the Making of the American Working Class*. London, 1991.

Rogin, Michael Paul. *Fathers and Children: Andrew Jackson and the Subjugation of the American Indian*. New York, 1975.

———. *Subversive Genealogy: The Politics and Art of Herman Melville*. New York, 1983.

Rohrbough, Malcolm. *Days of Gold: The California Gold Rush and the American Nation*. Berkeley, 1997.

Rolle, Andrew F. "California Filibustering and the Hawaiian Kingdom," *Pacific Historical Review* 19 (1950): 251–63.

Rollin, Michael Frederick. "The Divine Invasion: Manifest Destiny and the Westernization of Japanese Nationalism in the Late Tokugawa and Meiji Periods, 1853–1912." Master's Thesis, The University of Texas at San Antonio, 2002.

Rosaldo, Renato. "Imperialist Nostalgia," *Representations* 26 (Spring 1989): 107–22.

Rose, Anne C. *Beloved Strangers: Interfaith Families in Nineteenth-Century America*. Cambridge, MA, 2001.

———. *Victorian America and the Civil War*. New York, 1992.

Rosengarten, Frederic Jr. *Freebooters Must Die! The Life and Death of William Walker, the Most Notorious Filibuster of the Nineteenth Century.* Wayne, PA, 1976.

Rosenau, James N. *The Attentive Public and Foreign Policy: A Theory of Growth and Some New Evidence.* Princeton, 1968.

Ross, Steven J. *Workers on the Edge: Work, Leisure, and Politics in Industrializing Cincinnati, 1788–1890.* New York, 1985.

Rotundo, E. Anthony. *American Manhood: Transformations in Masculinity from the Revolution to the Modern Era.* New York, 1993.

Ryan, Mary. *Civic Wars: Democracy and Public Life in the American City during the Nineteenth Century.* Berkeley, 1997.

———. *Cradle of the Middle Class: The Family in Oneida County, New York, 1790–1865.* Cambridge, UK, 1981.

———. *The Empire of the Mother: American Writings about Domesticity, 1830–1860.* New York, 1982.

———. *Women in Public: Between Banners and Ballots, 1825–1880.* Baltimore, 1990.

Said, Edward. *Culture and Imperialism.* New York, 1993.

Sánchez-Eppler, Karen. "Raising Empires like Children: Race, Nation, and Religious Education," *American Literary History* 8 (1996): 399–425.

Saxton, Alexander. *The Rise and Fall of the White Republic: Class Politics and Mass Culture in Nineteenth-Century America.* London, 1990.

Scheckel, Susan. *The Insistence of the Indian: Race and Nationalism in Nineteenth-Century American Culture.* Princeton, 1998.

Schoonover, Thomas. *Dollars over Dominion: The Triumph of Liberalism in Mexican-United States Relations, 1861–1867.* Baton Rouge, 1978.

———. *Uncle Sam's War of 1898 and the Origins of Globalization.* Lexington, KY, 2003.

Schriber, Mary Suzanne. *Writing Home: American Women Abroad, 1830–1920.* Charlottesville, VA, 1997.

Schroeder, John H. *Mr. Polk's War: American Opposition and Dissent, 1846–1848.* Madison, 1973.

Scott, Anne Firor. *Natural Allies: Women's Associations in American History.* Urbana, 1991.

Scott, Joan. *Gender and the Politics of History.* New York, 1988.

———. "Gender: A Useful Category for Historical Analysis." *American Historical Review* 91 (December 1986): 1053–75.

Sellers, Charles. *The Market Revolution: Jacksonian America, 1815–1846.* New York, 1991.

Senkewicz, Robert M. *Vigilantes in Gold Rush San Francisco.* Stanford, CA, 1985.

Shearer, Ernest C. "The Carvajal Disturbances," *Southwestern Historical Quarterly* 55 (Oct. 1951): 201–30.

Sinha, Mrinalini. *Colonial Masculinity: The 'Manly Englishman' and the 'Effeminate Bengali' in the Late Nineteenth Century.* Manchester, UK, 1995.

Sklar, Kathryn Kish. *Catharine Beecher: A Study in American Domesticity.* New Haven, 1973.

Slotkin, Richard. *The Fatal Environment: The Myth of the Frontier in the Age of Industrialization, 1800–1890.* New York, 1985.

———. *Regeneration Through Violence: The Mythology of the American Frontier, 1600–1860.* Middletown, CT, 1973.

———. "Buffalo Bill's 'Wild West' and the Mythologization of the American Empire," in *Cultures of United States Imperialism,* Amy Kaplan and Donald E. Pease, eds. Durham, 1993, 164–81.

Smith, Elbert B. *The Presidency of James Buchanan.* Lawrence, 1975.

Smith, Harold F. *American Travelers Abroad: A Bibliography of Accounts Published before 1900.* Carbondale, IL, 1969.

Smith, Henry Nash. *Virgin Land: the American West as Symbol and Myth.* Cambridge, MA, 1950.

Smith, Page. *Daughters of a Promised Land: Women in American History.* Boston, 1970.

Smith, Peter H. *Talons of the Eagle: Dynamics of U.S.-Latin American Relations.* New York, 2000.

Smith-Rosenberg, Carroll. *Disorderly Conduct: Visions of Gender in Victorian America.* New York, 1985.

———. "Dis-Covering the Subject of the 'Great Constitutional Discussion,' 1786–1789," *Journal of American History* 79 (December 1992): 841–73.

Smits, Gregory. "Making Japanese by Putting on Clothes," in *Making Japanese.* Available online at: http://www.personal.psu.edu/faculty/g/j/gjs4/mj/ch4.htm.

Sobarzo, Horacio. *Cronica de la Aventura de Raousset-Boulbon en Sonora,* 2nd edition. Mexico D.F., 1980.

Stanley, Amy Dru. *From Bondage to Contract: Wage Labor, Marriage, and the Market in the Age of Slave Emancipation.* New York, 1998.

Stansell, Christine. *City of Women: Sex and Class in New York, 1789–1860.* Urbana, Ill, 1987.

Stanton, William. *The Leopard's Spots: Scientific Attitudes toward Race in America, 1815–1859.* Chicago, 1960.

Stellman, Louis J. *Sam Brannan: Builder of San Francisco.* New York, 1953.

Stepan, Nancy Leys, "Race and Gender: The Role of Analogy in Science," *ISIS* 77 (June 1986): 261–77.

Stephanson, Anders. *Manifest Destiny: American Expansion and the Empire of the Right.* New York, 1995.

Stevens, Sylvester. *American Expansion in Hawaii, 1842–1898.* Harrisburg, PA, 1945.

Stoler, Ann L. *Race and the Education of Desire: Foucault's History of Sexuality and the Colonial Order of Things.* Durham, 1995.

———. "Making Empire Respectable: The Politics of Sexual Morality in Twentieth-Century Colonial Cultures," *American Ethnologist* 16 (November 1989). 634–60.

———. "Tense and Tender Ties: The Politics of Comparison in North American History and (Post) Colonial Studies," *Journal of American History* 88 (December 2001): 829–65.

Stout, Joseph Allen. Jr. *Schemers and Dreamers: Filibustering in Mexico, 1848–1921.* Fort Worth, TX, 2002.

Stowe, Steven M. *Intimacy and Power in the Old South: Ritual in the Lives of the Planters*. Baltimore, 1987.

Stowe, William W. *Going Abroad: European Travel in Nineteenth-Century American Culture*. Princeton, 1994.

Strauss, W. Patrick. *Americans in Polynesia, 1783–1842*. East Lansing, MI, 1963.

Streeby, Shelly. *American Sensations: Class, Empire, and the Production of Popular Culture*. Berkeley, 2002.

Sundquist, Eric J. "The Literature of Expansion and Race," in *The Cambridge History of American Literature*, Sacvan Bercovitch, ed. New York, 1995, vol. 2: 127–328.

Susman, Warren I. " 'Personality' and the Making of Twentieth Century Culture," in *New Directions in American Intellectual History*, John Higham and Paul Conklin, eds. Baltimore, 1979, 212–26.

Tansey, Richard. "Southern Expansionism: Urban Interests in the Cuban Filibusters," *Plantation Society* 1 (June 1979): 227–51.

Theweleit, Klaus. *Male Fantasies. Vol 1. Women, Floods, Bodies, History*. Stephan Conway, translator. Minneapolis, 1987.

Thornton, Tamara Plakins. *Handwriting in America: A Cultural History*. New Haven, 1996.

Torgovnick, Marianna. *Gone Primitive: Savage Intellects, Modern Lives*. Chicago, 1990.

Tosh, John. "What Should Historians Do with Masculinity? Reflections on Nineteenth-Century Britain," *History Workshop Journal* 38 (Autumn 1994): 179–202.

Turner, Frederick Jackson. *Frontier and Section: Selected Essays of Frederick Jackson Turner*. Ray Allen Billington, ed. Englewood Cliffs, NJ, 1961.

Urban, Chester S. "New Orleans and the Cuba Question during the López Expeditions of 1849–1851: A Local Study in 'Manifest Destiny'," *Louisiana Historical Quarterly* 22 (1939): 1095–167.

Van Alstyne, Richard W. *The Rising American Empire*. New York, 1974.

Vance, William L. *America's Rome*. 2 volumes. New Haven, 1989.

Varg, Paul. *United States Foreign Relations, 1820–1860*. East Lansing, MI, 1979.

Varon, Elizabeth R. *We Mean to Be Counted: White Women and Politics in Antebellum Virginia*. Chapel Hill, 1998.

Vevier, Charles. "American Continentalism: An Idea of Expansion, 1845–1910," *American Historical Review* 65 (April 1960): 323–35.

Wald, Priscilla, *Constituting Americans: Cultural Anxiety and Narrative Form*. Durham, 1995.

———. "Terms of Assimilation: Legislating Subjectivity in the Emerging Nation," in *Cultures of United States Imperialism*, Amy Kaplan and Donald E. Pease, eds. Durham, 1993, 59–84.

Ward, John William. *Andrew Jackson: Symbol for an Age*. New York, 1953.

Warner, Michael. "Franklin and the Letters of the Republic," *Representations* 16 (Fall 1986): 110–30.

Watts, Steven. *The Republic Reborn: War and the Making of Liberal America, 1790–1820*. Baltimore, 1987.

Weber, David J. "'Scarce more than apes.' Historical Roots of Anglo-American Stereotypes of Mexicans in the Border Region," in *New Spain's Northern Frontier: Essays on Spain in the American West, 1540–1821,* David J. Weber, ed. Albuquerque, 1979, 295–307.

Weinberg, Albert. *Manifest Destiny: A Study of Nationalist Expansionism in American History,* 1935. Chicago, 1963.

Wexler, Laura. *Tender Violence: Domestic Visions in an Age of U.S. Imperialism.* Chapel Hill, 2000.

White, Deborah Gray. *Ar'n't I a Woman? Female Slaves in the Plantation South.* New York, 1985.

Widmer, Edward L. *Young America: The Flowering of Democracy in New York City.* New York, 1999.

Wilentz, Sean. *Chants Democratic: New York City and the Rise of the American Working Class, 1788–1850.* New York, 1984.

Wiley, Peter Booth. *Yankees in the Land of the Gods: Commodore Perry and the Opening of Japan.* New York, 1990.

Williams, William Appleman. *Empire as a Way of Life.* New York, 1980.

Wiltsee, Ernest A. *Gold Rush Steamers of the Pacific.* San Francisco, 1938.

Wyatt-Brown, Bertram. *Honor and Violence in the Old South.* New York, 1986.

———. *Southern Honor: Ethics and Behavior in the Old South.* New York, 1982.

Yacovone, Donald. "Abolitionists and the 'Language of Fraternal Love'," in *Meanings for Manhood: Constructions of Masculinity in Victorian America,* Mark C. Carnes and Clyde Griffen, eds. Chicago, 1990, 85–95.

Zboray, Ronald J. *A Fictive People: Antebellum Economic Development and the American Reading Public.* New York, 1993.

Zboray, Ronald J. and Mary Saracino Zboray. "Gender Slurs in Boston's Partisan Press during the 1840s," *Journal of American Studies* 34 (2000): 413–46.

Zorrilla, Luis G. *Historia de las relaciones entre México y los Estados Unidos de América, 1800–1958,* vol. 1. 1965. 2nd edition. Mexico, 1977.

Index